As we celebrate
our thirty years of הרבצת התורה
we pay tribute to our munificent benefactors

Mr. and Mrs. Ira and Ingeborg Rennert עמו״ש

by dedicating this special edition of
The Rav Shlomo Zalman Auerbach Hagadah
to them.

Their world-renowned philanthropy has been a major
factor in reclaiming the authentic Torah-true heritage
for thousands of our Jewish brethren.
Of particular note is their warmth, friendship, care
and concern to Yeshiva Derech Chaim at all times.
Their consistent devotion on behalf of our yeshiva
is always felt and sincerely appreciated.
They are truly always there for us.

We wish them good health, happiness, ברכה והצלחה
and much nachas from their children.

The Hanhala, Administration, Rebbeim
and Talmidim
of Yeshiva Derech Chaim

As we celebrate
our thirty years of הרבצת התורה
we pay tribute to our munificent benefactors
Mr. and Mrs. Rubin Schron עמו״ש
by dedicating this special edition of
The Rav Shlomo Zalman Auerbach Hagadah
to them.

They have been at the forefront of
Torah leadership that has transformed
the Jewish community.
Their generous support of Yeshivos Gedolos
in general, and in Yeshiva Derech Chaim
in particular, has indelibly affected
thousands of talmidim.
Their consistent devotion
on behalf of our yeshiva
is always felt and sincerely appreciated.
They are truly always there for us.

We wish them good health, happiness, ברכה והצלחה
and much nachas from their children.

The Hanhala, Administration, Rebbeim
and Talmidim
of Yeshiva Derech Chaim

לזכר ולע"נ

הרב משה יצחק ב"ר מאיר הכהן ז"ל

ב' מרחשון תשס"ה

איש יקר ושפל דרך הולך ישר
מלא בתורה יראה ואמונה צרופה

ת.נ.צ.ב.ה.

The Krasner Family

לעילוי נשמת האשה

מרת חוה פריימן ע"ה
בת החבר אברהם הקשר ז"ל

אם כל חיינו
שבכל מצב השכילה להיות עם כל חי
ללמד חכמת שעה ודורות

מסורה לבעלה הדגול ללא גבול
גידלה משפחה לתפארת
לפני השואה, בעיצומה ולאחריה
זכתה לראות בני חימשים בחייה
ואהבה את כולם
אהבה את האמת ושנאה שקר
ביתה היה מקלט לכל מדוכא ולכל מר נפש
מצאה דרך אל לב כל אחד ואחת
חסד ואמת האירה

נולדה בהמבורג כ"ה אלול תרס"א
נפטרה מיתת נשיקה בביתה בניו יורק
כ"ט אדר תשס"ד
בת מאה ושתים שנה

ת.נ.צ.ב.ה.

הרב אלכסנדר פריימן ורעיתו שושנה

לעילוי נשמת

החבר ישראל מאיר בן ר' יעקב זצ"ל

נפטר בשם טוב ובשיבה טובה
ערב חג הסוכות תשנ"ד

In memory of
Dr. Ernest Freeman זצ"ל

A person whose sterling qualities were hallowed by his incredible
עניוות, humility, that earned for him the title of עבד ה'.
He exemplified in his life the maxim of Chazal,
יפה תלמוד תורה עם דרך ארץ
He was a dedicated and caring physician, beloved and respected
by all his patients and all who came in contact with him.
His daily learning schedule was a model for all and upon his retiring
from his medical practice he expanded his learning schedule
to a full-time basis, setting an extraordinary example for
Torah learning, Torah teaching and Torah living.

He was a loving husband, father, grandfather, and great-grandfather
who inspired everyone with his exceptional מידות, warmth, and love.

A scion of illustrious Gaonim and Tzadikim, he carried on
the tradition of being a נאמן ביתו who radiated honesty,
truth and חסד in all his actions.

Rabbi and Mrs. Alfred A. Freeman
and Family

לזכות ולעילוי נשמת
נכדינו היקר והנעלה
הבחור אפרים מרדכי הכהן זצ"ל
בן הרב משה יצחק שליט"א
יארמוש

בעשרים ושתים שנותיו הקצרות
הוא עלה ונתעלה, והגיע לפסגות גבוהות
בתורה וביראה בעבודת ה' ובכל מדה נכונה.
קידש שם שמים בכל הליכותיו והאהיב את התורה
ועוסקיה בעיני כל רואיו.

נלב"ע לאחר שנזדכך ביסורים קשים
ביום שב"ק כ"ג סיון תשס"ד

ת.נ.צ.ב.ה.

Fishel Yosef and Rochel Leah Kipust

and

Dovid and Malka Yarmush

We dedicate this Hagadah
לע"נ הבחור החשוב
אפרים מרדכי ז"ל
בן הרב משה יצחק הכהן שליט"א

Ephraim Mordechai Yarmush ז"ל

Ephraim Mordechai accomplished in his short life what those much older strive to accomplish. His outstanding Middos Tovos, Limud Hatorah בהתמדה, Avodas Hashem and Ahavas Chessed were an inspiration to young and old alike. Wherever he went, he would light up the room with his big, warm smile, doling out encouraging words to all he met. He was מקבל his two and a half years of יסורים with אהבה. His only complaint was against himself. In his final months he lamented that during the past two years he frowned twice and cried once.
This was the life of a young yeshiva bochur who lived solely to serve his Creator to his utmost. Ephraim Mordechai Yarmush zt"l will always be remembered.

ת.נ.צ.ב.ה.

Dovid and Malka Yarmush
Fishel Yosef and Rochel Leah Kipust

Dedicated in loving memory of

רחל בת משה ע"ה

Rose Hirschman

of blessed memory

A woman of exceptional character,
Brimming with love for Hashem, His people and His Torah.
Her motto was, "Mitzvos are carfare",
And so she conducted her life,
always looking for opportunities to serve Hashem with joy.
She visited the sick and cheered them up.
She received everyone with a smile and joy
that left them with a warm feeling.
Her firm faith and trust inspired others.
Her proudest accomplishment was supporting
Torah and its scholars.
She returned her soul to its maker on
ט"ז חשון תשס"ד - November 11, 2003.
She will be sorely missed by all
who had the privilege to know her.

ת.נ.צ.ב.ה.

לעילוי הנשמות

יהודה שמואל ב"ר יצחק יעקב ע"ה ברוך ב"ר יוסף מאיר ע"ה
זיסל בת ר' אהרן ע"ה בלומא בת ר' איסר ע"ה

In loving memory of In loving memory of
Sam and Sadie Itzkowitz ע"ה   Bert and Blanche Vann ע"ה

They paved the way for generations of Torah observant Jewry.

In honor of the next generation of Torah observant Jewry

Aharon and Nesha Leah Itzkowitz
Yael Aviva, Shoshana and Yosef Yaakov Sholom

Yirmiyahu and Sima Itzkowitz
Zissel, Boruch Simcha, Yitzchok, Haddasa, Binyomin Mordechai,
Tziporah Aliza, Chaim Shmaya, Yehuda Shmuel, Yosef Meir
and Nechemia

Noach Nachman and Chaya Shaina Kupferstein
Boruch, Yisroel Zvi and Bluma Sora

Yehoshua Yonah and Rochel Leah Itzkowitz
Chaya, Boruch, Tova, Batya, Hillel, Avrohom Moshe Nosson
and Yehudis

Yitzchok Yaakov and Yocheved Itzkowitz
Yehuda Shmuel, Nechama, Benzion, Elazar Simcha, Chaya Bluma, Yisroel
Meir, Leah and Yechiel Dov

Yochanan and Adina Yael Itzkowitz
Rochel Chana, Aryeh and Eliyahu

Yisroel Yoel and Dvora Pessil Itzkowitz

Yosef and Shaindel Yitta Chaya Itzkowitz

This page is dedicated by
Naftali and Zelda Rivka Itzkowitz

This page is dedicated
in passionate, heartfelt appreciation
to my wife

Charna Tomor Shapiro שתחיה

"מצא אשה מצא טוב" (משלי יח)

Her inherent goodness is a daily inspiration to me
ואין טוב אלא תורה שנאמר
"כי לקח טוב נתתי לכם" (ברכות ה.)

She continues to lovingly encourage and support me
in the דרך of תורה
דרכיה דרכי נועם (משלי ג)
at the most wonderful Yeshiva
Derech Chaim
דרך חיים

May the Yeshiva continue
in its success for all generations.

Rabbi Dr. Rashi Shapiro

In honor of
our dear parents

Horav and Rebbitzen Yisroel Plutchok עמו״ש

and

Rabbi and Mrs. Yechezkel Gruber עמו״ש

Their love and caring for us
and each and every one of their children
is the shining example for us to follow.

May they have much נחת
from us and all their children.

Akiva and Brochie Gruber

In Appreciation

To the Roshei HaYeshiva

Horav Yisroel Plutchok שליט"א

and

Horav Mordechai Rennert שליט"א

and to the Administration

Rabbi Avi Geffner

and

Yanki Borchardt

for all that they do for all the Talmidim
and the entire Yeshiva.

Binyomin and Esther Pitterman
and Yona

לז״נ

הרב יהודה בן שלמה ברוך ע״ה

נפטר בשם טוב
ה׳ טבת תשכ״ג

Rabbi Julius Kreitman ע״ה

Beloved husband, father, brother and zeydie.
He was filled with אהבת ישראל and יראת שמים.
May he be a מליץ יושר for his family.

ת.נ.צ.ב.ה.

The Kreitman Family

In loving memory
of
husband, father
parents and grandparents

Ben Gross ע״ה

בנימין אייזיק

בן צבי הירש הכהן ע״ה

Joseph and Esther Friedman ע״ה

יוסף בן אברהם יצחק ע״ה

אסתר בת אברהם דוד ע״ה

Mrs. Renee Gross

and Family

In loving memory of our dear parents and brother

בצלאל עוזר ב"ר יעקב אריה ע"ה

ד' אייר תשל"ד

חנה בת ר' שלמה ע"ה

ח' סיון תשכ"ז

Charles and Chana Levy

אריה לייב ב"ר בצלאל עוזר ע"ה

ט"ו ניסן תשמ"ח

Louis Levy

משה ב"ר חיים יעקב ע"ה

ו' אדר תשל"ג

הינדא בת ר' מאיר אהרן ע"ה

י"ד טבת תש"מ

Morris and Helen Blumberg

ת.נ.צ.ב.ה.

Meir and Simma Levy

נעלה על זכרונינו עטרת ראשינו

ה"ה אבי מורי ואת בעלי
שנלקח מאתנו ביום ח׳ סיון תשמ"ח
ה"ה רב יעקב משה בן ר׳ בנימין יוסף ז"ל

ואנו תפלה שלא יתיבש המעין ולא יקצץ האילן
(תפלת החתם סופר זכותו יגן עלינו)

פעסל, שמשון דוד, וצביה פריש

לזכר עולם
לנשמת אבינו מורינו

ר׳ טובי-ה בן ר׳ משה ז״ל

שקבל כל אדם בסבר פנים יפות.
הוא סמל דברי חז״ל
״כל שרוח הבריות נוחה הימנו רוח המקום נוחה הימנו״

In memory of our dear father

Tibor Berk z"l

who personified the words of our Sages
"He who is pleasing to his fellow man
is pleasing also to God"

Dedicated by the

Berk and Lwowski families

In loving memory

לזכ"נ

משה בן אפרים יוסף ע"ה
י"ט טבת

פייגא מלכה בת מרדכי ע"ה
כ"ב שבט

אהרן מענדל בן נפתלי הרץ ע"ה
ט' ניסן

ת.נ.צ.ב.ה.

Peninah Leah Silbert

and family

לזכר נשמת

חי' פייגא בת נחום

שהלכה לעולמה
ג' אדר א' תשס"ה

ת.נ.צ.ב.ה.

משפחת געלב

THE ORANGE/WHISKEY CENTER

In loving memory of my parents

לע"נ ר' משה מנחם ב"ר אברהם ארי' ע"ה
נפטר כ"ה סיון תש"ס לפ"ק

ולע"נ מרת רחל לאה ב"ר שמעון נתן הכהן ע"ה
נפטרה כ"ח סיון תשס"ב לפ"ק

וויסענטאסקי
Mr. and Mrs. Joseph Wicentowsky

לזכות בנינו ונכדינו היקרים שיחיו

ר' יהואש אהרן ני"ו	ר' יצחק עקיבא ני"ו
מרת אילנא גאלדע תחי'	מרת אסתר תחי' ב"ר חיים יוסף הלוי ני"ו
ב"ר מאיר הירש הלוי ני"ו	ויוצ"ח לאה, שרה,
ויוצ"ח יהודית תחי' ומשה יחיאל ני'	צבי מאיר, רפאל אפרים וחנה ני"ו

מרת דינה דבורה תחי'
ובעלה ר' מנחם שאול ב"ר יוסף ברוך ני"ו
ויוצ"ח שרה לאה, רבקה בלימא, חנה, פריידל, צבי מאיר ונפתלי ני"ו
שיזכו לאריכת ימים ושנים טובים, ולעשות מצוות ומעשים טובים, ולהתעלות בתורה
וביראת שמים, באהבה וברצון ובשמחה ובטוב לב לקיים מצוות הבורא יתב"ש בשלימות,
וכן ירבה

ולעילוי נשמת משפחתינו

ר' יוסף נחמי' ב"ר סיני נח ע"ה - נפטר ד' תמוז תשנ"ז לפ"ק
מרת יהודית ב"ר יצחק עקיבא ע"ה - נפטרה ט' שבט תש"ס לפ"ק
ר' יצחק עקיבא ב"ר אביגדור משה ע"ה - נפטר כ"ט אלול תש"כ לפ"ק
מרת ליפקא (ליבא) ב"ר יהודא ליב ע"ה - נפטרה י"א כסלו תשכ"ב לפ"ק
ר' סיני נח ב"ר ישראל ע"ה - נפטר כ"ז חשון תשכ"ח לפ"ק
מרת פריידא ב"ר שמעון יוסף ע"ה - נפטרה ו' חשון תשל"ה לפ"ק

מאת ישראל שלמה ואשתו איטע אסתר ויעקב עקיבא אראנדזש

לזכר נשמת
האשה החשובה

שרה בת הרב משה ע"ה

ראש חודש סיון תשס"א

In loving memory
of

Mrs. Sarah Kaufman ע"ה

May she be a מליצה ישרה
for her entire משפחה

Eli Meir Kaufman

לזכר נשמת

ר' יוסף בנימין ב"ר זאב ע"ה

נפטר כ"ב ניסן, אחרון של פסח תשס"ג

ת.נ.צ.ב.ה.

In loving memory of

Jerome Schockett

בעל חסד ובעל צדקה

His מעשים טובים remain as an inspiration for us all.

Beverly Schockett and Family

In loving memory of my dear friend
Mrs. Hedy Kahn a"h ~ Channah Freidel bas Avroham a"h
23 Shevat 5765
Her beloved twin sister Zelda Leiba bas Avroham a"h
7 Adar I 5760
Her beloved daughter Tanya bas Moshe a"h
29 Elul 5754
and her cherished grandson, Tanya's young son Ari Binyomin ben Yosef a"h
23 Adar II 5763
May their memories be for a blessing.
May they be melitzei yosher for Klal Yisroel.

We should enjoy each day, live by the Torah way.
We should also say: We want Moshiach today!

A dear friend, who can find? Hedy was truly, one-of-a-kind!
She will be sorely missed. Always in my heart.

Mrs. Pearl Fiber-Berkowitz
of Washington Heights, NY formerly of Pelham Parkway, NY

לעילוי נשמת

Joseph Lieber יוסף בן חיים יהודה

נפטר ו' שבט תשמ"ג

Regine Lieber רבקה סרנא בת אברהם אביש הכהן

נפטרה כ"ב אדר תשכ"ט

Avrohom Lieber אברהם מרדכי בן יוסף

נפטר י"א אייר תשנ"ה

Chaim and Faigie Lieber

Dedicated in loving remembrance
of our honored grandparents

Zalman ben Kusheil

and

Belka bas Chaim Chafetz

Norman and Marsha Shine

In honor of
my dear friends

Rabbi Avi Geffner
and his Rebbetzin
and the whole Mishpacha

for doing on a daily basis
Kiddush ד׳
and giving comfort to all.

Steven M. Zukoff
Miami Beach, FL.

In honor of the first yahrzeit of our beloved husband, father and grandfather
ר׳ שמואל בן אהרן יוסף ז״ל
Reb Shmuel Rotter ז״ל
A peaceful, modest and kind-hearted mentsch.

He survived the horrors of the Holocaust and was zoche to build a beautiful yiddishe family. He lived his life with שמחת החיים, אמונה and a big, warm smile. He led our Pesach Seder with תמימות and sang "Old World" niggunim with joy in order to teach us the beauty of yiddishkeit. We will miss him at our Seder and every day of our lives.

יהי זכרו ברוך

And in memory of his parents and brothers
אהרן יוסף בן מיכאל ע״ה, מיכל בת יעקב ע״ה,
שלום בן אהרן יוסף ע״ה, מרדכי בן אהרן יוסף ע״ה ראטטר
who were murdered על קידוש ה׳ by the Nazis ימח שמם וזכרם

"שפוך עליהם זעמך, וחרון אפיך ישיגם" - (This was his powerful moment of the Seder)
May Hashem bring Moshiach and reunite all families, "לשנה הבאה בירושלים"
ת.נ.צ.ב.ה.

Temmy Rotter
Salzberg Family (N.Y.)   Shabat Family (Chicago)

לזכר נשמות

אמא וסבתא יקרה האשה הצנועה וטובת לב
מרת רבקה בת ר' צבי ע"ה Rosenfeld
נפטרה עש"ק י"ח ניסן, ב' דחול המועד פסח תשנ"ז

※ ※ ※

יוסף בן צבי ע"ה Ungar
נפטר כ"ב אדר תשס"ב

※ ※ ※

ומרת יוטא בת ר' צבי ע"ה Galandauer
נפטרה עש"ק י"ד תשרי, ערב סוכות תשנ"ד

※ ※ ※

ומרת חיה בת ר' מרדכי יהושע ע"ה Kalikstein
נפטרה ל' תשרי, א' דראש חודש מרחשון תשס"א

תהא נשמותיהם צרורות בצרור החיים ויהיו מליצי יושר לכל משפחותיהם

In honor of my

אשת חיל

Bassy תחי'

May we have many
healthy happy years together
עד מאה ועשרים שנה

Yosef Moshe Solkowitz

ספר זה הוקדש
לע"נ אבינו וזקננו היקר
צנוע ומעלי איש תם וישר ירא אלקים בלו"נ אהוב ונחמד לבריות
ר' חיים צבי בן ר' משה שמעון ז"ל יאנאווסקי
לע"נ אמנו וזקנתנו היקרה
מרת מרים בת ר' משה יוסף ע"ה
מנשים באהל תבורך
ששקדה כל ימיה על חינוך ביתה לתורה ויר"ש

זכותם תגן עלינו
"ולא ימוש ספר התורה מפינו ומפי זרעינו עד עולם"

ת.נ.צ.ב.ה.

דוד ופעריל טייכמאן ומשפחתם

לז"נ

הרבנית עדינה בת ישראל ע"ה

ז' טבת תשס"ג

In loving memory of our beloved mother
Rebbitzen Adina Ben-Porat
She dedicated her life to the support of Torah and to the כלל.
She served us with שמחה despite her years of great יסורים.
May she be a מליצה ישרה for her משפחה and for כלל ישראל.

Chaim and Esti Ben-Porat

In honor of the Roshei Yeshiva
Harav Yisroel Plutchok שליט״א
Harav Mordechai Rennert שליט״א
and their Rebbetzins עמו״ש
In appreciation for everything that they do
for the yeshiva, talmidim and Klal Yisroel.

And in recognition to Reb Avi Geffner נ״י
for his tireless work for the Yeshiva and for the Klal.

May the רבש״ע bentsch them with gezunt to continue
in their עד מאה ועשרים שנה, עבודת הקודש.

Dovid and Mila Wallk

לעילוי ולזכר נשמת
הילדה רחמה ליבא ע״ה
בת ר׳ אליעזר שלום נ״י
הייזלער

נפטרה י״ד סיון תשס״א

ת.נ.צ.ב.ה.

נדבת משה וחי' יוטא (מייזנער) גרינברגר
לעלוי נשמות הורינו

ר' עזריאל יהודה ב"ר משה ע"ה גרינברגר נפטר ט"ז ניסן (ב' פסח) תשס"ד
אסתר ניחה בת ר' מנשה ע"ה גרינברגר נפטרה י"ג סיון תשס"ד
ור' יעקב צבי ב"ר יוסף ע"ה מייזנער נפטר ר"ח כסלו (א' כסלו) תשס"ס
ת.נ.צ.ב.ה.

Dedicated in memory of our dear parents Isidor, Ella Greenberger and 'Hershel' Meisner. My father passed away on his english wedding anniversary, April 7th. His love for his wife, my mother, was so strong that she could not live without him and 8 weeks later she joined him in the world beyond. My father loved the holiday of Pesach and therefore it was quite appropriate for him to pass to the next world on the Yom Tov he so loved. My father-in-law was a devoted and loving husband and father. He passed away on Rosh Chodesh Kislev. As in life he never wanted to be מטריח anyone, so too, he passed away on a day that no הספדים were allowed. Had there been הספדים the funeral may have ended hours later than it actually did.

May they be מליצים ישרים for the entire family, may they be מתפלל for the sick and needy and may we all be זוכה to the coming of משיח במהרה בימינו אמן.

Moshe and Chaya Yita (Meisner) Greenberger

לז"נ

הרב יעקב שמעון בן ר' ברוך גאלדפיין ז"ל

יגע ועמל בתורה כל ימי חייו
למד תורה למאות תינוקות של בית רבן
קרב אלפים תחת כנפי השכינה

יה"ר שיהיה מליץ יושר לנו ולכל ישראל

מאת משפחתו

לזכרון ולעילוי נשמת
ר׳ חיים יוסף בן הרב נפתלי טייכמאן ע״ה
נפטר בשבת קודש כ״ז אייר תשמ״ה
הרב נפתלי בן רב שמואל ע״ה
נפטר ט׳ שבט תשכ״ח
רחל דינה בת רב דוד ע״ה
נפטרה ב׳ טבת תשכ״ז

מאת
דוד אליעזר טייכמאן

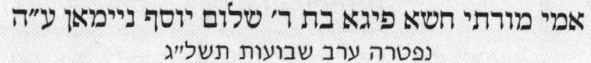

לזכר נשמת
אמי מורתי חשא פיגא בת ר׳ שלום יוסף ניימאן ע״ה
נפטרה ערב שבועות תשל״ג

אבי זקני ר׳ שלום יוסף בן ר׳ שימא גוטמאן קושנער ע״ה
נפטר כ״ד מרחשון תש״מ

אמי זקנתי גרונא בת יוסף יהושע קושנער ע״ה
נפטרה ב׳ אייר תשמ״ט

אבי זקני ר׳ צבי בן ר׳ יעקב ניימאן ע״ה
נפטר שב״ק שבעה עשר בתמוז תשנ״א

אבי זקני ר׳ יעקב בן ר׳ פינחס אייזיק קירשנביום ע״ה
נפטר י״ב אייר תשמ״ג

אמי זקנתי רבקה בת ר׳ מרדכי הכהן קירשנבוים ע״ה
נפטרה כ״ה מרחשון תשנ״ו

אבי זקני החבר יוסף בן החבר חיים זאב ברון ע״ה
נפטר ש״ק ב׳ דראש חודש אייר תשס״ב

דודי זקני ר׳ אברהם אשר בן ר׳ יוסף יהושע צימערמאן ע״ה
נפטר כ״ג מרחשון תשנ״ז

דודי זקני ר׳ שלמה בן ר׳ יוסף יהושע צימערמאן ע״ה
נפטר י״ח אלול תשס״ב

אליהו ניימאן ומשפחתו

לעילוי ולזכר נשמת

גיטל בת ר' יצחק אייזיק ע"ה

כ"ט חשון תשס"ה

ת.נ.צ.ב.ה.

משפחת שניידר

In memory of

לז"נ קלמן הירש בן זיסקינד
Karl H. Moskowitz

לז"נ אסתר בת בנימין
Elsbeth Kramer

לז"נ הרב נתן קרפל בן הרב משולם
Rabbi Charlie Weiss

לז"נ הרב נתנאל בן זלמן פנחס הכהן
Rabbi Nesanel Quinn זצ"ל

who influenced our lives greatly

Robert and Evelyn Moskowitz

לז"נ ר' משה בן ר' גדליה ע"ה
שמיני עצרת תשס"ג

ולז"נ עדינה מרים בת ר' שמואל הלוי
כ"ד חשון תשנ"ז

ולז"נ ישולא בן יעקב ע"ה

Nechama and Yochanan Ishakis

לעילוי הנשמות

רבקה לאה בת יהודה ליב ע"ה	ר' שלום ב"ר צבי הכהן ע"ה
Rivka Ray Blank	Ernest Hess
י"ט כסלו תשנ"ו	ב' דראש השנה תשנ"ה
ר' בנימין יעקב	ר' צבי אריה
ב"ר צבי אריה הלוי ע"ה	ב"ר משה הלוי ע"ה
Jerrald Blank	Harry Blank
י"ז אב תשמ"ה	ו' כסלו תש"מ

From
**Rabbi Yehuda and Keila Blank
and family**

לעילוי נשמת הבחורה היקרה
דבורה ע"ה בת אשר גדעון נ"י
שנקטפה בדמי ימיה

כ"ה תמוז תשס"א

צנועה ותמימה בכל מעשיה

כל שרוח הבריות נוחה הימנה
רוח המקום נוחה הימנו

שלמה פלאוט

לעילוי נשמת אבי מורי
הרב ר' מיכל בן ר' ניסן ז"ל
שישקא
ב' תשרי ה'תשל"ג

ולעילוי נשמת אמי מורתי
יענטא בת ר' יחיאל מיכל ע"ה
שישקא
ח' סיון ה'תשס"ב

ת.נ.צ.ב.ה.

נדבת בנם
ניסן צבי שישקא Szyszko

לז"נ
משה יעקב
בן הרב חיים ישראל ע"ה
In memory of
Moshe Shubert
נפטר בשם טוב

י"א אב תשס"ד

Always in our hearts

Mrs. Judith Shubert-Finkelstein
Boruch Shubert

לעילוי נשמת האשה
רבקה בת ר' משה דוד ע"ה
נפטרה י"ב אדר ה'תשס"ב

In memory of
Mrs. Rivka Tanenbaum A"H
February 24, 2002

אשה משארית הפליטה מחורבן יראפ
רוחה ועצמיותה העצומים
בנו בית שממנו הון כיבודים
קולות של שבח בקירוב נשמעים
היותם לה ולדורות לזכותים חשובים
הונצח ע"י בעלה
אפרים יהושע בן מנחם מנדל טעננבוים שי'
ובתה שרה אלטע
ונכדותי' פייגא אסתר ונחמה בלימה שי'
וע"י בנה ר' משה דוד מנחם מענדל ואשתו
מרת שושנה ובניהם בן ציון שמואל
ושלמה ברוך שיחיו

In honor of
my dear parents
Sam and Clarisse
Mizrahi

My deep thanks to you for everything. May Hashem bless you with good health and happiness for many years to come.

Love, your daughter
Allison

לעילוי נשמת הורינו
In loving memory of our Parents
ר' יעקב ב"ר צבי זאב קץ ז"ל
מרת חנה קץ ע"ה
בת ר' מנחם מנדל פלצקר ז"ל

ר' יחיאל מיכל ב"ר שלום לאנגנער ז"ל
מרת עטיל הענטיא לאנגנער ע"ה
בת ר' חיים יוסף רייטער ז"ל

Claire and Meyer Katz
Menucha and Hillel Hyman & family
Zev and Yocheved Katz & family
Shulamis and Mordechai Ginsburg & family

לעילוי ולזכר נשמת
ר' צבי יעקב ב"ר מרדכי לייב ע"ה
נפטר י"ח ניסן תשמ"ט

מרת רות בת ר' אריה ע"ה
נפטרה ו' חשון תשל"ט

זכו לגדל דורות לתורה ומצוות

הונצח ע"י
משפחת קעניגסבערג

לעילוי ולזכר נשמת האשה
חי' שרה בת ר' יוסף הכהן ע"ה
ה' כסלו תשנ"א
whose whole life
was giving to others

תנו לה מפרי ידיה
ויהללוה בשערים מעשיה

ת.נ.צ.ב.ה.

Yisocher and Estie Sussman
and family

In loving memory of our parents,
grandparents, brother and uncle

ר׳ אבא משה בן יעקב דוד ע״ה
יענטא בת ר׳ חיים ע״ה
ר׳ שמואל אלימלך
בן יחיאל מיכל ע״ה
פעראל בת רפאל דוד ע״ה
משה מיכל בן שמואל אלימלך ע״ה

Anshel and Fraidel Rennert
Refoel Dovid, Eliyohu Meir
and Rochel Sarah

לזכר נשמת
יוסף בן חיים לבוש ע״ה
ורעיתו
חוה רבקה בת זאב הכהן ע״ה
אלכסנדר בן צבי הירש שוץ ע״ה
ורעיתו
דבורה בת יוסף ע״ה

By their children
Barbara and Robert Schutz

לעילוי ולזכר נשמת
ר׳ אבא משה ב״ר יעקב דוד רעננערט ז״ל
נפטר ו׳ ניסן תשמ״ה

יענטא בת ר׳ חיים ע״ה
והאשה
נפטרה ד׳ שבט תשנ״ח

In memory of
Reb Abba Moshe and Yetta Rennert ע״ה

לעילוי ולזכר נשמת
ר׳ צבי ארי׳ בן ר׳ שמריהו ע״ה
נפטר י״ז טבת תשנ״ב
והאשה הינדה בת ר׳ שמואל הכהן ע״ה
נפטרה י״ג אדר א׳ תשס״ג

In memory of
Reb Hershel and Hilda Halberg ע״ה
Who have raised generations of Bnai Torah

Dedicated by Rabbi and Mrs. Yaakov
Dovid and Sarah Rennert and family

לזכר נשמת
ר׳ ישרא׳ בן ר׳ מאיר זצ״ל
בינה בת ר׳ דויד ע״ה
ר׳ בנימין ביינוש בן ר׳ ישרא׳ ז״ל
ר׳ מאיר בן ר׳ ישרא׳ ז״ל

יהא זכרם ברוך

ר׳ מיכא׳ ונחמה דרייפוס
ר׳ יואל דויד, ר׳ יעקב מאיר,
ורעותיהם
ר׳ משה נתן ושולמית

לעילוי נשמת
מיכל בן רב חיים זאב ע"ה
In memory of
Mr. Max Goldberg ע"ה
כ"ה טבת תש"ס
איש נאמן שומר תורה ומצוות, עוסק
בצרכי ציבור באמונה, יהי מליץ יושר
בעדינו ובעד כלל ישראל
In memory of the wonderful sedorim
we partook together with our family.

ת.נ.צ.ב.ה.

Mrs. Tillie Goldberg
Wayne and Susan Goldberg and Family
Milton and Fran Pfeiffer and Family
Howard Goldberg

In memory of our beloved parents
לעילוי נשמת
אליעזר בן חזקיהו שראגא פייוול ע"ה
ופייגא דאבא בת משה ע"ה
Louis and Frances Sobel ע"ה

Who along with the rest of the
שארית הפליטה devoted their lives
to successfully building a
Torah-true generation

Allan and Esther
Yarmush and family

לז"נ
שמעון בן החבר לוי יוסף ז"ל
מרים בת יעקב צבי ע"ה
פנחס בן יהודה לייב הכהן ז"ל
חי' רחל בת ר' מאיר ע"ה
דוב בער בן דוד ז"ל
פייגע בת ר' שלמה ע"ה

ובזכות
תהילה נשמה בת חנה
לרפואה שלימה

Aaron, Adina, Shamshi, Pinchos
and Dov Ber Rosenfeld

Dedicated in memory of our parents
ר' צבי הירש
בן קלונימוס קלמן ע"ה
חיה דבורה ב"ר פנחס ע"ה
Reb Zvi-Hersh and Chaya
Devorah Drebin

ת.נ.צ.ב.ה.

Mr. and Mrs. Kalman
Drebin

This dedication is sponsored by
Virtual Judaica, Inc.

Exhibition Hall:
1760 Fifty-third Street
Brooklyn, NY 11204

718-686-7937
www.virtualjudaica.com
info@virtualjudaica.com

In honor of
Jan, Orit
Barry, Shana
Gershon, Ahuva
Yair, Ariel
Avigayil, Noam
Talia, Ayelet, Yona,
Maytal and Saadia
שיחיו לימים טובים ארוכים

Susanne and Michael Wimpfheimer

In memory of
Arthur Selmar ע״ה
ר׳ עזריאל אבא בן דוד ע״ה
ט״ז חשון

In memory of
Shelly Seiff ע״ה
רחל סימא ע״ה
בת אברהם יהושע נ״י
כ׳ חשון

ת.נ.צ.ב.ה.

לזכר ולעילוי נשמת
חיים נחום בן יצחק דוב ע״ה
ה׳ חשון תשנ״ה

In loving memory of
Chaim Brownstein ע״ה

ת.נ.צ.ב.ה.

Daniel and Gila
Brownstein
and family

In loving memory of
George and Ruth Millman ע״ה
לזכר נשמת
Getzel ben Eliyahu ע״ה
ז׳ כסלו תשס״ד
Raizel Duba bas Chuna ע״ה
כ״ט ניסן תשי״ג
May they be מליצי ישרים
for the entire משפחה.

Reuven and Marcy Millman
and Family

לזכר נשמת
מרדכי ע״ה בן אברהם נ״י

In memory of
Edward Norman ע״ה
ג׳ תמוז תשס״ב

Mr. and Mrs. Nochum
Norman
and Family

לזכר נשמות
ר׳ דוד בן ר׳ שלמה הירש ע״ה
ר׳ אליהו אלכסנדר בן
ר׳ שמואל יעקב זאלצמאן ע״ה
חנה בת יקותיאל יהודה
זאלצמאן ע״ה

ת.נ.צ.ב.ה.

Mr. and Mrs. Shlomo
Hirsch

In fond memory of our parents,
grandparents and sister
צבי ב״ר בן ציון טרינק
ברכה מינה גיטה בת ר׳ יצחק טרינק
יהודה ב״ר שמריהו הכהן סארקין
צירל בת ר׳ נחום הכהן סארקין
חיה בת ר׳ יהודה הכהן סארקין

זאת נדבת
סימה לאה ויצחק שלמה
צבי, יהודה, נחום
ושמשון חיים סארקין

In honor of

Ema

who always makes
a spectacular Yom Tov
for the family.

**Dov and Debbie
Kagan**

In honor of
אשת חיל my

Brenda

באהבה,

Mark

In honor of
our dear children

**Dina Chana,
Rochel Leah,
Chaya Miriam**
and
Meir Yekusiel Yehuda

May the רבש״ע grant us
much נחת from them.

**Moshe and Marcia
Rosenfeld**

In honor of
our dear children

**Ada Gitel and Elimelech
Lipa and Leah**
and
Heshel Feivel

Ed and Shelly Raskin

לז"נ

Bubby Chames

חנה בת יצחק יעקב ע"ה

י"א אלול תשס"ג

לז"נ

Yaakov Chames

יעקב בן אברהם זאב

ז' אדר תשמ"ה

The Selmar Family

לז"נ

יגאל פנחס בן אברהם יצחק ליפשיטץ ע"ה

נפטר ביום הכפורים 5764

A devoted husband, father, grandfather and brother

A pure gentle soul

ת.נ.צ.ב.ה.

לז"נ

הב' אפרים מרדכי ז"ל
בן הרב משה יצחק הכהן
יארמוש שליט"א

מוקיר רבנן, קבל כל אדם בסבר פנים יפות, קיבל יסורים באהבה, השקיע נפשו בתורה, למד תורה מתוך הדחק

His שמחת החיים at all times was and will continue to be a חיזוק to all those who were זוכה to know him.

ת.נ.צ.ב.ה.

Itchie and Miriam Deutsch

In memory of
our beloved parents
who were מלא חסד and
supporters of
כלל ישראל for תורה

יצחק אליעזר בן אהרן

נפטר ל' ניסן תשנ"ג

מערא בת אברהם יעקב

נפטרה י"ד כסלו תשמ"ח

The Gertz and
Weissberger Families

לע"נ

הבחור החשוב אפרים מרדכי ז"ל
בן הרב משה יצחק הכהן שליט"א
Ephraim Yarmush ע"ה
who was taken from us at
the young age of 22.
He accomplished in his
short life what others take
a lifetime to achieve.

ת.נ.צ.ב.ה.

Yossi and Helene Klein

---

*In loving memory of our parents
and grandparents*

שלמה בן יעקב לייב ע"ה
שרה אלקה בת ר' דוב בער הכהן ע"ה

Our dear aunt

פיגא רחל בת אברהם וועלוועל ע"ה

our dear grandparents

אברהם וועלוועל בן יעקב דניאל ע"ה
אסתר לאה בת שמואל ישעיה ע"ה

*In honor of our dear brother,
Uncle Jeff*

ישראל אשר בן שלמה נ"י

The Winograd Family

לע"נ
אבי מורי
ר' אברהם משה הלפרן זצ"ל
בן ר' חיים הלפרן שליט"א
נפטר
ב' דראש חדש תמוז תשנ"ה

*Yanky and Blimi
Halpern*

לזכר נשמות

החה' רב מאיר בן נתן הכהן
חנה בת רב יצחק
רב יצחק בן יעקב
יענט בת רב דוד

*Dedicated by their beloved
children and grandchildren*
Ted and Eleanor Lomnitz
Yitzchok and Shulamis Lomnitz
Dovid Lomnitz

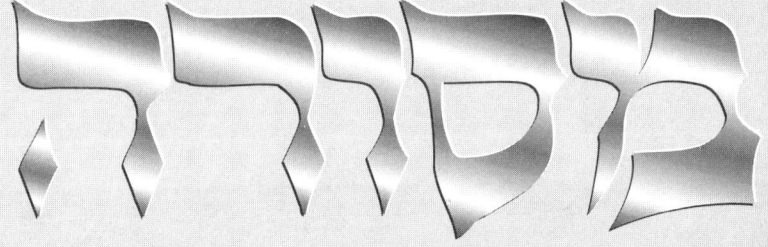

ArtScroll Mesorah Series®

Rabbi Nosson Scherman / Rabbi Meir Zlotowitz
General Editors

THE WASSERMAN EDITION

הגדה של פסח

THE PESACH HAGGADAH
with insights, halachic rulings and customs of
RABBI SHLOMO ZALMAN AUERBACH

Compiled by Rabbi Yisroel Bronstein
adapted into English by Rabbi David Oratz

Published by
Mesorah Publications, ltd

FIRST EDITION
First Impression . . . April 2005

Published and Distributed by
MESORAH PUBLICATIONS, Ltd.
4401 Second Avenue
Brooklyn, New York 11232

Distributed in Europe by
LEHMANNS
Unit E, Viking Business Park
Rolling Mill Road
Jarrow, Tyne & Wear NE32 3DP
England

Distributed in Australia & New Zealand by
GOLDS WORLD OF JUDAICA
3-13 William Street
Balaclava, Melbourne 3183
Victoria Australia

Distributed in Israel by
SIFRIATI / A. GITLER — BOOKS
6 Hayarkon Street
Bnei Brak 51127

Distributed in South Africa by
KOLLEL BOOKSHOP
Shop 8A Norwood Hypermarket
Norwood 2196, Johannesburg, South Africa

THE RAV SHLOMO ZALMAN HAGGADAH
© *Copyright 2005 by* MESORAH PUBLICATIONS, Ltd.
4401 Second Avenue / Brooklyn, N.Y. 11232 / (718) 921-9000 / www.artscroll.com

All rights reserved. *This text, the new translation, commentary, and prefatory comments — including the typographic layout, illustrations, charts, appendices, and cover design — have been edited and revised as to content, form and style and are fully protected against copyright infringement.*

No part of this book may be reproduced in any form — including photocopying and retrieval systems — *without* **written** *permission from the copyright holder, except by a reviewer who wishes to quote brief passages in connection with a review written for inclusion in magazines or newspapers.*

THE RIGHTS OF THE COPYRIGHT HOLDER WILL BE STRICTLY ENFORCED.

ISBN: 1-57819-062-2

Typography by CompuScribe at ArtScroll Studios, Ltd.
4401 Second Avenue / Brooklyn, N.Y. 11232 / (718) 921-9000

Printed in the United States of America by Noble Book Press

עֲטֶרֶת זְקֵנִים בְּנֵי בָנִים
The crown of elders is grandchildren
(*Mishlei* 17:6)

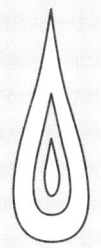

This Haggadah is dedicated
in loving memory of our dear parents

Joseph and Bess Wasserman ז"ל

יוסף בן דוב בער ע"ה   בילא בת יעקב ע"ה
ט' טבת תש"מ   י"ב סיון תשמ"ב

Sascha and Regina (Czaczkes) Charles ז"ל

שמריהו בן משה ע"ה   רבקה בת הרב יוסף הכהן ע"ה
י"ח אלול תשל"ב   ט"ו תמוז תשכ"ז

and in honor of our beloved children and grandchildren

Alan and Svetlana Wasserman
Sasha, Jesse, Talya, Jacob, and Bella

Mark and Anne Wasserman
Joseph, Bailey, Erin, Rebeccah, and Jordyn

Neil and Yael Wasserman
Yeshayahu, Shiri, Yonatan, and Ruth

Stuart and Rivka Berger
David, Gabrielle, and Jack

We are proud that the example, values, and legacy of our parents are so much at home in the lives of our children. How appropriate for a Pesach Haggadah, that unites generations.

Stanley and Ellen Wasserman

Preface

As members of the multitudes who were enlightened by the wisdom and warmed by the kindness of Maran Hagaon Harav Shlomo Zalman Auerbach זצוק״ל, we deem it a privilege to publish this volume, which collects his comments on the Haggadah and his halachic rulings on the Seder.

One of the most beloved *gedolim* and leading *poskim* of our time, Reb Shlomo Zalman was revered by great roshei hayeshivah and rabbanim and also by ordinary laymen and even little children. He was Rosh Yeshivas Kol Torah; responded orally and in writing to complex halachic queries day in, day out; and had his private intensive learning schedule; but he still managed to find time for the many people who consulted him on personal matters. It was typical of him that he considered a humble sanitation worker to be worthy of honor because "he merits to clean the streets of the Holy City."

His humility matched his greatness, but it could not mask his stature as one of the Torah giants of his era. This Haggadah is no more than an introduction to his clarity and depth of thought and his sensitivity to every segment of Klal Yisrael.

The material in this volume was collected by Rabbi Yisrael Bronstein, who has distinguished himself as an anthologizer of note. The original Hebrew version of this work has been and remains extremely popular in Israel, and we are certain that the English version will be accepted as a valuable contribution to the growing library of high quality English-language Judaica.

Without doubt, the Reb Shlomo Zalman Haggadah will enrich the Seder and Yom Tov of every family that has it. For being able to bring it to the public, we are grateful.

Rabbi Meir Zlotowitz   Rabbi Nosson Scherman
II Adar, 5765 / March 2005

Introduction

Praise to the Holy One, Blessed is He, Who allowed me to dwell in the tents of Torah. Now, He has graciously increased His favors to me, giving me the privilege of collecting the laws of the Seder and its customs. Clearly, His favors to me are undeserved.

I begin in the spirit of the words of the midrash (*Bereishis Rabbah* 97) which state: As the fish, growing in water, thirstily drink each new drop of rain, so too the Jewish People, growing in the waters of Torah, accept, thirstily, each new word of Torah, as if they had never heard words of Torah in their lives. Would my meager words be accepted with thirst. The Gemara (*Kiddushin* 13a) states: When Rav Assi passed away, the rabbis gathered in the study hall to collect all his teachings in order that they not be forgotten.

The words of Torah and the illuminating rulings of our master, Rav Shlomo Zalman Auerbach, of blessed memory, were greatly loved by the Jewish People. Now, many gather in the study hall to eternalize his teachings. The pure wellsprings of his Torah continue to quench the thirst of tens of thousands.

Therefore, using the words of our master as the final authority, I have undertaken to gather and select from the laws of Pesach, beginning with those pertaining to *Shabbos Hagadol* and continuing through those relevant to the last day of Pesach.

My first thanks are to my good friend, Rav Aharon Goldberg, grandson of our great teacher, who served him faithfully. He graciously shared with me so much of what he learned from his grandfather, including rulings, customs, halachic and Aggadic expositions. His marvelous memory is a veritable storehouse of the customs of his illustrious grandfather. Without his guidance, advice, and aid, this work would never have come to be. The words of *Mis-*

hlei, One with a good eye will be blessed (*Mishlei* 22:9), certainly apply to him. May Hashem reward him with *nachas* from all his offspring, as they follow in the footsteps of their fathers, and may he receive plentiful blessings forever.

Praise and thanks to Rav Shlomo Zalman's renowned disciple, Rav Avigdor Nebenzahl, rabbi of the Old City of Jerusalem. He spent much of his precious time reviewing this manuscript in his meticulous way, explaining many things with his insightful comments. May he be blessed with the Divine Light, and may he continue to spread his wealth of knowledge.

Great thanks and blessings to my friend Rav Yosef Shub, one of Rav Shlomo Zalman's closest disciples, for dedicating many hours in passing on the teachings of our master with great conscientiousness and wisdom.

With a great debt of gratitude I recognize the renowned *Roshei Yeshivah* and mentors whose sweet fruits I have eaten from and under whose wings I studied. These include Rav Baruch Mordechai Ezrachi, *Rosh Yeshivah* of Ateres Yisrael, and Rav Nosson Tzvi Finkel, *Rosh Yeshivah* of Mir. I drank from their Torah and they guided me in the path of Torah and fear of Heaven. With Hashem's blessing, may they reign many more years.

I express my limitless gratitude to my parents and in-laws who devoted themselves wholeheartedly to guiding their children in diligent Torah study and serving Hashem. They have done everything to remove from me any burdens and worries. May the Master of All compensate their work in full. I bless them with King David's blessing (*Tehillim* 92:15), "They will still be fruitful in old age, they will be vigorous and fresh," May they merit seeing their children and grandchildren to the *chuppah*, accomplished in Torah and good deeds. May Hashem bless them with good health and with joyful long years until the coming of *Mashiach*.

I take this opportunity to express my gratitude to my brother, Rav Yaakov Akiva, who teaches Torah in Yeshivah Tiferes Yaakov here in Yerushalayim. With great care he reviewed this entire work, and his marvelously clear and straightforward remarks clarified many important points for me. Many of those comments are cited in his name in the original Hebrew edition of this book. Hashem should continue to send him Heavenly blessings and may he see much *na-*

chas from his children as they continue in the ways of Hashem.

A special thank-you to the hosts of Torah, the administration of the Rav Zvi Pesach Frank Torah Institute and Library, and to its head, Rav Shabsi Dov Rosenthal. He and his institute were of great benefit to me. May Hashem grant him what his soul truly desires, to promulgate Torah and to strengthen it.

I would like to express my gratitude to Rav Yitzchak Kaufman, rabbi, *Rosh Kollel*, and more, who reviewed this book meticulously and made wonderful and enlightening comments. Similarly, I thank Rav Efraim Kirshenbaum for his wise guidance and advice.

I owe a great debt of gratitude to the renowned philanthropist Rav Nachum Meir Yaakov Weinreb, a lover of Torah and its scholars, who graciously took upon himself the cost of publishing the Hebrew version of this work, spreading the Torah teachings of our great master. May the merit of Rav Shlomo Zalman stand in his favor and that of his offspring, and may Hashem shower his house with blessings.

Praise to my good friend Rav Aaron Ilan, a storehouse of knowledge, who prepared an index for the Hebrew edition and was constantly available for help in any way.

This English edition opens up the Torah of Rav Shlomo Zalman Auerbach to an even wider audience. Thanks to Rabbi Dovid Oratz for translating this work and to Devorah Rhein for her help in editing.

A very special expression of gratitude to my wife and helpmate Chaya. Her wisdom and supreme skill in managing the house enable me to sit and study with peace of mind. Without her aid, this book would never have seen the light of day. In the immortal words of R' Akiva: What is mine is hers. May Hashem give us the merit to raise our children together in the path of Torah and fear of Heaven, with good health and Divine enlightenment. May we have only *nachas* and joy until the advent of *Mashiach*, speedily in our day. Amen.

Yisrael Bronstein
Rosh Chodesh Kislev 5765

Halachic Rulings Rav Shlomo Zalman Auerbach זצ"ל

◆§ Thirty Days Before Pesach

There is a Talmudic requirement that calls for asking about, and delving into, the laws of Pesach thirty days before Pesach (see *Pesachim* 6a; *Megillah* 4a). Rav Shlomo Zalman was asked: Can this requirement be fulfilled by studying *Yom Tov* laws as well, or does it have to be specifically the laws of Pesach?

He replied that it was clear that study of *Yom Tov* laws was not sufficient; one was required to study the laws specific to Pesach. However, one could supplement those laws with the laws of *Yom Tov*, so that he would know how to behave on *Yom Tov* as well.

He added: One could not say that because the general laws of *Yom Tov* are not specifically related to the upcoming holiday, studying its laws would be considered much like studying any tractate of Talmud. Study of other tractates is necessary, but is not included in the thirty-day requirement. In this case, however, he must clarify the laws of *Yom Tov* so that he will know what to do on the upcoming *Yom Tov* (*Ma'adanei Shlomo, Pesach*, p. 1).

Thirty days before Pesach, one may not use glue made from flour and water to bind books, out of concern that by the onset of Pesach it will not become disqualified to the degree that a dog would not eat it (*Mevakshei Torah* II, p. 552).

Rav Shlomo Zalman ruled that one may use money set aside for *ma'aser* (tithing) for the charity that supplies matzah for the poor.

In the past, there was a sum set by the community for this purpose and it was considered like a tax, and thus not eligible as *ma'aser* (see *Shulchan Aruch* 429:1 and *Mishnah Berurah* ad loc. 6). Today, however, there is no set sum that one must give for this cause. Accordingly, it can be considered like any other charity, and *ma'aser* funds may be used (*Ma'adanei Shlomo, Mo'adim, Inyanei Pesach*).

❧ The Blessing on Fruit Trees

If one did not recite the blessing the first time he saw the blossom on the fruit tree, he can recite the blessing the next time, even within thirty days of the first sighting (The same ruling applies to the blessing upon seeing the Great Sea and upon seeing a king.) (*Minchas Shlomo, Pesach* p. 6).

❧ Selling Chametz

Rav Shlomo Zalman was asked whether one could fully rely on selling true *chametz*, or should he only rely on it for difficult situations (e.g., great loss of money or the like). He responded that it is certainly preferable to finish all true *chametz* that one owns before Pesach, so as to avoid any question of the Torah prohibition against possessing *chametz* on Pesach. On the other hand, since the prohibition against eating *chametz* that remained over Pesach is only Rabbinic, it is fully permissible to rely on the sale of the storekeeper to be able to buy any product that he sold. In fact, when one has true *chametz* that he cannot consume before Pesach, it is a good idea to "sell" it to a storekeeper who has no choice but to sell the *chametz* in his store (*V'Aleihu Lo Yibol* I, page 166; also see *Ma'adanei Shlomo, Pesach,* p. 6).

Rav Shlomo Zalman was asked the following question concerning a storekeeper who died: The children of the deceased inherited the store and they transferred their share in the store to their mother through a halachically binding method. The store, however, was officially registered in the name of one of the children. Who has the obligation to sell the *chametz*?

He responded that according to Torah law the store belonged to the mother and to her only. Accordingly, the obligation to sell the *chametz* was hers alone, regardless of the officially registered owner of the store (*Ma'adanei Shlomo, Pesach*, p. 7).

When a resident of the Diaspora owns *chametz* in Israel and his agent sells it for him in Israel, the custom is that after Pesach ends [in Israel] the religious court acquires the *chametz* from the gentile. The *chametz* is thus in the possession of the court until the Jew does an act of acquisition for his *chametz* at a time when it is no longer Pesach for him. In this way, although the original owner of the *chametz* has an additional day of *Yom Tov,* the *chametz* that he had sold is technically not his until after his own Pesach is over.

Actually, however, this may not be necessary, for regarding the *chametz* that is *in Israel*, there could never have been a requirement for an extra day. Accordingly, it is possible to say that he may derive benefit on the eighth day of Pesach (while he is abroad) from his *chametz* in Israel. Further research on the topic is necessary, however (*Minchas Shlomo* II:58).

All year round, one should not sell *chametz* to a Jew who could conceivably eat or keep that *chametz* on Pesach. Selling to such a Jew transgresses the prohibition based on the verse (*Vayikra* 19:14): "You shall not place a stumbling block before a blind person" (in this case he is figuratively "blind" to the prohibition, and a "stumbling block" is placed before him). This is especially true for sales within thirty days of Pesach (see *Pesachim* 21b) (*Minchas Shlomo* I:44).

When fire breaks out on Pesach in the house of a gentile, it would seem permissible for the Jew to save the *chametz* that he himself sold to the gentile. Although he derives benefit from the knowledge that the *chametz* that he is saving will ultimately become his and he will then be able to eat it, this benefit is not really considered a "benefit," since at this moment the *chametz* belongs fully to the gentile (*Minchas Shlomo* II:55).

Rav Shlomo Zalman was asked how one could sell the crumbs in his books, being that apparently no gentile is interested in purchasing crumbs.

His response: A gentile is indeed interested in buying these crumbs, as well as even the *chametz* absorbed inside utensils, provided that he also acquires all the *chametz* of the large bakeries.

Furthermore, he must be paid for the bother of removing the *chametz* from these places. However, there is no real need to sell the crumbs inside books, since it is extremely unlikely that a person would ever eat the crumbs from his books. (See above General section, *Bedikas Chametz*)

When a person is unconscious as Pesach approaches, his caretakers should sell his *chametz* to a gentile for him. Since the *chametz* would otherwise become prohibited for any benefit, they are, in effect, fulfilling the mitzvah of returning a lost object. However, this may only apply when the *chametz* is actually transferred to the property of the gentile. Then there is no question that the gentile acquires the *chametz* at the time that it becomes prohibited to the Jew. When, however, it remains in the property of the Jew, the issue is quite complicated. If the person is mentally incompetent to effect a sale, it is far from clear that others can act as his agent without being appointed to do so. Only his wife, or the person designated to take care of his financial responsibilities, would clearly be allowed to sell the *chametz* (*Nachamu Ami*, Chapter 3 and notes there).

Actually, it is far from clear that a non-appointed agent can ever sell someone else's *chametz*. The Gemara in several places (e.g., *Bava Metzia* 12a) teaches that a non-appointed agent cannot act on behalf of a principal unless the matter is clearly advantageous to the principal. In the case of selling *chametz*, the alternative is transgressing a Torah prohibition and having the *chametz* become prohibited from benefit even after Pesach. It would thus seem to be clearly advantageous for the principal when a non-appointed agent sells the *chametz* on his behalf.

This would not apply to most non-religious Jews, however. If the seller knows that the principal would not agree to a full and proper sale, and would only agree to a *pro-forma* sale, then his sale of the principal's *chametz* is worthless. Accordingly, benefit from the *chametz* becomes prohibited (*Ma'adanei Eretz, Shevi'is* 1:20).

Yet even regarding religious Jews, who would agree to a full sale of their *chametz*, Rav Shlomo Zalman would not permit the *chametz* to be sold by a non-appointed agent. He ruled that the *chametz* of one who had forgotten to sell it should be burned — despite the fact that others sold the *chametz* for him. He based this on the view of

Ketzos Hachoshen (243:8), who rules that money [and, by extension, property] can never be *taken* from a principal without his knowledge even when it is completely to his advantage (reported by Rav Avigdor Nebenzahl).

A person who removes all *chametz* from his house has no reason to "sell *chametz*." In fact, "selling" under those circumstances could make the whole process seem a farce (*V'Aleihu Lo Yibol* I, p. 165).

∝§ Bedikas Chametz

If a person checked his pockets by sunlight and ascertained that there was no *chametz* in them, and then he was careful not to allow any more *chametz* into them, he need not check them again on the night of *bedikas chametz* (verbal responsum to *Rav Yehudah Weissenberg*).

The *Shulchan Aruch* (*Orach Chaim* 432:2) writes that one can check several buildings on the basis of one blessing. See *Mishnah Berurah* there 7, who explains that going from one building to another is not considered a break that requires a new blessing. He then cites *Chayei Adam* who qualifies this by stating that no new blessing is necessary because all the buildings are in one courtyard. When, however, a person is checking one building in one courtyard and another in another courtyard (such as his house and his shop), he must recite a second blessing when checking the building in the second courtyard. *Mishnah Berurah* concludes with the ruling of *Chok Yosef* and *Ma'amar Mordechai,* that no amount of going from one place to another requires a second blessing. Their reasoning is: Since all the buildings involve one mitzvah — for he is obligated to check all places containing *chametz* — it is all considered one long, continuing mitzvah.

Rav Shlomo Zalman ruled in accordance with this latter position (*V'Aleihu Lo Yibol*, p. 161).

When an agent performs a mitzvah for a principal, it is the agent who recites the blessing, not the principal. (See *Rambam, Hil. Berachos* 11:13; *K'neses Hagedolah, Orach Chaim* 585; *Terumos Hadeshen* 140, cited in *Teshuvos Kesav Sofer, Yoreh De'ah* 150.)

The reason is apparently similar to the reason given by *Beis Yosef* (432) for reciting a blessing on the removal of *chametz* but not on nullifying it. He explains that the Rabbis instituted a requirement to recite a blessing only for performing an action, or for saying something. Regarding *chametz* nullification, however, it is sufficient for a person to nullify in his heart without saying or doing a thing. Similarly, the principal cannot recite a blessing because he does nothing. Accordingly, if he *does* do something, such as beginning the *bedikah*, he may recite the blessing and then ask someone else to finish checking for *chametz*.

Now the question arises: How can the agent say, "and commanded us," when the house is not his, and he has no obligation whatsoever to check that house? (A similar question can be asked concerning an agent who places a mezuzah on the doorpost of someone else's house and recites the blessing.) This question was asked by *Magen Avraham* (432:6). His answer there (and in 167:40) seems to be based on an important principle stated by Ran (on *Rosh Hashanah* 29a). Ran explains why even a person who has already fulfilled a mitzvah (such as hearing the *shofar* on Rosh Hashanah) can perform that mitzvah again (i.e., blow the *shofar*) to free others from their obligation (*af al pi sheyatza motzi*). The reason for this is because all Jews are responsible for one another (*Kol Yisrael areivim zeh bazeh*). Accordingly, when a person does a mitzvah for the sake of another person's obligation, his responsibility for the other renders it as if he is doing the mitzvah *for himself*, "For since his friend did not fulfill his obligation it is as if he himself did not fulfill his obligation." In a similar vein, the principal is required to search for *chametz* in his own house, and when he does not fulfill his obligation, another individual is responsible for his requirement. When an individual chooses to fulfill this responsibility, and actually does the search, he can recite a blessing for his own responsibility to fulfill this mitzvah.

This is apparently the intention of the *Mishnah Berurah* (432:10) that writes that this individual is an agent for the blessing as well. For without this explanation, even if the agent can save the principal from transgressing by possessing *chametz*, why should he be able to recite the blessing? Similarly, this explains why the *Mishnah Berurah* writes (ibid.,:11) that if the principal recites the blessing and then he sends someone else to do the search, the second one does not recite a blessing, because an agent recites a blessing only for the principal's obligation to do so, and in this case he already recited a blessing.

(If he appointed two people, however, each of whom is to check one of two houses, then each one recites a blessing, for there is no connection between them.) (*Halichos Shlomo* 22:2, note 35, from a manuscript of Rav Shlomo Zalman.)

✥ Removal of Chametz

The *Shulchan Aruch* (440:2) rules that a Jew must erect a barrier at least ten handbreadths high in front of *chametz* in his house that belongs to a gentile. Today, most Jews sell their *chametz* to a gentile. Nevertheless, since it is so difficult to move all sorts of whiskeys and the like into a separate room and erect a ten-handbreadth-high barrier in front of it, is it sufficient to keep the *chametz* locked in a closet inside a drawer lower than ten handbreadths high? Alternatively, may it be left closed up in its own closet which is ten handbreadths high even though that is its normal place all year round?

Rav Shlomo Zalman ruled that it is quite clear that one may not leave the *chametz* closed up in its regular place together with permitted substances, even if the closet is ten handbreadths high. The reason for this is that the most important requirement is to have a clear separation between that which is your own and the *chametz* — which belongs to a gentile — out of concern that one may come to use the gentile's *chametz*.

Thus, although the area containing the *chametz* is either sold or rented, it must nevertheless be an area that a Jew will not enter on Pesach. Accordingly, all the true *chametz* should be gathered into one specific place and then closed up. This place is then sold or rented to the gentile. In addition, one should notify his family that that place was sold to the gentile. That would be sufficient even without a ten-handbreadth-high barrier. He must also hide the key or post a notice onto the entrance that the place belongs to the gentile (*Kovetz Kol HaTorah,* Nisan 5756, in a responsum to Rav Avraham Ehrentrau).

❧ Purging Utensils

Although a year-round utensil that is purged in boiling water to permit its use on Pesach must first be fully clean, one may purge a hot-water kettle even if it has a layer of calcium inside it. True, there is the far-fetched chance that a small crumb of *chametz* fell inside and was covered by the calcium. Yet, even if that were the case, we can assume that its taste has become spoiled and thus nullified (*Hagalas Keilim* 13:401, and note 385 ad loc., citing Rav Shlomo Zalman).

The general principle of purging is *Kebolo kach polto* (as it absorbs so shall it emit). Accordingly, a utensil that absorbed *chametz* through boiling liquid is purged in boiling water. A pressure cooker (whose cooking temperatures can greatly exceed 100 degrees Celsius — the boiling point of water) can nevertheless be purged in ordinary boiling water. This is so because the Sages set the general rule that rapidly boiling water purges. They did not limit this rule to situations in which the *chametz* was absorbed in similar temperatures. For example, the *chametz* may have originally become absorbed through a boiling liquid whose boiling point is higher than 100 degrees Celsius, and yet it can be purged in ordinary boiling water. Furthermore, the *chametz* may have been absorbed at sea level (where the boiling point of water is 100 degrees) and purged in the mountains (where the boiling point is lower). The same applies to pressure cookers; regardless of the temperature at which the *chametz* was absorbed it may be purged in ordinary boiling water (*Minchas Shlomo* 2:67).

False teeth should be thoroughly cleaned and then placed in a pot of boiled water which has been removed from the fire and whose temperature is now about 70 degrees Celsius (people do not eat or drink food whose temperature is higher than that). Generally speaking, utensils are not purged until twenty-four hours have passed since they have been used last, in order to prevent their reabsorbing the emitted taste. In this case, it is sufficient to "spoil" the water to be boiled by means of some substance such as kerosene (Rav Shlomo Zalman Auerbach, cited in *Nishmas Avraham* 1:451. Also see *Minchas Shlomo* 2:46, in the letter to *Chazon Ish*).

Kitchen sinks are generally made of enamel, and purging has no effect on them. [The same applies to formica countertops.] Marble countertops can be purged by means of pouring onto them hot water over a white-hot stone, or, at the very least, pouring onto them boiling water from the pot in which it was boiled (a private responsum to Rav Eliyahu Schlesinger).

Rav Shlomo Zalman said that the custom is to purge a marble countertop by pouring boiling water over it, even when it will be covered. This is a stringency in honor of Pesach (from the notes of his disciple, Rav Yosef Shub).

܀ Baking Matzos

Matzos must be baked with the intention of fulfilling the mitzvah of matzah. The halachic authorities of recent centuries debated over whether matzos baked by machine meet this requirement. Rav Shlomo Zalman stated that the custom of many was to be lenient in this regard and to consider it fully acceptable, especially if a Jew presses the button to activate the machine with the intention of making matzah (*Ma'adanei Shlomo, Pesach,* p. 9).

Matzos baked in a microwave oven are not acceptable for Seder matzos, because matzos must be baked by fire, and there is no "fire" in a microwave oven (Rav Shlomo Zalman, cited in *Seder He'aruch* 5:12).

Rav Ben-Zion Abba Shaul would not use an electric oven for baking matzos for the Seder. He felt that since the electric company controls the flow of electricity, there is a lack of "intent." Rav Shlomo Zalman permitted such matzos (*Orchos Rabbeinu* II p. 40 see there at length).

The *Shulchan Aruch* (459:2) rules: "And after working the dough and heating it up from contact, if it is left unworked it will become *chametz*."

Rav Shlomo Zalman explained that there is no set amount of time during which the dough becomes *chametz* when left unworked. Rather, as long as the dough is left standing in such a way that it is recognizably "unworked," we must fear that it indeed became *chametz*. This is generally over a minute, but it is not clear how much over a minute.

He added that many places have a *"reidler"* who stands at the end of the assembly line and makes the holes in the dough. He presses hard and as a result, there are often crumbs that become stuck onto the table. These crumbs come from worked dough, and they can actually remain on the table for several minutes without being worked. It is not clear whether they are nevertheless considered part of "worked dough" because he constantly does his work on that table, or whether it becomes necessary to change the paper on that table often (*Ma'adanei Shlomo, Pesach,* p. 10).

∾ Erev Pesach

It is forbidden to do any work for pay after noon on *Erev Pesach,* even if it is for the sake of Pesach and even if it is not considered *melachah* (one of the categories of work prohibited on Shabbos and *Yom Tov*). The only exception is if he is working to be able to buy food. Nevertheless, if one finds no one else to do work for the sake of Pesach in a permitted way [such as a gentile who does it for pay, or a Jew who does it for free], he may pay Jewish workers (*Shemiras Shabbos K'hilchasah* 42:43, and note 144 ad loc.).

When using romaine lettuce for *maror,* it is preferable not to clean the leaves by soaking them in a vinegar solution, even if only momentarily, and even if it is immediately washed off in water. According to the *Shulchan Aruch* (*Yoreh De'ah* 105:1), when a food is soaked in vinegar or brine long enough for it to have boiled were it to have been placed on the fire, it is considered "cooked" food (and *maror* should not be "cooked"; see *Orach Chaim* 473:5). For less than that time it is not considered "cooked," but the outer shell is said to have absorbed (as with cooking). Since a lettuce leaf has little or nothing left after the "outer shell" is removed, it is highly questionable whether it may be used for *maror* even after such short soaking (*Minchas Shlomo* 2:58; see *Beis Aharon V' Yisrael,* Shevat-Adar 5756 p. 62).

∾ When Erev Pesach Is Shabbos

At the Shabbos-morning meal of *Erev Pesach,* one who eats challah until the deadline for eating *chametz,* and then continues to eat the rest of the meal without any form of bread or matzah, is not required to recite separate blessings on the rest of the meal. Since *chametz* is forbidden at that time, one might think that the original blessing recited over the challah can thus not apply to the rest of the meal. However, as long as it is all one meal, no new blessings are required on the rest of the meal (*Shevus Yitzchak, Pesach,* p. 111).

When *Erev Pesach* falls out on Shabbos, one may brush his teeth (to rid all remnants of *chametz*) with an ordinary nylon-bristled toothbrush, but he may not use toothpaste (from the notes of Rav Yosef Shub; also see Rav Shlomo Zalman's notes to *Amirah L'Beis Yaakov,* 9).

After the Shabbos-morning meal on *Erev Pesach,* one may not give a gentile the *chametz* remnants to take out to the public domain, since that involves a Torah prohibition [for a Jew, when there is no *eruv*]. However, there are circumstances under which taking from one private domain to another by way of the public domain involves no more than a Rabbinic prohibition [for a Jew]. Under those circumstances, it could be permissable for the Jew to tell a gentile to take the *chametz* out of his house to the gentile's house (*Shemiras Shabbos K'hilchasah* 30:34 and citation from Rav Shlomo Zalman Auerbach in note 121 ad loc.; also see the addendum there).

The *Shulchan Aruch* (*Orach Chaim* 444) rules that when cooking food for use on Shabbos *Erev Pesach* it is forbidden to prepare any *chametz* products that can stick to the pot. Rama adds that in the event that one transgressed and prepared such food and it indeed stuck to the pot, if the pot cannot be wiped clean it may be washed lightly to remove the *chametz*. The *Mishnah Berurah* states that if it is necessary to wash it, it should preferably be washed by a gentile.

Rav Shlomo Zalman writes that at first it was clear to him that Rama referred exclusively to situations in which there was only a possibility of *chametz* remnants. In a case in which there were definite remnants, however, why shouldn't one be allowed to wash the pot? After all, no Jew would want to have any *chametz* remnants in his house over Pesach, despite the permissibility of nullifying the remnants or covering them with another utensil. Therefore it becomes a need of that day (which permits washing the utensil).

Nevertheless, he continued, from the language of Maharil, cited in *Chok Yaakov* 429:22, it appears that the ruling refers to definite *chametz* as well. Apparently, washing the utensil is nonetheless not considered a "need of that day," since the option of covering it with another utensil exists (*Shemiras Shabbos K'hilchasah* 28:167 and addendum there. Also see *Minchas Shlomo* 2:35).

According to *Pri Megadim* (*Eshel Avraham* 444:1), *shemurah matzah* is *muktzeh* on *Erev Pesach* that falls on Shabbos. Based on the context of what he says, it would seem that the prohibition applies to the daytime only, and not to the night, since the letter of the law does not prohibit eating matzah at night. Furthermore, it is clear that such matzah is not *muktzeh* on any other Shabbos (*Minchas Shlomo* 1:10; 2:49; also see *Shemiras Shabbos K'hilchasah* 20:65, and addendum there; for the category of *muktzeh*, see *Shemiras Shabbos K'hilchasah* 20:22 and note 65 there).

Regarding *seudah shelishis* (the third meal) on Shabbos *Erev Pesach*, Rav Shlomo Zalman did not agree with the view that permitted using matzah that was baked not for the sake of the mitzvah. He explained that the source for prohibiting matzah on *Erev Pesach* is the *Yerushalmi* cited in *Tur* 471. The *Yerushalmi* itself states that one cannot fulfill the mitzvah of matzah on Pesach for any matzah baked before noon of *Erev Pesach* — even when baked for the sake of the mitzvah (see *Tur* 458, and others). Thus, the reason for prohibiting eating matzah on *Erev Pesach* can *not* be its suitability for the mitzvah. Furthermore, even matzos that are baked *not* for the sake of the mitzvah must be carefully guarded to ensure that they do not become *chametz* — otherwise, such matzah would be prohibited to eat past an hour before noon on *Erev Pesach*. Although we are particular to ensure that the matzah be baked for the sake of the mitzvah, that is to follow a ruling acceptable to all. Actually, there are several views that maintain that even if they were not watched for the sake of the mitzvah, but only were protected from *chametz* (either from the time of harvest or at least from the time of grinding), they may still be used for the mitzvah (*Shemiras Shabbos K'hilchasah* 56:47).

The author of *Erev Pesach Shechal Lihiyos B'Shabbos* writes (in 21:5) that just as one is permitted to use boiled or fried matzah-meal products for *seudah shelishis,* so too, one may use a cake made from matzah meal, as long as it does not look like bread.

Rav Shlomo Zalman commented that there is nevertheless a difference between a matzah-meal cake and a boiled or fried matzah-meal product. Whereas the blessing on the latter two is *Mezonos* in any quantity, when making a meal (as defined in *Orach Chaim* 168) on the cake, he must wash, recite *Hamotzi,* and afterward recite *Bircas Hamazon* (in his notes at the end of the above-cited book).

Rama (296:8) rules that, ideally, a woman should not recite *Havdalah* for herself but, rather, listen to the *Havdalah* recited by a male. *Shemiras Shabbos K'hilchasah* (II 62:27) rules that when *Havdalah* is recited at the end of *Kiddush* on the Seder night, when everybody recites *Kiddush,* women may recite *Havdalah* as well. Based on the ruling of *Bi'ur Halachah* (296:8 s.v. *Lo yavdilu*), he concludes that she should nevertheless not recite the blessing over fire (*Borei me'orei ha'eish*). Rav Shlomo Zalman, however, disagreed and maintained that she could recite that blessing as well (reported by Rav Avigdor Nebenzahl.)

If one forgot to recite *Havdalah* in the *Kiddush* made on Saturday night, he should continue to recite the Haggadah until the second cup. He should then recite *Havdalah* over the second cup, i.e., he recites *Borei pri hagafen* over the wine, *Borei me'orei ha'eish* over the light of the candles, and the *Havdalah blessing* for *Yom Tov.* Then he drinks the wine.

If, only after drinking the second cup, one remembers that he did not recite *Havdalah,* he must recite *Havdalah* over wine before eating (or before continuing to eat if he already began eating). Even if he specifically had in mind not to drink any other wine — which obligates him to recite a new blessing on this cup — he need not be concerned that he appears to be adding a fifth cup. The reason is that since he may not eat until he recites *Havdalah,* we do not restrict him for unlikely reasons. If, however, he already ate the *afikoman* and then remembered that he did not recite *Havdalah,* he is not permitted to add another cup, and he must recite the *Havdalah* over the cup that he drinks after *Bircas Hamazon* (the fourth cup) (*Shemiras Shabbos K'hilchasah,* Chapter 62 and note 42, citing Rav Shlomo Zalman Auerbach).

When selling the *chametz* to a gentile in a year in which *Erev Pesach* falls out on Shabbos, the sale takes effect before Shabbos. Nevertheless, it is not necessary to specify that the sale does not include the *chametz* that will be eaten on Shabbos. When he eats the *chametz* on Shabbos, he is not considered to have "purchased" (i.e., acquired) the food from the gentile (which is prohibited on Shabbos). The reason for this permission is that he is merely eating normally and is not specifying any measure or sum. Furthermore, since the measuring will only take place after Pesach [if the gentile chooses to purchase all the *chametz*], the gentile does not care, and there is no chance of financial negotiations over that which was previously eaten (*Minchas Shlomo* 2:58).

Rav Shlomo Zalman was asked about hotels that serve their guests matzos for the Shabbos meals on *Erev Pesach*: Could one who does not want to eat matzah recite *Kiddush* in his room, eat challah or pita, being careful to leave no crumbs, continue the kosher-for- Pesach meal in the main dining room, and return to his room for *Bircas Hamazon*?

He replied that where that option exists it should be done. However, he added, it is preferable to eat more from the challah (or pita) before reciting *Bircas Hamazon* (*Moriah*, Teves 5756).

⤳ The Seder Night

If one has only one *shemurah matzah*, he may add a non-*shemurah matzah* to it for the *lechem mishneh* requirement. Although he cannot use this non-*shemurah matzah* to fulfill the requirement to eat *matzah* at the Seder, the matzah may be eaten, and so it can be used as a second matzah (*Shemiras Shabbos K'hilchasah* 55:14, citing Rav Shlomo Zalman Auerbach).

The general rule regarding the prohibition of *borer* (selecting) is that when one has a mixture of that which is needed and that which is not, it is permitted to select from the mixture that which is needed for "immediate use." Regarding the Seder, this means that shortly before *Kiddush* one may select that which is needed for *Kiddush*, for reciting the Haggadah, for matzah, *maror,* and the like, but not that which is needed for the meal, since that is beyond the requirement for "immediate use." This is apparently not the case in hotels, where they select everything they need even for the meal. I can see no leniency for this (*Minchas Shlomo* 2:58).

Ketzos Hashulchan (46, in *Badei Hashulchan* 2) uses the example of the second cup of wine at the Seder to prove that wine may be left uncovered for hours (as is the case while reciting the Haggadah) and yet be suitable for mitzvah use. Rav Shlomo Zalman disagrees. According to him, wine that is left uncovered for any appreciable amount of time should preferably not be used for a mitzvah. No proof can be brought from the second cup of wine at the Seder, he maintains, since it is a necessary part of reciting the Haggadah. Thus, it is no different from taking a very long time to recite the Haggadah. On the other hand, even if the wine is left uncovered for several hours while doing some unrelated mitzvah, such as learning Torah, it should not be used for mitzvah purposes (*Shemiras Shabbos K'hilchasah* 47:18 and note 90 there, citing Rav Shlomo Zalman Auerbach).

The *Shulchan Aruch* (472:5) rules that a student who is eating at the Seder of his rabbi should not recline unless he has that rabbi's permission, even if it is not the rabbi from whom he learned most of his Torah knowledge (*Rabbo Muvhak*).

Rav Shlomo Zalman explained that this applies as well to a rabbi from whom one heard lectures for a term. This applies even more so to a renowned Torah scholar. Furthermore, although it can be assumed that today all rabbis would permit leaning even without being asked, one should request permission of such rabbis before leaning (*Ma'adanei Shlomo, Pesach*, p. 11).

Concerning the above point, he added that there is no basis for a student refraining from having the Seder with his rabbi so that he is able to lean at the Seder. Quite the contrary; it is more important to demonstrate awe for one's rabbi than to lean at the Seder. This holds true even if one learns nothing from his rabbi at the Seder (from the notes of Rav Aharon Goldberg).

Rav Shlomo Zalman would stress that the Torah was given to human beings, and that for all mitzvos concerning eating we were commanded to eat normally, and not in some bizarre fashion. Accordingly, those who chew the entire quantity of matzah so that it may be consumed in one swallow may be eating in an abnormal manner known as *achilah gassah* (coarse forced eating) and is not fulfilling the mitzvah of eating matzah at all! (*Ma'adanei Shlomo, Pesach,* p. 11).

There is an apparent contradiction between two rulings of the *Mishnah Berurah*. Regarding *Karpas* (448:4) it states that one may recite the *Ha'adamah* blessing over *Karpas* for the sake of another person who will eat it, even if the one reciting the blessing does not eat it himself. Regarding the *lechem mishneh* requirement (to recite *Hamotzi* over two loaves of challah for each Shabbos meal), however, the *Mishnah Berurah* (273:19) rules that one may *not* recite the *Hamotzi* blessing for the sake of others who will eat from the challah when he himself will not.

Rav Shlomo Zalman explains this as follows: The main purpose in eating the *Karpas* is for the mitzvah, and for mitzvos one is allowed to recite the blessing for the sake of others, even if he himself will not perform that mitzvah. The main purpose of the challah on which *Hamotzi* is recited, however, is to have pleasure from a significant amount of food. One who does not partake of that challah is thus not permitted to recite the blessing (*Shemiras Shabbos K'hilchasah* 51:18).

One may weigh the matzah and *maror* on ordinary household scales (as opposed to commercial scales) for the purpose of determining the proper quantity that must be used to fulfill the mitzvah. This is so because weighing and measuring for the sake of a mitzvah is permitted, provided that it does not look like a business practice. Nevertheless, it is preferable to do so before *Yom Tov* (*Ma'adanei Shlomo, Pesach,* p. 12; also see *Shemiras Shabbos K'hilchasah* 29:38 and note 97 there, and addendum there).

The *Shulchan Aruch* (461:4) rules that one can fulfill the mitzvah of eating matzah with matzah soaked in water. The *Mishnah Berurah* (461:17) limits this permission to the old or infirm who cannot eat dry matzah. Even for these people, however, the matzah may not be soaked for twenty-four hours, for then it would be considered "cooked."

Rav Shlomo Zalman noted that even according to the *Mishnah Berurah*, soaking the matzah for a very short period of time to make chewing easier is fully permitted even for healthy people (provided that their custom is to eat soaked matzah the rest of Pesach as well). He added that he himself had been doing so for the last few years, and as long as the matzah is soaked for a short time only, there is no problem.

He also suggested keeping a little water in one's mouth to make the chewing easier (*Ma'adanei Shlomo, Pesach,* p. 12).

Rav Moshe Feinstein is cited in *Shevus Yitzchak* (*Pesach,* p. 117) as ruling that one who wants to use grape juice for the four cups should mix in one part wine to two parts grape juice, so that the drinking be in "a manner of freedom."

When Rav Shlomo Zalman was told of this ruling, he responded that this was a novel ruling which he had never heard from anyone else. Indeed, he maintained, grape juice is considered like wine in all respects, even with regard to the mitzvah of drinking "wine" for the enjoyment of *Yom Tov* (*Ma'adanei Shlomo, Pesach,* p. 13).

It once happened that the fourth cup of wine had a bad taste. As a result, a different wine, which had not previously been on the table, was brought out for a new fourth cup. Rav Shlomo Zalman ruled that a new blessing had to be recited on the wine (i.e., a fifth *Borei pri hagafen*). Since they knew that after the fourth cup it is prohibited to drink wine, their intent had been not to drink any other wine. Accordingly, they had to recite a new blessing on the new wine (as reported by his grandson, Rav Aharon Goldberg).

⋽ The Second Day of Yom Tov

Candles should be lit for the second day of *Yom Tov* (for residents of the Diaspora) after nightfall, and not toward evening on the first day. Strictly speaking, it is not forbidden to light the candles toward evening of the first day, since there is some need for light at that time. Nevertheless, since the main reason for lighting candles and for reciting the blessing over them is for the sake of the second day, and not for the slight need to have light on the first, it is preferable to light them after nightfall. This is even more true when there are electric lights in the room in which the candles are lit. In that case, the candles serve no real function for the first day, and they are only lit for the Rabbinic enactment (and custom) of lighting candles in honor of *Yom Tov*, which applies here only to the second night. In times of need, however, such as when one must leave the house shortly before nightfall, he may light the candles at that time even in a room lit by electric light. True, there is no benefit accruing to the first day of *Yom Tov* from those candles (because of the electric light), but when it is dark enough outside that if there would be a power outage he would benefit from those candles, he may light them then and recite a blessing. On the other hand, he may not light the candles when it is fully light outside (even though on a normal Friday it is permitted to light candles over an hour before sunset), because then there is no benefit whatsoever from that light for the first day of *Yom Tov* (*Minchas Shlomo* 2:58).

When a resident of the Diaspora is in Israel he must recite *Havdalah* at the end of the second day of *Yom Tov* (whereas an Israeli does not observe the second day and therefore recites *Havdalah* at the end of the first day). When the second day of *Yom Tov* is Shabbos [which can only occur on the last day of Pesach], both the resident of the Diaspora and the Israeli must recite *Havdalah* on Saturday night. *Havdalah* made by the Israeli, however, only separates from the sanctity of Shabbos, whereas the Diaspora resident's *Havdalah* separates from the sanctity of *Yom Tov* as well as Shabbos. Nevertheless, the Israeli is permitted to recite *Havdalah* for the Diaspora resident. The reason for this is that if the Diaspora resident would mention only Shabbos in his *Havdalah* and would forget to mention *Yom Tov* he would still fulfill his requirement for *Havdalah*. Hearing *Havdalah* recited by an Israeli who only mentions Shabbos certainly fulfills the requirement just as well (*Minchas Shlomo* 2:58).

A resident of Israel who is abroad for Pesach has no real obligation to keep a second day of *Yom Tov* as everyone else there does. Nevertheless, he is not permitted to publicly show that he is not keeping a second day of Pesach. If, however, he can leave the room in which the second Seder is being conducted, leaving the impression that he is attending a Seder elsewhere, he need not participate in a second Seder (*Yom Tov Sheni K'hilchaso* 3:28 and note 84 there citing Rav Shlomo Zalman).

A resident of Israel who is abroad for Pesach and is participating in a second Seder should be careful not to allow seventy-two minutes to pass from the time he drank his first cup of wine until he begins his meal. If he cannot, then he should recite an after-blessing for that first cup of wine (ibid., note 85, citing Rav Shlomo Zalman; see the discussion regarding *The Long Break Between Kiddush and the Meal*).

A resident of Israel who is abroad for Pesach is not supposed to be called to the Torah on the second day. If he cannot avoid it, however, he may recite a blessing over the Torah. The same applies on the additional day celebrated abroad at the end of Pesach — even if that day is a day on which the Torah is not read in Israel (i.e., it is neither Monday nor Thursday). The blessing is nevertheless not considered to have been made in vain, for it is not a personal blessing, but rather a blessing recited for the congregation (ibid., Chapter 9, note 13, citing Rav Shlomo Zalman).

◈§ Medicine and Illness on Pesach

Just because a medicine has a bitter taste does not mean it is automatically considered "not suitable for human use." There are examples of other liquids that no person would drink that Rambam categorizes as "drink" (see Rambam, *Tumas Adam* 10:2). Accordingly, one should not make such decisions on his own and should consult a Rabbinic authority (*Minchas Shlomo* 1:17).

A person who will be taking care of a sick person all night long on the Seder night might find it very difficult to stay awake without eating. Under such difficult circumstances, he may eat after midnight (providing that he ate the *afikoman* before midnight) (*Nishmas Avraham* IV 478:1).

A sick person, or a doctor, who could not fulfill any of the Seder mitzvos before midnight should conduct the Seder after midnight. He may not, however, recite the blessings over matzah and *maror* at that time. Furthermore, although he drinks each of the four cups in its proper place in the Haggadah, he recites a blessing only on the first and third cups. Ordinarily, a separate blessing is recited on each of the four cups, since each one involves a mitzvah of its own. In this case, however, it is not clear whether he is indeed fulfilling the mitzvah of four cups. If he is not, then the extra blessings could be in vain. Accordingly, he should follow the ruling of the *Shulchan Aruch* and recite a new blessing over the wine only when there is a clear break (i.e., for the first and third cups) (*Nishmas Avraham* I:477).

When it was publicized that a specific vitamin was produced from a *chametz* base, Rav Shlomo Zalman was asked about the status of baby formulas and other products which contained this vitamin.

He replied that the vitamin was produced through a chemical process whereby the *chametz* base becomes unsuitable even for the consumption of a dog. Furthermore, at the end of the process, when the vitamin is produced, the vitamin itself is not a food and it is only edible when mixed with other foods. Accordingly, the vitamin itself is not *chametz*.

(Even foods that are totally inedible are nevertheless forbidden when given importance (*achshvei*). See, however, *Yad Avraham* (on *Rama, Yoreh De'ah* 155:3) to ascertain why this does not apply here.)

Rav Shlomo Zalman added that even the importance which the factory gives to the vitamin by adding it to the product is not considered *achshvei*. By the time the consumer buys it, the vitamin is nullified by the product, and there is no concept of *achshvei* in a mixture, as Rosh states (cited in *Shulchan Aruch* 442:9). (There is no reason to differentiate between *chametz* and other prohibitions.)

Thus, there is no problem giving this formula to infants (but not adults). It should be prepared on Pesach in special utensils used only for the infant (*Ma'adanei Shlomo, Pesach* p. 8).

Any medications containing *chametz* which have a somewhat pleasant taste (such as syrups, or medicines meant to be sucked or chewed, that have some *chametz* in them) may not be taken on Pesach. This applies even when the quantity of actual *chametz* is small. They may not even be kept in the house (without selling them). Only when there is a danger to life can such medications be used (*Shemiras Shabbos K'hilchasah* 40:74).

There is greater room for leniency, however, for a tiny quantity of *chametz* that is mixed with bitter substances and sweetened with a coating of sugar. Since the only "pleasure" in that medicine is from the sugar coating, it could be considered not in the normal manner of eating, and thus permitted (Rav Shlomo Zalman Auerbach, cited ibid., note 163).

Any pill or serum for injection containing *chametz* can be fully permitted on Pesach, provided that before Pesach it had been rendered inedible even for a dog. When not rendered inedible, it is preferable to have serum injected by a gentile and have the intent not to acquire it. As for a pill, it can be permitted for one who is a *choleh she'ein bo sakanah* (i.e., one who is laid up in bed or with pains all over his body) since it is not the normal manner of benefiting from the *chametz* ingredient. Ideally, one should wrap the pill in very fine paper and swallow that. It is then considered "benefit in a non-standard fashion," which is permitted for a *choleh she'ein bo sakanah* (unpublished responsa presented by Rav Aharon Goldberg).

One who must buy a medicine on Pesach that is true *chametz* [such as one whose life is in danger] should not pay for it on Pesach, and he should have in mind not to acquire it legally. He then does not have to limit himself to buying the precise quantity that he needs, and he is permitted to use the remainder after Pesach (*Nishmas Avraham* 1:450).

Concerning the sick woman who believes in a special diet (which includes *chametz*) to cure her illness: Although the doctors claim that this diet has no effect on her condition, it appears that their own treatment for this serious illness has no long-term effect and involves suffering for most people. Accordingly, it should be left to the patient to determine the methods that help her most. This does not apply, however, to prohibited foods [such as *chametz*] and other prohibitions. *Ohr Same'ach* writes regarding Yom Kippur that when the Gemara states that the sick person's opinion overrides the opinion of doctors, that applies only to eating and drinking, areas in which a person can know his own needs. Regarding medicine, however, when experts say that he needs medicine, their opinions override that of the patient (*Minchas Shlomo* 2:82).

~§ The Prohibition to See or Find Chametz

Rav Shlomo Zalman was asked whether it was permissible to keep in one's possession over Pesach children's artwork made with dried noodles glued onto cardboard boxes (see *Pesachim* 45b). He replied that one could be lenient on two conditions: (1) that it was well glued and was unlikely to fall off, and (2) that it was painted, and thereby rendered inedible even for a dog (*Ma'adanei Shlomo, Pesach* p. 7).

Rav Shlomo Zalman was asked to explain the prohibition of *chametz she'avar alav haPesach* (*chametz* over which Pesach passed — *chametz* that was not sold and remained in the possession of a Jew). Such *chametz* was prohibited even after Pesach as a punishment (see *Mishnah Berurah* 448:7). Yet, even the *chametz* of one who was out of town for reasons beyond his control, or of one who was in the hospital and was incapable of taking care of his *chametz*, also becomes prohibited. Why would they be punished for circumstances beyond their control?

Rav Shlomo Zalman explained that it was not the *person* who was punished; rather, a punishment was decreed on the *chametz*! In other words, all *chametz* for which a solution was supposed to have been found was decreed to be "*chametz she'avar alav haPesach*" and prohibited. Accordingly, even when someone searches for *chametz*, finds nothing, nullifies whatever he missed, and then finds *chametz* in the middle of Pesach, he must get rid of the *chametz* that he finds. This is true even though he had no way to know about this *chametz*, for he searched for it, nullified it, etc. Since nothing was done with the *chametz* itself (i.e. it was not sold), one must get rid of it. So too, regarding the *chametz* of one who was very sick before Pesach and recovered on Pesach. It becomes prohibited as a "punishment" for the *chametz* as well (*Ma'adanei Shlomo, Pesach* p. 7).

Any soap may be used on Pesach, even if it has no special certification for Pesach. In our times, soap contains sharp ingredients that render it inedible even for a dog (*Me'or HaShabbos* II, Letters, letter 29:6).

It was publicized that carbon dioxide gas requires certification for Pesach because it can be made from wheat, and thus be considered *chametz*. Rav Shlomo Zalman disagreed, stating that gas can never be considered *chametz* since it has no substance, and because a dog would not eat it (*V'aleihu Lo Yibol* I, p. 164).

It is fully permissible for an Ashkenazic Jew to purchase on Pesach legumes and cakes baked like matzah (from a dough containing flour and other ingredients besides water — known as *matzah ashirah*, rich matzah) to serve to Sephardic guests (for whom these products are permitted). Although the reason given by the *Mishnah Berurah* for prohibiting "rich matzah" for a healthy person is out of concern that any amount of water mixed with the other ingredients could render it *chametz,* that applies only to the prohibition to eat it. That prohibition is more severe than the prohibition against possessing *chametz,* so we are not concerned in this case (*V'Aleihu Lo Yibol* I, p. 167).

৵ Blessings

It is the custom of Sephardim to recite *Hamotzi* on matzah only on Pesach and not for the rest of the year. Some of them recite *Hamotzi* even the rest of the year, but only on matzah left over from Pesach (*Sdei Chemed; Ma'areches Haberachos* 1:10). It is our custom, however, to always treat matzah as if it were bread unless it crumbles of its own accord in the mouth (unpublished responsum of Rav Shlomo Zalman to Rav Zvi Mendlowitz).

"Matzah brei" is a fried mixture of pieces of matzah mixed with eggs, milk, or water. If it is fried so that the oil covers the whole mixture, it is considered as if it was boiled (for what difference is there between boiling in water and boiling in oil?) and the *Mezonos* blessing is recited. *Magen Avraham*'s doubt (in 168:36) as to whether it is considered *Mezonos* or *Hamotzi* applies only to ordinary frying. In that case, it should be eaten only as part of a meal in which *Hamotzi* had been previously recited for matzah. On the other hand, if only a little bit of oil (or oil spray) was used just so that the matzah brei will not stick to the pan, one recites *Hamotzi* over it and afterward recites *Bircas Hamazon*. However, if one boils the pieces of matzah for a half minute or so and then fries the mixture, the blessing is *Mezonos* (*Kuntres Hateshuvos* in *V'sein Berachah* 11).

The proper blessing on any product made from potato starch is *Shehakol*. Nevertheless, if one recites *Ha'adamah* instead, even on a potato-starch cake, he need not recite a new blessing (*Kuntres Hateshuvos* in *V'sein Berachah* 3).

❧ Customs

Rav Shlomo Zalman ruled that when a woman gets married she follows the customs of her husband, whether that involves greater stringency or greater leniency. For example, an Ashkenazi woman (who does not eat legumes on Pesach) who marries a Sephardi man (who does) may now eat legumes on Pesach. Normally, one who changes a custom must first undergo a special procedure of *Hataras Nedarim* (permitting vows), but a woman who changes her custom because of marriage need not do so. Since she has no way of knowing whom she will ultimately marry, the original custom of her father's house applies to her only until marriage.

However, he added, a husband may relinquish his rights in this regard, and she can then continue her old customs. Indeed, it is quite common for a husband to relinquish his right to have his wife pray according to his custom (*Nusach Ashkenaz, Nusach Sephard, Edot Hamizrach,* etc.) and allow her to continue praying as before.

If, however, she began following her husband's custom when she first got married and then decided to revert to her original custom, the situation is somewhat different. Her husband can still relinquish his right and permit her, but she will then require *Hataras Nedarim*, as would anyone else changing his custom. Similarly, if she first continued her old custom (with her husband's permission) and now wants to accept the custom of her husband, she requires *Hataras Nedarim* as well (*Yom Tov Sheni K'hilchaso* 19:18. Also see *Halichos Beisah* 18:12).

Miscellaneous

The rule is that one who says *"V'sein berachah"* 101 times can thereafter assume that he remembered to make the springtime change from *V'sein tal u'matar livrachah* to *V'sein berachah* in his *Shemoneh Esrei*. Accordingly, if after finishing *Shemoneh Esrei* he is uncertain whether he in fact said it right, he need not repeat *Shemoneh Esrei*.

Rav Shlomo Zalman ruled that one may say *"V'sein berachah"*

101 times on Pesach itself. Normally, it is forbidden to prepare on *Yom Tov* for the weekdays. This is permitted, nevertheless, because any form of speech is not considered a preparatory act (*Me'or Ha-Shabbos* II, Letters, 28:4).

In some synagogues, there is a set of cards, prominently posted, which notifies the congregation what to say at various times of the year. One card, displayed until Pesach, says "*V'sein tal u'matar livrachah*, and another, displayed from Pesach, says *V'sein berachah*. Rav Shlomo Zalman ruled that it is permitted to change the cards on *Yom Tov* itself, even though one does not actually start saying *V'sein berachah* until after *Yom Tov*, during the *Ma'ariv* prayer, which is no longer *Yom Tov*. This too is not considered preparation for the weekdays, since this serves to notify people — now — what the law is. This notification aids a person who might have to pray alone in his home and might otherwise forget to make the change (*Me'or HaShabbos* II, Letters, 39:1).

On the last day of Pesach, one may speak about the *chametz* he intends to eat after Pesach. In general, it is permitted on Shabbos and *Yom Tov* to talk about matters that do not involve prohibited work (*melachah*), but involve other prohibitions (such as *chametz* on Pesach, and eating on Yom Kippur). It is only regarding *melachah* that the Sages even prohibited speech, for one should feel on Shabbos [and *Yom Tov*] that all one's work has been completed. When one speaks about weekday work on Shabbos he cannot feel as if his work has been completed. This does not apply, however, to speaking about eating after Yom Kippur or eating *chametz* after Pesach (as cited in *Shemiras Shabbos K'hilchasah* 29:160 and addendum there).

On *chol hamo'ed*, it is permitted to cook for *chol hamo'ed* meals as well as for *Yom Tov* meals, but not to prepare for after *Yom Tov*. In Israel, *Yom Tov* ends on different days for residents of Israel and for residents of the Diaspora visiting Israel. The question therefore arises whether a resident of Israel can cook on *chol hamo'ed* for the meal that a guest from abroad will eat on his last day of *Yom Tov*, which for the resident of Israel is after *Yom Tov*.

Rav Shlomo Zalman ruled that since the guest from abroad was a guest and could not cook for himself, the resident of Israel could cook his subsequent meals for him even on *chol hamo'ed* if he would not be able to cook for his guest after his own *Yom Tov*. On the other hand, a resident of Israel who is abroad for Pesach would not be allowed to cook on *chol hamo'ed* for the last-day meal of residents of the Diaspora. Since they are in their own place, they can cook for themselves and there is no need for the resident of Israel to cook for them (*Minchas Shlomo* 2:58).

The law is that one may generally not invite a gentile to a *Yom Tov* meal. The reason for this is the concern that one may come to add more food to be cooked for the gentile on *Yom Tov*, and cooking on *Yom Tov* is only permitted for Jews. Rav Shlomo Zalman was asked about inviting a couple, one of whom was a gentile who had undergone a non-kosher conversion. Although the "convert" was technically a gentile, there was the hope that as a result of the invitation the couple would strengthen their religious practice, including eventually undergoing a kosher conversion.

Rav Shlomo Zalman replied that in a certain respect this situation was worse than the standard case of a gentile. In this case, the gentile believed that he was actually Jewish, so there is a greater possibility of adding food to cook for him. If, however, the couple shows up without an invitation, there is room for leniency based on the permission of the *Mishnah Berurah* (512:10) for serving an uninvited gentile. Although we have stated that there is a greater chance in this case for adding food to be cooked, it is counterbalanced by the mitzvah of *kiruv* (bringing closer to Judaism).

Rav Shlomo Zalman added that in earlier years it was customary to invite honored gentiles (such as consuls) to the Seder. He explained that the reason, apparently, was to prevent ill-feeling toward Jews, especially since it was well known that Pesach was a time for such invitations. Perhaps, he concluded, this counterbalanced the concern of adding food to be cooked in these circumstances (*Shulchan Shlomo, Yom Tov* 512:8).

Those who do not use any flour products other than plain matzah (i.e., they do not use the "rich matzah" mentioned above) on Pesach should not cook in utensils in which other flour-based products were used (although Sephardim do use such products) (*Erev Pesach Shechal B'Shabbos*, Chapter 4, note 4).

☙ The Seventh Day of Pesach

A person once erred in his recital of *Kiddush* on the seventh night of Pesach, saying *Shehecheyanu*. Before drinking the wine, he realized his error. He knows that if the unnecessary *Shehecheyanu* is considered a "break" between the blessing and the wine he must recite a new *Borei pri hagafen*. What should he do in this particular case?

Rav Shlomo Zalman ruled that it was not considered a break. He explained that a break that requires a new blessing is one which involves taking the mind away from the blessing. In this case, however, the person thought that he was required to recite the *Shehecheyanu*, and so there was no taking the mind away from the blessing (*Mikraei Kodesh, Pesach* 1:62; see further *Shemiras Shabbos K'hilchasah* II:47, note 215).

☙ When The Last day of Pesach Falls Out on Friday

When the last day of Pesach falls out on Friday, it is prohibited to use *chametz* utensils for the Shabbos meals, even though Shabbos is no longer Pesach (*Me'or HaShabbos* II, Letters, letter 33).

A person may cook legumes on Friday, the last day of Pesach, for tomorrow's Shabbos meal, provided that there are Sephardic Jews (who eat legumes on Pesach) who could visit on Friday and eat those legumes. Even when there are no Sephardic Jews available, it is not clear that he may not cook the legumes on Friday. It is certainly permitted for one who adopts the stringency of not eating soaked matzah (*gebrokts*) to cook such food for Shabbos. This applies even in Israel when the last day of Pesach is the seventh day of Pesach (and there is no custom to eat soaked matzah on that day). The reason for permission is because there are so many Jews who eat soaked matzah all of Pesach, and since any of those could have stopped by on Friday, he is permitted to cook soaked matzah (*Me'or HaShabbos* II, Letters, letter 33, based on the ruling of Rav Y.M. Tukachinsky in *Luach Eretz Yisrael*).

Customs and Practices of Rav Shlomo Zalman Auerbach זצ"ל

◆§ Matzos Before Pesach

In Rav Shlomo Zalman's household, matzah was not eaten from Purim until the Seder night (Rav Yosef Shub, citing Rav Baruch Auerbach).

He would wake up very early to supervise the baking of the matzos, and he participated in the actual baking. When asked how he could go before reciting the morning prayers, he answered that since it was needed for a mitzvah, it was certainly permitted (*Halichos Shlomo, Tefillah* 2, *Orchos Halachah*, note 23).

His eldest son, Rav Shmuel, would bring him the matzah baked on *Erev Pesach* ("*Matzas Mitzvah*") to use at the Seder, and he greatly encouraged this practice (Rav Yosef Shub, citing Rav Baruch Auerbach).

◆§ The Blessing on Fruit Trees

The *Shulchan Aruch* (226:1) writes, "He who goes out in the days of Nisan and sees [fruit] trees blossoming recites the blessing 'Blessed are You, Hashem, our God, Who did not withhold anything from His universe and He created in it creatures that are good and trees that are good, to cause mankind pleasure with them.'"

Rav Shlomo Zalman was very careful to recite this blessing, and he once remarked that, from his thirteenth birthday and on, he never missed reciting it (*Halichos Shlomo, Tefillah* 23, *Orchos Halachah*, note 121).

He would recite this blessing only upon seeing two fruit trees. He would recite the blessing even on Shabbos (ibid.).

If the tree had not yet blossomed, as long as there were leaves — even just the beginning of a bloom — he would recite the blessing (ibid.).

∽§ Shabbos Hagadol

One of the many explanations given for the name *Shabbos Hagadol*, the Great Shabbos, is as follows: The Torah (*Vayikra* 23:15) writes: "You shall count for yourselves from the morrow of the *Shabbos*." The *Shabbos* referred to in this verse is the subject of an ongoing dispute found in the Talmud (*Menachos* 65a). The Sadducees said that this refers to the first *Shabbos* (Saturday) during Pesach, and that the counting of the Omer begins on the morrow, i.e., the first Sunday of Pesach. *Chazal*, on the other hand, maintain that the *Shabbos* reference is to the first day of Pesach, which is an appropriate reference because Pesach is also a *rest day*. Accordingly, we start counting the Omer from the second day of Pesach, the morrow of *Shabbos*, i.e., the first day of *Yom Tov*.

Thus, when comparing the two rest days, the weekly Shabbos, and the once-yearly first day of Pesach, the weekly Shabbos can be entitled *Shabbos Hagadol* — the great and holy Shabbos (*HaShabbos Hagadol V'hakadosh* — see the *Retzei* addition recited on Shabbos in the Grace After Meals). On the Shabbos preceding Pesach this comparison and subsequent differentiation becomes evident. First, we celebrate *Shabbos Hagadol*, the great rest day. This is followed by the first day of Pesach, a day which, when seen from the perspective of prohibited activities, is a minor rest day.

Additionally, it is well known that many practices were instituted to counter the errors of the Sadducees. Accordingly, it makes sense to say that it was called "*Shabbos Hagadol*" to correct the erroneous notions of the Sadducees and thereby strengthen the tradition of the Sages of the Oral Law (from a lecture on the laws of Pesach given by Rav Shlomo Zalman in 1970 and published in *Kuntres Seder Pesach*[1]).

---

1. This reason can also be found in *Bnei Yissachar,* Nisan 3:2, citing *Shemen Hamor.*

The *Shulchan Aruch* (430:1; see also *Mishnah Berurah* ad loc.) discusses the custom to recite a portion of the Haggadah (from *Avadim hayinu* through *l'chaper al avonoseinu*) on the afternoon of *Shabbos Hagadol*. The Gra's (ad loc.) custom was not to recite the Hagaddah because therein it states: "It [the Haggadah] applies only when matzah and *maror* are before you — i.e., at the Seder." On this Shabbos, Rav Shlomo Zalman followed the custom of the Gra, but, in preparing for Pesach, he did not refrain from studying the Haggadah at other times (Rav Yosef Shub, citing Rav Baruch Auerbach, the son of Rav Shlomo Zalman).

∽§ Selling the Chametz

It is customary to sell one's *chametz* by empowering the local rabbi to act as an agent to sell the *chametz* to a gentile before Pesach. In this manner, at the onset of Pesach, when one is prohibited from owning any *chametz*, a person technically owns no *chametz*. It is the gentile who owns it, and there are no restrictions on him.

The problem is that this sale is seemingly a legal device to get around a prohibition, known as *ha'aramah,* evading the law. Generally speaking, although we permit *ha'aramah* for *d'rabbanan* (Rabbinic prohibitions), we do not permit *ha'aramah* for *d'oraysa* (Biblical prohibitions). For example: Animal feed is generally *chametz*, and some animals resist feed to which they are unaccustomed. Is it permitted to sell an entire herd to a gentile for Pesach so that the gentile — the new owner — can feed them *chametz* feed? Of course, after Pesach the animals will revert to the Jewish owner and he will have benefited from their being fattened with *chametz* feed. In this case the *Bechor Shor* (to *Pesachim* 21) prohibits this as a *ha'aramah* in a Torah prohibition.

We ask: Why is this any different than the standard sale of *chametz* to a gentile, which apparently involves *ha'aramah* in the *d'oraysa* prohibition of "No *chametz* may be seen in your possession" (*Shemos* 13:7; also see ibid., 12:19)? *Bechor Shor* answers that, in fact, only a Rabbinic prohibition is involved. From the Torah perspective, it is sufficient to nullify one's *chametz* by saying the requisite, "Any *chametz* which is in my possession shall be nullified like the dust of the earth ...". In spite of the nullification, the

Sages forbade retaining the *chametz* (nullified) in one's possession, but this (Rabbinic) prohibition is removed when the *chametz* is sold to a gentile. On the other hand, the animals sold to the gentile were not first nullified, and they were only sold to be able to feed them *chametz*. Since that involves a Torah prohibition, the *ha'aramah* is forbidden.

This answer does not solve all the problems related to selling *chametz* to a gentile, and many have questioned the above approach. For example: The owner of a large cookie concern sells all his *chametz* to a gentile. On the night before Pesach, he recites, "Any *chametz* which is in my possession ... shall be nullified and become ownerless." Now, obviously, he doesn't really mean to make his business "ownerless." Only the remainder of his *chametz*, "which I did or did not see," is made ownerless, but certainly not the *chametz* which was sold to a gentile by means of a legally binding contract. The question then remains unanswered: How can one sell his *chametz* to a gentile when a *ha'aramah* is forbidden for Torah prohibitions?

We must therefore postulate that selling the *chametz* does not involve *ha'aramah*. Only when the sale is a legal apparatus to circumvent a prohibition is it considered a *ha'aramah*. The sale of *chametz* to a gentile is a full legal sale, and each person should know that he is signing a completely binding legal contract. Indeed, if the gentile brings the full sum of money and fulfills all the other conditions set into the contract by our Sages, the *chametz* will in fact belong to the gentile. Accordingly, those who sell their *chametz* should know that it is neither a legal loophole nor a *ha'aramah*, but a fully binding sale, and he should have clear intent to sell it.

Many people who sell their *chametz* have no such intention. Nevertheless, as long as there is a legally binding bill of sale, the seller's unstated intention is not relevant. Let us illustrate this point by means of a bridegroom who signs a *kesubah* document at his wedding and later claims that he had no idea what he was signing. His claim has no legal validity, for we tell him, "You knew that you were signing a *kesubah* and not an autograph sheet, and if you signed it, you are obligated by what it says." Similarly, one who signs a contract in a foreign language cannot claim that he does not know what he signed; if he knew that he was signing a contract, it is his responsibility to make sure to understand what he is signing or be bound by his signature in any case. Thus, any *chametz* may be sold to a gentile, because the sale is a legally binding sale, with or without the seller's realization (from a lecture on the laws of Pesach given by Rav Shlomo Zalman in 1970 and published in *Kuntres Seder Pesach*).

Rav Shlomo Zalman was very strict concerning the rooms and closets (containing *chametz*) which were sold to the gentile. He would not allow opening them and removing from them even a non-*chametz* product because, in his opinion, that would make a farce of the whole sale (reported by his grandson, Rav Aharon Goldberg[1]).

On the night of *bedikas chametz*, Rav Shlomo Zalman used to sell his *chametz* through the *gabbai* of the Gra Shul. He specified the places in which he stored his *chametz* and he made sure to pay the *gabbai* for his trouble (from an article by Rav Yosef Shub, published in *Peninei HaShabbos. Vayikra* 5759[2]).

ᴥ§ Bedikas Chametz

The first mishnah in tractate *Pesachim* states: "The evening of the fourteenth [of Nisan — the night before Pesach] we must search for the *chametz* by the light of a candle." Although he ruled that it was permissible to use a flashlight, Rav Shlomo Zalman personally was particular about using a candle (in accordance with the language of the mishnah) and he encouraged others to do so as well (Rav Yosef Shub).[3]

On the other hand, he always left on the electric lights in the room in which he was searching — even replacing burnt-out bulbs before the search. He would say, "The format of the mitzvah as required by the Sages is with a candle, but one sees clearly by means of electric light" (from his grandson, Rav Aharon Goldberg).[4]

---

1. Some permit specifically stipulating to the gentile that he is able to go occasionally into the sold space. Rav Aharon Goldberg reports that his grandfather was not convinced that even such a stipulation would work.

2. See there for a lengthy explanation on the source of the custom to pay money.

3. Also see *Shevus Yitzchak* 4.

4. See Rav Y.Y. Neuwirth's article in *Moriah*, Nisan 5752.

Customarily, the entire house is meticulously cleaned before the search for *chametz* begins, and this might delay the search. This is not proper. One should begin the search at the proper time (as soon as it is dark, right after the *Ma'ariv* prayers), even if members of the household are still cleaning other areas of the house (Rav Shlomo Zalman Auerbach, cited in *V'Aleihu Lo Yibol*).

Rav Shomo Zalman was asked: Since our custom is to clean the entire house before Pesach, what is the purpose of *bedikas chametz*? Is the house not checked already? Rav Shlomo Zalman responded that the requirement is to verify by candlelight that indeed every place was well cleaned and checked, ascertaining that there is no *chametz* in the house. Similarly, one must search each of his closets verifying that it has been thoroughly cleaned (Rav Shlomo Zalman, replying to his son, Rav Yaakov, cited in *Mevakshei Torah, Pesachim* II p. 532; see also *Kovetz Kol HaTorah*, Nisan 5756, and *Shevus Yitzchak*, p. 36).

The language of the blessing recited for *bedikas chametz* is "*al biur chametz*," i.e., the removal of, not the searching for, *chametz*. Even one who cleaned the entire house very thoroughly — and has already removed all *chametz* — recites this blessing, for it is always possible that one spot was forgotten, and in the course of the *bedikah*, *chametz* will be discovered (*Ma'adanei Shlomo, Pesach* p. 4. Also see *Mevakshei Torah, Pesachim*).

The primary intent of the mitzvah of *bedikas chametz* (and the accompanying blessing) is to search dwelling places. Nevertheless, other places — e.g., suitcases, clothing pockets, cars, etc. — must be checked as well, although (if they are the only places being checked) no blessing is recited (Rav Shlomo Zalman, cited in *Shevus Yitzchak* 4:2).

Although one generally expresses his joy in fulfilling a mitzvah that recurs from year to year by reciting the *Shehecheyanu* ("Who has kept us alive...") blessing, it is not recited for *bedikas chametz*, for there is no real pleasure involved in its fulfillment. Instead, when one recites *Shehecheyanu* on the Seder night (at the end of *Kiddush*), his intent should be that it applies to all the mitzvos that are connected to the holiday (from a lecture on the laws of Pesach given by Rav Shlomo Zalman in 1970 and published in *Kuntres Seder Pesach*).

It is customary to leave pieces of *chametz* in places where they will be found by the searcher. The *Mishnah Berurah* (432:13) cites the custom of the Ari to leave specifically ten pieces of *chametz*.

Rav Shlomo Zalman's wife used to place the ten pieces around the house, and after she died, Rav Shlomo Zalman asked his grandson, Rav Aharon Goldberg, to continue the custom.

"Yet I must emphasize that one should not make a minor point greater than the major point. Many people carefully wrap the ten pieces in plastic and other coverings, and store them safely until the *chametz* is burned the next day. At the same time, they have a basket filled with bread, which is neither closed nor in a safe place, and children are walking around unsupervised with their *chametz*. What is so special about those ten pieces? Of course, it is an ancient custom to carefully wrap the ten pieces, and one should never make light of ancient customs. Yet the important thing is to take great care of *all* the *chametz* that is still in the house. The main requirement is that all the bread must be closed away, and certainly not moved from place to place" (from a lecture on the laws of Pesach given by Rav Shlomo Zalman in 1970 and published in *Kuntres Seder Pesach*).

Rav Shlomo Zalman did not search for *chametz* in his books. He conceded that some authorities were stringent on this point (notably *Chazon Ish, Hilchos Pesach* 116:18), but did not understand a reason for stringency: If crumbs might be found inside the books, they were nullified, and since people do not eat old crumbs from books there is no cause for further concern. Indeed, even if one were to find a piece of cookie or candy inside a book it generally becomes unappetizing and he would not eat it (*Ma'adanei Shlomo, Pesach,* p. 5).

On the other hand, his son Rav Azriel reports that he was careful not to bring his books to the table for the duration of the holiday. This was apparently based on the concern that crumbs might fall out and mix with food at the table, and actually be eaten (although he was not concerned with the possibility of choosing to eat crumbs *by themselves*) (see *Rema,* end of 447, and *Darchei Chaim V'Shalom* 571).

The custom in Yerushalayim is that the sale of *chametz* to the gentile takes effect on the fourteenth day of Nisan (*Erev Pesach*).

Accordingly, the *chametz* still belongs to the Jew the night before, at the time of *bedikas chametz*. Nevertheless, the custom is not to search in those rooms or closets in which pure *chametz*, sold to the gentile, will be stored. Why doesn't the Rabbinic requirement to search for *chametz* in *all* one's property apply here?

The answer is that the Sages instituted a requirement to search for *chametz* in places where *chametz might* be found. When he *knows* that *chametz* is to be found there, there is no requirement to search. How can he "search for" what is certainly there?

This is seen from the fact that people leave *chametz* on a table to be eaten from until the next morning. Obviously, they do not search for this *chametz,* because they know that it will be removed before Pesach. For this reason, after the search one says, "Any *chametz* which is in my possession that I did not see and remove, nor know about..." (*Ma'adanei Shlomo, Pesach* p. 3).

The Gemara (*Pesachim* 6a) states that one who leaves his house more than thirty days before Pesach, and has no intention of returning until after Pesach, has no obligation to search for *chametz.* (He is required to search if he intends to return before the end of Pesach or if he leaves within thirty days of Pesach.) Although the implication of the Gemara (see *Rashi* ad loc.) is that he is leaving for a distant place, the same laws apply to one leaving home but staying in the same city. (*Ma'adanei Shlomo, Pesach* p. 4. See there for why "in our days" the same laws apply even when not far away.)

Yeshivah students [who go home within thirty days of Pesach] should perform *bedikas chametz* in their dormitory room on the night before their departure (as reported by Rav Yosef Shub).

One who will be staying in a hotel for Pesach, and arrives there before the night of the fourteenth of Nisan, must perform *bedikas chametz* in his room. Although generally we are not concerned with tiny crumbs that might have been left in the room, there is still the chance that he might come to eat them (*Minchas Shlomo* II:58; *Kovetz Kol HaTorah*, Nisan 5756).

If in the hotel room a refrigerator containing *chametz* has been provided, even though the *chametz* items do not belong to the guest, since he has the option to purchase them, they must be removed from the room (*Minchas Shlomo*, ibid.).

✃ Burning the Chametz

There is a dispute in the mishnah in *Pesachim* (21a) whether *chametz* must be burned, or other methods of destruction are acceptable. The *Shulchan Aruch* (445:1) rules in accordance with the Sages, that any method is sufficient. *Rema* (ad loc.) adds that, nevertheless, the custom is to burn the *chametz*, in accordance with the view of R' Yehudah. (See also *Mishnah Berurah* 445:10.)

If one wishes to follow the custom of burning the *chametz*, he should burn at least a *kezayis* of *chametz* in its natural state without pouring any kerosene or lighting fluid on it. Pouring lighting fluid or kerosene on *chametz* renders it unfit for a dog's consumption, and therefore no longer prohibited as "*chametz*." Although there are other opinions that pouring fuel onto the *chametz* can be seen as the beginning of the burning process, it is preferable not to use kerosene or lighting fluid (from a lecture on the laws of Pesach given by Rav Shlomo Zalman in 1970 and published in *Kuntres Seder Pesach*).

Rav Shlomo Zalman himself was very careful not to use any kerosene or lighting fluid at all. In addition, he was particular about burning his *chametz* in his own separate fire to make sure that it would burn completely (from his grandson, Rav Aharon Goldberg).

There is an interesting paradox in this matter. The rule is that any *chametz* (before the time of prohibition) which a dog would not consume is not prohibited, even on Pesach itself. Another rule is that, according to Torah law, *chametz* should be burned until it is charcoal, and per Rabbinic law until it turns to dust. These standards are from the laws of *nosar* (portions of sacrifices remaining after the prescribed eating periods) regarding which the Torah writes (*Vayikra* 7:17): "What is left over shall be burned in the fire" (see *Tosafos, Pesachim* 26b s.v. *Bishlah*). The following difficulty presents itself, in light of these two laws, when burning *chametz* at the time designated by Halachah, which is before its time of prohibition.

While burning the *chametz*, well before it reaches the charcoal stage it is no longer suitable for a dog's consumption. If so, it is no longer considered *chametz*, and it may even be kept over Pesach. However, one has not yet fulfilled the mitzvah of "burning" *chametz*, because, at the very least, "burning" means rendering it to charcoal. Indeed, if another Jew were to ask him for that partially burned *chametz* (which a dog would no longer eat) it would be permissible to give it to him. Accordingly, how does one ever fulfill the requirement of burning *chametz*? (From a lecture on the laws of Pesach given by Rav Shlomo Zalman in 1970 and published in *Kuntres Seder Pesach*. See also *Minchas Shlomo* I:15.)

Rav Shlomo Zalman would burn the *lulav* along with his *chametz* (Rav Yosef Shub, citing Rav Baruch Auerbach).

✦§ The Fast of the Firstborn

It is customary for the firstborn male (of either parent) to fast on *Erev Pesach*, or at least to partake in a meal served in honor of a mitzvah, such as a *siyum,* a festive meal celebrating the completion of a Talmud tractate. It is sufficient for the firstborn to eat any minimum quantity at such a "meal" in order to be considered a participant, and then he may continue eating the rest of the day (Rav Shlomo Zalman Auerbach, cited in *V'Aleihu Lo Yibol* I p. 174. Cf. *Minchas Yitzchak* IX:45).

In difficult situations, the firstborn may be included in the *siyum* via the telephone, and thereby be relieved of fasting (*Ma'adanei Shlomo, Pesach* p. 2; also see *Minchas Shlomo* I:9, concerning answering *amen* to a blessing heard over the telephone).

There are several powerful questions on the subject of the fast of the firstborn: (a) The firstborn were saved on the night of the Seder, so why do we fast the day before? If you say that it is to avoid fasting on a festival day, it can be argued that *Erev Pesach* is also a festival day, because it is the day on which the *pesach* sacrifice was brought, and, indeed, after midday, many types of work are forbidden! (b) The miracle of being saved applied equally to male and female firstborn, so why is it only firstborn males who fast? (c) Among the Egyptians, if there was no firstborn, then the oldest in the household died. Among the Jews, this household elder was saved as well. Why does such an elder have no obligation to fast? (d) More fundamentally: Why does *today's* firstborn have to fast? It was the firstborn *at that time* that was saved, so perhaps they and all their offspring should fast. What connection is there to *today's* firstborn? In response, we must realize that this fast is different. Until the sin of the Golden Calf, it was the firstborn who performed the Divine service. Indeed, at Sinai, when the Torah was given, the firstborn brought the sacrifices. Only after the sin of the Golden Calf was the priesthood transferred from the firstborn to the *Kohanim*.

Now, as the term *Pesach* denotes, the main commemoration of the miracle of Pesach is that Hashem passed over (*pasach*) the homes of the Jews and did not kill their firstborn. As a result, the firstborn became sanctified and privileged to perform the Divine service. However, not all firstborn were given this privilege; the Torah specifies that *service* should be performed by males only.

Let us try and imagine the shame of the firstborn on the first *erev Pesach* after the sin of the Golden Calf. More animals were sacrificed that day than on any other day of the year. The Gemara (*Pesachim* 64b) relates, in fact, that they slaughtered "two times 600,000" animals. Now, who would have been more fitting to sacrifice these animals than the firstborn? Why, the very name "Pesach" is based on the miracle in which the Jewish firstborn were saved — and through that miracle they were sanctified for Divine service. Instead, it was the *Kohanim* who performed the service, while the firstborn stood outside, ashamed before their brothers. What shame and pain they must have felt!

Apparently, this was the source for the fast of the firstborn on the day on which the *pesach* offering was sacrificed. On such a day, how could they have found any pleasure in food or drink? Even in future generations, the firstborn would say to themselves, "By right, we should be the ones sacrificing the offerings, but because of our sins and the sins of our ancestors we cannot." So how could they eat on such a day? Thus, the true purpose of this fast is to recall the sin of the Golden Calf which caused the firstborn to lose their right to Divine service. As a result, only the firstborn males fast, because only they had been give the privilege of serving[1] (from a lecture on the laws of Pesach given by Rav Shlomo Zalman in 1970 and published in *Kuntres Seder Pesach*).

---

1. Rav Shlomo Zalman's disciple, Rav Avigdor Nebenzahl, points out that several difficulties still remain: a) Why do firstborn *Kohanim* fast? b) Since this is a fast representing mourning, how can one fast on this day when, as mentioned above, it too is considered a *Yom Tov*?

☙ Korban Pesach

Erev Pesach afternoon Rav Shlomo Zalman would go to the *Kosel Hama'aravi*, where he would recite the *Korban Pesach* service (Rav Yosef Shub, citing Rav Baruch Auerbach).

☙ When Erev Pesach Falls on Shabbos

When *erev Pesach* falls on Shabbos, compliance with the Shabbos requirement of three meals is problematic. At least two meals must include bread products on which the *Hamotzi* blessing is recited. The problem is that, on the one hand, it is prohibited to eat matzah on *erev Pesach* and, on the other hand, *chametz* may only be eaten in the morning hours — and even then there is the danger of crumbs spreading.

Rav Shlomo Zalman's family would eat challah in a covered courtyard in front of the house, and then move inside to finish the meal by eating kosher-for-Pesach food (but not matzah). They would recite the *Bircas Hamazon* inside (as reported by Rav Shlomo Zalman's grandson, Rav Aharon Goldberg).

Thus they satisfied the morning-meal requirement. They would then take a short break. They fulfilled the requirement of the third meal in accordance with the *Mishnah Berurah* (444:8, ibid.) with leaving the house again to partake of challah outdoors, and again finishing the rest of the meal inside.

☙ Candle-Lighting

In Rav Shlomo Zalman's house the custom was to light the holiday candles before sunset, emphasizing that they are being lit in honor of the festival (*Kol HaTorah*, Nisan 5756, as reported by his grandson, Rav Pinchas Bondy). Others have the custom of lighting the candles when the men return from the synagogue.

☙ Preparations for the Seder

As a rule, it goes against the spirit of Judaism to live on a grand scale and, for example, to dine using gold and silver dishes. This applies even more so now that we live in exile [even here in Israel]. The exception to this rule is Pesach night, when we rejoice and act as if we actually left Egypt and collected all the wealth of the Egyptians. On this night everything is permitted — and moreso —

it's a mitzvah! It is a night to live grandly and show that we are now free (from a lecture on the laws of Pesach given by Rav Shlomo Zalman in 1970 and published in *Kuntres Seder Pesach*).

Rav Shlomo Zalman had several silver utensils which he inherited, and he would use them only on the Seder night. The same applied to a beautiful armchair that he received as a gift (*Kuntres Seder Pesach,* note 42).

Matzah and other bread products may not be eaten until a small portion of it is set aside as *challah*. (In the times of the *Beis HaMikdash, challah* was given to the *Kohen;* today it is burned.) If the matzah bakery did not remove *challah*, a *kezayis*-sized piece should be removed at home. The initial *challah* requirement, however, only applies when a volume of approximately five pounds of flour is prepared in one batch. Smaller quantities are exempt. When one has a larger quantity which became obligated in this mitzvah, and then a smaller quantity is separated, such as when one buys only one matzah, *challah* is taken, but a smaller piece is sufficient (Rav Shlomo Zalman, cited in *Shemiras Shabbos K'hilchasah* 42:48).

Rav Shlomo Zalman would separate *challah* on behalf of anyone who forgot to separate his own (from a letter provided by his grandson, Rav Aharon Goldberg; also see *Minchas Shlomo* 3:133).

Selecting matzos for the Seder may involve the prohibition of *borer* (selection). When one has a package of matzos containing whole and broken matzos, he may select one matzah at a time until he finds three whole matzos that are fitting to use at the Seder. This does not transgress the prohibition of *borer*. If, however, one has a mixture (i.e., they are not lying together in a package) of whole and broken matzos, he may not remove the broken pieces and leave the whole matzos. The broken matzos are unsuitable for the mitzvah at the Seder, and by taking them away he is *selecting* the bad from the good, thus transgressing the prohibition of *borer*. On the other hand, if he already has his three matzos for the Seder, and the reason for his further separating the broken matzos from the whole ones is simply because the whole ones are nicer to serve, then he may remove the broken pieces (*Shemiras Shabbos K'hilchasah* 3:28, 70, and 72, citing Rav Shlomo Zalman Auerbach).

Some people burn the edge of a broken matzah so that it will be fully "baked" all around, which, in their opinion, makes it a *shleimah,* a whole matzah. Rav Shlomo Zalman found no source for such a practice. He commented, however, that if it is done, it should be done well, so that at least it looks like a whole matzah. Furthermore, it should not be done on Yom Tov itself since it is only permissible to cook on Yom Tov food to prepare it for eating; not to prepare it only so one can use it for a mitzvah (Rav Shlomo Zalman, cited in Meor HaShabbos I, 9:11; also see the appendix volume to Shemiras Shabbos K'hilchasah 55:35).

⋅§ The Seder Plate

The Seder plate has, in additon to the three matzos, a piece of *maror, charoses, karpas,* a "foreleg," and an egg. The "foreleg" is in commemoration of the *pesach* sacrifice, and the egg commemorates the *chagigah* sacrifice that accompanied it. Some make sure that the egg is roasted, in deference to the view of *Ben Teima* (*Pesachim* 70b) that the *chagigah* must be roasted. We use a "foreleg" corresponding to the arm of a human which reminds us of Hashem's "outstretched arm" in Egypt, an integral element of the Exodus (see *Shemos* 6:6). Today, people use any sort of roasted meat [or chicken] to commemorate the *pesach* sacrifice. However, when we recite in the Haggadah "Pesach — why did our fathers eat a *pesach* offering?" we may not point to this meat, because that appears as sanctifying meat outside of the *Beis HaMikdash*, which is prohibited. Similarly, our custom is not to eat roast meat at the Seder, so that it not appear as if we are eating actual sacrifices (from a lecture on the laws of Pesach given by Rav Shlomo Zalman in 1970 and published in *Kuntres Seder Pesach*).

Rav Shlomo Zalman would set the "Seder plate" on top of the matzah cover, placing each of the six items in small dishes and arranging them according to the pattern of the Ari, as indicated:
(Rav Yosef Shub, citing Rav Baruch Auerbach).

Although the Gra arranged the Seder plate in the order in which each item is taken, our custom is to follow the order of the Ari. This order is based on Kabbalistic mysteries, and we do not know the reason for it (from a lecture on the laws of Pesach given by Rav Shlomo Zalman in 1970 and published in *Kuntres Seder Pesach*).

The egg on Rav Shlomo Zalman's Seder plate was hard boiled (not roasted), and he would eat it at the meal (Rav Yosef Shub, citing Rav Shlomo Zalman's son, Rav Baruch Auerbach).

Rav Shlomo Zalman set a Seder plate before each male at the table (*Kol HaTorah,* Nisan 5756, as reported by Rav Shlomo Zalman's grandson, Rav Pinchas Bondy).

Rav Shlomo Zalman used hand-s*hemurah* matzos for the Seder (Rav Yosef Shub, citing Rav Shlomo Zalman's son, Rav Baruch Auerbach).

✑ Pesach Customs

Rav Shlomo Zalman would eat *gebrokts*, "soaked" matzah products on Pesach (Rav Yosef Shub, citing Rav Baruch Auerbach).

Rav Shlomo Zalman's custom was not to eat any food that fell on the floor. Similarly, any utensils that fell on the floor would be washed before further use (ibid.).

Rav Shlomo Zalman did not use potato starch on Pesach because of its resemblance to flour. Likewise, he would not eat anything that had the appearance of a *chametz* cake (reported by Rav Aharon Goldberg).

✑ The Seventh Day of Pesach

Rav Shlomo Zalman would eat a third holiday meal on the last day(s) of Pesach (the eight day outside *Eretz Yisrael*), in accordance with the custom of the Gra (*Kol HaTorah*, Nisan 5756, citing his grandson, Rav Pinchas Bondy).

✑ Starting the Seder

It is customary to wear a white *kittel* for the Seder. Even a *chasan* in his first year of marriage, as well as a mourner, can wear a *kittel* for the Seder (Rav Yosef Shub, citing Rav Shlomo Zalman's son, Rav Baruch Auerbach; cf. *Igros Moshe, Yoreh De'ah* 4:61).

Rav Shlomo Zalman himself wore a white Jerusalem caftan, known as a "v*eiser chalat*" (Rav Yosef Shub, citing Rav Baruch Auerbach).

All those assembled at Rav Shlomo Zalman's Seder would announce each new section of the Haggadah (e.g. *Kaddesh, U're-chatz,* etc.) as it was reached (Rav Yosef Shub, citing Rav Shlomo Zalman's son, Rav Baruch Auerbach).

⋑ The Seder

☐ Kaddesh

Women, who were included in the salvation from Egypt, are obligated in all the precepts of Pesach. Thus, they are also obligated in *Kiddush,* the first of the Seder's obligatory four cups of wine.[1]

There are three customs regarding who recites *Kiddush* at the Seder: (1) The master of the house recites *Kiddush* for all the assembled, and they fulfill their *Kiddush* requirement through his recital. They must listen to his *Kiddush* with the intent to fulfill their requirement and answer *amen* after each blessing.[2] (2) All the assembled recite *Kiddush* quietly, along with the master of the house.[3] (3) Each participant (women as well as men) recites his

---

1. The Gemara (*Pesachim* 106a) derives a woman's obligation in the *Kiddush* for Shabbos from the verse: *Remember the Sabbath day to sanctify it* (*Shemos* 20:8). There is no corresponding source regarding *Kiddush* for *Yom Tov.* R' Akiva Eiger (*Responsa,* 1 and *Hashmatos* ad loc.) states that "most of our women" are stringent, and have accepted upon themselves most of the time-bound mitzvos (*mitzvos asei she'hazeman gerama*), including *Kiddush* for *Yom Tov* (cf. *Sha'agas Aryeh* 66; see *Orchos Chaim* 188:3; *Ben Ish Chai,* Second Year, *Bereishis* 11; also see *Pischei Teshuvah* 529:2 and *Shulchan Aruch HaRav* 271:5).

Shemiras Shabbos K'hilchasah, Chapter 47, note 26 cites Rav Shlomo Zalman Auerbach as stating that, according to the explanation of R' Akiva Eiger, Sephardic women, who follow the view of *Beis Yosef* not to recite *berachos* for time-bound mitzvos, should not recite their own *Kiddush* for any *Yom Tov* other than Pesach. Pesach is the exception, for the reason stated in the text.

2. *Shulchan Aruch, Orach Chaim* 472:22, based on the Gemara (*Berachos* 53a). See *Mishnah Berurah* 124:21 concerning *Baruch Hu U'Varuch Shemo.*

3. *Vayaged Moshe* 15:7.

own *Kiddush*, separately.[1] Rav Shlomo Zalman Auerbach followed the first custom, but nevertheless instructed all the participants of the Seder to raise their own cup of wine during *Kiddush* as if they were reciting their own *Kiddush*. This reinforces the awareness that *Kiddush* is the first of the four cups (*Shemiras Shabbos K'hilchasah* 47, note 26).

According to Rav Shlomo Zalman, grape juice may be used for the four cups. He personally would mix wine with grape juice (*Kuntres Seder Pesach* note 49).[2]

A woman who recites her own *Kiddush* should not recite *Shehecheyanu*, as she has already recited it when she lit the candles. If she does not recite her own *Kiddush*, but fulfills her obligation through another person's recital, she may answer *amen* to his *Shehecheyanu*. Nevertheless, before reciting *Kiddush* in his house Rav Shlomo Zalman would always instruct the women of his household not to answer *amen* to his *Shehecheyanu* (*Minchas Shlomo* II:58, and note contained in ibid.:60).

It was Rav Shlomo Zalman's custom to stand while reciting Friday-night *Kiddush*, but to sit for the *Yom Tov*-night *Kiddush*. When *Yom Tov* fell on Friday night, he would stand (Rav Yosef Shub, citing Rav Baruch Auerbach).[3]

---

1. Ibid., 6.

2. Cf. *Haggadah Kol Dodi* Laws of the Seder 3:8, where Rav Dovid Feinstein quotes his father, Rav Moshe Feinstein, who says that the four-cups requirement is fulfilled only with wine that intoxicates. Also see *Shevus Yitzchak*, *Pesach*, p. 117, which cites Rav Moshe Feinstein as requiring a minimum of one-third wine in a mixture with grape juice to insure that the person drink "in a manner of freedom (*derech cherus*)." See, however, *Ma'adanei Shlomo*, *Pesach* p. 13, citing Rav Shlomo Zalman's response to the above requirement: "This is a new ruling the likes of which we have never heard; we find that grape juice is equivalent to wine in all respects." Also see *Seder Pesach K'hilchasah* II Chapter 3 note 25, citing Rav Chaim Kanievsky as stating that the Chazon Ish used to drink grape juice for the four cups. Similarly, *Teshuvos V'hanhagos* II, *Orach Chaim* 243 states that the Tchebiner Rav, Rav Dov Berish Wiedenfeld, also drank grape juice for the four cups.

3. *Shulchan Aruch, Orach Chaim* 271:10 rules that one should stand while reciting *Kiddush* on Friday night. *Mishnah Berurah*, ad loc. 45, explains that *Vayechulu* is a testimony that God created the world in six days and rested on the seventh, and testimony requires standing (see *Devarim* 19:17). Since one does not recite *Vayechulu* on *Yom Tov* night (unless it falls on Friday night) there is no reason to stand. See *Rema* and *Mishnah Berurah* op. cit. for other customs.

When reciting *Kiddush* on *Motzaei Shabbos, Havdalah* is added, and one recites the *berachah* of *borei me'orei ha'eish* over the candles. Two candles should not be placed together for this purpose, because separating them afterward is a possible transgression of the prohibition to extinguish fire. If only the two flames touch, however, one is permitted separate them (*Yom Tov Sheni K'hilchasah*, Chapter 1, note 16, citing Rav Shlomo Zalman Auerbach, based on *Rosh, Beitzah* 2:17).

If one mistakenly concludes the *Havdalah* portion with the words, *"hamavdil bein kodesh l'chol"* (as is the case on ordinary *Motzaei Shabbosos*), rather than *"hamavdil bein kodesh l'kodesh,"* he must repeat the entire blessing and conclude it properly (Rav Shlomo Zalman, cited in *Si'ach Halachah* 25:9).

If one mistakenly recites the *borei minei besamim* blessing, it does not invalidate the *Kiddush/Havdalah* in any way (cited in *Shemiras Shabbos K'hilchasah*, Chapter 62, note 49).

Before *Kiddush*, Rav Shlomo Zalman would announce that all participants should listen to the *Shehecheyanu* with the intent of applying it to all of the mitzvos of the evening: making a Seder, eating the *karpas* and dipping it in salt water, eating matzah, eating *maror*, leaning, reciting the story of the Exodus, drinking the four cups of wine, abstaining from *chametz,* etc. (reported by his grandson, Rav Aharon Goldberg).

In the *Shehecheyanu* blessing, the customary pronunciation is: *la'zeman hazeh,* not *le'zeman hazeh* (*Halichos Shlomo* 23, note 68; cf. *Mishnah Berurah* 676:1).

Drinking the Kiddush wine

Due to its dual nature, while drinking the wine, one should have in mind to fulfill both mitzvah requirements: *Kiddush* and the first of the Seder's four cups (from a lecture on the laws of Pesach given by Rav Shlomo Zalman in 1970).

☐ U'rechatz

The custom in Rav Shlomo Zalman's home was for all participants to wash.[1] The custom of others is that only the head of the household washes.[2]

If one mistakenly recited the blessing *al netilas yadayim* after this washing, he must nevertheless repeat the blessing when he washes later before eating the matzah. One should preferably touch something unclean (such as shoes), so that there is now a definite obligation to wash again, and thus, there is no question of an unnecessary blessing (*Rivevos Efrayim*, I:301, citing Rav Shlomo Zalman Auerbach).

☐ Karpas

The term "*karpas*" is not mentioned at all in the Gemara, which only states that in addition to *maror* there is a mitzvah to eat another vegetable (the blessing over which is ... *adamah*) and to dip it in a liquid. *Maharil* (cited in *Magen Avraham* 473:4) is the first to say that the custom is to take a vegetable called "*karpas*" (which is spelled with the same letters as *samech perech*, alluding to the 600,000 males who were enslaved). Although the vegetable the Maharil referred to was celery, the custom is to eat any vegetable [other than *maror*]. Some use a cucumber, others a potato; what is important is that it be a vegetable on which the blessing *borei pri ha'adamah* is recited (from a lecture on the laws of Pesach given by Rav Shlomo Zalman Auerbach in 1970).

Rav Shlomo Zalman himself used to use celery at his Seder until there was an insect problem in celery. As a result, in later years he used cucumbers (as related by his son, Rav Shmuel Auerbach).

Rav Shlomo Zalman did not recline while eating the *karpas* (Rav Yosef Shub, citing Rav Shlomo Zalman's son, Rav Baruch Auerbach).

---

1. As reported by his grandson, Rav Aharon Goldberg.
2. *Maharil, Minhagim, Seder Haggadah*, citing *Maharash*. This is also the implication of *Rambam, Hil. Chametz U'matzah* 8:1; also see *Shulchan Aruch* 473:6.

☐ Yachatz

Rav Shlomo Zalman would not allow the children in his house to steal the *afikoman* (Rav Yosef Shub, citing Rav Shlomo Zalman's son, Rav Baruch Auerbach).

☐ Maggid

Rav Shlomo Zalman would not make lengthy explanations during the Haggadah. He would simply translate the words and say some basic *divrei Torah* (as related by his disciple, Rav Avigdor Nebenzahl; also see *Kol HaTorah,* Nisan 5756, citing Rav Pinchas Bondy).

At Rav Shlomo Zalman's Seder, the second cup of wine was poured before reciting *Ha lachma anya*,[1] even though many Haggadahs direct one to pour the wine between *Ha lachma anya* and *Mah nishtanah*.

Ha lachma anya

Rav Shlomo Zalman used to add the words, "*Bivehilu yatzanu miMitzrayim*" — "We left Egypt in haste" — immediately before beginning *Ha lachma anya*.[2]

After saying "*kol ditzrich yesei v'yifsach*" — "whoever is in need, let him come and partake of the Pesach," Rav Shlomo Zalman would explain that this is said in reference to the *pesach* sacrifice.[3]

Covering the matzos

Although many sources require removing the Seder plate, Rav Shlomo Zalman would not do so; he would merely cover the matzos.[4]

Mah Nishtanah

At Rav Shlomo Zalman's Seder, each child would ask the *Mah*

---

1. *Kol HaTorah Journal*, Nisan 5756, citing his grandson, Rav Pinchas Bondy.
2. Ibid. This appears in the version of the Haggadah used by the Rambam.
3. Cited by his son, Rav Azriel Auerbach.
4. Rav Yosef Shub, citing Rav Shlomo Zalman's son, Rav Baruch Auerbach. Also see above, s.v. *Why are the matzos sometimes covered*...

nishtanah individually, and then everybody would recite it together.[1]

After the *Mah nishtanah*, Rebbetzin Auerbach would give nuts to the children.[2]

Dam va'esh ...

As each of the words, *dam, va'eish, v'simros ashan* (blood, fire, and pillars of smoke), is said, a bit of wine is removed from the cup. Rav Shlomo Zalman would pour it from the cup;[3] others use a finger to remove it.[4] The same was done in the following paragraphs, as each of the plagues is mentioned and for each word of Rabbi Yehudah's mnemonic.

Lefichach

At Rav Shlomo Zalman's seder, all the participants would lift their cups and hold them until finishing the blessing of *Ga'al Yisrael*.[5]

Baruch ... asher gaalanu

Rav Shlomo Zalman recited this blessing while seated.[6]

☐ Motzi

Rav Shlomo Zalman used three matzos.[7]

---

1. Rav Yosef Shub, citing Rav Shlomo Zalman's son, Rav Baruch Auerbach. Cf. *Rema* 473:7; also see *Hagahos Chasam Sofer* ad loc.
2. Rav Yosef Shub, citing Rav Shlomo Zalman's son, Rav Baruch Auerbach.
3. Ibid.
4. *Mishnah Berurah* 473:74.
5. *Shulchan Aruch* 473:7; *Mishnah Berurah* ad loc. 77; cf. *Aruch Hashulchan* ad loc. 23 who cites the custom of putting the cup down when reciting *Hallel* and raising it again it for the entire *berachah*. [When the cup is put down the matzos should be uncovered.]
6. *Vayaged Moshe* 22:27, who says that some have the custom of reciting it while standing. Rav Aharon Goldberg says that his grandfather, Rav Shlomo Zalman, would recite it while seated.
7. The prevalent practice is to use three matzos, but some have the custom to use just two, as for any other Shabbos or holiday. The reason for three matzos is that although we fulfill the mitzvah of eating matzah with the broken piece of matzah, two complete "loaves" are still required as is the case on any Shabbos or holiday. Accordingly, we recite the *Hamotzi* blessing (first, in accordance with its status of being the standard blessing) over all three to satisfy the requirement of two complete "loaves." Then we put down the bottom matzah

☐ Matzah

Each participant should eat the requisite amount using matzah from each of the two matzos (additional matzos may be added as necessary) while leaning to the left. The matzos are not dipped into salt.[1]

The matzah must be eaten before midnight (*chatzos*). According to Rav Shlomo Zalman, this ideally should be considered the mid-point between nightfall (*not* sunset) and dawn — about twenty minutes *before* the time listed in the calendars (*Minchas Shlomo* Vol. II 58:19).

☐ Maror

Rav Shlomo Zalman would use romaine lettuce for *maror* (Rav Yosef Shub, in the name of Rav Shlomo Zalman's son, Rav Baruch).[2]

The lettuce requires cleaning and checking for insect infestation, but it should not be cleaned by soaking it in vinegar, since that disqualifies the lettuce from use as *maror* (*Minchas Shlomo* II:58).

When the Seder night is Friday night, the lettuce should be cleaned and checked earlier in the day. When not done before Shabbos, it may be checked on Shabbos, but any small insects found attached to the lettuce should be removed along with a piece of lettuce (*Shemiras Shabbos K'hilchasah* 3:36, citing Rav Shlomo Zalman).

☐ Korech

Some recite the paragraph זֵכֶר לְמִקְדָּשׁ כְּהִלֵּל, *In remembrance of the Temple we do as Hillel did*, before eating the "sandwich." Rav

---

and recite the *al achilas matzah* blessing over the top complete matzah and the second fragment-matzah (from a lecture on the laws of Pesach given by Rav Shlomo Zalman Auerbach in 1970).

1. *Rema* (475:1). Rav Shlomo Zalman (in his 1970 lecture on the laws of Pesach printed in *Kuntres Seder Pesach*) cites two views: One is that salt is nevertheless placed on the table to fulfill the custom based on the verse (*Vayikra* 2:13): "...The salt of your God's covenant... on your every offering shall you offer salt." The second is that it not even be brought to the table.

2. He also permitted using lettuce grown in hothouses where the growing medium is separated from the earth (*Minchas Shlomo* II:4).

Shlomo Zalman would recite it *after* eating the "sandwich."[1]

☐ Shulchan Orech

Rav Shlomo Zalman was particular about finishing *Hallel* before *chatzos*.[2]

Rav Shlomo Zalman did not lean during the meal (Rav Yosef Shub, citing Rav Shlomo Zalman's son, Rav Baruch).[3]

☐ Tzafun

Some have the custom to put the *afikoman* on their shoulders, in memory of the Exodus. Rav Shlomo Zalman did not (as reported by his grandson, Rabbi Aharon Goldberg).

Rav Shlomo Zalman did not follow the custom that some have of leaving a piece of the *afikoman* for the future[4] (as reported by his grandson, Rav Aharon Goldberg).

---

1. As reported by his grandson, Rabbi Pinchas Bondy, and recorded in *Kol HaTorah*, Nisan 5756.
According to Hillel, the blessings recited earlier on the matzah and on the *maror* are needed for *Korech*, and thus, one cannot speak — or even recite a paragraph — until *after* finishing *Korech* (see *Biur Halachah*, 475:1 s.v. *v'omer*). Indeed, although *Korech* is *eaten* "In remembrance of the Temple we do as Hillel did," oral recitation of that remembrance is not necessarily required. If one wants, he may say it after finishing *Korech* (from a lecture on the laws of Pesach given by Rav Shlomo Zalman in 1970, published in *Kuntres Seder Pesach*).

2. We have noted above that Rav Shlomo Zalman calculated *chatzos* as the midpoint between nightfall (*tzeis hakochavim*) and dawn, and not the midpoint between sunset (*shkiah*) and dawn. His calculation sets *chatzos* about twenty minutes earlier than the standard calculation. He was particular to finish eating the *afikoman* before this time. Regarding the recital of *Hallel*, however, he was more lenient, and he was particular only to finish before *chatzos* according to the standard calculation (*Kol HaTorah*, Nisan 5756, citing Rav Shlomo Zalman's grandson, R' Pinchas Bondy).

3. *Rema* (476:1) rules that one should preferably lean for the entire meal. Above (s.v. *concerning the requirement to lean*), however, we have quoted Rav Shlomo Zalman as stating that really there should be no requirement to lean nowadays. Yet we refrain from canceling a custom which prevailed at the time of our Sages. He concluded that for situations where there never was a universal custom, leaning is not necessary nowadays (see there). Apparently, leaning during the meal falls into that category.

4. See *Teshuvos Mishneh Sachir* II:122, who writes that the *afikoman* should never be left over on the first night of Pesach, for it has the laws of the *pesach*

☐ Barech

At שְׁפֹךְ חֲמָתְךָ, *Pour your wrath*..., some stand when opening the door and say, "*Baruch Haba*" (Welcome); at Rav Shlomo Zalman's Seder they sat, but said, "*Baruch Haba*" (Rav Yosef Shub, citing Rav Baruch Auerbach).

☐ Hallel

Some hold the wine cup while reciting *Hallel*. Rav Shlomo Zalman did not (Rav Yosef Shub, citing Rav Baruch Auerbach).

Rav Shlomo Zalman followed the Ashkenazic custom regarding the end of *Hallel*, reciting יְהַלְלוּךָ, *They shall praise You*, until just before the closing blessing. He recited יִשְׁתַּבַּח שְׁמְךָ, *May Your Name be praised*, later in the Haggadah, with a closing blessing, just before the drinking of the fourth cup (Rav Avigdor Nebenzahl).

☐ Nirtzah

After the Seder, some say *Shir HaShirim*, because of its connection to the Exodus (see *Rema* 490:9 and *Mishnah Berurah* there 17). Rav Shlomo Zalman followed this custom (Rav Yosef Shub, citing Rav Baruch Auerbach).

---

offering. He concludes that those who have this custom should only follow it when celebrating a second night of Pesach (such as in the Diaspora). Since the requirement is only Rabbinic, the restrictions are more lenient.

עֶרֶב פֶּסַח – Erev Pesach

Laws of the Search for *Chametz*

1. One must begin the search immediately at the beginning of the night of the fourteenth of Nisan. It is proper for one to begin just after *tzeis hakochavim,* even before the light of day has completely subsided, so that he not delay the search or forget about it (*Orach Chayim* 431:1 and *Mishnah Berurah* §1).

2. It is forbidden to begin a meal or to begin a bath or to do any kind of work starting from a half-hour before nighttime. However, a snack — that is, a *k'beitzah* or less of bread, or fruit in any amount — is permitted at this time. When the actual time for the search arrives one should not spend much time eating even a snack, as this would cause a delay in the start of the search (432:2 and *Mishnah Berurah* §2, 5-6).

3. It is also forbidden to engage in Torah study once the time for the search has arrived. (There are those who forbid this also during the half-hour *before* nightfall. This applies only in private, however, and not, for instance, to someone who gives a short *shiur* in a *beis midrash* after *Ma'ariv.* If someone asks a person who is not learning to remind him about the search when the proper time comes, he may also learn during this half-hour interval) (ibid. *Mishnah Berurah* §7).

4. Any place into which it is possible that *chametz* might have been brought must be searched. Even places not normally used for *chametz,* but where there is a reasonable possibility that *chametz* may happen to have been brought there, require a search. This includes houses, yards (except in cases where one can assume that leftover food is eaten by animals or birds), nooks and crevices as far as the hand can reach, and whatever containers might have once been used for holding *chametz.* In a situation where a search in a particular place would entail great difficulty, it is possible to be lenient and sell that place to a non-Jew, so that it would not require a search. The details of these rules may be found in *Orach Chayim* 433:3,5 and *Mishnah Berurah* §23.

5. Pockets of garments must be searched, even if one feels confident that he has never put any *chametz* in them, because one often does so without realizing it (433:11 and *Mishnah Berurah* §47).

6. One should clean up the house before the search is begun. It is customary to clean the whole house on or before the 13th of Nisan, so that the search can be started without delay at nightfall of the 14th. It is also customary to take a feather with which to dust out the *chametz* from holes and crevices (ibid. and *Mishnah Berurah* §46).

Note: Source references within the laws refer to *Shulchan Aruch Orach Chayim,* unless otherwise noted.

7. It is preferable to use a single wax candle for the search. A search done by the light of a torch is not valid at all, but one done using a candle made of tallow is valid. The validity of a search done by the light of an oil candle is a matter of dispute between halachic authorities (433:2 and *Mishnah Berurah* §10). Contemporary authorities rule that one may use a flashlight for the search.
8. It is customary to place several pieces of bread (taking care that they should not crumble) in safe places around the house, where they may be found by the person conducting the search. (The *Arizal* wrote that *ten* pieces should be used.) Some halachic authorities write that this practice is not obligatory, and the *Taz* in fact advises against it, lest the pieces become lost. (The *Pischei Teshuvah*, however, notes that nowadays, when the entire house is rid of *chametz* before the search, there is a sound halachic basis for the practice of placing some *chametz* around the house to provide something for which to search.) (432:2, *Mishnah Berurah* §13 and *Shaar Hatziun* ad loc.)
9. There is a controversy as to whether one must search those rooms which are to be sold to a non-Jew with the *chametz*. The custom is to be lenient in this regard, although it would be preferable that in this circumstance the *chametz* be sold *before* the search (436, *Mishnah Berurah* §32).

Laws of the *Berachah* over the Search

1. Some say that it is proper to wash the hands before reciting the *berachah* for the search, but this is only for the sake of cleanliness (432, *Mishnah Berurah* §1).
2. One must not speak between the *berachah* and the onset of the search. If he spoke about matters unrelated to the search, he must repeat the *berachah* (432:1, *Mishnah Berurah* §5).
3. One should not speak about matters unrelated to the search until he completes the search, so that one may devote his entire concentration to the task at hand. If he did, however, speak about unrelated matters after beginning the search, he need not repeat the *berachah*. Furthermore, it is altogether permitted to speak about any matters related to the search at this point (ibid.).
4. Immediately after the search one should recite the כָּל חֲמִירָא declaration, annulling all the *unknown chametz* in his possession. If one does not understand the Aramaic content of this declaration, he should say it in Hebrew or English or whatever language he does understand. If one said it in Aramaic, so long as he has a basic understanding of what the declaration means, though he may not understand the translation of every word, the annulment is valid. One who does not understand the content at all, and thinks he is reciting a prayer of some sort, has not annulled his *chametz* (434:2 and *Mishnah Berurah* §8).

Laws of *Erev Pesach*

1. Prayers are held early on *erev Pesach* in order to allow people to finish eating before the end of the fourth hour of the day (*Mishnah Berurah* 429:13).

2. אֵל אֶרֶךְ אַפַּיִם, לַמְנַצֵּחַ, and מִזְמוֹר לְתוֹדָה are not said on *erev Pesach* (*Orach Chayim* 429:2).

3. It is forbidden to eat *chametz* after a third of the halachic day has passed. The duration of the day can be calculated in various ways. One should consult a competent Halachic authority or a reliable Jewish calendar (443:1 and *Mishnah Berurah* §8).

4. The deadline for ridding one's property of *chametz* and deriving benefit from the *chametz* is at the end of the *fifth* hour of the halachic day (*Mishnah Berurah* §9).

5. Immediately after a third of the day has passed, one should burn the remaining *chametz* and then recite the second כָּל חֲמִירָא declaration, annulling *all* the *chametz* in his possession. This declaration must not be delayed past the start of the sixth hour, for at that time the annulment no longer has any validity (434:2). See **"Burning the *Chametz*"** below.

6. If *erev Pesach* falls on a Shabbos, the *chametz* should be burned on the day before *erev Pesach* (Friday) in the morning, at the same time as other years. However, the כָּל חֲמִירָא declaration should not be said until the 14th of Nisan, i.e. Shabbos morning, after the last *chametz* meal has been eaten (444:2).

7. One should take care that all food utensils not *kashered* for Pesach have been thoroughly cleaned, so that they do not contain any *chametz* residue, and they should be placed out of reach for the duration of Pesach (440:2; end of 442, *Mishnah Berurah* 433:23).

8. Those utensils too hard to clean from *chametz* residue should be sold together with the *chametz*. (Only the *residue itself* should be sold, not the utensil, so as to avoid the necessity of immersing the utensil in a *mikveh* when it is repurchased from the non-Jew.) These utensils should also be placed in a room where they are out of reach, or together with the *chametz* that is being sold (ibid.).

9. After halachic noon it is forbidden to do any work (מְלָאכָה). If someone's clothing tore at that time, and he needs that article of clothing for *Yom Tov*, he may make a minor repair for himself, even if it involves expert workmanship. Someone else may also do it for him at no charge (*Orach Chayim* 468, *Mishnah Berurah* §5).

10. Any manner of work which is forbidden on *Chol Hamoed* is also forbidden on *erev Pesach* afternoon, although it is permissible for one to have a non-Jew do these things for him (*Mishnah Berurah* §7).

11. One should cut his nails and have his hair cut before noon. If, however, he neglected to do so, he may have his hair cut by a non-Jew even after noon, and he may cut his own nails (*Mishnah Berurah* §5).
12. Any matzah which one could use for fulfilling the mitzvah of matzah at the Seder may not be eaten all day on *erev Pesach,* even if that matzah has been crumbled or ground into flour and mixed with water or juices. Some people have a custom not to eat matzah from *Rosh Chodesh* Nisan (471:2, *Mishnah Berurah* §10).
13. A child who is too young to understand the story of the Exodus may be fed matzah on *erev Pesach* (471:2 and *Mishnah Berurah* §13).
14. Although we consider matzah with folds or bubbles to be unfit for Pesach use, these may also not be eaten on *erev Pesach* (*Mishnah Berurah* §12).
15. Matzah that has been prepared by adding juices into the dough (such as egg matzah or fruit-juice matzah) may be eaten on *erev Pesach*. (Note: It is the Ashkenazi practice to avoid such matzos whenever the eating of *chametz* is forbidden, except for the sick or elderly.)
16. From the beginning of the *halachic* tenth hour of the day, only snacks such as fruits and vegetables may be eaten. One should be careful, however, not to fill himself up on these either, to preserve one's appetite for the matzah at the Seder (471:1 and *Mishnah Berurah* 7).
17. The Gemara says that a small amount of wine can also cause satiety, but a large amount stimulates the appetite. *Be'ur Halachah* concludes that the amount of wine one may drink depends on his individual nature, and that a person should not drink (after the tenth hour) an amount of wine that he feels may make him feel sated (471:1 and *Be'ur Halachah* ad loc.).

Fast of the Firstborn

1. There is a custom for firstborn males to fast on *erev Pesach,* even if they are firstborn to only one of their parents. If the firstborn son is a minor, the father fasts in his place. If the father is a firstborn himself (and thus has to fast in his own right), the mother fasts for the child. (See *Orach Chayim* 270 and *Mishnah Berurah* ad loc. for the details of this law.)
2. If the firstborn has a headache or similar infirmity he does not have to fast. Similarly, if the fast is likely to cause him to be unable to fulfill the evening's mitzvos of matzah, *maror,* and the four cups of wine properly, it is better for him not to fast. In either of these cases, however, he should limit his eating to small amounts rather than eating full meals (470 and *Mishnah Berurah* ad loc.).
3. There is a controversy among the halachic authorities as to whether a firstborn may eat at a meal served in honor of a mitzvah, and this issue

depends on the local custom. The generally accepted practice is to permit eating at a festive meal at the completion of a *mesechta*, even if the first-born himself did not participate in the learning (*Mishnah Berurah* §10).

Burning the *Chametz*

1. The *chametz* should preferably not be burned until the day of the 14th of Nisan, after the last *chametz* meal has been eaten. If someone is concerned that the *chametz* found in the search may become lost or find its way back into the rest of the house if it is left too long, he should burn it at night, and he is considered to have fulfilled the Torah commandment to destroy *chametz* on *erev Pesach* (תַּשְׁבִּיתוּ) (*Orach Chayim* 445:1, *Mishnah Berurah* §6).

2. If one has *hoshanos* which had been used on Sukkos, he should use them to feed the flame burning the *chametz*, so that they may be used for yet another mitzvah (*Mishnah Berurah* §7).

3. The *chametz* must be burned (until it is completely charred) before the beginning of the sixth hour, and thereupon the declaration of annulment (כָּל חֲמִירָא) is recited. The annulment is ineffective if it is recited once the sixth hour has begun (*Mishnah Berurah* §1,6).

4. One should not recite the annulment declaration before his *chametz* has been fully burned, so that he will be able to fulfill the mitzvah of תַּשְׁבִּיתוּ (burning the *chametz*) with *chametz* that still belongs to him (443:2).

בדיקת חמץ

The *chametz* search is initiated with the recitation of the following blessing:

בָּרוּךְ אַתָּה יהוה אֱלֹהֵינוּ מֶלֶךְ הָעוֹלָם, אֲשֶׁר קִדְּשָׁנוּ בְּמִצְוֹתָיו, וְצִוָּנוּ עַל בִּעוּר חָמֵץ.

Upon completion of the *chametz* search, the *chametz* is wrapped well and set aside to be burned the next morning and the following declaration is made. The declaration must be understood in order to take effect; one who does not understand the Aramaic text may recite it in English, Yiddish or any other language. Any *chametz* that will be used for that evening's supper or the next day's breakfast or for any other purpose prior to the final removal of *chametz* the next morning is not included in this declaration.

כָּל חֲמִירָא וַחֲמִיעָא דְּאִכָּא בִרְשׁוּתִי, דְּלָא חֲמִתֵּהּ וּדְלָא בְעַרְתֵּהּ וּדְלָא יָדַעְנָא לֵהּ, לִבָּטֵל וְלֶהֱוֵי הֶפְקֵר כְּעַפְרָא דְאַרְעָא.

ביעור חמץ

The following declaration, which includes all *chametz* without exception, is to be made after the burning of leftover *chametz*. It should be recited in a language which one understands. When *Pesach* begins on *Motzaei Shabbos*, this declaration is made on *Shabbos* morning. Any *chametz* remaining from the *Shabbos* morning meal is flushed down the drain before the declaration is made.

כָּל חֲמִירָא וַחֲמִיעָא דְּאִכָּא בִרְשׁוּתִי, דַּחֲזִתֵּהּ וּדְלָא חֲזִתֵּהּ, דַּחֲמִתֵּהּ וּדְלָא חֲמִתֵּהּ, דְּבִעַרְתֵּהּ וּדְלָא בִעַרְתֵּהּ, לִבָּטֵל וְלֶהֱוֵי הֶפְקֵר כְּעַפְרָא דְאַרְעָא.

עירוב תבשילין

It is forbidden to prepare on *Yom Tov* for the next day even if that day is the Sabbath. If, however, Sabbath preparations were started before *Yom Tov* began, they may be continued on *Yom Tov*. *Eruv tavshilin* constitutes this preparation. A matzah and any cooked food (such as fish, meat or an egg) are set aside on the day before *Yom Tov* to be used on the Sabbath and the blessing is recited followed by the declaration [made in a language understood by the one making the *eruv*]. If the first days of Pesach fall on Thursday and Friday, an *eruv tavshilin* must be made on Wednesday.

[In *Eretz Yisrael*, where only one day *Yom Tov* is in effect, the *eruv* is omitted.]

בָּרוּךְ אַתָּה יהוה אֱלֹהֵינוּ מֶלֶךְ הָעוֹלָם, אֲשֶׁר קִדְּשָׁנוּ בְּמִצְוֹתָיו, וְצִוָּנוּ עַל מִצְוַת עֵרוּב.

SEARCH FOR CHAMETZ

The *chametz* search is initiated with the recitation of the following blessing:

Blessed are You, HASHEM, our God, King of the universe, Who has sanctified us with His commandments, and commanded us concerning the removal of chametz.

Upon completion of the *chametz* search, the *chametz* is wrapped well and set aside to be burned the next morning and the following declaration is made. The declaration must be understood in order to take effect; one who does not understand the Aramaic text may recite it in English, Yiddish or any other language. Any *chametz* that will be used for that evening's supper or the next day's breakfast or for any other purpose prior to the final removal of *chametz* the next morning is not included in this declaration.

Any chametz which is in my possession which I did not see, and remove, nor know about, shall be nullified and become ownerless, like the dust of the earth.

BURNING THE CHAMETZ

The following declaration, which includes all *chametz* without exception, is to be made after the burning of leftover *chametz*. It should be recited in a language which one understands. When *Pesach* begins on *Motzaei Shabbos*, this declaration is made on *Shabbos* morning. Any *chametz* remaining from the *Shabbos* morning meal is flushed down the drain before the declaration is made.

Any chametz which is in my possession which I did or did not see, which I did or did not remove, shall be nullified and become ownerless, like the dust of the earth.

ERUV TAVSHILIN

It is forbidden to prepare on *Yom Tov* for the next day even if that day is the Sabbath. If, however, Sabbath preparations were started before *Yom Tov* began, they may be continued on *Yom Tov*. *Eruv tavshilin* constitutes this preparation. A matzah and any cooked food (such as fish, meat or an egg) are set aside on the day before *Yom Tov* to be used on the Sabbath and the blessing is recited followed by the declaration [made in a language understood by the one making the *eruv*]. If the first days of Pesach fall on Thursday and Friday, an *eruv tavshilin* must be made on Wednesday.

[In *Eretz Yisrael*, where only one day *Yom Tov* is in effect, the *eruv* is omitted.]

Blessed are You, HASHEM, our God, King of the universe, Who sanctified us with His commandments and commanded us concerning the commandment of eruv.

בְּהָדֵין עֲרוּבָא יְהֵא שָׁרֵא לָנָא לַאֲפוּיֵי וּלְבַשּׁוּלֵי וּלְאַצְלוּיֵי וּלְאַטְמוּנֵי וּלְאַדְלוּקֵי שְׁרָגָא וּלְתַקָּנָא וּלְמֶעְבַּד כָּל צָרְכָּנָא, מִיּוֹמָא טָבָא לְשַׁבַּתָּא לָנָא וּלְכָל יִשְׂרָאֵל הַדָּרִים בָּעִיר הַזֹּאת.

הדלקת נרות

The candles are lit and the following blessings are recited.
When Yom Tov falls on *Shabbos*, the words in parentheses are added.

בָּרוּךְ אַתָּה יהוה אֱלֹהֵינוּ מֶלֶךְ הָעוֹלָם, אֲשֶׁר קִדְּשָׁנוּ בְּמִצְוֹתָיו, וְצִוָּנוּ לְהַדְלִיק נֵר שֶׁל [שַׁבָּת וְשֶׁל] יוֹם טוֹב.

בָּרוּךְ אַתָּה יהוה אֱלֹהֵינוּ מֶלֶךְ הָעוֹלָם, שֶׁהֶחֱיָנוּ וְקִיְּמָנוּ וְהִגִּיעָנוּ לַזְּמַן הַזֶּה.

It is customary to recite the following prayer after the kindling.
The words in brackets are included as they apply.

יְהִי רָצוֹן לְפָנֶיךָ, יהוה אֱלֹהַי וֵאלֹהֵי אֲבוֹתַי, שֶׁתְּחוֹנֵן אוֹתִי [וְאֶת אִישִׁי, וְאֶת בָּנַי, וְאֶת בְּנוֹתַי, וְאֶת אָבִי, וְאֶת אִמִּי] וְאֶת כָּל קְרוֹבַי; וְתִתֶּן לָנוּ וּלְכָל יִשְׂרָאֵל חַיִּים טוֹבִים וַאֲרוּכִים; וְתִזְכְּרֵנוּ בְּזִכְרוֹן טוֹבָה וּבְרָכָה; וְתִפְקְדֵנוּ בִּפְקֻדַּת יְשׁוּעָה וְרַחֲמִים; וּתְבָרְכֵנוּ בְּרָכוֹת גְּדוֹלוֹת; וְתַשְׁלִים בָּתֵּינוּ; וְתַשְׁכֵּן שְׁכִינָתְךָ בֵּינֵינוּ. וְזַכֵּנִי לְגַדֵּל בָּנִים וּבְנֵי בָנִים חֲכָמִים וּנְבוֹנִים, אוֹהֲבֵי יהוה, יִרְאֵי אֱלֹהִים, אַנְשֵׁי אֱמֶת, זֶרַע קֹדֶשׁ, בַּיהוה דְּבֵקִים, וּמְאִירִים אֶת הָעוֹלָם בַּתּוֹרָה וּבְמַעֲשִׂים טוֹבִים, וּבְכָל מְלֶאכֶת עֲבוֹדַת הַבּוֹרֵא. אָנָּא שְׁמַע אֶת תְּחִנָּתִי בָּעֵת הַזֹּאת, בִּזְכוּת שָׂרָה וְרִבְקָה וְרָחֵל וְלֵאָה אִמּוֹתֵינוּ, וְהָאֵר נֵרֵנוּ שֶׁלֹּא יִכְבֶּה לְעוֹלָם וָעֶד, וְהָאֵר פָּנֶיךָ וְנִוָּשֵׁעָה. אָמֵן.

Through this eruv may we be permitted to bake, cook, fry, insulate, kindle flame, prepare for, and do anything necessary on the festival for the sake of the Sabbath — for ourselves and for all Jews who live in this city.

LIGHTING THE CANDLES

The candles are lit and the following blessings are recited.
When Yom Tov falls on Shabbos, the words in parentheses are added.

Blessed are You, HASHEM, our God, King of the universe, Who has sanctified us with His commandments, and commanded us to kindle the flame of the (Sabbath and the) festival.

Blessed are You, HASHEM, our God, King of the universe, Who has kept us alive, sustained us, and brought us to this season.

It is customary to recite the following prayer after the kindling.
The words in brackets are included as they apply.

May it be Your will, HASHEM, my God and God of my forefathers, that You show favor to me [my husband, my sons, my daughters, my father, my mother] and all my relatives; and that You grant us and all Israel a good and long life; that You remember us with a beneficent memory and blessing; that You consider us with a consideration of salvation and compassion; that You bless us with great blessings; that You make our households complete; that You cause Your Presence to dwell among us. Privilege me to raise children and grandchildren who are wise and understanding, who love HASHEM and fear God, people of truth, holy offspring, attached to HASHEM, who illuminate the world with Torah and good deeds and with every labor in the service of the Creator. Please, hear my supplication at this time, in the merit of Sarah, Rebecca, Rachel, and Leah, our mothers, and cause our light to illuminate that it not be extinguished forever, and let Your countenance shine so that we are saved. Amen.

סדר אמירת קרבן פסח
RECITAL OF THE KORBAN PESACH

סדר אמירת קרבן פסח

After *Minchah*, many customarily recite the following passages that describe the קׇרְבַּן פֶּסַח, *pesach* offering:

רִבּוֹן הָעוֹלָמִים, אַתָּה צִוִּיתָנוּ לְהַקְרִיב קׇרְבַּן הַפֶּסַח בְּמוֹעֲדוֹ בְּאַרְבָּעָה עָשָׂר יוֹם לַחֹדֶשׁ הָרִאשׁוֹן, וְלִהְיוֹת כֹּהֲנִים בַּעֲבוֹדָתָם וּלְוִיִּים בְּדוּכָנָם וְיִשְׂרָאֵל בְּמַעֲמָדָם קוֹרְאִים אֶת הַהַלֵּל. וְעַתָּה בַּעֲוֹנוֹתֵינוּ חָרַב בֵּית הַמִּקְדָּשׁ וּבָטֵל קׇרְבַּן הַפֶּסַח, וְאֵין לָנוּ לֹא כֹהֵן בַּעֲבוֹדָתוֹ וְלֹא לֵוִי בְדוּכָנוֹ וְלֹא יִשְׂרָאֵל בְּמַעֲמָדוֹ, וְלֹא נוּכַל לְהַקְרִיב הַיּוֹם קׇרְבַּן פֶּסַח. אֲבָל אַתָּה אָמַרְתָּ וּנְשַׁלְּמָה פָרִים שְׂפָתֵינוּ. לָכֵן יְהִי רָצוֹן מִלְּפָנֶיךָ יהוה אֱלֹהֵינוּ וֵאלֹהֵי אֲבוֹתֵינוּ שֶׁיִּהְיֶה שִׂיחַ שִׂפְתוֹתֵינוּ חָשׁוּב לְפָנֶיךָ כְּאִלּוּ הִקְרַבְנוּ אֶת הַפֶּסַח בְּמוֹעֲדוֹ וְעָמַדְנוּ עַל מַעֲמָדוֹ, וְדִבְּרוּ הַלְוִיִּים בְּשִׁיר וְהַלֵּל לְהוֹדוֹת לַיהוה. וְאַתָּה תְּכוֹנֵן מִקְדָּשְׁךָ עַל מְכוֹנוֹ, וְנַעֲשֶׂה וְנַקְרִיב לְפָנֶיךָ אֶת הַפֶּסַח בְּמוֹעֲדוֹ, כְּמוֹ שֶׁכָּתַבְתָּ עָלֵינוּ בְּתוֹרָתֶךָ עַל יְדֵי מֹשֶׁה עַבְדְּךָ כָּאָמוּר:

שמות יב:א-יא

וַיֹּאמֶר יהוה אֶל מֹשֶׁה וְאֶל אַהֲרֹן בְּאֶרֶץ מִצְרַיִם לֵאמֹר. הַחֹדֶשׁ הַזֶּה לָכֶם רֹאשׁ חֳדָשִׁים רִאשׁוֹן הוּא לָכֶם לְחׇדְשֵׁי הַשָּׁנָה. דַּבְּרוּ אֶל כׇּל עֲדַת יִשְׂרָאֵל לֵאמֹר בֶּעָשֹׂר לַחֹדֶשׁ הַזֶּה וְיִקְחוּ לָהֶם אִישׁ שֶׂה לְבֵית אָבֹת שֶׂה לַבָּיִת. וְאִם יִמְעַט הַבַּיִת מִהְיוֹת מִשֶּׂה וְלָקַח הוּא וּשְׁכֵנוֹ הַקָּרֹב אֶל בֵּיתוֹ בְּמִכְסַת נְפָשֹׁת אִישׁ לְפִי אׇכְלוֹ תָּכֹסּוּ עַל הַשֶּׂה. שֶׂה תָמִים זָכָר בֶּן שָׁנָה יִהְיֶה לָכֶם מִן הַכְּבָשִׂים וּמִן הָעִזִּים תִּקָּחוּ.

הגדה של פסח [78]

RECITAL OF THE KORBAN PESACH

After *Minchah,* many customarily recite the following passages that describe the קׇרְבַּן פֶּסַח, *pesach* offering:

Master of the universe, You commanded us to bring the pesach offering at its set time, on the fourteenth day of the first month; and that the Kohanim be at their assigned service, the Levites on their platform, and the Israelites at their station reciting the Hallel. But now, through our sins, the Holy Temple is destroyed, the pesach offering is discontinued, and we have neither Kohen at his service, nor Levite on his platform, nor Israelite at his station. So we are unable to bring the pesach offering today. But You said: "Let our lips compensate for the bulls" — therefore, may it be Your will, HASHEM, our God and the God of our forefathers, that the prayer of our lips be considered by You as if we had brought the pesach offering at its set time, had stood at its station, and the Levites had uttered song and Hallel, to thank HASHEM. And may You establish Your sanctuary on its prepared site, that we may ascend and bring the pesach offering before You at its set time — as You have prescribed for us in Your Torah, through Moshe, Your servant, as it is said: in Your Torah, through Moshe, Your servant, as it is said:

Shemos 12:1-11

And HASHEM said to Moshe and Aharon in the land of Egypt, saying: This month shall be for you the beginning of the months, it shall be for you the first of the months of the year. Speak to the entire assembly of Israel saying: On the tenth of this month, they shall take for themselves — each man — a lamb or kid for each fathers' house, a lamb or kid for the household. But if the household will be too small for a lamb or kid, then he and his neighbor who is near his house shall take according to the number of people; everyone according to what he eats shall be counted a lamb/kid. An unblemished lamb or kid, a male, within its first year shall it be for you; from the sheep or goats shall you take it.

וְהָיָה לָכֶם לְמִשְׁמֶרֶת עַד אַרְבָּעָה עָשָׂר יוֹם לַחֹדֶשׁ הַזֶּה וְשָׁחֲטוּ אֹתוֹ כֹּל קְהַל עֲדַת יִשְׂרָאֵל בֵּין הָעַרְבָּיִם. וְלָקְחוּ מִן הַדָּם וְנָתְנוּ עַל שְׁתֵּי הַמְּזוּזֹת וְעַל הַמַּשְׁקוֹף עַל הַבָּתִּים אֲשֶׁר יֹאכְלוּ אֹתוֹ בָּהֶם. וְאָכְלוּ אֶת הַבָּשָׂר בַּלַּיְלָה הַזֶּה צְלִי אֵשׁ וּמַצּוֹת עַל מְרֹרִים יֹאכְלֻהוּ: אַל תֹּאכְלוּ מִמֶּנּוּ נָא וּבָשֵׁל מְבֻשָּׁל בַּמָּיִם כִּי אִם צְלִי אֵשׁ רֹאשׁוֹ עַל כְּרָעָיו וְעַל קִרְבּוֹ. וְלֹא תוֹתִירוּ מִמֶּנּוּ עַד בֹּקֶר וְהַנֹּתָר מִמֶּנּוּ עַד בֹּקֶר בָּאֵשׁ תִּשְׂרֹפוּ. וְכָכָה תֹּאכְלוּ אֹתוֹ מָתְנֵיכֶם חֲגֻרִים נַעֲלֵיכֶם בְּרַגְלֵיכֶם וּמַקֶּלְכֶם בְּיֶדְכֶם וַאֲכַלְתֶּם אֹתוֹ בְּחִפָּזוֹן פֶּסַח הוּא לַיהוה.

Some recite the following ten Scriptural passages as part of the recital of the *korban pesach*. Others continue on p. 90.

שמות יב:כא-כח

וַיִּקְרָא מֹשֶׁה לְכָל זִקְנֵי יִשְׂרָאֵל וַיֹּאמֶר אֲלֵהֶם מִשְׁכוּ וּקְחוּ לָכֶם צֹאן לְמִשְׁפְּחֹתֵיכֶם וְשַׁחֲטוּ הַפָּסַח. וּלְקַחְתֶּם אֲגֻדַּת אֵזוֹב וּטְבַלְתֶּם בַּדָּם אֲשֶׁר בַּסַּף וְהִגַּעְתֶּם אֶל הַמַּשְׁקוֹף וְאֶל שְׁתֵּי הַמְּזוּזֹת מִן הַדָּם אֲשֶׁר בַּסַּף וְאַתֶּם לֹא תֵצְאוּ אִישׁ מִפֶּתַח בֵּיתוֹ עַד בֹּקֶר. וְעָבַר יהוה לִנְגֹּף אֶת מִצְרַיִם וְרָאָה אֶת הַדָּם עַל הַמַּשְׁקוֹף וְעַל שְׁתֵּי הַמְּזוּזֹת וּפָסַח יהוה עַל הַפֶּתַח וְלֹא יִתֵּן הַמַּשְׁחִית לָבֹא אֶל בָּתֵּיכֶם לִנְגֹּף. וּשְׁמַרְתֶּם אֶת הַדָּבָר הַזֶּה לְחָק לְךָ וּלְבָנֶיךָ עַד עוֹלָם. וְהָיָה כִּי תָבֹאוּ אֶל הָאָרֶץ אֲשֶׁר יִתֵּן יהוה לָכֶם כַּאֲשֶׁר דִּבֵּר וּשְׁמַרְתֶּם אֶת הָעֲבֹדָה הַזֹּאת. וְהָיָה כִּי יֹאמְרוּ אֲלֵיכֶם בְּנֵיכֶם מָה הָעֲבֹדָה הַזֹּאת לָכֶם. וַאֲמַרְתֶּם זֶבַח פֶּסַח הוּא לַיהוה אֲשֶׁר פָּסַח עַל בָּתֵּי בְנֵי יִשְׂרָאֵל בְּמִצְרַיִם בְּנָגְפּוֹ אֶת מִצְרַיִם וְאֶת בָּתֵּינוּ הִצִּיל וַיִּקֹּד הָעָם וַיִּשְׁתַּחֲווּ. וַיֵּלְכוּ וַיַּעֲשׂוּ בְּנֵי יִשְׂרָאֵל כַּאֲשֶׁר צִוָּה יהוה אֶת מֹשֶׁה וְאַהֲרֹן כֵּן עָשׂוּ.

שמות יב:מג-נ

וַיֹּאמֶר יהוה אֶל מֹשֶׁה וְאַהֲרֹן זֹאת חֻקַּת הַפָּסַח כָּל בֶּן נֵכָר לֹא יֹאכַל בּוֹ. וְכָל עֶבֶד אִישׁ מִקְנַת כָּסֶף וּמַלְתָּה

It shall be yours for examination until the fourteenth day of this month; the entire congregation of the assembly of Israel shall slaughter it in the afternoon. They shall take some of its blood and they shall place it on the two doorposts and on the lintel of the houses in which they will eat it. They shall eat the meat on that night — roasted over the fire — and matzos; with bitter herbs shall they eat it. You shall not eat it partially roasted or cooked in water; only roasted over fire — its head, its legs, with its innards. You shall not leave any of it until morning; any of it that is left until morning you shall burn in the fire. So shall you eat it: your loins girded, your shoes on your feet, and your staff in your hand; you shall eat it in haste — it is a pesach offering to HASHEM.

<small>Some recite the following ten Scriptural passages as part of the recital of the *korban pesach*. Others continue on p. 91.</small>

Shemos 12:21-28

Moshe called to all the elders of Israel and said to them, "Draw forth or buy yourselves sheep for your families, and slaughter the pesach offering. You shall take a bundle of hyssop and dip it into the blood that is in the basin, and touch the lintel and the two doorposts with some of the blood that is in the basin, and as for you, you shall not leave the entrance of your house until morning. HASHEM will pass through to smite Egypt, and He will see the blood that is on the lintel and the two doorposts; and HASHEM will pass over the entrance and He will not permit the destroyer to enter your homes to smite. You shall observe this matter as a decree for yourself and for your children forever.

"It shall be that when you come to the land that HASHEM will give you, as He has spoken, you shall observe this service. And it shall be that when your children say to you, 'What is this service to you?' You shall say, 'It is a pesach feast-offering to HASHEM, Who passed over the houses of the Children of Israel in Egypt when He smote the Egyptians, but He saved our households,' " and the people bowed their heads and prostrated themselves. The Children of Israel went and did as HASHEM commanded Moshe and Aharon, so did they do.

Shemos 12:43-50

HASHEM said to Moshe and Aharon, "This is the decree of the pesach offering: no alienated person may eat from it. Every slave of a man, who was bought for money, you shall circumcise

אֹתוֹ אָז יֹאכַל בּוֹ. תּוֹשָׁב וְשָׂכִיר לֹא יֹאכַל בּוֹ. בְּבַיִת אֶחָד יֵאָכֵל לֹא תוֹצִיא מִן הַבַּיִת מִן הַבָּשָׂר חוּצָה וְעֶצֶם לֹא תִשְׁבְּרוּ בוֹ. כָּל עֲדַת יִשְׂרָאֵל יַעֲשׂוּ אֹתוֹ.

וְכִי יָגוּר אִתְּךָ גֵּר וְעָשָׂה פֶסַח לַיהוה הִמּוֹל לוֹ כָל זָכָר וְאָז יִקְרַב לַעֲשֹׂתוֹ וְהָיָה כְּאֶזְרַח הָאָרֶץ וְכָל עָרֵל לֹא יֹאכַל בּוֹ. תּוֹרָה אַחַת יִהְיֶה לָאֶזְרָח וְלַגֵּר הַגָּר בְּתוֹכְכֶם. וַיַּעֲשׂוּ כָּל בְּנֵי יִשְׂרָאֵל כַּאֲשֶׁר צִוָּה יהוה אֶת מֹשֶׁה וְאֶת אַהֲרֹן כֵּן עָשׂוּ.

ויקרא כג:ד-ה

אֵלֶּה מוֹעֲדֵי יהוה מִקְרָאֵי קֹדֶשׁ אֲשֶׁר תִּקְרְאוּ אֹתָם בְּמוֹעֲדָם. בַּחֹדֶשׁ הָרִאשׁוֹן בְּאַרְבָּעָה עָשָׂר לַחֹדֶשׁ בֵּין הָעַרְבַּיִם פֶּסַח לַיהוה.

במדבר ט:א-יד

וַיְדַבֵּר יהוה אֶל מֹשֶׁה בְמִדְבַּר סִינַי בַּשָּׁנָה הַשֵּׁנִית לְצֵאתָם מֵאֶרֶץ מִצְרַיִם בַּחֹדֶשׁ הָרִאשׁוֹן לֵאמֹר. וְיַעֲשׂוּ בְנֵי יִשְׂרָאֵל אֶת הַפָּסַח בְּמוֹעֲדוֹ. בְּאַרְבָּעָה עָשָׂר יוֹם בַּחֹדֶשׁ הַזֶּה בֵּין הָעַרְבַּיִם תַּעֲשׂוּ אֹתוֹ בְּמוֹעֲדוֹ כְּכָל חֻקֹּתָיו וּכְכָל מִשְׁפָּטָיו תַּעֲשׂוּ אֹתוֹ. וַיְדַבֵּר מֹשֶׁה אֶל בְּנֵי יִשְׂרָאֵל לַעֲשֹׂת הַפָּסַח. וַיַּעֲשׂוּ אֶת הַפֶּסַח בָּרִאשׁוֹן בְּאַרְבָּעָה עָשָׂר יוֹם לַחֹדֶשׁ בֵּין הָעַרְבַּיִם בְּמִדְבַּר סִינַי כְּכֹל אֲשֶׁר צִוָּה יהוה אֶת מֹשֶׁה כֵּן עָשׂוּ בְּנֵי יִשְׂרָאֵל. וַיְהִי אֲנָשִׁים אֲשֶׁר הָיוּ טְמֵאִים לְנֶפֶשׁ אָדָם וְלֹא יָכְלוּ לַעֲשֹׂת הַפֶּסַח בַּיּוֹם הַהוּא וַיִּקְרְבוּ לִפְנֵי מֹשֶׁה וְלִפְנֵי אַהֲרֹן בַּיּוֹם הַהוּא. וַיֹּאמְרוּ הָאֲנָשִׁים הָהֵמָּה אֵלָיו אֲנַחְנוּ טְמֵאִים לְנֶפֶשׁ אָדָם לָמָּה נִגָּרַע לְבִלְתִּי הַקְרִיב אֶת קָרְבַּן יהוה בְּמוֹעֲדוֹ בְּתוֹךְ בְּנֵי יִשְׂרָאֵל.

וַיֹּאמֶר אֲלֵהֶם מֹשֶׁה עִמְדוּ וְאֶשְׁמְעָה מַה יְּצַוֶּה יהוה לָכֶם. וַיְדַבֵּר יהוה אֶל מֹשֶׁה לֵּאמֹר. דַּבֵּר אֶל בְּנֵי יִשְׂרָאֵל לֵאמֹר אִישׁ אִישׁ כִּי יִהְיֶה טָמֵא לָנֶפֶשׁ אוֹ בְדֶרֶךְ רְחֹקָה לָכֶם אוֹ לְדֹרֹתֵיכֶם וְעָשָׂה פֶסַח לַיהוה. בַּחֹדֶשׁ הַשֵּׁנִי בְּאַרְבָּעָה עָשָׂר יוֹם בֵּין הָעַרְבַּיִם יַעֲשׂוּ אֹתוֹ עַל מַצּוֹת וּמְרֹרִים יֹאכְלֻהוּ. לֹא יַשְׁאִירוּ מִמֶּנּוּ עַד בֹּקֶר וְעֶצֶם לֹא יִשְׁבְּרוּ בוֹ כְּכָל חֻקַּת הַפֶּסַח יַעֲשׂוּ אֹתוֹ: וְהָאִישׁ אֲשֶׁר

him; then he may eat from it. A sojourner and a hired laborer may not eat from it. In one house shall it be eaten; you shall not remove any of the meat from the house to the outside, and you shall not break a bone in it. The entire assembly of Israel shall perform it.

"When a proselyte sojourns among you he shall make the pesach offering for HASHEM; each of his males shall be circumcised, and then he may draw near to perform it and he shall be like the native of the land; no uncircumcised male may eat from it. One law shall there be for the native and the proselyte who lives among you." All the Children of Israel did as HASHEM had commanded Moshe and Aharon, so did they do.

Vayikra 23:4-5

These are the appointed festivals of HASHEM, the holy convocations, which you shall designate in their appropriate time. In the first month on the fourteenth of the month in the afternoon is the time of the pesach offering to HASHEM.

Bamidbar 9:1-14

HASHEM spoke to Moses, in the Wilderness of Sinai, in the second year from their exodus from the land of Egypt, in the first month, saying: "The Children of Israel shall make the pesach offering in its appointed time. On the fourteenth day of this month in the afternoon shall you make it, in its appointed time; according to all its decrees and laws shall you make it."

Moshe spoke to the Children of Israel to make the pesach offering. They made the pesach offering in the first [month], on the fourteenth day of the month, in the afternoon, in the Wilderness of Sinai; according to everything that HASHEM had commanded Moses, so the Children of Israel did.

There were men who had been contaminated by a human corpse and could not make the pesach offering on that day; so they approached Moshe and Aharon on that day. And those men said to him, "We are unclean through contact with a dead person; why should we be deprived of offering Hashem's sacrifice in its time among the Children of Israel?"

Moshe said to them, "Stand and I will hear what HASHEM will command you."

HASHEM spoke to Moshe, saying, "Speak to the Children of Israel, saying: If any man will become contaminated through a human corpse or on a distant road, whether you or your generations, he shall make the pesach offering for HASHEM, in the second month, on the fourteenth day, in the afternoon, shall they make it; with matzos and bitter herbs shall they eat it. They shall not leave over from it until morning nor shall they break a bone of it; like all the decrees of the pesach offering shall they make it. But a man who

הוּא טָהוֹר וּבְדֶרֶךְ לֹא הָיָה וְחָדַל לַעֲשׂוֹת הַפֶּסַח וְנִכְרְתָה הַנֶּפֶשׁ הַהִוא מֵעַמֶּיהָ כִּי קָרְבַּן יְהוָֹה לֹא הִקְרִיב בְּמֹעֲדוֹ חֶטְאוֹ יִשָּׂא הָאִישׁ הַהוּא. וְכִי יָגוּר אִתְּכֶם גֵּר וְעָשָׂה פֶסַח לַיהוָֹה כְּחֻקַּת הַפֶּסַח וּכְמִשְׁפָּטוֹ כֵּן יַעֲשֶׂה חֻקָּה אַחַת יִהְיֶה לָכֶם וְלַגֵּר וּלְאֶזְרַח הָאָרֶץ.

במדבר כח:טז

וּבַחֹדֶשׁ הָרִאשׁוֹן בְּאַרְבָּעָה עָשָׂר יוֹם לַחֹדֶשׁ פֶּסַח לַיהוָֹה.

דברים טז:א-ח

שָׁמוֹר אֶת חֹדֶשׁ הָאָבִיב וְעָשִׂיתָ פֶּסַח לַיהוָֹה אֱלֹהֶיךָ כִּי בְּחֹדֶשׁ הָאָבִיב הוֹצִיאֲךָ יְהוָֹה אֱלֹהֶיךָ מִמִּצְרַיִם לָיְלָה. וְזָבַחְתָּ פֶּסַח לַיהוָֹה אֱלֹהֶיךָ צֹאן וּבָקָר בַּמָּקוֹם אֲשֶׁר יִבְחַר יְהוָֹה לְשַׁכֵּן שְׁמוֹ שָׁם. לֹא תֹאכַל עָלָיו חָמֵץ שִׁבְעַת יָמִים תֹּאכַל עָלָיו מַצּוֹת לֶחֶם עֹנִי כִּי בְחִפָּזוֹן יָצָאתָ מֵאֶרֶץ מִצְרַיִם לְמַעַן תִּזְכֹּר אֶת יוֹם צֵאתְךָ מֵאֶרֶץ מִצְרַיִם כֹּל יְמֵי חַיֶּיךָ. וְלֹא יֵרָאֶה לְךָ שְׂאֹר בְּכָל גְּבֻלְךָ שִׁבְעַת יָמִים וְלֹא יָלִין מִן הַבָּשָׂר אֲשֶׁר תִּזְבַּח בָּעֶרֶב בַּיּוֹם הָרִאשׁוֹן לַבֹּקֶר. לֹא תוּכַל לִזְבֹּחַ אֶת הַפָּסַח בְּאַחַד שְׁעָרֶיךָ אֲשֶׁר יְהוָֹה אֱלֹהֶיךָ נֹתֵן לָךְ. כִּי אִם אֶל הַמָּקוֹם אֲשֶׁר יִבְחַר יְהוָֹה אֱלֹהֶיךָ לְשַׁכֵּן שְׁמוֹ שָׁם תִּזְבַּח אֶת הַפֶּסַח בָּעָרֶב כְּבוֹא הַשֶּׁמֶשׁ מוֹעֵד צֵאתְךָ מִמִּצְרָיִם. וּבִשַּׁלְתָּ וְאָכַלְתָּ בַּמָּקוֹם אֲשֶׁר יִבְחַר יְהוָֹה אֱלֹהֶיךָ בּוֹ וּפָנִיתָ בַבֹּקֶר וְהָלַכְתָּ לְאֹהָלֶיךָ. שֵׁשֶׁת יָמִים תֹּאכַל מַצּוֹת וּבַיּוֹם הַשְּׁבִיעִי עֲצֶרֶת לַיהוָֹה אֱלֹהֶיךָ לֹא תַעֲשֶׂה מְלָאכָה.

יהושע ה:י-יא

וַיַּחֲנוּ בְנֵי יִשְׂרָאֵל בַּגִּלְגָּל וַיַּעֲשׂוּ אֶת הַפֶּסַח בְּאַרְבָּעָה עָשָׂר יוֹם לַחֹדֶשׁ בָּעֶרֶב בְּעַרְבוֹת יְרִיחוֹ. וַיֹּאכְלוּ מֵעֲבוּר הָאָרֶץ מִמָּחֳרַת הַפֶּסַח מַצּוֹת וְקָלוּי בְּעֶצֶם הַיּוֹם הַזֶּה.

מלכים ב כג:כא-כב

וַיְצַו הַמֶּלֶךְ אֶת כָּל הָעָם לֵאמֹר עֲשׂוּ פֶסַח לַיהוָֹה אֱלֹהֵיכֶם כַּכָּתוּב עַל סֵפֶר הַבְּרִית הַזֶּה. כִּי לֹא נַעֲשָׂה כַּפֶּסַח

is pure and was not on the road and had refrained from making the pesach offering, that soul shall be cut off from its people, for he had not offered HASHEM's offering in its appointed time; that man will bear his sin. When a convert shall dwell with you, and he shall make a pesach offering to HASHEM, according to the decree of the pesach offering and its law, so shall he do; one decree shall be for you, for the proselyte and the native of the Land."

Bamidbar 28:16

In the first month, on the fourteenth day of the month, shall be a pesach offering to HASHEM.

Devarim 16:1-8

You shall observe the month of springtime and perform the pesach offering for HASHEM, your God, for in the month of springtime HASHEM, your God, took you out of Egypt at night. You shall slaughter the pesach offering to HASHEM, your God, from the flock, [and also offer] cattle, in the place where HASHEM will choose to rest His Name. You shall not eat leavened bread with it, for seven days you shall eat matzos because of it, bread of affliction, for you departed from the land of Egypt in haste — so that you will remember the day of your departure from the land of Egypt all the days of your life.

No leaven of yours shall be seen throughout your boundary for seven days, nor shall any of the flesh that you offer on the afternoon before the first day remain overnight until morning. You may not slaughter the pesach offering in one of your cities that HASHEM, your God, gives you; except at the place that HASHEM, your God, will choose to rest His Name, there shall you slaughter the pesach offering in the afternoon, when the sun descends, the appointed time of your departure from Egypt. You shall roast it and eat it in the place that HASHEM, your God, will choose, and in the morning you may turn back and go to your tents. For a six-day period you shall eat matzos and on the seventh day shall be an assembly to HASHEM, your God; you shall not perform any labor.

Yehoshua 5:10-11

The Children of Israel encamped at Gilgal and performed the pesach offering on the fourteenth day of the month in the evening, in the plains of Yericho. They ate from the grain of the land on the day after the pesach offering, matzos and roasted grain, on this very day.

II Melachim 23:21-22

The king then commanded the people, saying, "Perform the pesach offering unto HASHEM your God, as written in this Book of the Covenant." For such a pesach offering had not been

הַזֶּה מִימֵי הַשֹּׁפְטִים אֲשֶׁר שָׁפְטוּ אֶת יִשְׂרָאֵל וְכָל יְמֵי מַלְכֵי יִשְׂרָאֵל וּמַלְכֵי יְהוּדָה: כִּי אִם בִּשְׁמֹנֶה עֶשְׂרֵה שָׁנָה לַמֶּלֶךְ יֹאשִׁיָּהוּ נַעֲשָׂה הַפֶּסַח הַזֶּה לַיהוה בִּירוּשָׁלָם:

דברי הימים ב ל:א-כ

וַיִּשְׁלַח יְחִזְקִיָּהוּ עַל כָּל יִשְׂרָאֵל וִיהוּדָה וְגַם אִגְּרוֹת כָּתַב עַל אֶפְרַיִם וּמְנַשֶּׁה לָבוֹא לְבֵית יהוה בִּירוּשָׁלָם לַעֲשׂוֹת פֶּסַח לַיהוה אֱלֹהֵי יִשְׂרָאֵל. וַיִּוָּעַץ הַמֶּלֶךְ וְשָׂרָיו וְכָל הַקָּהָל בִּירוּשָׁלָם לַעֲשׂוֹת הַפֶּסַח בַּחֹדֶשׁ הַשֵּׁנִי. כִּי לֹא יָכְלוּ לַעֲשׂתוֹ בָּעֵת הַהִיא כִּי הַכֹּהֲנִים לֹא הִתְקַדְּשׁוּ לְמַדַּי וְהָעָם לֹא נֶאֶסְפוּ לִירוּשָׁלָם. וַיִּישַׁר הַדָּבָר בְּעֵינֵי הַמֶּלֶךְ וּבְעֵינֵי כָּל הַקָּהָל: וַיַּעֲמִידוּ דָבָר לְהַעֲבִיר קוֹל בְּכָל יִשְׂרָאֵל מִבְּאֵר שֶׁבַע וְעַד דָּן לָבוֹא לַעֲשׂוֹת פֶּסַח לַיהוה אֱלֹהֵי יִשְׂרָאֵל בִּירוּשָׁלָם כִּי לֹא לָרֹב עָשׂוּ כַּכָּתוּב: וַיֵּלְכוּ הָרָצִים בָּאִגְּרוֹת מִיַּד הַמֶּלֶךְ וְשָׂרָיו בְּכָל יִשְׂרָאֵל וִיהוּדָה וּכְמִצְוַת הַמֶּלֶךְ לֵאמֹר בְּנֵי יִשְׂרָאֵל שׁוּבוּ אֶל יהוה אֱלֹהֵי אַבְרָהָם יִצְחָק וְיִשְׂרָאֵל וְיָשֹׁב אֶל הַפְּלֵיטָה הַנִּשְׁאֶרֶת לָכֶם מִכַּף מַלְכֵי אַשּׁוּר. וְאַל תִּהְיוּ כַּאֲבוֹתֵיכֶם וְכַאֲחֵיכֶם אֲשֶׁר מָעֲלוּ בַּיהוה אֱלֹהֵי אֲבוֹתֵיהֶם וַיִּתְּנֵם לְשַׁמָּה כַּאֲשֶׁר אַתֶּם רֹאִים: עַתָּה אַל תַּקְשׁוּ עָרְפְּכֶם כַּאֲבוֹתֵיכֶם תְּנוּ יָד לַיהוה וּבֹאוּ לְמִקְדָּשׁוֹ אֲשֶׁר הִקְדִּישׁ לְעוֹלָם וְעִבְדוּ אֶת יהוה אֱלֹהֵיכֶם וְיָשֹׁב מִכֶּם חֲרוֹן אַפּוֹ: כִּי בְשׁוּבְכֶם עַל יהוה אֲחֵיכֶם וּבְנֵיכֶם לְרַחֲמִים לִפְנֵי שׁוֹבֵיהֶם וְלָשׁוּב לָאָרֶץ הַזֹּאת כִּי חַנּוּן וְרַחוּם יהוה אֱלֹהֵיכֶם וְלֹא יָסִיר פָּנִים מִכֶּם אִם תָּשׁוּבוּ אֵלָיו: וַיִּהְיוּ הָרָצִים עֹבְרִים מֵעִיר לָעִיר בְּאֶרֶץ אֶפְרַיִם וּמְנַשֶּׁה וְעַד זְבֻלוּן וַיִּהְיוּ מַשְׂחִיקִים עֲלֵיהֶם וּמַלְעִגִים בָּם. אַךְ אֲנָשִׁים מֵאָשֵׁר וּמְנַשֶּׁה וּמִזְּבֻלוּן נִכְנְעוּ וַיָּבֹאוּ לִירוּשָׁלָם. גַּם בִּיהוּדָה הָיְתָה יַד הָאֱלֹהִים לָתֵת לָהֶם לֵב אֶחָד לַעֲשׂוֹת מִצְוַת הַמֶּלֶךְ וְהַשָּׂרִים בִּדְבַר יהוה. וַיֵּאָסְפוּ יְרוּשָׁלַםִ עַם רָב לַעֲשׂוֹת אֶת חַג הַמַּצּוֹת בַּחֹדֶשׁ הַשֵּׁנִי קָהָל לָרֹב מְאֹד. וַיָּקֻמוּ וַיָּסִירוּ אֶת הַמִּזְבְּחוֹת אֲשֶׁר בִּירוּשָׁלָם וְאֵת כָּל הַמְקַטְּרוֹת הֵסִירוּ וַיַּשְׁלִיכוּ לְנַחַל קִדְרוֹן. וַיִּשְׁחֲטוּ הַפֶּסַח

celebrated since the days of the Judges who judged Israel, and all the days of the kings of Israel and the kings of Yehudah; but in the eighteenth year of King Yoshiyahu this Pesach was celebrated unto HASHEM in Yerushalayim.

II Divrei Hayamim 30:1-20

Chizkiyahu then sent word to all of Israel and Yehudah, and also wrote letters to Ephraim and Menasheh to come to the Temple of HASHEM in Yerushalayim to perform the pesach offering to HASHEM, God of Israel. For the king and his officers and all the congregation had conferred and decided to perform the pesach offering in the second month, for they had not been able to perform it at its [proper] time, for the Kohanim had not yet sanctified themselves in sufficient numbers, and the people had not been gathered to Yerushalayim by then. The matter was deemed proper by the king and all of the congregation. They established the matter to make an announcement throughout all of Israel, from Beer-sheva to Dan, to come and perform the pesach offering unto HASHEM, God of Israel, in Yerushalayim, because for a long time they had not done in accordance with what was written.

The runners went throughout all of Israel and Yehudah with the letters from the hand of the king and his leaders, and by order of the king, saying, "Return to HASHEM, the God of Avraham, Yitzchak and Yisrael, and He will return to the remnant of you that still remains from the hands of the kings of Ashur. Do not be like your fathers and brothers who betrayed HASHEM, the God of their forefathers, so that He made them into a desolation, as you see. Do not stiffen your necks now as your fathers did! Reach out to HASHEM and come to His Sanctuary, which He has sanctified forever, and worship HASHEM, your God, so that His burning wrath may turn away from you! For when you return to HASHEM, your brothers and sons will be regarded with mercy by their captors, and [will be allowed] to return to this land, for HASHEM your God is gracious and merciful, and He will not turn His face away from you if you return to Him!"

The runners passed from city to city in the land of Ephraim and Menasheh up to Zevulun but people laughed at them and mocked them. However, some people from Asher, Menasheh and Zevulun humbled themselves and came to Yerushalayim. Also in Yehudah the hand of God was upon them, instilling them all with a united heart to follow the commandment of the king and the leaders regarding the word of HASHEM.

So a great crowd assembled in Jerusalem to observe the Festival of Matzos in the second month — a very large congregation. They got up and removed the altars that were in Yerushalayim, they also removed all the incense altars and threw them into the Kidron Ravine. They slaughtered the pesach offering on the

בְּאַרְבָּעָה עָשָׂר לַחֹדֶשׁ הַשֵּׁנִי וְהַכֹּהֲנִים וְהַלְוִיִּם נִכְלְמוּ וַיִּתְקַדְּשׁוּ וַיָּבִיאוּ עֹלוֹת בֵּית יהוה: וַיַּעַמְדוּ עַל עָמְדָם כְּמִשְׁפָּטָם כְּתוֹרַת מֹשֶׁה אִישׁ הָאֱלֹהִים הַכֹּהֲנִים זֹרְקִים אֶת הַדָּם מִיַּד הַלְוִיִּם. כִּי רַבַּת בַּקָּהָל אֲשֶׁר לֹא הִתְקַדָּשׁוּ וְהַלְוִיִּם עַל שְׁחִיטַת הַפְּסָחִים לְכֹל לֹא טָהוֹר לְהַקְדִּישׁ לַיהוה. כִּי מַרְבִּית הָעָם רַבַּת מֵאֶפְרַיִם וּמְנַשֶּׁה יִשָּׂשכָר וּזְבֻלוּן לֹא הִטֶּהָרוּ כִּי אָכְלוּ אֶת הַפֶּסַח בְּלֹא כַכָּתוּב כִּי הִתְפַּלֵּל יְחִזְקִיָּהוּ עֲלֵיהֶם לֵאמֹר יהוה הַטּוֹב יְכַפֵּר בְּעַד. כָּל לְבָבוֹ הֵכִין לִדְרוֹשׁ הָאֱלֹהִים יהוה אֱלֹהֵי אֲבוֹתָיו וְלֹא כְּטָהֳרַת הַקֹּדֶשׁ. וַיִּשְׁמַע יהוה אֶל יְחִזְקִיָּהוּ וַיִּרְפָּא אֶת הָעָם.

דברי הימים ב לה:א-יט

וַיַּעַשׂ יֹאשִׁיָּהוּ בִירוּשָׁלִַם פֶּסַח לַיהוה וַיִּשְׁחֲטוּ הַפֶּסַח בְּאַרְבָּעָה עָשָׂר לַחֹדֶשׁ הָרִאשׁוֹן: וַיַּעֲמֵד הַכֹּהֲנִים עַל מִשְׁמְרוֹתָם וַיְחַזְּקֵם לַעֲבוֹדַת בֵּית יהוה: וַיֹּאמֶר לַלְוִיִּם הַמְּבִינִים לְכָל יִשְׂרָאֵל הַקְּדוֹשִׁים לַיהוה תְּנוּ אֶת אֲרוֹן הַקֹּדֶשׁ בַּבַּיִת אֲשֶׁר בָּנָה שְׁלֹמֹה בֶן דָּוִיד מֶלֶךְ יִשְׂרָאֵל אֵין לָכֶם מַשָּׂא בַּכָּתֵף עַתָּה עִבְדוּ אֶת יהוה אֱלֹהֵיכֶם וְאֵת עַמּוֹ יִשְׂרָאֵל. וְהָכִינוּ לְבֵית אֲבוֹתֵיכֶם בְּמַחְלְקוֹתֵיכֶם בִּכְתָב דָּוִיד מֶלֶךְ יִשְׂרָאֵל וּבְמִכְתַּב שְׁלֹמֹה בְנוֹ. וְעִמְדוּ בַקֹּדֶשׁ לִפְלֻגּוֹת בֵּית הָאָבוֹת לַאֲחֵיכֶם בְּנֵי הָעָם וַחֲלֻקַּת בֵּית אָב לַלְוִיִּם. וְשַׁחֲטוּ הַפָּסַח וְהִתְקַדְּשׁוּ וְהָכִינוּ לַאֲחֵיכֶם לַעֲשׂוֹת כִּדְבַר יהוה בְּיַד מֹשֶׁה. וַיָּרֶם יֹאשִׁיָּהוּ לִבְנֵי הָעָם צֹאן כְּבָשִׂים וּבְנֵי עִזִּים הַכֹּל לַפְּסָחִים לְכָל הַנִּמְצָא לְמִסְפַּר שְׁלֹשִׁים אֶלֶף וּבָקָר שְׁלֹשֶׁת אֲלָפִים אֵלֶּה מֵרְכוּשׁ הַמֶּלֶךְ. וְשָׂרָיו לִנְדָבָה לָעָם לַכֹּהֲנִים וְלַלְוִיִּם הֵרִימוּ חִלְקִיָּה וּזְכַרְיָהוּ וִיחִיאֵל נְגִידֵי בֵּית הָאֱלֹהִים לַכֹּהֲנִים נָתְנוּ לַפְּסָחִים אַלְפַּיִם וְשֵׁשׁ מֵאוֹת וּבָקָר שְׁלֹשׁ מֵאוֹת. וְכָנַנְיָהוּ וּשְׁמַעְיָהוּ וּנְתַנְאֵל אֶחָיו וַחֲשַׁבְיָהוּ וִיעִיאֵל וְיוֹזָבָד שָׂרֵי הַלְוִיִּם הֵרִימוּ לַלְוִיִּם לַפְּסָחִים חֲמֵשֶׁת אֲלָפִים וּבָקָר חֲמֵשׁ מֵאוֹת.

fourteenth of the second month, and the Kohanim and Levites felt humiliated and sanctified themselves and brought burnt-offerings to the Temple of HASHEM. They stood at their ordained positions, in accordance with the Torah of Moshe, the man of God — the Kohanim threw the blood [on the Altar], [taking it] from the hands of the Levites. For there were many in the congregation who had not sanctified themselves, and the Levites took charge of slaughtering the pesach offering for anyone who was not pure, to sanctify it to HASHEM. For many of the people — many from Ephraim, Menasheh, Yissachar and Zevulun — had not purified themselves, and they ate the pesach offering not in accordance with that which is written; but Chizkiyahu prayed for them, saying, "May the benevolent HASHEM grant atonement for whoever sets his heart to seek out God, HASHEM, the God of his forefathers, though without the purity required for the sacred." HASHEM listened to Chizkiyahu and absolved the people.

II Divrei Hayamim 35:1-19

Yoshiyahu made the pesach offering to HASHEM. They slaughtered the pesach offering on the fourteenth day of the first month.

He set up the Kohanim according to their divisions, and he encouraged them in the service of the Temple of HASHEM. He then said to the Levites, who taught all of Israel, who were consecrated to HASHEM, "Place the Holy Ark in the Temple that Shlomo son of David, the king of Israel, built. Then you will no longer have any carrying on your shoulder; so now serve HASHEM your God and His people Israel. Organize yourselves by your fathers' families, according to your divisions, in accordance with the written instructions of David king of Israel and the written instructions of his son Shlomo. Stand in the Sanctuary according to the groupings of your fathers' families near your kinsmen, the populace, and the Levites' fathers' family division. Slaughter the pesach offering; sanctify yourselves and prepare your kinsmen to act in accordance with the word of HASHEM, through Moshe."

Yoshiyahu donated animals of the flock — sheep and goats — to the populace, all of them for pesach offerings for those who were present, in the amount of thirty thousand, in addition to three thousand [head of] cattle; all this was from the personal property of the king. His officers also contributed voluntarily to the populace, to the Kohanim and to the Levites. Chilkiyah, Zecharyahu and Yechiel, the managers of the Temple of God, gave two thousand six hundred [sheep] to the Kohanim for pesach offerings, and three hundred [head of] cattle. Cananyahu, together with his brethren Shemaiah and Nesanel, and Chashavyahu, Yeiel and Yozabad, officers of the Levites, donated five thousand [sheep] for pesach [offerings] for the Levites, and five hundred [head of] cattle.

וַתִּכּוֹן הָעֲבוֹדָה וַיַּעַמְדוּ הַכֹּהֲנִים וְהַלְוִיִּם עַל עָמְדָם עַל מַחְלְקוֹתָם כְּמִצְוַת הַמֶּלֶךְ. וַיִּשְׁחֲטוּ הַפֶּסַח וַיִּזְרְקוּ הַכֹּהֲנִים מִיָּדָם וְהַלְוִיִּם מַפְשִׁיטִים. וַיָּסִירוּ הָעֹלָה לְתִתָּם לְמִפְלַגּוֹת לְבֵית אָבוֹת לִבְנֵי הָעָם לְהַקְרִיב לַיהוה כַּכָּתוּב בְּסֵפֶר מֹשֶׁה וְכֵן לַבָּקָר. וַיְבַשְּׁלוּ הַפֶּסַח בָּאֵשׁ כַּמִּשְׁפָּט וְהַקֳּדָשִׁים בִּשְּׁלוּ בַּסִּירוֹת וּבַדְּוָדִים וּבַצֵּלָחוֹת וַיָּרִיצוּ לְכָל בְּנֵי הָעָם. וְאַחַר הֵכִינוּ לָהֶם וְלַכֹּהֲנִים כִּי הַכֹּהֲנִים בְּנֵי אַהֲרֹן בְּהַעֲלוֹת הָעוֹלָה וְהַחֲלָבִים עַד לָיְלָה וְהַלְוִיִּם הֵכִינוּ לָהֶם וְלַכֹּהֲנִים בְּנֵי אַהֲרֹן. וְהַמְשֹׁרְרִים בְּנֵי אָסָף עַל מַעֲמָדָם כְּמִצְוַת דָּוִיד וְאָסָף וְהֵימָן וִידֻתוּן חוֹזֵה הַמֶּלֶךְ וְהַשֹּׁעֲרִים לְשַׁעַר וָשָׁעַר אֵין לָהֶם לָסוּר מֵעַל עֲבֹדָתָם כִּי אֲחֵיהֶם הַלְוִיִּם הֵכִינוּ לָהֶם. וַתִּכּוֹן כָּל עֲבוֹדַת יהוה בַּיּוֹם הַהוּא לַעֲשׂוֹת הַפֶּסַח וְהַעֲלוֹת עֹלוֹת עַל מִזְבַּח יהוה כְּמִצְוַת הַמֶּלֶךְ יֹאשִׁיָּהוּ. וַיַּעֲשׂוּ בְנֵי יִשְׂרָאֵל הַנִּמְצְאִים אֶת הַפֶּסַח בָּעֵת הַהִיא וְאֶת חַג הַמַּצּוֹת שִׁבְעַת יָמִים. וְלֹא נַעֲשָׂה פֶסַח כָּמֹהוּ בְּיִשְׂרָאֵל מִימֵי שְׁמוּאֵל הַנָּבִיא וְכָל מַלְכֵי יִשְׂרָאֵל לֹא עָשׂוּ כַּפֶּסַח אֲשֶׁר עָשָׂה יֹאשִׁיָּהוּ וְהַכֹּהֲנִים וְהַלְוִיִּם וְכָל יְהוּדָה וְיִשְׂרָאֵל הַנִּמְצָא וְיוֹשְׁבֵי יְרוּשָׁלָיִם. בִּשְׁמוֹנֶה עֶשְׂרֵה שָׁנָה לְמַלְכוּת יֹאשִׁיָּהוּ נַעֲשָׂה הַפֶּסַח הַזֶּה.

כָּךְ הָיְתָה עֲבוֹדַת קָרְבַּן הַפֶּסַח בְּבֵית אֱלֹהֵינוּ בְּיוֹם אַרְבָּעָה עָשָׂר בְּנִיסָן:

אֵין שׁוֹחֲטִין אוֹתוֹ אֶלָּא אַחַר תָּמִיד שֶׁל בֵּין הָעַרְבַּיִם. עֶרֶב פֶּסַח, בֵּין בְּחֹל בֵּין בְּשַׁבָּת, הָיָה הַתָּמִיד נִשְׁחָט בְּשֶׁבַע וּמֶחֱצָה וְקָרֵב בִּשְׁמוֹנָה וּמֶחֱצָה. וְאִם חָל עֶרֶב פֶּסַח לִהְיוֹת עֶרֶב שַׁבָּת הָיוּ שׁוֹחֲטִין אוֹתוֹ בְּשֵׁשׁ וּמֶחֱצָה וְקָרֵב בְּשֶׁבַע וּמֶחֱצָה. וְהַפֶּסַח אַחֲרָיו.

כָּל אָדָם מִיִּשְׂרָאֵל, אֶחָד הָאִישׁ וְאֶחָד הָאִשָּׁה, כָּל שֶׁיָּכוֹל לְהַגִּיעַ לִירוּשָׁלַיִם בִּשְׁעַת שְׁחִיטַת הַפֶּסַח הָיָב בְּקָרְבַּן פֶּסַח.

Thus the service was in order. The Kohanim were stationed at their positions and the Levites in their divisions, in accordance with the king's orders. They slaughtered the pesach offering, and the Kohanim threw [the blood, which they had taken] from their hands, while the Levites were flaying. They removed the parts that were to be offered up — in order to give [flesh of the pesach offering] to the family groups of the populace — to offer them up before HASHEM, as is written in the Book of Moshe; and similarly for the cattle. They cooked the pesach offering over the fire according to the law, and they cooked the [other] sacrificial meat in pots and cauldrons and pans, and distributed it quickly to all the populace. Afterwards they prepared [the pesach offering] for themselves and for the Kohanim, because the Kohanim — the descendants of Aharon — were busy burning burnt-offerings and fats until nighttime, so now the Levites prepared for themselves and for the Kohanim, the descendants of Aharon.

The singers, the descendants of Asaf, stood at their positions — according to the decree of David, Asaf, Heiman and Yedusun the king's seer — with the gate-keepers at every gate; they did not have to leave their own tasks, for their brother Levites had prepared for them. The entire service of HASHEM was thus well organized on that day, to perform the pesach offering and to bring up burnt-offerings upon the Altar of HASHEM, in accordance with the command of King Yoshiyahu. So the Children of Israel who were present performed the pesach offering at that time, and then the Festival of Unleavened Bread for seven days. Such a pesach offering had not been celebrated since the days of Shmuel Hanavi. None of the kings of Israel performed like the pesach offering that Yoshiyahu did with the Kohanim, the Levites, all of Yehudah and Israel who were present, and the inhabitants of Yerushalayim. It was in the eighteenth year of Yoshiyahu's reign that this pesach offering was performed.

This was the service of the pesach offering on the fourteenth of Nisan:

We may not slaughter it until after the afternoon tamid offering. On the eve of Pesach, whether on a weekday or on Shabbos, the tamid offering would be slaughtered at seven and a half hours [after daybreak], and offered at eight and a half hours. But when erev Pesach fell on Friday, they would slaughter it at six and a half hours, and offer it at seven and a half. [In either case] the pesach offering [was slaughtered] after it.

Every Jew, male or female, whoever is able to reach Yerushalayim in time to slaughter the pesach, is obligated to bring the pesach offering.

מְבִיאוֹ מִן הַכְּבָשִׂים אוֹ מִן הָעִזִּים, זָכָר תָּמִים בֶּן שָׁנָה, וְשׁוֹחֲטוֹ בְּכָל מָקוֹם בָּעֲזָרָה, אַחַר גְּמַר עֲבוֹדַת תָּמִיד הָעֶרֶב וְאַחַר הֲטָבַת הַנֵּרוֹת.
וְאֵין שׁוֹחֲטִין הַפֶּסַח, וְלֹא זוֹרְקִין הַדָּם, וְלֹא מַקְטִירִין הַחֵלֶב, עַל הֶחָמֵץ.

שָׁחַט הַשּׁוֹחֵט, וְקִבֵּל דָּמוֹ הַכֹּהֵן שֶׁבָּרֹאשׁ הַשּׁוּרָה בִּכְלִי שָׁרֵת, וְנוֹתֵן לַחֲבֵרוֹ, וַחֲבֵרוֹ לַחֲבֵרוֹ. כֹּהֵן הַקָּרוֹב אֵצֶל הַמִּזְבֵּחַ זוֹרְקוֹ זְרִיקָה אַחַת כְּנֶגֶד הַיְסוֹד, וְחוֹזֵר הַכְּלִי רֵיקָן לַחֲבֵרוֹ, וַחֲבֵרוֹ לַחֲבֵרוֹ. מְקַבֵּל אֶת הַמָּלֵא וּמַחֲזִיר אֶת הָרֵיקָן. וְהָיוּ הַכֹּהֲנִים עוֹמְדִים שׁוּרוֹת וּבִידֵיהֶם בָּזִיכִין שֶׁכֻּלָּן כֶּסֶף אוֹ כֻלָּן זָהָב. וְלֹא הָיוּ מְעֹרָבִים. וְלֹא הָיוּ לַבָּזִיכִין שׁוּלַיִם, שֶׁלֹּא יַנִּיחוּם וְיִקְרֹשׁ הַדָּם.

אַחַר כָּךְ תּוֹלִין אֶת הַפֶּסַח בְּאֻנְקְלָיוֹת, וּמַפְשִׁיט אוֹתוֹ כֻּלּוֹ, וְקוֹרְעִין בִּטְנוֹ וּמוֹצִיאִין אֵמוּרָיו – הַחֵלֶב שֶׁעַל הַקֶּרֶב, וְיוֹתֶרֶת הַכָּבֵד, וּשְׁתֵּי הַכְּלָיוֹת, וְהַחֵלֶב שֶׁעֲלֵיהֶן, וְהָאַלְיָה לְעֻמַּת הָעָצֶה. נוֹתְנָן בִּכְלִי שָׁרֵת וּמוֹלְחָן וּמַקְטִירָן הַכֹּהֵן עַל הַמַּעֲרָכָה, חֶלְבֵי כָּל זֶבַח וָזֶבַח לְבַדּוֹ. בַּחֹל, בַּיּוֹם וְלֹא בַּלַּיְלָה שֶׁהוּא יוֹם טוֹב. אֲבָל אִם חָל עֶרֶב פֶּסַח בַּשַּׁבָּת, מַקְטִירִין וְהוֹלְכִין כָּל הַלַּיְלָה. וּמוֹצִיא קְרָבָיו וּמְמַחֶה אוֹתָן עַד שֶׁמֵּסִיר מֵהֶן הַפֶּרֶשׁ.

שְׁחִיטָתוֹ וּזְרִיקַת דָּמוֹ וּמִחוּי קְרָבָיו וְהֶקְטֵר חֲלָבָיו דּוֹחִין אֶת הַשַּׁבָּת, וּשְׁאָר עִנְיָנָיו אֵין דּוֹחִין.

בְּשָׁלֹשׁ כִּתּוֹת הַפֶּסַח נִשְׁחָט. וְאֵין כַּת פְּחוּתָה מִשְּׁלֹשִׁים אֲנָשִׁים. נִכְנְסָה כַּת אַחַת, נִתְמַלְּאָה הָעֲזָרָה, נוֹעֲלִין אוֹתָהּ. וּבְעוֹד שֶׁהֵם שׁוֹחֲטִין

It may be brought from sheep or from goats, an unblemished male in its first year. It may be slaughtered anywhere in the Temple Courtyard, after the completion of the afternoon tamid offering, and after the kindling of the Menorah's lamps.

We may not slaughter the pesach, nor throw its blood [onto the Altar], nor burn its fats [on the Altar], if chametz is in our possession.

Someone [even a non-Kohen] would slaughter [the animal]. The Kohen at the head of the line [closest to the animal] would receive its blood in a sanctified vessel and pass it to his colleague, and he to his colleague. The Kohen closest to the Altar would throw it, with one throwing, at the base [of the Altar], then return the vessel to his colleague, and he to his colleague. He would first accept the full one, then return the empty one. The Kohanim would stand in lines, [all the Kohanim of each line] holding either silver or golden vessels. But they would not mix [two types of vessels in one line]. The vessels did not have flat bottoms, lest one would put down a vessel [and forget it], thus causing the blood to congeal.

Following this, they would suspend the pesach from hooks. They would skin it completely, tear open its stomach and remove the organs ordained for the Altar — the suet covering the stomach, the diaphragm with the liver, the two kidneys and the suet upon them, and [in the case of a lamb] the tail opposite the kidneys. They would place [these organs] in a sanctified vessel and salt them, then a Kohen would burn them on the Altar fire. The portions of each offering [would be placed on the fire] separately. On a weekday, [this would be done] by day and not at night when the festival had already begun. But when erev Pesach fell on Shabbos, they would burn [the organs] during the entire night. They would remove the innards and squeeze them until all their wastes were removed.

Slaughtering it, throwing its blood, squeezing out its innards, and burning its fats [on the Altar] supersede Shabbos; but its other requirements do not supersede [Shabbos].

The pesach is slaughtered in three groups, no group comprising less than thirty men. The first entered, filling the Courtyard; then they closed the gates. For as long as they

וּמַקְרִיבִין, הַכֹּהֲנִים תּוֹקְעִין, הֶחָלִיל מַכֶּה לִפְנֵי הַמִּזְבֵּחַ, וְהַלְוִיִּים קוֹרְאִין אֶת הַהַלֵּל. אִם גָּמְרוּ קֹדֶם שֶׁיַּקְרִיבוּ כֻּלָּם, שָׁנוּ; אִם שָׁנוּ, שִׁלְּשׁוּ. עַל כָּל קְרִיאָה תָּקְעוּ הֵרִיעוּ וְתָקְעוּ. גָּמְרָה כַּת אַחַת לְהַקְרִיב, פּוֹתְחִין הָעֲזָרָה, יָצְאָה כַּת רִאשׁוֹנָה, נִכְנְסָה כַּת שְׁנִיָּה, נָעֲלוּ דַּלְתוֹת הָעֲזָרָה. גָּמְרָה, יָצְאָה שְׁנִיָּה וְנִכְנְסָה שְׁלִישִׁית. כְּמַעֲשֵׂה הָרִאשׁוֹנָה כָּךְ מַעֲשֵׂה הַשְּׁנִיָּה וְהַשְּׁלִישִׁית.

אַחַר שֶׁיָּצְאוּ כֻּלָּן רוֹחֲצִין הָעֲזָרָה מִלִּכְלוּכֵי הַדָּם, וַאֲפִלּוּ בַּשַּׁבָּת. אַמַּת הַמַּיִם הָיְתָה עוֹבֶרֶת בָּעֲזָרָה, שֶׁכְּשֶׁרוֹצִין לְהָדִיחַ הָרִצְפָּה סוֹתְמִין מְקוֹם יְצִיאַת הַמַּיִם וְהִיא מִתְמַלֵּאת עַל כָּל גְּדוֹתֶיהָ, עַד שֶׁהַמַּיִם עוֹלִין וְצָפִין וּמְקַבְּצִין אֲלֵיהֶם כָּל דָּם וְלִכְלוּךְ שֶׁבָּעֲזָרָה. אַחַר כָּךְ פּוֹתְחִין הַסְּתִימָה וְיוֹצְאִין הַמַּיִם עִם הַלִּכְלוּךְ, נִמְצֵאת הָרִצְפָּה מְנֻקָּה, זֶהוּ כְּבוֹד הַבַּיִת.

יָצְאוּ כָּל אֶחָד עִם פִּסְחוֹ וְצָלוּ אוֹתָם. כֵּיצַד צוֹלִין אוֹתוֹ? מְבִיאִין שַׁפּוּד שֶׁל רִמּוֹן, תּוֹחֲבוֹ מִתּוֹךְ פִּיו עַד בֵּית נְקוּבָתוֹ, וְתוֹלֵהוּ לְתוֹךְ הַתַּנּוּר וְהָאֵשׁ לְמַטָּה, וְתוֹלֶה כְּרָעָיו וּבְנֵי מֵעָיו חוּצָה לוֹ, וְאֵין מְנַקְּרִין אֶת הַפֶּסַח כִּשְׁאָר בָּשָׂר.

בַּשַּׁבָּת אֵינָן מוֹלִיכִין אֶת הַפֶּסַח לְבֵיתָם, אֶלָּא כַּת הָרִאשׁוֹנָה יוֹצְאִין בְּפִסְחֵיהֶן וְיוֹשְׁבִין בְּהַר הַבַּיִת, הַשְּׁנִיָּה יוֹצְאִין עִם פִּסְחֵיהֶן וְיוֹשְׁבִין בַּחֵיל, וְהַשְּׁלִישִׁית בִּמְקוֹמָהּ עוֹמֶדֶת. חָשְׁכָה, יָצְאוּ וְצָלוּ אֶת פִּסְחֵיהֶן.

כְּשֶׁמַּקְרִיבִין אֶת הַפֶּסַח בָּרִאשׁוֹן מַקְרִיבִין עִמּוֹ בְּיוֹם אַרְבָּעָה עָשָׂר זֶבַח שְׁלָמִים, מִן הַבָּקָר אוֹ מִן הַצֹּאן, גְּדוֹלִים אוֹ קְטַנִּים, זְכָרִים אוֹ נְקֵבוֹת, וְהִיא נִקְרֵאת חֲגִיגַת אַרְבָּעָה עָשָׂר, עַל זֶה נֶאֱמַר בַּתּוֹרָה,

slaughtered and offered [the pesach], the Kohanim would blow the shofar, the flute would play before the Altar, and the Levites would recite Hallel. If they completed [Hallel] before all had brought their offerings, they repeated it. If they completed [Hallel] a second time, they would recite it a third time. For each recitation, they blew tekiah, teruah, tekiah. When the first group was done offering, they opened the Courtyard [gates]. The first group left, the second group entered, and the Courtyard gates were closed. When they were done, the second group left and the third group entered. Like the procedure of the first, so was the procedure of the second and third.

After all [three groups] had left, they [the Kohanim] would wash the [stone] Courtyard [floor] of the blood, even on Shabbos. A channel of water passed through the Courtyard. When they wished to wash the floor, they would block the outlet, causing the water to overflow and gather all the bloods and other waste matter in the Courtyard. Then they would remove the blockage and the water with the waste would run out. Thus, the floor would be clean. And this is the manner of cleansing the Temple.

They left, each with his pesach, and roasted them. In what manner was it roasted? They would bring a pomegranate wood spit, thrust it through its mouth to its anus and suspend it inside the oven with the fire below it. Its legs and innards were suspended outside [its body cavity]. They would not purge the pesach in the same manner as other meat.

On Shabbos they would not carry the pesach [meat] to their homes. Rather, the first group would go out [of the Courtyard] with their pesach offerings and remain on the Temple Mount. The second group would go out and remain within the Cheil [a ten-cubit-wide area, just outside the Courtyard walls]. The third group would remain where they were. When it became dark, they would leave [for their homes] and roast their pesach offerings.

When they would bring the pesach offering, they would bring with it — on the fourteenth of Nisan — a peace-offering, either from the cattle herd or from the flock, old or young, male or female. This is called "the festive offering of the fourteenth." Regarding this the Torah states:

וְזָבַחְתָּ פֶּסַח לַיהוה אֱלֹהֶיךָ צֹאן וּבָקָר.¹ וְלֹא קְבָעָהּ הַכָּתוּב חוֹבָה אֶלָּא רְשׁוּת בִּלְבָד, מִכָּל מָקוֹם הִיא כְּחוֹבָה מִדִּבְרֵי סוֹפְרִים, כְּדֵי שֶׁיְּהֵא הַפֶּסַח נֶאֱכָל עַל הַשֹּׂבַע. אֵימָתַי מְבִיאִין עִמּוֹ חֲגִיגָה? בִּזְמַן שֶׁהוּא בָּא בְּחֹל, בְּטָהֳרָה וּבְמוּעָט. וְנֶאֱכֶלֶת לִשְׁנֵי יָמִים וְלַיְלָה אֶחָד, וְדִינָהּ כְּכָל תּוֹרַת זִבְחֵי שְׁלָמִים, טְעוּנָה סְמִיכָה וּנְסָכִים וּמַתַּן דָּמִים שְׁתַּיִם שֶׁהֵן אַרְבַּע וּשְׁפִיכַת שְׁיָרִים לַיְסוֹד.

זֶהוּ סֵדֶר עֲבוֹדַת קָרְבָּן פֶּסַח וַחֲגִיגָה שֶׁעָמוֹ בְּבֵית אֱלֹהֵינוּ שֶׁיִּבָּנֶה בִּמְהֵרָה בְּיָמֵינוּ, אָמֵן. אַשְׁרֵי הָעָם שֶׁכָּכָה לּוֹ, אַשְׁרֵי הָעָם שֶׁיהוה אֱלֹהָיו.²

אֱלֹהֵינוּ וֵאלֹהֵי אֲבוֹתֵינוּ, מֶלֶךְ רַחֲמָן רַחֵם עָלֵינוּ, טוֹב וּמֵטִיב הִדָּרֶשׁ לָנוּ. שׁוּבָה אֵלֵינוּ בַּהֲמוֹן רַחֲמֶיךָ בִּגְלַל אָבוֹת שֶׁעָשׂוּ רְצוֹנֶךָ. בְּנֵה בֵיתְךָ כְּבַתְּחִלָּה וְכוֹנֵן מִקְדָּשְׁךָ עַל מְכוֹנוֹ. וְהַרְאֵנוּ בְּבִנְיָנוֹ וְשַׂמְּחֵנוּ בְּתִקּוּנוֹ. וְהָשֵׁב שְׁכִינָתְךָ לְתוֹכוֹ, וְהָשֵׁב כֹּהֲנִים לַעֲבוֹדָתָם וּלְוִיִּים לְשִׁירָם וּלְזִמְרָם, וְהָשֵׁב יִשְׂרָאֵל לִנְוֵיהֶם. וְשָׁם נַעֲלֶה וְנֵרָאֶה וְנִשְׁתַּחֲוֶה לְפָנֶיךָ. וְנֹאכַל שָׁם מִן הַזְּבָחִים וּמִן הַפְּסָחִים אֲשֶׁר יַגִּיעַ דָּמָם עַל קִיר מִזְבַּחֲךָ לְרָצוֹן. יִהְיוּ לְרָצוֹן אִמְרֵי פִי וְהֶגְיוֹן לִבִּי לְפָנֶיךָ, יהוה צוּרִי וְגֹאֲלִי.³

---

(1) *Devarim* 16:2. (2) *Tehillim* 144:15. (3) 19:15.

And you shall slaughter the pesach offering to HASHEM, your God, from the flock and cattle.[1] Yet the Torah did not establish this as an obligation, but only as a voluntary offering. Nevertheless, it was made obligatory by the Rabbis, in order that the pesach offering be eaten in satiety. When may the festive-offering be brought with it [the pesach]? When it [the pesach] is brought on a weekday, in purity and there are few. It may be eaten for two days and the included night, its laws being the same as the laws of other peace-offerings. It requires semichah, libations, two [Altar] applications of blood that are equivalent to four, and pouring the remainder [of the blood] at the [Altar's] base.

This is the order of the pesach offering and the festive-offering brought with it in the Temple of our God — may it be rebuilt speedily, in our days — Amen. Praiseworthy is the people for whom this is so; praiseworthy is the people whose God is HASHEM.[2]

Our God and the God of our forefathers, O merciful King, have mercy on us; O good and beneficent One, let Yourself be sought out by us; return to us in Your yearning mercy for the sake of the forefathers who did Your will. Rebuild Your House as it was at first, and establish Your Sanctuary on its prepared site; show us its rebuilding and gladden us in its perfection. Return Your Shechinah to it; restore the Kohanim to their service, the Levites to their song and music; and restore Israel to their dwellings. And there may we ascend and appear and prostrate ourselves before You. There we shall eat of the peace offerings and pesach offerings whose blood will gain the sides of Your Altar for favorable acceptance. May the expressions of my mouth and the thoughts of my heart find favor before You, HASHEM, my Rock and my Redeemer.[3]

הַהֲכָנוֹת לַסֵּדֶר – Preparing for the Seder

Preparing Wine for the Four Cups

1. It is preferable to use red wine, if it is not inferior in quality to the white wine available (472:11).
2. One may use boiled wine or wine to which flavoring has been added, although it is preferable to use pure, unboiled wine so long as it is not of inferior quality (472:2 and *Mishnah Berurah* 39-40).

Karpas

1. One should use the vegetable called *karpas,* because this word is an anagram of the words ס׳, 60 (referring to the 600,000 Jews), and פֶּרֶךְ, *worked hard*. However, any vegetable may be used other than those which may be used for *maror*.
2. One should prepare salt water or Kosher for Pesach vinegar in which to dip the *karpas*. (If the Seder night falls on Shabbos, the salt water should be made beforehand. If one forgot to do so, he may prepare the minimum amount of salt water on Shabbos, immediately prior to the meal, making sure that he puts less than 66 percent salt in the mixture.) (473:4 and *Mishnah Berurah* 19, 21).

Maror

1. There are five vegetables which the Mishnah (*Pesachim* 2:6) mentions which may be used for *maror*: *chazeres* (lettuce), *ulshin* (endives), *tamcha* (horse-radish), *charchavinah* and *maror*. One may use either the leaves or the stalks of these species. While one may not use their roots, the thick, hard part of the root (as the horseradish root) has the same status as the stalk. The leaves may not be used after they have dried out, but the stalk may be used when dry. Neither may be used if it has been soaked in water or any other liquid for 24 hours.

    Since the Mishnah lists the varieties in order of preference, and *chazeres* precedes *tamcha,* it should be more preferable to use lettuce than horseradish. However, since lettuce is extremely hard to rid of all the bugs that infest it, if one is unable to check and cleanse the lettuce thoroughly he should use horseradish instead (473:5, *Mishnah Berurah* ad loc.).

2. The horseradish should be ground, as eating a whole piece of horseradish constitutes a danger to one's well-being and is not a fulfillment of the mitzvah. However, the ground horseradish should not be left open for a long time after, as this causes all its bitterness to dissipate (ibid.).

3. The *Mishnah Berurah* records that the *Gra* used to leave the grinding of the horseradish until after he came home from shul on the Seder night, and then left it covered until the beginning of the Seder. (Note: The grinding of these vegetables on *Yom Tov* should be done differently than usual. See *Orach Chayim* 504.) When the Seder night comes out on Shabbos, when such grinding is forbidden, the horseradish should be prepared before

Shabbos and left covered until the beginning of the Seder. (Nowadays many people prepare the horseradish before *Yom Tov* even when it is not Shabbos, since its sharpness can be preserved quite well in a closed container. This is the practice of *Maran* R' Schach as well.) (ibid.)

4. If someone is too ill or delicate to eat the entire *k'zayis* of horseradish at one time, he may spread it out over a period of *Kedei Achilas Peras* (approx. 2-9 minutes).

Charoses

1. *Charoses* should be prepared with fruits which are used in *Tanach* as metaphors for Israel — such as figs (see *Shir Hashirim* 2:13), nuts (ibid., 6:11) and apples (ibid., 8:5). It is also customary to use almonds, because the Hebrew word for almond (שָׁקֵד) also means *swift*, and is thus a reminder of God's speedy deliverance of the Jews from Egypt. One should also put in pieces of ginger and cinnamon, to symbolize the straw that was used by the Jewish slaves to prepare bricks. The *charoses* should have a thick consistency, as a reminder of the mortar that the Egyptians forced the Jews to prepare. However, just before it is used (to dip the *maror*) some wine should be poured into it, as a remembrance of the blood that played an important role in the Exodus (and also to make it more usable as a dip). When the Seder is held on Shabbos the wine should be put into the *charoses* before Shabbos. If one forgot to do so, he may do it differently than usual, and should add enough wine to made a loose consistency (504).

Two Cooked Foods

1. After the destruction of the Temple the Sages instituted the practice of placing two kinds of cooked foods on the Seder table, one to commemorate the meat of the *pesach* offering and the other to commemorate the meat of the *chagigah* offering — both of which were sacrificed in the Temple on the fourteenth of Nisan and eaten at the Seder. The custom has developed that one of the two foods should be meat, customarily a shankbone (corresponding to the human arm, symbolizing the "outstretched arm" of Hashem) that has been roasted on the fire (as the *pesach* meat was). The second food is customarily an egg, because the Aramaic word for *egg* (בֵּיעָא) is related to the Aramaic word for *desire* — God *desired* (בָעָא) to take us out of Egypt with an outstretched *arm*. The egg can be cooked or roasted in any way (as the *chagigah* was), although some have the custom to roast it specifically.

Rema writes that many have the custom to eat eggs at the Seder. He explains that eggs are traditionally eaten by mourners, and they are eaten at this time as a commemoration of the destruction of the Temple. The *Mishnah Berurah*, citing *Gra*, says that we eat the egg of the Seder plate, since, as noted above, it symbolizes the *chagigah* offering. (According to this explanation, only the egg on the Seder plate needs to be eaten, but this custom subsequently became popularly extended to include the eating of eggs in general.) (473:4, *Mishnah Berurah* ad loc.; 470:2, *Mishnah Berurah* 11.)

2. It is best to boil or roast these two foods before *Yom Tov*. If this was neglected, they may be prepared on *Yom Tov*. If they were prepared on *Yom Tov*, the foods must be eaten on that day of *Yom Tov*, as one may only cook food on *Yom Tov* if it will be eaten that same day. The two foods will thus have to be prepared anew for the second Seder (ibid.).

Making Arrangements for Reclining

1. The seats of those who must recline while drinking the wine and eating the matzah should be prepared in a manner that will enable comfortable reclining on one's left side (472:2).

Preparing the Cups

1. The cups should be whole (not chipped or broken) and clean, and should be able to hold at least a *revi'is*. Since it is preferable to drink a majority of the wine in the cup for each of the four cups, it is advisable not to use a very large cup. This applies to the cups used by all the participants in the Seder, including women and children (who have reached the age of training in mitzvos). (472:14, 15; *Mishnah Berurah* 33.)

Preparing the Table

1. The table should be set with elegant and luxurious articles according to one's means. Although it is usually proper to use moderation in this regard out of mourning for the Temple, on Pesach it is encouraged, as this serves as yet another demonstration of our freedom. The table should be set in advance so that the Seder can get underway without delay (so the children should not become too tired) (472:1,2; *Mishnah Berurah* 6).

The Beginning of the Seder

1. Although, as mentioned above, the Seder should begin as promptly as possible, *Kiddush* should not be said before dark (*tzeis hakochavim*) (472:1).

2. It is customary for the leader to wear a *kittel* for the Seder (ibid., *Mishnah Berurah* 12).

3. Only one Seder plate is set, before the leader of the Seder. There are several different opinions as to how the Seder plate should be arranged (see diagrams on page 40).

4. The children should be kept awake at least until after reciting עֲבָדִים הָיִינוּ, so that they should hear the basic story of the Exodus. Children who have reached the age of training in mitzvos must participate in all the practices of the entire Seder. (However they must only consume a cheekful of wine, according to the size of their own mouths, for each required cup. Furthermore, there is an opinion that holds that they need not drink the four cups of wine at all.) (472:15; *Mishnah Berurah* §46, 47.)

Reclining

1. One should not recline on his back or stomach, but only on his left side. This applies to left-handed people as well (472:3, *Mishnah Berurah* ad loc.).
2. Someone who is in mourning for a relative should also recline, although he should do so in a less luxurious manner than usual. It is also customary for a mourner not to wear a *kittel* for the Seder, although some opinions permit it (*Mishnah Berurah* 13).
3. The custom is that women do not recline (472:4).
4. A student in the presence of his *rebbi* — or any person in the presence of a great, recognized rabbinical figure — should not recline. This holds true only if they are seated at the same table. (According to some opinions, a student in the presence of his *rebbi* should ask for permission to recline even if he is sitting at a separate table.) (472:5, *Mishnah Berurah* 18.)
5. A son must recline in the presence of his father, even if his father is also his *rebbi* (472:5).
6. If one forgot to recline for any of the places in the Seder which call for reclining, he has not fulfilled that mitzvah, and it must be performed again. *Raaviah* maintains, however, that since eating in a reclining position is not a sign of freedom and leisure in our culture, the practice need not be followed. Although we do not follow the *Raaviah's* opinion, when redoing one of the mitzvos might lead to a halachic complication, this opinion is adopted and the mitzvah in question is not done over. These exceptions will be noted in appropriate places in the Haggadah (472:7, *Mishnah Berurah* 20).

Drinking the Four Cups

1. Even if one dislikes wine or suffers discomfort when drinking it, he should force himself to drink the four cups (unless it will actually make him ill). The wine may be diluted, as long as it remains fit to be used as *Kiddush* wine.
2. It is preferable to drink the entire cup of wine each time. The minimum amount that *must* be consumed is a majority of a *revi'is*, although there is an opinion that one must drink most of the wine in the cup, if the cup is larger than a *revi'is*. The requisite amount of wine should be drunk all at once, or at the very most within a time span of *kedei achilas pras* (approx. 2-9 minutes) (472:9, *Mishnah Berurah* 30, 33, 34).
3. The four cups must be drunk in their appropriate places in the Seder: one for *Kiddush*, one after *Maggid*, one for *bentching*, and one for *Hallel* (472:8).

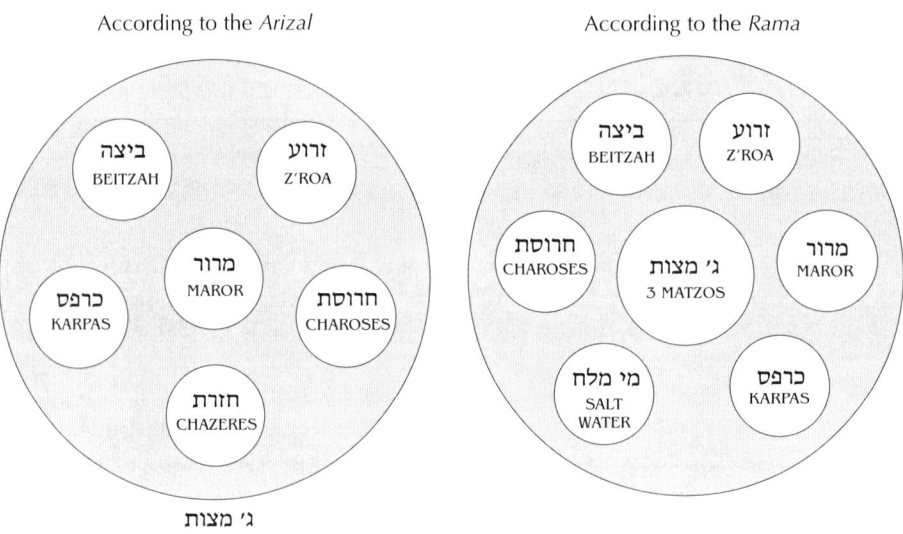

סימני הסדר
The Order of the Seder

KADDESH	*Sanctify* the day with the recitation of Kiddush.	קדש
URECHATZ	*Wash* the hands before eating Karpas.	ורחץ
KARPAS	Eat a **vegetable** dipped in salt water.	כרפס
YACHATZ	**Break** the middle matzah. Put away larger half for Afikoman.	יחץ
MAGGID	**Narrate** the story of the Exodus from Egypt.	מגיד
RACHTZAH	*Wash* the hands prior to the meal.	רחצה
MOTZI	Recite the blessing, **Who brings forth**, over matzah as a food.	מוציא
MATZAH	Recite the blessing over **Matzah**.	מצה
MAROR	Recite the blessing for the eating of the **bitter herbs**.	מרור
KORECH	Eat the **sandwich** of matzah and bitter herbs.	כורך
SHULCHAN ORECH	The **table prepared** with the festive meal.	שלחן עורך
TZAFUN	Eat the afikoman which had been **hidden** all during the Seder.	צפון
BARECH	Recite Bircas Hamazon, the **blessings** after the meal.	ברך
HALLEL	Recite the **Hallel** Psalms of praise.	הלל
NIRTZAH	Pray that God **accept** our observance and speedily send the Messiah.	נרצה

קַדֵּשׁ

Kiddush should be recited and the Seder begun as soon after synagogue services as possible — however, not before nightfall.
Each participant's cup should be poured by someone else to symbolize the majesty of the evening, as though each participant had a servant.

Some recite the following before *Kiddush*:

הֲרֵינִי מוּכָן וּמְזֻמָּן לְקַדֵּשׁ עַל הַיַּיִן, וּלְקַיֵּם מִצְוַת כּוֹס רִאשׁוֹן מֵאַרְבַּע כּוֹסוֹת. לְשֵׁם יִחוּד קֻדְשָׁא בְּרִיךְ הוּא וּשְׁכִינְתֵּיהּ, עַל יְדֵי הַהוּא טָמִיר וְנֶעְלָם, בְּשֵׁם כָּל יִשְׂרָאֵל. וִיהִי נֹעַם אֲדֹנָי אֱלֹהֵינוּ עָלֵינוּ, וּמַעֲשֵׂה יָדֵינוּ כּוֹנְנָה עָלֵינוּ, וּמַעֲשֵׂה יָדֵינוּ כּוֹנְנֵהוּ.

On Friday night begin here:

[וַיְהִי עֶרֶב וַיְהִי בֹקֶר]

יוֹם הַשִּׁשִּׁי. וַיְכֻלּוּ הַשָּׁמַיִם וְהָאָרֶץ וְכָל צְבָאָם. וַיְכַל אֱלֹהִים בַּיּוֹם הַשְּׁבִיעִי מְלַאכְתּוֹ אֲשֶׁר עָשָׂה, וַיִּשְׁבֹּת בַּיּוֹם הַשְּׁבִיעִי מִכָּל מְלַאכְתּוֹ אֲשֶׁר עָשָׂה. וַיְבָרֶךְ אֱלֹהִים אֶת יוֹם הַשְּׁבִיעִי וַיְקַדֵּשׁ אֹתוֹ, כִּי בוֹ שָׁבַת מִכָּל מְלַאכְתּוֹ אֲשֶׁר בָּרָא אֱלֹהִים לַעֲשׂוֹת.[1]

On all nights continue here:

סַבְרִי מָרָנָן וְרַבָּנָן וְרַבּוֹתַי:

בָּרוּךְ אַתָּה יהוה אֱלֹהֵינוּ מֶלֶךְ הָעוֹלָם, בּוֹרֵא פְּרִי הַגָּפֶן:

בּוֹרֵא פְּרִי הַגָּפֶן
Who creates the fruit of the vine

In addition to being used for the regular *Yom Tov Kiddush*, this cup of wine also serves another purpose. It is the first of the four cups of wine that were instituted by the Sages for the Seder. According to the Midrash, these four cups correspond to the four expressions of redemption used by God in His promise to Moshe in *Shemos* 6:6-7: 1) "I shall *take you out* from under the burdens of Egypt; 2) I shall

KADDESH

Kiddush should be recited and the Seder begun as soon after synagogue services as possible — however, not before nightfall.
Each participant's cup should be poured by someone else to symbolize the majesty of the evening, as though each participant had a servant.

Some recite the following before Kiddush:

Behold, I am prepared and ready to recite the *Kiddush* over wine, and to fulfill the mitzvah of the first of the Four Cups. For the sake of unification of the Holy One, Blessed is He, and His Presence, through Him Who is hidden and inscrutable — [I pray] in the name of all Israel. May the pleasantness of my Lord, our God, be upon us — may He establish our handiwork for us; our handiwork may He establish.

On Friday night begin here:

(And there was evening and there was morning)
The sixth day. Thus the heaven and the earth were finished, and all their array. On the seventh day God completed His work which He had done, and He abstained on the seventh day from all His work which He had done. God blessed the seventh day and hallowed it, because on it He abstained from all His work which God created to make.[1]

On all nights continue here:

By your leave, my masters and teachers:

Blessed are You, HASHEM, our God, King of the universe, Who creates the fruit of the vine.

---

(1) *Bereishis* 1:31-2:3.

---

rescue you from their servitude; 3) I shall *redeem* you with an outstretched arm and with great judgments; 4) I shall *take you to Me* for a people and I shall be a God to you."

Why did the Sages choose wine as the medium to express the four expressions of redemption? Many people experience discomfort from drinking so much wine. Why not institute a ceremony using four fruits, four nuts, or even four matzos? Surely this would also spur the children's curiosity, providing us the opportunity to explain the four expressions of redemption and their significance on this night.

[On Friday night include all passages in parentheses.]

בָּרוּךְ אַתָּה יהוה אֱלֹהֵינוּ מֶלֶךְ הָעוֹלָם, אֲשֶׁר בָּחַר בָּנוּ מִכָּל עָם, וְרוֹמְמָנוּ מִכָּל לָשׁוֹן, וְקִדְּשָׁנוּ בְּמִצְוֹתָיו. וַתִּתֶּן לָנוּ יהוה אֱלֹהֵינוּ בְּאַהֲבָה [שַׁבָּתוֹת לִמְנוּחָה וּ]מוֹעֲדִים לְשִׂמְחָה, חַגִּים וּזְמַנִּים לְשָׂשׂוֹן, אֶת [יוֹם הַשַּׁבָּת הַזֶּה וְאֶת] יוֹם חַג הַמַּצּוֹת הַזֶּה, זְמַן חֵרוּתֵנוּ [בְּאַהֲבָה] מִקְרָא קֹדֶשׁ, זֵכֶר לִיצִיאַת מִצְרָיִם, כִּי בָנוּ

We must know that the four expressions of redemption are not mere repetitive variations of the same theme. They each build upon the other, each creating additional levels of joy: First, "I shall take you out from under the burdens of Egypt," which is a relief from physical labor. Second, "I shall rescue you from their servitude" — this indicates the absolution of all servility. Third, "I shall redeem you with an outstretched arm," which refers to the physical extrication of the Jews from the land of Egypt. Fourth, " I shall take you to Me for a people," which indicates the *spiritual* elevation of the Jews on becoming God's chosen people. (In the future, when the redemption will be complete, there will be a fifth cup, corresponding to the additional level of (ibid., 8), "I shall *bring* you to the land ...") Each expression builds on the effects of the previous one, intensifying the redemption process.

Correspondingly, the Sages instituted the four cups of wine. If four nuts (or four fruits) would be eaten at the Seder, there would be four unrelated acts of eating nuts. The first nut or fruit is tasty, the second less so (but certainly not more so), and for the third or fourth there is almost no interest. With wine, however, the effect of drinking the four cups is cumulative; each cup intensifies the feelings of joy and exhilaration over the four-step process of redemption (from a lecture on the laws of Pesach given by Rav Shlomo Zalman in 1970).

זֵכֶר לִיצִיאַת מִצְרָיִם
In commemoration of the Exodus from Egypt

This phrase, which makes perfect sense in the context of the *Kiddush* for Pesach, also appears in the regular *Kiddush* for Shabbos. This is in accordance with the Gemara (*Pesachim* 117b) which

[On Friday night include all passages in parentheses.]

Blessed are You, HASHEM, our God, King of the universe, Who has chosen us from all nations, exalted us above all tongues, and sanctified us with His commandments. And You, HASHEM, our God, have lovingly given us (Sabbaths for rest,) holidays for rejoicing, feasts and seasons for joy, (this Sabbath day and) this Feast of Matzos, the season of our freedom (in love,) a holy convocation in commemoration of the Exodus from Egypt. For You

---

requires mentioning the Exodus in the Shabbos *Kiddush*. Indeed, the Torah itself establishes the connection and writes (*Devarim* 5:15): "And you shall remember that you were a slave in the land of Egypt, and Hashem, your God, has taken you out from there ... therefore, Hashem, your God, has commanded you to make the Sabbath day." Let us expound on the connection between Shabbos and the Exodus from Egypt.

We must differentiate between two classes of miracles as perceived by the early commentaries. When a miracle occurs to a righteous person as a result of his own good deeds, he recognizes the miracle which has been performed for him. On the other hand, if the miracle is not the result of his meritorious deeds, but of other factors, such as the exceptional merit of his ancestors or the merit of others, then, "Even the person himself who experiences the miracle is unaware of the miracle" (*Niddah* 31a). Rashi, citing the Midrash, gives an example of this in his commentary to *Bereishis* 19:17, where the Torah relates that the angel who was about to destroy Sodom warned Lot and his wife not to look back as they escaped from the city. Rashi explains, "You did evil along with them, and it is only through the merit of Avraham that you are being saved, not through your own merit. It is inappropriate for you to see their punishment while you are being saved."

The Jews at the time of the Exodus had sunk to the forty-ninth level of impurity and were bereft of all merit. The Midrash relates that the angels protested the injustice of the Jews' salvation. Why are the Jews being saved? Both Jews and Egyptians were idolaters! By all rights, they should have been unaware of the miracles being performed for them. As with Lot and his wife, they should have been told "not to look." Yet the Jews were granted miraculous displays of

God's might, so that "even a simple maidservant saw more of God's glory than the prophet Yechezkel" (*Mechilta, Parashas HaShirah* 3). How did they merit this?

Furthermore, the Torah itself testifies (*Devarim* 34:11-12): "All the signs and wonders ... in the land of Egypt ... that Moshe performed before the eyes of all Israel." Not only did they do nothing to deserve these miracles, but were also granted the vision to see all the signs and wonders with such great clarity!

It would seem that all this was not a result of their own merit, but rather a means to implant in their hearts — and in the hearts of all ensuing generations — the firm belief in the existence of God. Indeed, the miracles were not necessary for getting the Jews out of Egypt. They could have exited Egypt through natural means as well, and certainly Hashem could have brought them straight to the Land of Israel without their ever having to cross the sea. Yet Hashem desired to harden the heart of Pharaoh to increase the "supernaturalness" of the Exodus so that the belief in Hashem would be firmly implanted in the hearts of the Jewish People.

In contrast, throughout history there have been those who denied that the world had a Creator Who created the world in six days, and that He is the Master of the Universe Who controls all of creation. Others assumed that after He created the world He gave it over to be ruled by the laws of nature, and He no longer controls the world. Still others do not admit that the Creator created the world in six days; they admit only a creation of primeval matter at some point after which all else evolved without any Divine intervention.

We, on the other hand, believe that the Glory of Hashem fills the entire universe. We believe that He constantly renews the universe's power of existence, and that if He would hide His countenance from the world, the world would return to its primordial state. Accordingly, as part of our prayers we say the verse (*Nechemiah* 9:6): "...You give them all life," meaning, only You give life to every moment of Creation, so that the world is constantly renewed. This verse continues, "And the heavenly legion bows to You," which indicates that all of Creation is subservient to Hashem.

The reason for keeping the seventh day as a day of rest, in commemoration of Hashem "resting" on the seventh day of Creation, is to emphasize His role as Creator. Those who subscribe to the heresies mentioned above see no point to Shabbos.

To further refute these heresies, Hashem showed His people all the miracles He performed in Egypt. Indeed, they did not deserve to see these miracles in their own merit. Rather, Hashem demonstrated these miracles to instill in them the clear belief in an active God Who is the Master of the Universe, a God Who controls the course of events every second, every day. Thus, these miracles were different from all other miracles that occurred to the Jewish people throughout the ages.

As is well known, the Jordan River was split for the Jewish Nation as they entered the Land of Israel (see *Yehoshua* 3:16), and R' Pinchas ben Yair also split a river (see *Chullin* 7a). Yet these miracles occurred as a result of the temporary cessation of the laws of nature, i.e., the water stopped flowing and thus "the waters descending from upstream stood still" (*Yehoshua,* ibid.). On the other hand, the miracles in Egypt involved an active change in the laws of nature. The Sea of Reeds was split so that "Straight as a wall stood the running water" (*Exodus* 15:8). In other words, the water was *still* "running water," and yet it stood "straight as a wall"!

Similarly, in the plague of blood, the water did not *mix* with blood; rather, the water changed its very nature and *became* blood. The same is true for all of the plagues. As a result of seeing the laws of nature completely change, the people firmly believed that Hashem re-creates the world each second. He is in full control, and only He has the power to change anything at will.

Once His identity as Creator was firmly established in their minds, (due to the fantastic miracles of the Exodus) it became clear that He created the world in six days and rested on the seventh. We, too, rest in recognition of His rest. This, then, is the connection between Shabbos and the Exodus.

This concept resolves many other difficulties. The Gemara says that a gentile who totally refrains from any *melachah* on Shabbos has transgressed a capital crime (*Sanhedrin* 58b). Before the Exodus from Egypt, there was no commandment to keep Shabbos, so this theoretically would apply to *anyone* who refrained from *melachah* on Shabbos; he was considered guilty of a capital crime. We ask, Why? If keeping Shabbos testifies to the Creation, what is wrong with keeping Shabbos?

According to our approach, however, the answer is clear. Before witnessing all the miracles in Egypt they could not yet fully comprehend the true essence of Shabbos, and thus they could not fulfill the mitzvah. This is similar to the Gemara's statement (*Yoma* 69a) that Yirmiyahu and Daniel could not use the words "powerful and awesome" regarding Hashem because they questioned where His

בְּחַרְתָּ וְאוֹתָנוּ קִדַּשְׁתָּ מִכָּל הָעַמִּים, [וְשַׁבָּת] וּמוֹעֲדֵי קָדְשֶׁךָ [בְּאַהֲבָה וּבְרָצוֹן] בְּשִׂמְחָה וּבְשָׂשׂוֹן הִנְחַלְתָּנוּ. בָּרוּךְ אַתָּה יהוה, מְקַדֵּשׁ [הַשַּׁבָּת וְ]יִשְׂרָאֵל וְהַזְּמַנִּים.

On Saturday night, add the following two paragraphs:

בָּרוּךְ אַתָּה יהוה אֱלֹהֵינוּ מֶלֶךְ הָעוֹלָם, בּוֹרֵא מְאוֹרֵי הָאֵשׁ.

בָּרוּךְ אַתָּה יהוה אֱלֹהֵינוּ מֶלֶךְ הָעוֹלָם, הַמַּבְדִּיל בֵּין קֹדֶשׁ לְחוֹל, בֵּין אוֹר לְחֹשֶׁךְ, בֵּין יִשְׂרָאֵל לָעַמִּים, בֵּין יוֹם הַשְּׁבִיעִי לְשֵׁשֶׁת יְמֵי הַמַּעֲשֶׂה. בֵּין קְדֻשַּׁת שַׁבָּת לִקְדֻשַּׁת יוֹם טוֹב הִבְדַּלְתָּ, וְאֶת יוֹם הַשְּׁבִיעִי מִשֵּׁשֶׁת יְמֵי הַמַּעֲשֶׂה קִדַּשְׁתָּ, הִבְדַּלְתָּ וְקִדַּשְׁתָּ אֶת עַמְּךָ יִשְׂרָאֵל בִּקְדֻשָּׁתֶךָ. בָּרוּךְ אַתָּה יהוה, הַמַּבְדִּיל בֵּין קֹדֶשׁ לְקֹדֶשׁ.

---

power and awesomeness were. They certainly must have *believed* that Hashem was powerful and awesome. Yet one cannot praise Hashem's essence, since no creature is capable of perceiving His essence. Rather, we can only praise the attributes reflected in the actions that we can perceive. Since they saw no sign of His power and awesomeness, they could not praise Him with those attributes. The same applies to keeping Shabbos. Even though they believed in Hashem as a Creator, and believed that He rested on the seventh day, they could still not keep Shabbos. Only after it was proved to them beyond the shadow of a doubt that all of Creation had a Creator could they keep Shabbos.

This also explains why the Shabbos before Pesach is called *Shabbos Hagadol* — the Great Shabbos. Only after seeing the miracles in Egypt could the Jewish people acquire the deep understanding of, and belief in, a Creator. Only then could they comprehend the *purpose* of keeping Shabbos. Thus, it was the miracles of Egypt that caused us to keep all the Shabbosos of the year, and were it not for those miracles we would not have merited the mitzvah of Shabbos at all.

This idea connects the end of the Torah to its beginning. The Torah

have chosen and sanctified us above all peoples, (and the Sabbath) and Your holy festivals (in love and favor), in gladness and joy have You granted us as a heritage. Blessed are You, HASHEM, Who sanctifies (the Sabbath,) Israel, and the festive seasons.

> On Saturday night, add the following two paragraphs:
>
> Blessed are You, HASHEM, our God, King of the universe, Who creates the illumination of the fire.
>
> Blessed are You, HASHEM, our God, King of the universe, Who distinguishes between sacred and secular, between light and darkness, between Israel and the nations, between the seventh day and the six days of activity. You have distinguished between the holiness of the Sabbath and the holiness of a Festival, and have sanctified the seventh day above the six days of activity. You distinguished and sanctified Your nation, Israel, with Your holiness. Blessed are You, HASHEM, Who distinguishes between holiness and holiness.

---

ends (*Devarim* 34:11-12), "All the signs and wonders that Hashem sent him to perform in the land of Egypt ... that Moshe performed before the eyes of all Israel." It begins (*Bereishis* 1:1), "In the beginning of God's creating the heavens and the earth ...." This hints that the purpose of all the signs and wonders was to reinforce the clear understanding that it was God Who created the heavens and the earth.

Furthermore, we can now explain why the month of Nisan is called *Rosh Chadashim,* the premier month, the month from which all other months are counted (see *Shemos* 12:2). The Gemara (*Rosh Hashanah* 10b) teaches us that even if we count the years of the world from the month of Tishrei (supporting the opinion that the world was created in Tishrei), nevertheless, we count the months from Nisan, as stated by the Torah. The reason for this is as explained above: The complete changing of the laws of nature which reached its crescendo in the month of Nisan was to teach *Bnei Yisrael* and their offspring forever after that the world was created by a Creator. It was this lesson that sanctified this month to be the premier month (cf. *Derashos HaRan*) (published in the magazine section of *Yated Ne'eman,* Pesach edition 5757).

On all nights conclude here:

בָּרוּךְ אַתָּה יהוה אֱלֹהֵינוּ מֶלֶךְ הָעוֹלָם, שֶׁהֶחֱיָנוּ וְקִיְּמָנוּ וְהִגִּיעָנוּ לַזְּמַן הַזֶּה.

The wine should be drunk without delay while reclining on the left side. It is preferable to drink the entire cup, but at the very least, most of the cup should be drained.

שֶׁהֶחֱיָנוּ וְקִיְּמָנוּ וְהִגִּיעָנוּ לַזְּמַן הַזֶּה
Who has kept us alive, sustained us, and brought us to this season

It is proper to ponder the exalted nature of this night. No other night can compare to this night. It is a "night [that] shines like the day" (*Tehillim* 139:12), "a night of anticipation" (*Shemos* 12:42) — a night which God awaits and a night which we await, a night anticipated in every generation. There are countless mitzvos fulfilled on this night. There are several Torah mitzvos, and many more rabbinic mitzvos. When we recite *Shehecheyanu*, we are thanking God for bringing us to this exalted time. Accordingly, one should have in mind all the Torah and rabbinic mitzvos fulfilled on this night: All the details of the Seder, the four cups, leaning, even eating *karpas* and dipping it; indeed, every movement performed on this night (from a lecture on the laws of Pesach given by Rav Shlomo Zalman in 1970).

☙ The Long Break Between Kiddush and the Meal

All year long, a person must eat his meal immediately after reciting *Kiddush* (see *Pesachim* 101a). Apparently, the same should apply to the night of the Seder. Nevertheless, it is virtually impossible to find a Seder today in which less than an hour or two pass between *Kiddush* and the meal. After all, we recite the Haggadah at length, and "he who tells more is praised." How do we ignore the requirement to serve the meal immediately after *Kiddush*?

The answer is that the purpose of the Seder night is to sanctify — *l'kadeish* (from the same root as *Kiddush*) — this night. From this perspective, reciting the Haggadah can be considered merely an extension of *Kiddush*. This is compared to one who recites *Kiddush* and, because he cleaves so devotedly to God, takes a while to wash for the meal. Then he recites the blessing of *Al netilas yadayim* slowly

On all nights conclude here:

Blessed are You, HASHEM, our God, King of the universe, Who has kept us alive, sustained us, and brought us to this season.

The wine should be drunk without delay while reclining on the left side. It is preferable to drink the entire cup, but at the very least, most of the cup should be drained.

---

and meticulously, followed by a recitation of *Mizmor l'David, Hashem ro'i lo echsar* with great devotion. A great deal of time may pass, and yet it is all one long chain of *l'kadeish,* sanctification.

Additionally, the entire order of Seder night is preparatory to the internalization and self-involvement which the Talmud requires: "In every generation a person must consider himself as if he personally had gone out of Egypt" (*Pesachim* 116b). He must recount the miracles and wonders that occurred *to him* on this night. Therefore the *Kiddush,* the Haggadah recitation, and the festive meal are all intertwined in the pursuit of this theme.

Finally, our Sages tell us that matzah is called *lechem oni — she'onim alav devarim harbeh,* a bread which facilitates much discussion, with questions and answers. Thus, we declare, "*Ha lachma anya*" ("This is the bread of affliction"), well before we eat it. This declaration emphasizes the connection between recounting the story of the Exodus and this "bread" which we eat: We must "discuss many things" (i.e., recount the story of the Exodus) before eating the matzah (see *Pesachim* 115b). Since reciting the section of *Maggid* is merely a preparation for eating the matzah, it is considered as if *Kiddush* was recited with the intention to eat immediately. Thus, far from being an interruption before the meal, the Haggadah is itself the preparation for, and the beginning of, the meal.

This also accounts for why *Al hagefen*, the blessing after wine, is not recited after *Kiddush,* despite the long break before the meal which would normally mandate reciting this blessing before seventy-two minutes pass (see *Shulchan Aruch, Orach Chaim* 184:5 and *Mishnah Berurah* ad loc.). Here, too, the meal actually begins after *Kiddush,* with the recitation of the Haggadah (from a lecture on the laws of Pesach given by Rav Shlomo Zalman in 1970, with additions as published in *Pa'amei Kol Torah*; see also *Minchas Shlomo* I, 18:10).

Furthermore, since all year long *Kiddush* is normally followed

וּרְחַץ

The head of the household — according to many opinions,
all participants in the Seder — washes his hands as if to eat bread
[pouring water from a cup, twice on the right hand and twice on the left],
but without reciting a blessing.

---

immediately by the meal, one generally does not recite *Al hagefen*. Accordingly, if one would recite this blessing specifically this night, it would seem as if he is cutting all ties to the meal, and that the *Kiddush* is indeed separate from the meal (responsum printed in *Kol Torah* journal, Nisan 5756).[1]

וּרְחַץ / *U'rechatz*

◈§ Why do we wash before eating karpas?

The *Shulchan Aruch* (*Orach Chaim* 158:4) rules that one must wash his hands not only before the eating of bread, but before the eating of any food that has been wetted by one of the "seven liquids" (water, wine, olive oil, etc.). However, since there are opinions that this washing is not applicable nowadays (see *Mishnah Berurah* 158:20), as in all cases of doubt in *berachos* a blessing is not recited.

The halachah to wash one's hands before eating wet food in general is not universally practiced, and *Magen Avraham* (158:8) defends those who are lax, although he does not condone it. [Rav Shlomo Zalman's grandson, Rav Aaron Goldberg, reports that his grandfather was among those who demonstrated some laxity in this halachah.] Indeed, it seems inconsistent to suddenly observe this halachah at the Seder, yet not observe it all year round (see *Taz* 473:6).

A justification might be that, according to some, only the leader washes his hands, when a pitcher of water is brought to him. Thus, this

---

1. His son, Rav Azriel Auerbach, however, is quoted as saying that Rav Shlomo Zalman always drank some wine before the end of the 72-minute period, and that in his last Seder he actually recited *Al hagefen*. It should be noted, however, that *Yom Tov Sheni K'hilchaso* cites Rav Shlomo Zalman as questioning whether it is appropriate to stop in the middle of reciting the Haggadah to taste anything. He writes that Rav Shlomo Zalman ruled that one who wishes to be stringent and taste additional wine, or *Karpas* (of which he would privately eat less than a *kezayis* in the middle of *Maggid* — *Haggadas Arzei Halevanon*), or anything else during the Haggadah recital, should do so privately, without publicizing that he is being stringent beyond the accepted norms.

U'RECHATZ

The head of the household — according to many opinions, all participants in the Seder — washes his hands as if to eat bread [pouring water from a cup, twice on the right hand and twice on the left], but without reciting a blessing.

washing may be seen as part of the regal deportment which is customary at the Seder and not necessarily a ritual requirement.

The preferred explanation (based on the writings of the *Rishonim*), is that *U'rechatz* is a function of the exalted nature of "this night." We were fortunate to become sanctified and purified on this night in which we left Egypt, when God redeemed us and we became "children to Hashem" (*Devarim* 14:1). Our new status demands that we be especially meticulous on this night about all areas of halachic observance. Accordingly, the washing of the hands before eating wetted food, although it may not be so carefully observed throughout the year, is practiced by all on this night (from a lecture on the laws of Pesach given By Rav Shlomo Zalman in 1970).

This is also why it is called *U'rechatz* (*and* wash). The "and" connects it to the preceding *Kaddesh*; i.e., we are stringent about washing the hands for wetted food, which continues the sanctification experienced during *Kaddesh*. Furthermore, this explains why here it is called *U'rechatz*, implying a command, whereas washing for the matzah is called *Rachtzah*, a more casual form. Only regarding washing over wetted food, about which so many are lax all year round, are we commanded, Wash! Washing over bread (or matzah), however, is practiced all year round, and accordingly, needs no special urgency (from an unpublished manuscript cited in the notes to the above-cited lecture published as *Kuntres Seder Pesach*, by *Kol Torah Yeshivah*).

ও§ *How much wetted food requires washing?*

This requirement to wash for a piece of *karpas* whose volume is smaller than a *kezayis* (i.e., less than the volume of half an egg) has ramifications that extend far beyond the Seder night. The *Mishnah Berurah* (158:20), in its first edition, states that there is no need to wash the hands on wetted foods whose volume is less than a *kezayis*. The logic is as follows: After eating a minimum of a *kezayis* of bread, one is required to recite the *Bircas Hamazon*. However, the obligation

כַּרְפַּס

All participants take a vegetable other than *maror* and dip it into salt water. A piece smaller in volume than half an egg should be used. The following blessing is recited [with the intention that it also applies to the *maror* which will be eaten during the meal] before the vegetable is eaten.

בָּרוּךְ אַתָּה יהוה אֱלֹהֵינוּ מֶלֶךְ הָעוֹלָם, בּוֹרֵא פְּרִי הָאֲדָמָה.

to wash and recite the blessing *al netilas yadayim* applies only to a minimum of a double *kezayis* (the volume of an egg). When eating only a *kezayis*, though the accepted ruling is to wash without a blessing, many authorities say there is no obligation to wash at all. Now, although the later authorities rule that one should be stringent and wash his hands before eating wetted food, there is no basis to adopt this stringency when eating less than a *kezayis* of wetted food, since even for bread it is far from clear that washing is required for less than a *kezayis*. In later editions of the *Mishnah Berurah*, however, a note is made that retracts this position, with a reference to the laws of washing before *karpas*. He reasons that one who washes before wetted foods, itself a stringency, should be consistent and also be stringent for less than a *kezayis*.

This has ramifications as well for those who are normally not stringent about washing before wetted foods. The *Shulchan Aruch* (603:1) rules that during the *Aseres Yemei Teshuvah* (the ten days from Rosh Hashanah through Yom Kippur) it is appropriate to conduct oneself with greater stringency than the rest of the year. Accordingly, it is appropriate for those who are not stringent about washing for wetted foods all year round to be stringent during the *Aseres Yemei Teshuvah* and, based on this correction of the *Mishnah Berurah*, to be strict on less than a *kezayis* as well (from a lecture on the laws of Pesach given by Rav Shlomo Zalman in 1970).

כַּרְפַּס / Karpas

◆§ **When reciting the blessing for karpas, why should one have the intention that it apply also for maror?**

Mishnah Berurah (473:20) writes that when reciting *Borei pri*

KARPAS

All participants take a vegetable other than *maror* and dip it into salt water. A piece smaller in volume than half an egg should be used. The following blessing is recited [with the intention that it also applies to the *maror* which will be eaten during the meal] before the vegetable is eaten.

Blessed are You, HASHEM, our God, King of the universe, Who creates the fruits of the earth.

---

ha'adamah over the *karpas* one should have the intention that it apply to the *maror* as well. Apparently, the basis for this requirement is as follows: Just as performing the mitzvah of eating matzah requires a special blessing of *Al achilas matzah* and the ordinary blessing of *Hamotzi,* so too, the mitzvah of eating *maror* requires a special blessing of *Al achilas maror* and the ordinary blessing of *Ha'adamah*. However, a person is not required to recite a new *Ha'adamah* blessing for each vegetable that he eats. Simply, he should have the *maror* in mind when reciting the *Ha'adamah* blessing over the *karpas*.

The question arises, however, why this is any different from the four cups of wine. Ashkenazi Jews recite a separate blessing for each cup on the presumption that each one is a separate mitzvah (see *Rema* 474:1, and *Mishnah Berurah* ad loc. 4). Why, then, should the *maror* and the *karpas* be any different? Each one is a separate mitzvah, and thus, a separate *borei pri ha'adamah* should be required for each. Furthermore, whereas the mitzvah of *maror* is mentioned in the Torah (*Bamidbar* 9:11), the mitzvah of *karpas* is rabbinic. Accordingly, the greater importance of *maror* should certainly require its own blessing![1] (from a lecture on the laws of Pesach given by Rav Shlomo Zalman Auerbach in 1970).

---

1. A possible answer to this question can be suggested from what Rav Shlomo Zalman wrote in *Minchas Shlomo* I:18, where he differentiates between the blessing on wine and the blessings on other foods. Whereas the blessings on other foods are for the pleasure of consuming the food, the blessing on wine is that and more. In the blessing on wine we also thank God for making wine available for us to use to fulfill mitzvos. Accordingly, one who dislikes wine and finds no pleasure in it would still recite the *Borei pri hagafen* blessing when reciting *Kiddush* or *Havdalah*. Thus, the blessing can be recited for each cup individually, because each one is its own mitzvah, while for other foods, such as *maror* and *karpas*, it would be preferable to recite only one blessing.

יַחַץ

The head of the household breaks the middle matzah in two. He puts the smaller part back between the two whole matzos, and wraps up the larger part for later use as the *afikoman*. Some briefly place the *afikoman* portion on their shoulders, in accordance with the Biblical verse recounting that Israel left Egypt carrying their matzos on their shoulders, and say בְּבֶהָלוּ יָצָאנוּ מִמִּצְרַיִם, "In haste we went out of Egypt."

מַגִּיד

Some recite the following before *Maggid*:

הִנְנִי מוּכָן וּמְזוּמָן לְקַיֵּם הַמִּצְוָה לְסַפֵּר בִּיצִיאַת מִצְרַיִם. לְשֵׁם יִחוּד קֻדְשָׁא בְּרִיךְ הוּא וּשְׁכִינְתֵּיהּ, עַל יְדֵי הַהוּא טָמִיר וְנֶעְלָם, בְּשֵׁם כָּל יִשְׂרָאֵל. וִיהִי נֹעַם אֲדֹנָי אֱלֹהֵינוּ עָלֵינוּ, וּמַעֲשֵׂה יָדֵינוּ כּוֹנְנָה עָלֵינוּ, וּמַעֲשֵׂה יָדֵינוּ כּוֹנְנֵהוּ:

יַחַץ / Yachatz

◆§ Why don't we break the matzah closer to the time it is eaten?

The matzah is broken early in the Seder because of the dual nature of *"lechem oni."* The Torah (*Devarim* 16:3) refers to matzah as *"lechem oni,"* bread of poverty, to teach us that "just as a poor man usually eats only broken pieces of bread (because he cannot afford a complete loaf), so too, the matzah we eat on Pesach night should be broken" (*Pesachim* 116a).

Another interpretation of *lechem oni* is given by the Gemara (ibid.). According to that understanding, *oni* is related to the root *anah*, to recite. Matzah is "bread over which many words are recited." The story of the Exodus, which is elaborated on during the course of the Haggadah, takes place around the matzah, which is prominently displayed on the Seder table.

In order to fulfill both interpretations of *lechem oni* at the same time, the matzah is broken, thus transformed into "bread of poverty," before the start of the recitation of the Haggadah, when the matzah becomes the "bread over which many words are recited" [See our discussion following *Kiddush* above, s.v. The Long Break ... for a different perspective on this issue] (from a lecture on the laws of Pesach given by Rav Shlomo Zalman Auerbach in 1970).

YACHATZ

The head of the household breaks the middle matzah in two. He puts the smaller part back between the two whole matzos, and wraps up the larger part for later use as the *afikoman*. Some briefly place the *afikoman* portion on their shoulders, in accordance with the Biblical verse recounting that Israel left Egypt carrying their matzos on their shoulders, and say בְּבְהִלוּ יָצְאנוּ מִמִּצְרָיִם, *"In haste we went out of Egypt."*

MAGGID

Some recite the following before *Maggid*:

Behold, I am prepared and ready to fulfill the mitzvah of telling of the Exodus from Egypt. For the sake of the unification of the Holy One, Blessed is He, and His presence, through Him Who is hidden and inscrutable – [I pray] in the name of all Israel. May the pleasantness of my Lord, our God, be upon us – may He establish our handiwork for us; our handiwork may He establish.

מַגִּיד / Maggid

◆§ **Why is no blessing recited for fulfilling the mitzvah of recounting the Exodus?**

The Torah commands us to "recall the day you went out of Egypt" (*Devarim* 16:3), specifically on the night of the fifteenth of Nisan (*Rambam, Hil. Chametz U'matzah* 7:1). The question therefore arises: Why do we not recite a blessing over this mitzvah, much as we recite blessings over the mitzvos of eating matzah and *maror*? The *Rishonim* answer that we have already fulfilled this mitzvah when reciting in *Kiddush,* "in commemoration of the Exodus from Egypt"; thus it is too late to recite a blessing here (Rabbeinu Yerucham, *Nesiv* 5:4, citing Rabbeinu Peretz; *Avudraham* citing Rif).

This answer requires further clarification. It has been said that there are two separate mitzvos: *Zechirah,* Mentioning the Exodus, which applies each and every day and night, and *Sippur,* telling the story of the Exodus on the Seder night. See, e.g., *Haggadah of the Roshei Yeshivah* (Book Two) p. 66. Accordingly, perhaps by reciting, "in commemoration of the Exodus from Egypt," one fulfills the obligation of mentioning, but certainly not the obligation of telling.

We preface our answer with some general information concerning the mitzvah of mentioning the Exodus all year round, and *sippur,* the

[At Rav Shlomo Zalman's Seder, the second cup was now poured. Before reciting הָא לַחְמָא עַנְיָא, Rav Shlomo Zalman would say: בִּבְהִלוּ יָצָאנוּ מִמִּצְרַיִם.] The broken matzah is lifted for all to see as the head of the household begins with the following brief explanation of the proceedings.

הָא לַחְמָא עַנְיָא דִי אֲכָלוּ אַבְהָתָנָא בְּאַרְעָא

unique mitzvah of this night. The Halachah accords with R' Elazar ben Azaryah that there is an obligation to mention the Exodus each and every day and night. The essence of this mitzvah is to say, "He has taken us out of Egypt." We fulfill this mitzvah in the morning prayers when we say the third paragraph of *Shema, Vayomer Hashem el Moshe . . .,* followed by *Emes v'yatziv,* and in evening prayers when we say the third paragraph of *Shema* followed by *Emes v'emunah.*

According to the *Tur (Orach Chaim* 66, citing *Yerushalmi;* see *Mishnah Berurah* 66:53), one must also mention "splitting the Sea of Reeds" and "the plague of the firstborn." It is important to know that a person must mention all three each day and night — and, each time, have the intention to fulfill the mitzvah. Each morning, before reciting the *Shemoneh Esrei,* we say, "From Egypt You redeemed us, Hashem, our God, and from the house of slavery You liberated us. All their first-born You slew... the Sea of Reeds You split." Similarly, each night we say (in a different order), "Who struck with His anger all the firstborn of Egypt and removed His nation from their midst to eternal freedom; Who brought His children through the split part of the Sea of Reeds."

That is the daily requirement of *zechirah.* There is a separate mitzvah that applies to the night of the fifteenth of Nisan only, the mitzvah to tell the story of the Exodus. The essence of this mitzvah is expressed by Rabban Gamliel below: "Whoever has not explained the following three things on Pesach has not fulfilled his duty, namely: PESACH — the *pesach* sacrifice; MATZAH — the unleavened bread; MAROR — the bitter herbs." The requirement is to *explain;* to elaborate on the details of this night. First we explain the *pesach* sacrifice, "Why did our fathers eat a *pesach* offering during the period when the Temple stood? Because the Holy One, Blessed is He, passed over the houses of our fathers in Egypt." Then we elaborate on the matzah: "Because the dough of our fathers did not have time to become leavened." Lastly, we speak about *maror,* and continue explaining and illustrating to the best of our ability. All year long, the requirement is merely to "mention"; on the night of Pesach, however, the obligation is to explain and elaborate. Indeed, if one does not "tell the tale," he does not fulfill the mitzvah.

True, in this teaching of Rabban Gamliel the phrase "has not fulfilled

[At Rav Shlomo Zalman's Seder, the second cup was poured.
Before reciting *This is the bread of affliction* . .
., Rav Shlomo Zalman would say, *In haste we went out of Egypt*.]
The broken matzah is lifted for all to see as the head of the household
begins with the following brief explanation of the proceedings.

This is the bread of affliction that our fathers ate in

---

his duty" is generally explained as not fulfilling his duty *in the ideal sense*, yet the mitzvah is indeed fulfilled in a lesser sense. That, however, applies only to these three fundamental elements. The essence of the requirement of *sippur*, however, is to explain and elaborate by means of questions and answers, and even if there is no one of whom to ask questions, one must explain and elaborate to oneself.

Now that we have explained the basic difference between the two mitzvos, the question stands out even more sharply: How is it possible to do, as the above-cited *Rishonim* say, that one fulfills the mitzvah of *sippur* through mentioning the Exodus in *Kiddush* or in the evening prayers?

We will attempt to answer the question of why no blessing is recited on the mitzvah of *sippur* through a new understanding of the two mitzvos. First, the reason why no blessing is recited for the general mitzvah of mentioning the Exodus is that it is impossible. As soon as one recites the blessing, saying, "...Who has sanctified us with His commandments and commanded us to mention the Exodus from Egypt," he has mentioned the Exodus and has already fulfilled the mitzvah! As for the mitzvah of *sippur*, it is not truly an independent mitzvah. Rather, it is a *continuation* of the mitzvah of *zechirah*, mentioning the Exodus. The mitzvah to "recall the day you went out of Egypt" is a foundation stone of the Torah. This is what the Holy One, Blessed is He, commands us: On the fifteenth of Nisan one must tell the story of the Exodus, and the rest of the year there is a daily and nightly obligation. On the night of Pesach one must explain and elaborate until everything that transpired is made clear, whereas the rest of the year, each morning and night, there is only a need to briefly review. Since, however, they are both essentially one mitzvah, and there can be no blessing recited on the mitzvah all year round, no blessing is recited for the mitzvah of *sippur* on the Seder night either (from a lecture on the laws of Pesach given by Rav Shlomo Zalman in 1970).

⏵ *Why are the matzos sometimes covered and sometimes uncovered?*

It is important to study in preparation of the Seder and not to

דְמִצְרָיִם. כָּל דִכְפִין יֵיתֵי וְיֵכוֹל, כָּל דִצְרִיךְ יֵיתֵי וְיִפְסַח. הָשַׁתָּא הָכָא, לְשָׁנָה הַבָּאָה בְּאַרְעָא דְיִשְׂרָאֵל. הָשַׁתָּא עַבְדֵי, לְשָׁנָה הַבָּאָה בְּנֵי חוֹרִין.

The Seder plate is removed and the second of the four cups of wine is poured. [Rav Shlomo Zalman would not remove the the Seder plate, he would only cover the matzos. As noted, the wine for the second cup was poured before הָא לַחְמָא עַנְיָא was recited.]

The youngest present asks the reasons for the unusual proceedings of the evening. [At Rav Shlomo Zalman's Seder, each child would individually ask the Four Questions, then everyone would recite them as a group.]

מַה נִּשְׁתַּנָּה הַלַּיְלָה הַזֶּה מִכָּל הַלֵּילוֹת?
שֶׁבְּכָל הַלֵּילוֹת אָנוּ אוֹכְלִין חָמֵץ וּמַצָּה, הַלַּיְלָה הַזֶּה – כֻּלּוֹ מַצָּה.

---

stumble blindly through the Haggadah. For example, here the Haggadah says to uncover the matzos, so people uncover them; elsewhere the Haggadah says to cover them, and people cover them — but the need to understand never crosses their mind. Only one who studies the laws understands that the matzos, in their role as "bread over which many words are recited" [see the discussion at *Yachatz,* p. 120] should actually be uncovered for the entire recital of *Maggid.*

There are two exceptions to this rule. The first is when we make *Kiddush.* Just as we generally cover the challos when we recite *Kiddush* so as not to "shame" the challos, so too tonight; rather than shame the matzah when holding the wine, we cover it [since the challos or matzos are seemingly overlooked by making *Kiddush* first, as the blessing *Hamotzi* generally takes precedence over the blessing *Hagafen*]. When *Kiddush* is over, however, we revert to the natural atmosphere for reciting the Haggadah — with uncovered matzos.

The second exception is based on the requirement stated in the Gemara (*Pesachim* 116b) to "remove the table" to stimulate the children to ask why it is being removed before eating. This was relevant in earlier times, when people ate on individual small tables

the land of Egypt. Whoever is hungry, let him come and eat; whoever is in need, let him come and partake of the *pesach*. Now, we are here; next year may we be in the Land of Israel! Now, we are slaves; next year may we be free men!

<small>The Seder plate is removed and the second of the four cups of wine is poured. [Rav Shlomo Zalman would not remove the the Seder plate, he would only cover the matzos. As noted, the wine for the second cup was poured before *This is the bread of affliction* . . . was recited.]
The youngest present asks the reasons for the unusual proceedings of the evening. [At Rav Shlomo Zalman's Seder, each child would individually ask the Four Questions, then everyone would recite them as a group.]</small>

Why is this night different from all other nights?

1. For on all other nights we may eat *chametz* and matzah, but on this night – only matzah.

(and perhaps today for anyone who eats that way). Today, we stimulate the children's curiosity by covering the matzos. Why are the matzos being covered when just a bit earlier the matzah was broken in two, as if to eat? Thus, the matzos are uncovered for the duration of *Maggid* except when holding the wine cup or when, in Talmudic times, "the table" would have been removed (cited by Rav Shlomo Zalman's son, Rav Azriel Auerbach).

כָּל דִכְפִין יֵיתֵי וְיֵכוֹל
Whoever is hungry, let him come and eat

A *chagigah* sacrifice would accompany the *pesach* sacrifice, so that one would feel satiated before eating the *pesach* offering. One who was already satiated, however, did not eat from the *chagigah*, but instead proceeded directly to eat the *pesach* sacrifice. The Haggadah comes to teach us how it will be in the future, when the Temple is rebuilt and sacrifices will once again be offered: *Whoever is hungry, let him come and eat* from the *chagigah* and other foods, and only *whoever is in need* — i.e., who is neither hungry nor full — *let him come and partake of the pesach*, eating a *kezayis*-size piece when satiated (Rav Shlomo Zalman Auerbach, citing *Rash* of Amsterdam, as recorded by Rav Shlomo Zalman's grandson, Rav Aharon Goldberg).

שֶׁבְּכָל הַלֵּילוֹת אָנוּ אוֹכְלִין שְׁאָר יְרָקוֹת, הַלַּיְלָה הַזֶּה – מָרוֹר.

שֶׁבְּכָל הַלֵּילוֹת אֵין אָנוּ מַטְבִּילִין אֲפִילוּ פַּעַם אֶחָת, הַלַּיְלָה הַזֶּה – שְׁתֵּי פְעָמִים.

שֶׁבְּכָל הַלֵּילוֹת אָנוּ אוֹכְלִין בֵּין יוֹשְׁבִין וּבֵין מְסֻבִּין, הַלַּיְלָה הַזֶּה – כֻּלָּנוּ מְסֻבִּין.

הַלַּיְלָה הַזֶּה – שְׁתֵּי פְעָמִים
But on this night — twice

How can a child ask about dipping twice? At this point in the Seder, he has only seen the *karpas* dipped into salt water, and has yet to see the *maror* either eaten or dipped. The answer must be that when a child sees *maror* and *charoses* on the Seder plate, which was placed on the table at the beginning of the night, it stands to reason that he would ask his father what they are. His father replies that the *maror* is dipped into the *charoses*. When the son then sees the *karpas* dipped into salt water, he asks his father why on this night we dip twice. This is a fulfillment of the mitzvah of "And you shall tell your son on that day...."

A basic requirement of the Seder is to make many changes and signs to pique the children's curiosity. Not only does this insure that they remain awake, but it also serves to make them ask questions — which promotes the father's answers. Thus, telling the story of the Exodus takes on a question and answer format. This is a superb pedagogical method which insures that the lesson will enter the child's heart and be remembered forever (from a lecture on the laws of Pesach given by Rav Shlomo Zalman in 1970, published in *Kuntres Seder Pesach*).

⊱ Concerning the requirement to lean

The reason for the Talmudic requirement to lean on the left side is that, in those days, wealthy and important people always ate while leaning on their left side. In our days, however, even the wealthiest and most important people no longer eat in this way. As a rule, however, anything the Sages institute is not for us to cancel, and therefore the practice should be continued. Furthermore, this presents an opportunity for the child to ask his father, "Why is this night different," and allows the father to answer that we lean as an expression of freedom.

2. For on all other nights we eat many vegetables, but on this night – we eat *maror*.

3. For on all other nights we do not dip even once, but on this night – twice.

4. For on all other nights we eat either sitting or reclining, but on this night – we all recline.

Although the requirement of leaning still applies, there are certain circumstances in which we are lenient, as ruled by the *Shulchan Aruch* and *Rema*. For example, *Rema* (472:4) states that "our women ... do not customarily lean." To explain: The Gemara (*Pesachim* 107a) rules that a woman who is so subservient to her husband that she is like his maid should not lean, but women who have importance in their own right are obligated to lean. Now, it is well known that our women have been considered for many generations to be "women of importance" — no woman is her husband's maid! Nevertheless, they customarily do not lean because they rely on the view of Ravyah, that in our days there is no obligation to lean.

This view raises two fundamental questions. First, according to Ravyah, now neither men nor women have an obligation to lean, since it is no longer considered "a manner of freedom." Yet only women rely on this view and not men. Why is this so? Furthermore, all the other early authorities dispute Ravyah and require leaning even for those who are uncomfortable with leaning (most of us are indeed less comfortable that way). In their view, a law instituted by the Rabbis cannot be canceled, as mentioned above. We ask: Since women are equally obligated in the mitzvos of the Seder night (matzah, *maror*, etc.), for they were equally included in the miraculous redemption, why should they rely on a lenient opinion regarding leaning, while men cannot?

The answer is that, today, there should be no obligation for anyone to lean, since it serves no function. Nevertheless, we refrain from canceling a custom instituted by the Sages. Regarding women, however, there was *never* a universal custom to lean, as mentioned above; only "women of importance" leaned. Thus, we can revert to the basic law, according to which leaning is not necessary in our times[1] (from a lecture on the laws of Pesach given by Rav Shlomo Zalman in 1970, published in *Kuntres Seder Pesach*).

Rav Shlomo Zalman himself would use a special armchair for that

---

1. He concluded: "This is the real truth in explaining the matter."

The Seder plate is returned. The matzos are kept uncovered as the Haggadah is recited in unison. The Haggadah should be translated if necessary, and the story of the Exodus should be amplified upon.

עֲבָדִים הָיִינוּ לְפַרְעֹה בְּמִצְרָיִם, וַיּוֹצִיאֵנוּ יהוה אֱלֹהֵינוּ מִשָּׁם בְּיָד חֲזָקָה

---

night with a pillow placed on the left arm. He would lean slightly to the left onto the pillow (Torah section of the Hebrew *Yated Ne'eman*, *Parashas Metzora* 5763).

עֲבָדִים הָיִינוּ לְפַרְעֹה בְּמִצְרָיִם
We were slaves to Pharaoh in Egypt

First we were slaves to Pharaoh in Egypt, and then Hashem took us from there to be subservient to Him; going out from Egypt forces us to be subservient to Hashem.

Even more fundamentally, at the Exodus, Hashem appeared personally before all the Children of Israel, so that even the most lowly of slaves saw a more direct vision of Godliness than Yechezkel saw in his vision of the Divine Chariot (*Yechezkel* 1). Indeed, each and every one of them pointed at Him and said (*Shemos* 15:2): "This is my God and I will beautify Him." This revelation was so complete that, for all time, it gave the Jewish Nation the strength to resist any prophet who comes — even bearing "signs" and miracles — intending to tear them away from their belief in God. The paradox was that although the people were not worthy, Hashem nevertheless revealed Himself to them and changed the course of nature to show His greatness. As explained, this set the underlying foundation for their keeping the Torah and cleaving to Him, and, for this reason, the Torah speaks so much of commemorating the Exodus from Egypt.

And yet, it is important to recognize that Hashem has no interest in changing the course of nature (see *Shabbos* 53b: "How inferior this man was, for the natural order was changed on his behalf." Also see ibid., 118b). Indeed, "all the works of Creation were created according to the form they desired" (*Chullin* 60a), with no intention to change them. Even when the Holy One, Blessed is He, changed the form of the moon, the Gemara (*Shevuos* 9a) tells us that He said, "Bring a sacrifice to atone for Me, for I have diminished the moon." All this is because the world was created as a perfect entity, there was no element of evil or damage in God's creation of the world. Accordingly,

The Seder plate is returned. The matzos are kept uncovered as the Haggadah is recited in unison. The Haggadah should be translated if necessary, and the story of the Exodus should be amplified upon.

We were slaves to Pharaoh in Egypt, but HASHEM our God took us out from there with a mighty hand

He does not want any fundamental changes in the natural order.

In this vein, *Koheles* (3:14) says: "I realized that whatever *Elokim* does will last forever." *Koheles* referred to God with this name, because, numerically, *Elokim* equals *teva,* nature. Nothing can be added to His world and nothing can be subtracted from it; God has acted so that [man] should stand in awe of Him" (see Rashi ad loc. who cites several examples).

Accordingly, even when Hashem changed the natural order for the sake of the Exodus, it was only to show His greatness, so that we would learn to stand in awe of Him. This is why *Maharal* (*Gevuros Hashem* 2) writes that the requirement to retell the Exodus is fulfilled only by delving into the wonders of Hashem. It is only the deeper understanding of those wonders which brings about the awe of Hashem, which is the purpose of all Creation (from an unpublished manuscript presented by his grandson, Rav Aharon Goldberg).

The answer to the Mah Nishtanah

The son asked his father four questions, including, "On all other nights we do not dip even once, but on this night — twice." The father apparently answers all four questions with the all-purpose answer: "*Avadim hayinu l'Faroh b'Mitzrayim* — We were slaves to Pharaoh in Egypt," and Hashem took us out. The son's curiosity may still be unsatisfied. How does this answer why we dip twice? Because we were slaves we have to dip twice!

Actually, the main requirement is for the father to answer and to explain each of the four questions of the *Mah Nishtanah*. By answering the four questions with only a general, superficial answer like, "We were slaves to Pharaoh in Egypt and Hashem took us out," he obviously has not fulfilled his mitzvah of "and you shall tell your son on that day. . . ." Superficial answers will not penetrate, and if they do, they will be quickly forgotten. Rather, the obligation is to use a question and answer format, and to make the answer as concrete as possible.

Accordingly, one makes many changes on this night. These changes lead to questions, and then the questions are answered properly: "Why do we eat matzah? Because Hashem took us out of

וּבִזְרוֹעַ נְטוּיָה. וְאִלּוּ לֹא הוֹצִיא הַקָּדוֹשׁ בָּרוּךְ הוּא אֶת אֲבוֹתֵינוּ מִמִּצְרַיִם, הֲרֵי אָנוּ וּבָנֵינוּ וּבְנֵי בָנֵינוּ מְשֻׁעְבָּדִים הָיִינוּ לְפַרְעֹה בְּמִצְרָיִם. וַאֲפִילוּ כֻּלָּנוּ חֲכָמִים, כֻּלָּנוּ נְבוֹנִים, כֻּלָּנוּ זְקֵנִים, כֻּלָּנוּ יוֹדְעִים אֶת הַתּוֹרָה, מִצְוָה עָלֵינוּ לְסַפֵּר בִּיצִיאַת מִצְרָיִם. וְכָל הַמַּרְבֶּה לְסַפֵּר בִּיצִיאַת מִצְרַיִם, הֲרֵי זֶה מְשֻׁבָּח.

מַעֲשֶׂה בְּרַבִּי אֱלִיעֶזֶר וְרַבִּי יְהוֹשֻׁעַ וְרַבִּי אֶלְעָזָר בֶּן עֲזַרְיָה וְרַבִּי עֲקִיבָא וְרַבִּי טַרְפוֹן שֶׁהָיוּ מְסֻבִּין בִּבְנֵי בְרַק, וְהָיוּ מְסַפְּרִים בִּיצִיאַת מִצְרַיִם כָּל אוֹתוֹ הַלַּיְלָה.

Egypt in great haste and the dough was not allowed to rise into bread. Why do we eat *maror*? Because *maror* means bitter, and the Egyptians embittered our lives. Why do we lean? We lean to show that we are free men. Ah! You ask why we dip twice? Now that's a good question, a question which the Gemara (*Pesachim* 110b) itself asks, and there are two reasons. The first, as the Gemara there explains, is so that you, my son, should notice the change and ask about the changes made on this night. Then, to answer your question, I will be able to explain the Exodus from Egypt. In addition, dipping exemplifies freedom and wealth; a poor man eats his bread and has nothing in which to dip it, whereas a wealthy man is served meat and all sorts of delicacies accompanied by an array of sauces and dips.

"As to why we dip the *maror* in *charoses,* in addition to the deep secrets involved, there are simple answers as well: It nullifies the poison of the *maror,* and the consistency of the *charoses* is reminiscent of the mortar with which they used to build." All this can be found in the last chapter of Gemara *Pesachim* (from a lecture on the laws of Pesach given by Rav Shlomo Zalman in 1970).

וְהָיוּ מְסַפְּרִים בִּיצִיאַת מִצְרַיִם כָּל אוֹתוֹ הַלַּיְלָה
They discussed the Exodus from Egypt all that night

According to Maharal, one does not fulfill the mitzvah of telling the

and an outstretched arm. Had not the Holy One, Blessed is He, taken our fathers out from Egypt, then we, our children, and our children's children would have remained subservient to Pharaoh in Egypt. Even if all of us were wise, all of us understanding, all of us old, all of us knowledgeable in the Torah – it would be an obligation upon us to tell the story about the Exodus from Egypt. The more one expands upon the discussion of the Exodus, the more he is praiseworthy.

It happened that Rabbi Eliezer, Rabbi Yehoshua, Rabbi Elazar ben Azaryah, Rabbi Akiva, and Rabbi Tarfon were gathered (at the Seder) in Bnei Brak. They discussed the Exodus from Egypt all that night

---

story of the Exodus (see above, end of s.v. *Avadim hayinu...*) by merely reading the Haggadah. Rather, in each generation, one must delve deeply into the wondrous things that Hashem did for us at that particular time in our history.

Hashem took us out of Egypt "to eternal freedom" (from the daily *Ma'ariv* prayers). This is true despite the Gemara's statement (*Megillah* 14a) that "We are still enslaved to Achashverosh" (i.e., we are still not free to do as we please with no concern for the reaction of the world powers). The main redemption from Egypt was a spiritual redemption; at first we were Pharaoh's slaves — even our spirit was enslaved to him — then we left Egypt for eternal freedom to be the servants of Hashem, with our spirits subservient only to His Torah and His service. Accordingly, we will soon say in the Haggadah, "Had He given us the Torah, but not brought us into the Land of Israel, it would have sufficed us." For only the Torah gives us our power, regardless of whether we are physically free as well.

This is also how we should understand the verse (*Shemos* 1:14): "They embittered their lives." The Egyptians, through enslaving the Jews, embittered the very essence of their lives — the Torah and mitzvos, of which it is said, "For they are our life and the length of our days" (from the daily *Ma'ariv* prayers). It was from this form of enslavement that they were taken out to eternal freedom: to be sanctified and exalted above all other nations by becoming the servants of Hashem; to become His chosen people, a kingdom of *Kohanim,* and a holy nation.

עַד שֶׁבָּאוּ תַלְמִידֵיהֶם וְאָמְרוּ לָהֶם, רַבּוֹתֵינוּ הִגִּיעַ זְמַן קְרִיאַת שְׁמַע שֶׁל שַׁחֲרִית.

אָמַר רַבִּי אֶלְעָזָר בֶּן עֲזַרְיָה, הֲרֵי אֲנִי כְּבֶן שִׁבְעִים שָׁנָה, וְלֹא זָכִיתִי שֶׁתֵּאָמֵר יְצִיאַת מִצְרַיִם בַּלֵּילוֹת, עַד שֶׁדְּרָשָׁהּ בֶּן זוֹמָא, שֶׁנֶּאֱמַר, לְמַעַן תִּזְכֹּר אֶת יוֹם צֵאתְךָ מֵאֶרֶץ מִצְרַיִם כֹּל יְמֵי חַיֶּיךָ.[1] יְמֵי חַיֶּיךָ הַיָּמִים, כֹּל יְמֵי חַיֶּיךָ הַלֵּילוֹת. וַחֲכָמִים

If only a person would realize how much more holy the Jewish People are than the other nations, it would be impossible to sin. As it is written in Kabbalistic works, if not for the sin of Adam the idolaters would have the appearance of animals, and this will indeed be the case after the final redemption. For it is only sin that blurs the difference in appearance between Jews and idolaters. As a result, one needs great powers of discernment to grasp the difference, and thus it is easy to sin.

The main distinction of the Jewish People is that the Holy One, Blessed is He, is with them everywhere, even in their greatest misfortunes. Thus, Hashem said to Yaakov as he descended to Egypt (*Bereishis* 46:4): "I shall descend with you to Egypt and I shall surely bring you up." Similarly, the verse says (*Tehillim* 46:8): "Hashem, Master of Legions, is with us, a stronghold for us is the God of Yaakov, Selah."

This idea is further developed by *Yalkut Shimoni* (*I Shmuel,* 117 and *Tehillim* 850): One verse (*I Shmuel* 12:22) says: "For Hashem shall not forsake His people for the sake of His great Name," and a second verse (*Tehillim* 94:14) says, "For Hashem will not cast off His people, nor will He forsake His heritage." The two verses indicate that, although His people do not have their own merit, Hashem will not forsake them because they are His people, His heritage, and for the sake of His great Name. One who ponders all this will draw closer to the Holy One, Blessed is He; he will cleave to His Torah and distance himself from sin (from an unpublished manuscript presented by his grandson, Rav Aharon Goldberg).

until their students came and said to them: "Our teachers, the time has come for the reading of the morning *Shema*."

Rabbi Elazar ben Azaryah said: I am like a seventy-year-old man, but I could not succeed in having the Exodus from Egypt mentioned every night, until Ben Zoma expounded it, as it says: "In order that you may remember the day you left Egypt all the days of your life."[1] The phrase "the days of your life" indicates only the days; the addition of the word "all" includes the nights as well. But the [other] Sages

(1) *Devarim* 16:3.

יְמֵי חַיֶּיךָ הַיָּמִים, כֹּל יְמֵי חַיֶּיךָ הַלֵּילוֹת
The phrase "the days of your life" indicates only the days; the addition of the word "all" includes the nights as well.

Sha'agas Aryeh (12) asks why women are not obligated in the mitzvah of *Zechiras Yetzias Mitzrayim*, mentioning the Exodus each morning and night. *Rambam* (*Hil. Krias Shema* 1:3) rules that, after all, the obligation extends to both morning and night (see the discussion above, as to why no blessing is recited when recounting the Exodus), and thus it is apparently a mitzvah that is not time-bound, and women should be obligated as well. He answers that there are two separate obligations: one that applies only to the day and a second that applies only to the evening. Accordingly, if one forgot to mention the Exodus by day he cannot compensate by reciting it that night, since the mentioning of it at night is a separate obligation. This identification of two separate mitzvos also results in identifying *each* one as a time-bound mitzvah, and thus women are not obligated.

This answer is difficult to accept. The division of the mitzvah into night and day obligations does not make them two separate obligations, much as the obligation to recite *Shema* is seemingly divided, "When you lie down and when you rise" (*Devarim* 6:7), and yet considered by Rambam (Introduction to *Hilchos Krias Shema*) to be one mitzvah. Accordingly, it remains unclear why women do not mention the Exodus both morning and evening (*Haggadas Arzei Halevanon*, p. 70).

אוֹמְרִים, יְמֵי חַיֶּיךָ הָעוֹלָם הַזֶּה, כֹּל יְמֵי חַיֶּיךָ לְהָבִיא לִימוֹת הַמָּשִׁיחַ.

בָּרוּךְ הַמָּקוֹם, בָּרוּךְ הוּא. בָּרוּךְ שֶׁנָּתַן תּוֹרָה לְעַמּוֹ יִשְׂרָאֵל, בָּרוּךְ הוּא. כְּנֶגֶד

לְהָבִיא לִימוֹת הַמָּשִׁיחַ
Includes the days of Mashiach

Regarding the mitzvah to remember the Exodus from Egypt, it says, "'kol yemei chayecha' — haleilos," which literally means: All the days of your life — the nights. In other words, this verse teaches that the nights are included in the requirement of *zechiras yetzias Mitzrayim*. The lesson is taught in a somewhat cryptic manner. However, regarding the days of *Mashiach* it says, "'kol yemei chayecha' **l'havi liyemos haMashiach**," which means: All the days of your life *includes* the days of *Mashiach*. The lesson is similar, but the text is a bit more specific in explaining the extrapolation. Why the addition of *l'havi*?

The answer is that according to Ben Zoma, there are two separate requirements — to mention the Exodus by day, and to mention it by night — as has been discussed several times before. According to Ben Zoma, the extra word "all" teaches the night requirement in addition to the ordinary day requirement. The Sages, however, when they learn from the extra word "all" the requirement to mention the Exodus in the days of *Mashiach* they are not adding to the original requirement. "All" teaches that the obligation will apply to that period *as well*, i.e., it is part of the original requirement, not an addition to it (cited by his grandson, Rav Aharon Goldberg).

לְהָבִיא לִימוֹת הַמָּשִׁיחַ
Includes the days of Mashiach

The Gemara (*Berachos* 12b) states: Ben Zoma asked the Sages how they can say that in the days of *Mashiach* there is still an obligation to mention the Exodus: The verse (*Yirmiyahu* 23: 7-8) explicitly states, "Behold, days are coming — the word of Hashem — when people will no longer swear, 'As Hashem lives, Who brought the Children of Israel up from the land of Egypt,' but rather, 'As Hashem lives, Who brought up and brought back the offspring of the House of Israel from the land

declare that "the days of your life" would mean only the present world; the addition of "all" includes the days of Mashiach.

Blessed is the Omnipresent; Blessed is He. Blessed is the One Who has given the Torah to His people Israel; Blessed is He. Concerning

---

of the North and from all the lands wherein He had dispersed them.'" The Sages replied: The verse does not mean that there will no longer be *any* mention of leaving Egypt, just that it will be secondary to the mentioning of the great redemption at the End of Days.

Rav Shlomo Zalman said that he had heard the following explanation: The true dispute between Ben Zoma and the Sages is regarding how grave the situation will be at that time. According to Ben Zoma, the people will have sunk so low — the lack of belief in God will be so great — that Hashem will have to demonstrate His dominion over the world by totally changing the natural order of the world and defying the laws of nature for an entire year (corresponding to the length of the ten-plague period in Egypt). This, in turn, will cause people to forget about the miracles that occurred in Egypt. The Sages, however, maintain the situation will reach such a nadir that miracles will be necessary, but not to the degree that the Exodus will be forgotten. This idea is also expressed by the verse in *Michah* (7:15) regarding the End of Days: "As in the days when you left the land of Egypt I will show it wonders." In other words: You remember the Exodus from Egypt, but even to those who have forgotten I will show wonders (ibid.).

בָּרוּךְ שֶׁנָּתַן תּוֹרָה לְעַמּוֹ יִשְׂרָאֵל
Blessed is the One Who has given the Torah to His people Israel

Why do we bless Him for giving us the Torah, when He gave us the Torah only after the other nations rejected it? We know the famous Midrash: The Torah says (*Devarim* 33:2): "Hashem came from Sinai — having shone forth to them from Seir, having appeared from Mount Paran." This means that Hashem offered the Torah to the other nations before giving it to Israel. We ask: If Torah was given to Israel only by default, why the blessing?

The answer is that only the Jewish People are inherently tied to the

אַרְבָּעָה בָנִים דִּבְּרָה תוֹרָה – אֶחָד חָכָם, וְאֶחָד רָשָׁע, וְאֶחָד תָּם, וְאֶחָד שֶׁאֵינוֹ יוֹדֵעַ לִשְׁאוֹל.

חָכָם מָה הוּא אוֹמֵר? מָה הָעֵדֹת וְהַחֻקִּים וְהַמִּשְׁפָּטִים אֲשֶׁר צִוָּה יהוה אֱלֹהֵינוּ אֶתְכֶם?¹ וְאַף אַתָּה אֱמָר לוֹ כְּהִלְכוֹת הַפֶּסַח,

---

Torah. Thus, even had another nation accepted the Torah, it would have been a superficial connection much as the connection gentiles have to the seven Noahide laws. Accordingly, we bless Hashem for connecting us to the Torah so securely.

With this idea we can also answer another question. The Torah ends with the verse (*Devarim* 34:12): "And for all the strong hand and for all the great awesomeness that Moshe performed before the eyes of all of Israel." Rashi explains that *before the eyes of all of Israel* refers to the fact "that his heart inspired him to break the Tablets before their eyes, as it says, 'And I smashed them before your eyes.' " The mind of the Holy One, Blessed is He, was in accord with the mind of Moshe about this. Now why would the Torah end with an idea that brings up Israel's iniquity?

According to our approach, however, the Torah ends with the greatest praise of Israel: Moshe demonstrated that if the Jewish People are not worthy of the Torah, there is no place for any Torah. Accordingly, the shattered Tablets are placed in the Ark along with the second Tablets, thus demonstrating the praise, rather than the shame, of the Jewish People (*Sefer Hazikaron Mevakshei Torah, Yom Tov*, p.553, from an unpublished manuscript of Rav Shlomo Zalman Auerbach).

בָּרוּךְ שֶׁנָּתַן תּוֹרָה לְעַמּוֹ יִשְׂרָאֵל
Blessed is the One Who has given the Torah to His people Israel

Our Sages comment on the verse (*Tehillim* 68:35): "Acknowledge invincible might to God," that man can give invincible might to the Heavenly Host, or, Heaven forbid, the reverse. We also find in the Gemara that the Holy One, Blessed is He, cries tears (so to speak) over one who is capable of studying Torah but does not do so.

Now, would the heart of any human being possessing the slightest

four sons does the Torah speak – one is wise, one is wicked, one is simple and one is unable to ask.

The wise son – what does he say? "What are the testimonies, decrees and ordinances which HASHEM, our God, has commanded you?"[1] Therefore, explain to him the laws of the *pesach* offering:

---
(1) *Devarim* 6:20.

---

level of sensitivity not melt at the thought of bringing tears to his father's eyes? This is even more so regarding the Holy One, Blessed is He. After a father begets a child, the child can exist without his father. The Holy One, Blessed is He, however, needs only to turn His attention away from the world momentarily and the entire world will end. Accordingly, it is crucial for a person to rouse himself to Torah study (*Sefer Hazikaron Mevakshei Torah, Yom Tov*, p. 325, from the personal notes of Rav Shlomo Zalman Auerbach).

כְּנֶגֶד אַרְבָּעָה בָנִים דִּבְּרָה תוֹרָה
Concerning four sons does the Torah speak

The Torah's language concerning the question of the wise son is (*Devarim* 6:20): "If your son will ask you tomorrow, *leimor*, saying..." The word *leimor* may also be interpreted as, if he asks, he truly seeks an answer. He asks in anticipation of *leimor*, that an answer will be told to him. Furthermore, he is asking *tomorrow* — he is not overly preoccupied with his question; first he does what is required of him, then he asks — much as the Jewish People first said (*Shemos* 24:7), "We will do," and only afterwards, "We will hear."

On the other hand, the wicked son asks (*Shemos* 12:26), "And it shall be that when your children will say to you, 'What is this service to you?'" The wicked son *says*, he does not *ask*. Furthermore, he says so immediately, and does not wait for tomorrow (Rav Aharon Goldberg citing his grandfather).

וְאַף אַתָּה אֱמָר לוֹ כְּהִלְכוֹת הַפֶּסַח
Therefore, explain to him the laws of the pesach offering ....

The father must explain to his son in such a way that he does not forget that one must not eat after the *afikoman*, meaning that,

אֵין מַפְטִירִין אַחַר הַפֶּסַח אֲפִיקוֹמָן.

רָשָׁע מָה הוּא אוֹמֵר? מָה הָעֲבֹדָה הַזֹּאת לָכֶם?[1] לָכֶם וְלֹא לוֹ, וּלְפִי שֶׁהוֹצִיא אֶת עַצְמוֹ מִן הַכְּלָל, כָּפַר בְּעִקָּר – וְאַף אַתָּה הַקְהֵה אֶת שִׁנָּיו וֶאֱמָר לוֹ, בַּעֲבוּר זֶה עָשָׂה יהוה לִי בְּצֵאתִי מִמִּצְרָיִם.[1] לִי וְלֹא לוֹ, אִלּוּ הָיָה שָׁם לֹא הָיָה נִגְאָל.

תָּם מָה הוּא אוֹמֵר? מַה זֹּאת? וְאָמַרְתָּ אֵלָיו, בְּחֹזֶק יָד הוֹצִיאָנוּ יהוה מִמִּצְרַיִם מִבֵּית עֲבָדִים.[2]

וְשֶׁאֵינוֹ יוֹדֵעַ לִשְׁאוֹל, אַתְּ פְּתַח לוֹ. שֶׁנֶּאֱמַר,

---

although the father must explain thoroughly, if he spends too much time explaining they will have to go straight to eating the *afikoman,* and bypass the meal. Therefore we classify the father's obligation: Explain in such a way that he does not forget that one must not eat after the *afikoman* (Rav Aharon Goldberg citing his grandfather).

וְשֶׁאֵינוֹ יוֹדֵעַ לִשְׁאוֹל, אַתְּ פְּתַח לוֹ
As for the son who is unable to ask,
you must initiate the subject for him

Many have asked why *you,* אַתְּ, is written in the feminine form (אַתְּ, *at,* rather than אַתָּה, *attah*). One can answer in the following manner: *Sefer Hachinuch* (*Mitzvah* 21) writes that the requirement to tell the Exodus story applies to women as well. *Minchas Chinuch* (ad loc.) questions how women can be obligated in this mitzvah, since women are not obligated in time-bound mitzvos and the mitzvah to tell the Exodus story is limited to this night (also see above s.v. *Yemei*

that one may not eat dessert after the final taste of the *pesach* offering.

The wicked son – what does he say? "Of what purpose is this service to you?"[1] – [implying] "to you," but not to him. By excluding himself from the community of believers, he denies the basic principle of Judaism. Therefore, blunt his teeth and tell him: "It is because of this that HASHEM did so for me when I went out of Egypt."[1] "For me," but not for him – had he been there, he would not have been redeemed.

The simple son – what does he say? "What is this?" Tell him: "With a strong hand did HASHEM take us out of Egypt, from the house of bondage."[2]

And as for the son who is unable to ask, you must initiate the subject for him, as it says:

---

(1) *Shemos* 12:26. (2) *Shemos* 13:8.

---

chayecha hayamim). He answers that this limitation is overridden by the fact that they, too, were included in the miracle of the Exodus, and thus they must be obligated as well.

This reasoning may be also applied to the son who is unable to ask. One might say that, being the essence of the mitzvah to tell the Exodus story is through question and answer, apparently with the son who is unable to ask, the mitzvah cannot be fulfilled properly. This is inconceivable. He, too, was included in the miracle — he must be included in the mitzvah as well. If necessary make special considerations for him, and initiate the question for him, but he must be included. In this respect he can be compared to women, who would otherwise have no obligation, yet must be included, because they, too, were included in the miracle. Therefore, the feminine form of you (*at*) is used to indicate this comparison (Rav Aharon Goldberg citing his grandfather).

וְהִגַּדְתָּ לְבִנְךָ בַּיּוֹם הַהוּא לֵאמֹר, בַּעֲבוּר זֶה עָשָׂה יהוה לִי בְּצֵאתִי מִמִּצְרָיִם.[1]

יָכוֹל מֵרֹאשׁ חֹדֶשׁ, תַּלְמוּד לוֹמַר בַּיּוֹם הַהוּא. אִי בַּיּוֹם הַהוּא, יָכוֹל מִבְּעוֹד יוֹם, תַּלְמוּד לוֹמַר בַּעֲבוּר זֶה. בַּעֲבוּר זֶה לֹא אָמַרְתִּי אֶלָּא בְּשָׁעָה שֶׁיֵּשׁ מַצָּה וּמָרוֹר מֻנָּחִים לְפָנֶיךָ.

מִתְּחִלָּה, עוֹבְדֵי עֲבוֹדָה זָרָה הָיוּ אֲבוֹתֵינוּ, וְעַכְשָׁו קֵרְבָנוּ הַמָּקוֹם לַעֲבוֹדָתוֹ.

וְהִגַּדְתָּ לְבִנְךָ . . . בַּעֲבוּר זֶה עָשָׂה ה' לִי
You shall tell your son . . . "It is because of this that Hashem did so for me . . ."

He says, "that Hashem did so for me." In other words, one must tell the son who is unable to ask that all the miracles were performed in our merit. However, one must also be aware of another line of thought. One should know that the Torah continues (*Shemos* 13:9), "And it will be for you a sign on your arm and for a remembrance between your eyes — so that Hashem's Torah may be in your mouth — for with a strong hand Hashem removed you from Egypt." In other words, because of Hashem's *strong hand* He paid no attention to the claim of the angels comparing the Jewish People and the Egyptian nation (*Yalkut Shimoni* 234), "These worship idols and these worship idols." Perhaps there was not enough merit to warrant their redemption. Why, then, did Hashem redeem them? "So that Hashem's Torah may be in your mouth," i.e., that you accept His Torah, and so that "you will worship God on this mountain." Thus, the entire justification of the Exodus from Egypt was for the Jewish People to be able to receive the Torah, not because of their merits (Rav Aharon Goldberg citing his grandfather).

יָכוֹל מֵרֹאשׁ חֹדֶשׁ
One might think from the first day of Nissan

The root of all sanctity is the month of Nisan. The sanctity of every festival is dependent upon the proclamation of Sanhedrin sanctifying

You shall tell your son on that day, saying: "It is because of this that HASHEM did so for me when I went out of Egypt."[1]

One might think [that the obligation to discuss the Exodus commences] from the first day of the month of Nisan, but the Torah says: "You shall tell your son on that day." But the expression "on that day" could be understood to mean only during the daytime; therefore the Torah adds: "It is because of this that HASHEM did so for me when I went out of Egypt." The pronoun "this" implies something tangible, thus, "You shall tell your son" applies only at the time when matzah and *maror* lie before you – at the Seder.

Originally our ancestors were idol worshipers, but now the Omnipresent has brought us near to His

---

(1) *Shemos* 13:8.

---

the month in which it falls *(Kiddush Hachodesh)*, and the first month — the one from which all are counted — is the month of Nisan. The Torah states this explicitly *(Shemos* 12:2): "This month shall be for you the beginning of the months, it shall be for you the first of the months of the year." Only after the first month — Nisan — is sanctified is it possible to then sanctify, for example, the seventh month (Tishrei).

On a deeper level, it would seem that Pesach itself sanctifies its own month. The Torah commands us *(Devarim* 16:1): "Guard the month of springtime," which our Sages *(Rosh Hashanah* 21a) explain as a requirement that Pesach occur at the time of the ripening of the crop. The obligation to *guard* requires adding an extra month to the standard twelve-month year when otherwise Pesach would occur earlier than the time of the ripening of the crop. Thus, we see that the sanctification of the month itself, and the very determination of which month it is, depends on Pesach. Accordingly, this night of Pesach is the night that sanctifies the month, and from which all the subsequent months are sanctified (from an unpublished manuscript provided by his grandson, Rav Aharon Goldberg).

שֶׁנֶּאֱמַר, וַיֹּאמֶר יְהוֹשֻׁעַ אֶל כָּל הָעָם, כֹּה אָמַר יהוה אֱלֹהֵי יִשְׂרָאֵל, בְּעֵבֶר הַנָּהָר יָשְׁבוּ אֲבוֹתֵיכֶם מֵעוֹלָם, תֶּרַח אֲבִי אַבְרָהָם וַאֲבִי נָחוֹר, וַיַּעַבְדוּ אֱלֹהִים אֲחֵרִים. וָאֶקַּח אֶת אֲבִיכֶם אֶת אַבְרָהָם מֵעֵבֶר הַנָּהָר, וָאוֹלֵךְ אוֹתוֹ בְּכָל אֶרֶץ כְּנָעַן, וָאַרְבֶּה אֶת זַרְעוֹ, וָאֶתֵּן לוֹ אֶת יִצְחָק. וָאֶתֵּן לְיִצְחָק אֶת יַעֲקֹב וְאֶת עֵשָׂו, וָאֶתֵּן לְעֵשָׂו אֶת הַר שֵׂעִיר לָרֶשֶׁת אוֹתוֹ, וְיַעֲקֹב וּבָנָיו יָרְדוּ מִצְרָיִם.[1]

בָּרוּךְ שׁוֹמֵר הַבְטָחָתוֹ לְיִשְׂרָאֵל, בָּרוּךְ הוּא. שֶׁהַקָּדוֹשׁ בָּרוּךְ הוּא חִשַּׁב אֶת הַקֵּץ, לַעֲשׂוֹת כְּמָה שֶׁאָמַר לְאַבְרָהָם אָבִינוּ בִּבְרִית בֵּין הַבְּתָרִים, שֶׁנֶּאֱמַר, וַיֹּאמֶר לְאַבְרָם, יָדֹעַ תֵּדַע כִּי גֵר יִהְיֶה זַרְעֲךָ בְּאֶרֶץ לֹא לָהֶם, וַעֲבָדוּם וְעִנּוּ אֹתָם, אַרְבַּע מֵאוֹת שָׁנָה. וְגַם אֶת הַגּוֹי אֲשֶׁר יַעֲבֹדוּ דָּן אָנֹכִי, וְאַחֲרֵי כֵן יֵצְאוּ בִּרְכֻשׁ גָּדוֹל.[2]

The matzos are covered and the cups lifted as the following paragraph is proclaimed joyously. Upon its conclusion, the cups are put down and the matzos are uncovered.

וְהִיא שֶׁעָמְדָה לַאֲבוֹתֵינוּ וְלָנוּ, שֶׁלֹּא אֶחָד בִּלְבָד עָמַד עָלֵינוּ לְכַלּוֹתֵנוּ. אֶלָּא שֶׁבְּכָל דּוֹר וָדוֹר עוֹמְדִים עָלֵינוּ לְכַלּוֹתֵנוּ, וְהַקָּדוֹשׁ בָּרוּךְ הוּא מַצִּילֵנוּ מִיָּדָם.

צֵא וּלְמַד מַה בִּקֵּשׁ לָבָן הָאֲרַמִּי לַעֲשׂוֹת לְיַעֲקֹב אָבִינוּ, שֶׁפַּרְעֹה לֹא גָזַר

service, as it says: Yehoshua said to all the people, "So says HASHEM, God of Israel: Your fathers always lived beyond the Euphrates River, Terach the father of Avraham and Nachor, and they served other gods. Then I took your father Avraham from beyond the river and I had him travel through all the land of Canaan. I multiplied his offspring and gave him Yitzchak. To Yitzchak I gave Yaakov and Esav, to Esav I gave Mount Seir to inherit, but Yaakov and his children went down to Egypt."[1]

Blessed is He Who keeps His pledge to Israel; Blessed is He! For the Holy One, Blessed is He, calculated the End in order to do as He said to our father Avraham at the Bris bein Habesarim, as it says: He said to Avram, "Know with certainty that your offspring will be aliens in a land not theirs, they will serve them, and they will oppress them four hundred years; but also upon the nation which they shall serve will I execute judgment, and afterwards they shall go out with great possessions."[2]

The matzos are covered and the cups lifted as the following paragraph is proclaimed joyously. Upon its conclusion, the cups are put down and the matzos are uncovered.

And it is this that has stood by our fathers and us. For not only one has risen against us to annihilate us, but in every generation they rise against us to annihilate us. But the Holy One, Blessed is He, rescues us from their hand.

Go and learn what Lavan the Aramean attempted to do to our father Yaakov! For Pharaoh decreed

(1) *Yehoshua* 24:2-4. (2) *Bereishis* 15:13-14.

צֵא וּלְמַד מַה בִּקֵּשׁ לָבָן הָאֲרַמִּי לַעֲשׂוֹת
Go and learn what Lavan the Aramean attempted to do

Although there is no explicit verse in the story of Yaakov and Lavan

אֶלָּא עַל הַזְּכָרִים, וְלָבָן בִּקֵּשׁ לַעֲקוֹר אֶת הַכֹּל.
שֶׁנֶּאֱמַר:
אֲרַמִּי אֹבֵד אָבִי, וַיֵּרֶד מִצְרַיְמָה וַיָּגָר שָׁם
בִּמְתֵי מְעָט, וַיְהִי שָׁם לְגוֹי, גָּדוֹל עָצוּם וָרָב.[1]

which states that Lavan wished to kill our father Yaakov, the verse *An Aramean attempted to destroy my father* testifies that this is so. This occurs in each generation; the nations plot against us, but not necessarily with our knowledge. This may be understood from the verse (*Tehillim* 117:1): "Praise Hashem, all nations; extol Him, all the states! For His kindness has overwhelmed *us* ..." Now, why should the nations praise Him when "His kindness has overwhelmed *us*"? The well-known answer is that the nations know very well the evil plots they have planned for us, and when Hashem protects the Jewish People, they realize that Hashem knows everything (Rav Aharon Goldberg citing his grandfather).

וַיְהִי שָׁם לְגוֹי, גָּדוֹל עָצוּם וָרָב
And there he became a nation —
great, mighty, and numerous.

Hoshea (2:1) prophesies, "The number of the Children of Israel will be like the sand of the sea, which can neither be measured nor counted; and it will happen that in the place [of their exile] where it was said to them, 'You are not My people,' it will be said to them, 'Children of the living God.' "

Can neither be measured nor counted is no mere poetic statement. The Gemara (*Yoma* 22b) derives from this statement that it is prohibited to count the Jewish People, and according to one view, counting the Jewish People transgresses *two* prohibitions: (a) "neither be measured, (b) nor counted." Elsewhere (*Berachos* 62b), we find a similar point made: The Gemara states that Hashem said that he would cause King David to stumble in a matter "that even schoolchildren know, as is written (*Shemos* 30:12): 'When you take a census of the Children of Israel according to their numbers, every man shall give Hashem an atonement for his soul so that there will not be a plague among them when counting them.' " Thus, it is clear that counting the Jewish People is forbidden, and even when counting to

> only against the males, and Lavan attempted to uproot everything, as it says:
>
> > An Aramean attempted to destroy my father, and he descended to Egypt and sojourned there, with few people; and there he became a nation – great, mighty, and numerous.[1]

(1) *Devarim* 26:5.

---

fulfill God's command, still an atonement is required for their soul.

Now, this seems very strange. Why is it that counting the Jewish People is harmful to them, to the degree that it even brings a plague upon them? We find no such harm befalling the gentiles who constantly count their populations!

Another problem: The verse in *Hoshea* is the subject of further discussion in *Yoma* 22a. The Gemara points out a contradiction: The number of the Children of Israel is first compared to the sand of the sea — a finite, countable number — and then it concludes that it can neither be counted nor measured! The answer given is that the comparison to the sand refers to when they are not doing God's will (and thus they are of a finite number) whereas when they do God's will they will be too numerous to be counted or measured.

Now, this too is difficult to understand, for it implies that the verse deprecates the Children of Israel (at least in the beginning). Yet our Sages teach us that this prophecy of Hoshea was after he had begun speaking in their favor. If so, why did he start with, "The number of the Children of Israel will be like the sand of the sea," referring to a situation in which the Jewish People do not do God's will?

The answer to these questions is the fundamental difference between the Jewish Nation and the gentiles. The greatness of gentile nations is determined by their size and power, quantities that are easily measured. The Jewish People, on the other hand, have different criteria. For them the main criterion is not the physical but the spiritual.

The Gra, in his commentary on *Mishlei* (3:15), elaborates on this idea the verse states that Torah "is more precious than pearls." The Gra explains that just as the value of a pearl increases significantly the larger it is, so with Torah the quality multiplies along with the quantity. The same applies to the Jewish People. The Torah says (*Vayikra* 26:8): "Five of you will pursue a hundred, and a hundred of

וַיֵּרֶד מִצְרַיְמָה – אָנוּס עַל פִּי הַדִּבּוּר.
וַיָּגָר שָׁם – מְלַמֵּד שֶׁלֹּא יָרַד יַעֲקֹב אָבִינוּ לְהִשְׁתַּקֵּעַ בְּמִצְרַיִם, אֶלָּא לָגוּר שָׁם. שֶׁנֶּאֱמַר, וַיֹּאמְרוּ אֶל פַּרְעֹה, לָגוּר בָּאָרֶץ בָּאנוּ, כִּי אֵין מִרְעֶה לַצֹּאן אֲשֶׁר לַעֲבָדֶיךָ, כִּי כָבֵד הָרָעָב בְּאֶרֶץ כְּנָעַן, וְעַתָּה יֵשְׁבוּ נָא עֲבָדֶיךָ בְּאֶרֶץ גֹּשֶׁן.[1]
בִּמְתֵי מְעָט – כְּמָה שֶׁנֶּאֱמַר, בְּשִׁבְעִים נֶפֶשׁ יָרְדוּ אֲבֹתֶיךָ מִצְרָיְמָה, וְעַתָּה שָׂמְךָ יהוה אֱלֹהֶיךָ כְּכוֹכְבֵי הַשָּׁמַיִם לָרֹב.[2]

---

you will pursue ten thousand." Whereas the ratio of 5 to 100 is 1:20, the ratio of 100 to 10,000 is 1:100. This indicates that for the Jewish People an increase in quantity brings about a qualitative change as well. Accordingly, a person cannot count the Jewish People, for it is not their physical number that is of importance; if the Jewish People follow God's will, then even one of them can defeat all their enemies. The opposite, Heaven forbid, is true as well: They are not governed by *mazal* and the natural course of events holds no sway over them, so that, Heaven forbid, even when they are the majority they are defeated, as the verse says (*Devarim* 32:30): "How can one pursue a thousand and two cause a myriad to flee?"

Accordingly, any counting of the Jewish People harms their sanctity and transgresses a prohibition, and thus, an atonement for each soul is necessary. Otherwise it would appear as if the Jewish People also are concerned with the physical.

We can now return to the words of Hoshea: "The number of the Children of Israel." Even when the Jewish People are on the level where they are merely a number, they still are part of Hashem, and are "Children of the living God," as it says (*Vayikra* 16:16): "...that dwells with them amid their contamination." This teaches us that the *Shechinah*, so to speak, *dwells* among them even when they have contaminated themselves.

Of course when a son sins, his father wants him to realize the error of his ways on his own, but if he does not, his father will force this realization to the best of his ability. This applies to the Jewish People

And he descended to Egypt – compelled by Divine decree.

He sojourned there – this teaches that our father Yaakov did not descend to Egypt to settle, but only to sojourn temporarily, as it says: They (the sons of Yaakov) said to Pharaoh: "We have come to sojourn in this land because there is no pasture for the flocks of your servants, because the famine is severe in the Land of Canaan. And now, please let your servants dwell in the land of Goshen."[1]

With few people – as it is says: With seventy persons, your forefathers descended to Egypt, and now HASHEM, your God, has made you as numerous as the stars of heaven.[2]

---

(1) *Bereishis* 47:4. (2) *Devarim* 10:22.

---

as well. Even when they are at a very low level, for the sake of His great Name Hashem will not abandon His people. The Gemara (*Kiddushin* 70b) expresses this in a similar manner: The Jewish People have an additional advantage over the gentile nations, as indicated by the verse (*Yirmiyahu* 31:32): "I will be a God for them and they will be a people for Me." Rashi explains that even though they are not *now* My people, as a result of bringing them close to Me they will become "a people for Me."

We find a similar idea regarding the Exodus from Egypt. On the verse (*Devarim* 16:3): "For you departed from the land of Egypt in haste," *Mahari Mintz* writes that although the people were in a very lowly state, as soon as the Holy One, Blessed is He, showed them a sign for the good, they immediately raised their level of sanctity. Thus, their haste was not haste in running *away*, but rather for the sake of (*Shemos* 3:12): "You will serve God on the mountain." Accordingly, Hoshea concludes that even those on the lowest level cannot be changed for others, rather they will be "like the sand of the sea, which can neither be measured nor counted; and it will happen that in the place [of their exile] where it was said to them, 'You are not my people'..." (*Sefer Hazikaron Mevakshei Torah, Yom Tov*, p. 62, from an unpublished manuscript of Rav Shlomo Zalman Auerbach).

וַיְהִי שָׁם לְגוֹי — מְלַמֵּד שֶׁהָיוּ יִשְׂרָאֵל מְצֻיָּנִים שָׁם.

גָּדוֹל עָצוּם — כְּמָה שֶׁנֶּאֱמַר, וּבְנֵי יִשְׂרָאֵל פָּרוּ וַיִּשְׁרְצוּ וַיִּרְבּוּ וַיַּעַצְמוּ בִּמְאֹד מְאֹד, וַתִּמָּלֵא הָאָרֶץ אֹתָם.[1]

וָרָב — כְּמָה שֶׁנֶּאֱמַר, רְבָבָה כְּצֶמַח הַשָּׂדֶה נְתַתִּיךְ, וַתִּרְבִּי וַתִּגְדְּלִי וַתָּבֹאִי בַּעֲדִי עֲדָיִים, שָׁדַיִם נָכֹנוּ וּשְׂעָרֵךְ צִמֵּחַ, וְאַתְּ עֵרֹם וְעֶרְיָה; וָאֶעֱבֹר עָלַיִךְ וָאֶרְאֵךְ מִתְבּוֹסֶסֶת בְּדָמָיִךְ, וָאֹמַר לָךְ, בְּדָמַיִךְ חֲיִי, וָאֹמַר לָךְ, בְּדָמַיִךְ חֲיִי.[2]

וַיָּרֵעוּ אֹתָנוּ הַמִּצְרִים, וַיְעַנּוּנוּ, וַיִּתְּנוּ עָלֵינוּ עֲבֹדָה קָשָׁה.[3]

וַיָּרֵעוּ אֹתָנוּ הַמִּצְרִים — כְּמָה שֶׁנֶּאֱמַר, הָבָה נִתְחַכְּמָה לוֹ, פֶּן יִרְבֶּה, וְהָיָה כִּי תִקְרֶאנָה

וָאֹמַר לָךְ, בְּדָמַיִךְ חֲיִי
And I said to you: "Through Your blood shall you live!"

"Through your blood" is written in the plural form (*b'damayich*). Accordingly, our Sages explain that it refers to two bloods: the blood of the *pesach* sacrifice and the blood of circumcision. These two mitzvos were given to the Jewish People so that they could merit redemption through them. The following is Rav Shlomo Zalman's explanation as to why these two mitzvos were specifically chosen.

It is well known that all of Creation is dependent upon fulfilling the mitzvos, as is written (*Yirmiyahu* 33:25): "If My covenant with the night and with the day would not be, had I not set up the laws of heaven and earth [i.e., the laws of the Torah]."

Ramban, in his introduction to *Sefer Hamitzvos*, explains that each individual mitzvah has its own portion of the Creation to which it imparts the power of existence. Furthermore, the number of positive commandments corresponds to the 248 limbs of a person, and the

There he became a nation – this teaches that the Israelites were distinctive there.

Great, mighty – as it says: And the Children of Israel were fruitful, increased greatly, multiplied, and became very, very mighty; and the land was filled with them.[1]

Numerous – as it says: I made you as numerous as the plants of the field; you grew and developed, and became charming, beautiful of figure; your hair grown long; but you were naked and bare. And I passed over you and saw you downtrodden in your blood and I said to you: "Through your blood shall you live"; and I said to you: "Through your blood shall you live."[2]

The Egyptians did evil to us and afflicted us; and imposed hard labor upon us.[3]

The Egyptians did evil to us – as it says: Let us deal with them wisely lest they multiply and, if we happen

---

(1) *Shemos* 1:7. (2) *Yechezkel* 16:7,6. (3) *Devarim* 26:6.

---

365 negative commandments correspond to the sinews in his body. Thus, a person must conclude that his very existence is dependent upon the mitzvos, and he must constantly keep in mind that each limb "demands," so to speak, that he keep its corresponding mitzvah.

As a corollary of this principle, it can be said that fulfilling a mitzvah in its natural manner maintains nature, but fulfilling a mitzvah that goes *beyond* the natural course of events brings about supernatural events. Accordingly, when the People of Israel required supernatural aid to redeem them from their slavery before the designated time, they were given two mitzvos whose fulfillment goes beyond their nature. The first, circumcision, required them to inflict a wound upon themselves. The second, the *pesach* sacrifice, put them in danger, as the verse says (*Shemos* 8:22): "If we were to slaughter the deity of Egypt in their sight, will they not stone us?" Thus, these two mitzvos brought about the supernatural Exodus from Egypt (*Haggadas Arzei Halevanon,* page 141).

מִלְחָמָה, וְנוֹסַף גַּם הוּא עַל שֹׂנְאֵינוּ, וְנִלְחַם בָּנוּ, וְעָלָה מִן הָאָרֶץ.[1]

וַיְעַנּוּנוּ – כְּמָה שֶׁנֶּאֱמַר, וַיָּשִׂימוּ עָלָיו שָׂרֵי מִסִּים, לְמַעַן עַנֹּתוֹ בְּסִבְלֹתָם, וַיִּבֶן עָרֵי מִסְכְּנוֹת לְפַרְעֹה, אֶת פִּתֹם וְאֶת רַעַמְסֵס.[2]

וַיִּתְּנוּ עָלֵינוּ עֲבֹדָה קָשָׁה – כְּמָה שֶׁנֶּאֱמַר, וַיַּעֲבִדוּ מִצְרַיִם אֶת בְּנֵי יִשְׂרָאֵל בְּפָרֶךְ.[3]

וַנִּצְעַק אֶל יהוה אֱלֹהֵי אֲבֹתֵינוּ, וַיִּשְׁמַע יהוה אֶת קֹלֵנוּ, וַיַּרְא אֶת עָנְיֵנוּ, וְאֶת עֲמָלֵנוּ, וְאֶת לַחֲצֵנוּ.[4]

וַנִּצְעַק אֶל יהוה אֱלֹהֵי אֲבֹתֵינוּ – כְּמָה שֶׁנֶּאֱמַר, וַיְהִי בַיָּמִים הָרַבִּים הָהֵם וַיָּמָת מֶלֶךְ מִצְרַיִם, וַיֵּאָנְחוּ בְנֵי יִשְׂרָאֵל מִן הָעֲבֹדָה, וַיִּזְעָקוּ, וַתַּעַל שַׁוְעָתָם אֶל הָאֱלֹהִים מִן הָעֲבֹדָה.[5]

וַיִּשְׁמַע יהוה אֶת קֹלֵנוּ – כְּמָה שֶׁנֶּאֱמַר, וַיִּשְׁמַע אֱלֹהִים אֶת נַאֲקָתָם, וַיִּזְכֹּר אֱלֹהִים אֶת בְּרִיתוֹ אֶת אַבְרָהָם, אֶת יִצְחָק, וְאֶת יַעֲקֹב.[6]

וַיַּרְא אֶת עָנְיֵנוּ – זוֹ פְּרִישׁוּת דֶּרֶךְ אֶרֶץ, כְּמָה שֶׁנֶּאֱמַר, וַיַּרְא אֱלֹהִים אֶת בְּנֵי יִשְׂרָאֵל, וַיֵּדַע אֱלֹהִים.[7]

וְאֶת עֲמָלֵנוּ – אֵלּוּ הַבָּנִים, כְּמָה שֶׁנֶּאֱמַר,

עֲמָלֵנוּ אֵלּוּ הַבָּנִים
Our burden refers to the children

How does "burden" refer to children? "Burden" (*amal*) in Hebrew can have two meanings: a) a burden that is undertaken willingly in the sense of "Man was born to toil (*amal*)" (*Iyov* 5:7); "You should toil

to be at war, they may join our enemies and fight against us and then leave the country.¹

And they afflicted us – as it says: They set taskmasters over them in order to oppress them with their burdens; and they built Pisom and Raamses as treasure cities for Pharaoh.²

They imposed hard labor upon us – as it says: The Egytians subjugated the Children of Israel with hard labor.³

We cried out to HASHEM, the God of our fathers; and HASHEM heard our cry and saw our affliction, our burden and our oppression.⁴

We cried out to HASHEM, the God of our fathers – as it says: It happened in the course of those many days that the king of Egypt died; and the Children of Israel groaned from the servitude and cried; their cry because of the servitude rose up to God.⁵

HASHEM heard our cry – as it says: God heard their groaning, and God recalled His covenant with Avraham, with Yitzchak, and with Yaakov.⁶

And saw our affliction – that is the disruption of family life, as it says: God saw the Children of Israel and God knew.⁷

Our burden – refers to the children, as it says:

---

(1) *Shemos* 1:10. (2) *Shemos* 1:11. (3) *Shemos* 1:13. (4) *Devarim* 26:7. (5) *Shemos* 2:23. (6) *Shemos* 2:24. (7) *Shemos* 2:25.

(*amel*) in Torah" (*Toras Kohanim, Bechukosai* 1:1); "Fortunate is he who toils (*amal*) in Torah" (*Yalkut Shimoni, Iyov* 42:928), "We toil (*amelim*) and receive reward" (from the *Hadran* at the end of each tractate). In each of these examples, *amal* clearly refers to the rewarding toil of challenges and struggles in everyday life. b) On the other hand, *amal* can also refer to sinfulness, in the sense of, "And he saw no perversity (*amal*) in Israel" (*Bamidbar* 23:21).

In our context, it cannot refer to sinfulness, but rather to a burden undertaken willingly (as opposed to slavery). Children can indeed be

כָּל הַבֵּן הַיִּלּוֹד הַיְאֹרָה תַּשְׁלִיכֻהוּ, וְכָל הַבַּת תְּחַיּוּן.[1]

וְאֶת לַחֲצֵנוּ — זוֹ הַדְּחַק, כְּמָה שֶׁנֶּאֱמַר, וְגַם רָאִיתִי אֶת הַלַּחַץ אֲשֶׁר מִצְרַיִם לֹחֲצִים אֹתָם.

וַיּוֹצִאֵנוּ יהוה מִמִּצְרַיִם בְּיָד חֲזָקָה, וּבִזְרֹעַ נְטוּיָה, וּבְמֹרָא גָּדֹל, וּבְאֹתוֹת וּבְמֹפְתִים.[2]

וַיּוֹצִאֵנוּ יהוה מִמִּצְרַיִם — לֹא עַל יְדֵי מַלְאָךְ, וְלֹא עַל יְדֵי שָׂרָף, וְלֹא עַל יְדֵי שָׁלִיחַ, אֶלָּא הַקָּדוֹשׁ בָּרוּךְ הוּא בִּכְבוֹדוֹ וּבְעַצְמוֹ. שֶׁנֶּאֱמַר, וְעָבַרְתִּי בְאֶרֶץ מִצְרַיִם בַּלַּיְלָה הַזֶּה, וְהִכֵּיתִי כָל בְּכוֹר בְּאֶרֶץ מִצְרַיִם מֵאָדָם וְעַד בְּהֵמָה, וּבְכָל אֱלֹהֵי מִצְרַיִם אֶעֱשֶׂה שְׁפָטִים, אֲנִי יהוה.[3]

וְעָבַרְתִּי בְאֶרֶץ מִצְרַיִם בַּלַּיְלָה הַזֶּה — אֲנִי וְלֹא מַלְאָךְ. וְהִכֵּיתִי כָל בְּכוֹר בְּאֶרֶץ מִצְרַיִם — אֲנִי וְלֹא שָׂרָף.

וּבְכָל אֱלֹהֵי מִצְרַיִם אֶעֱשֶׂה שְׁפָטִים — אֲנִי וְלֹא הַשָּׁלִיחַ. אֲנִי יהוה — אֲנִי הוּא, וְלֹא אַחֵר.

---

a burden, but one that most people take upon themselves with eagerness and enthusiasm (from an unpublished manuscript of Rav Shlomo Zalman presented by his grandson, Rav Aharon Goldberg).

[See *Yalkut Shimoni, Shemos* 165 concerning Amram's statement referring to children, "We are toiling (*amelim*) in vain."]

וַיּוֹצִאֵנוּ ה' מִמִּצְרַיִם
Hashem took us out of Egypt

We say, "Hashem took us out of Egypt, not through an angel, not through a seraph, not through a messenger, but the Holy One,

Every son that is born you shall cast into the river, but every daughter you shall let live.¹

Our oppression – refers to the pressure expressed in the words: I have also seen how the Egyptians are oppressing them.

Hashem took us out of Egypt with a mighty hand and with an outstretched arm, with great fear, with signs and with wonders.²

Hashem took us out of Egypt – not through an angel, not through a seraph, not through a messenger, but the Holy One, Blessed is He, in His glory, Himself, as it says: I will pass through the land of Egypt on that night; I will slay all the firstborn in the land of Egypt from man to beast; and upon all the gods of Egypt will I execute judgments; I, Hashem.³

"I will pass through the land of Egypt on that night" – I and no angel; "I will slay all the firstborn in the land of Egypt" – I and no seraph; "And upon all the gods of Egypt will I execute judgments" – I and no messenger; "I, Hashem" – it is I and no other.

---

(1) *Shemos* 1:22. (2) *Devarim* 26:8. (3) *Shemos* 12:12.

Blessed is He, in His glory, Himself." If the main result of the Exodus, over which we exult, would have been the transition from slavery to freedom, it would not matter who took us out. However, the main result of the Exo-dus was not a transition, but that we became a new breed; the birth of a new nation, a nation as different from the gentiles as night is from day.

Similarly, the verse says (*Devarim* 4:34): "Or has any god ever miraculously come to take for himself a nation from amidst a nation...." Our Sages explain that "to take for himself a nation from amidst a nation" can be compared to a shepherd who sticks his hand into the womb of an animal to pull out her child.

Accordingly, it is a new birth, not merely freedom from slavery. We achieved an exalted level of sanctity greater than that of the angels, and thus required Hashem to personally save us in all His glory.

בְּיָד חֲזָקָה – זוֹ הַדֶּבֶר, כְּמָה שֶׁנֶּאֱמַר, הִנֵּה יַד יהוה הוֹיָה בְּמִקְנְךָ אֲשֶׁר בַּשָּׂדֶה, בַּסּוּסִים בַּחֲמֹרִים בַּגְּמַלִּים בַּבָּקָר וּבַצֹּאן, דֶּבֶר כָּבֵד מְאֹד.[1]

וּבִזְרֹעַ נְטוּיָה – זוֹ הַחֶרֶב, כְּמָה שֶׁנֶּאֱמַר, וְחַרְבּוֹ שְׁלוּפָה בְּיָדוֹ, נְטוּיָה עַל יְרוּשָׁלָיִם.[2]

וּבְמֹרָא גָּדֹל – זוֹ גִּלּוּי שְׁכִינָה, כְּמָה שֶׁנֶּאֱמַר, אוֹ הֲנִסָּה אֱלֹהִים לָבוֹא לָקַחַת לוֹ גוֹי מִקֶּרֶב גּוֹי, בְּמַסֹּת, בְּאֹתֹת, וּבְמוֹפְתִים, וּבְמִלְחָמָה, וּבְיָד חֲזָקָה, וּבִזְרוֹעַ נְטוּיָה, וּבְמוֹרָאִים גְּדֹלִים, כְּכֹל אֲשֶׁר עָשָׂה לָכֶם יהוה אֱלֹהֵיכֶם בְּמִצְרַיִם לְעֵינֶיךָ.[3]

וּבְאֹתוֹת – זֶה הַמַּטֶּה, כְּמָה שֶׁנֶּאֱמַר, וְאֶת הַמַּטֶּה הַזֶּה תִּקַּח בְּיָדֶךָ, אֲשֶׁר תַּעֲשֶׂה בּוֹ אֶת הָאֹתֹת.[4]

וּבְמֹפְתִים – זֶה הַדָּם, כְּמָה שֶׁנֶּאֱמַר, וְנָתַתִּי מוֹפְתִים בַּשָּׁמַיִם וּבָאָרֶץ:

<small>As each of the words דָּם, blood, אֵשׁ, fire, and עָשָׁן, smoke, is said, a bit of wine is removed from the cup, with the finger or by pouring. [Rav Shlomo Zalman would pour some wine from his cup.]</small>

דָּם וָאֵשׁ וְתִימְרוֹת עָשָׁן.[3]

דָּבָר אַחֵר – בְּיָד חֲזָקָה, שְׁתַּיִם. וּבִזְרֹעַ נְטוּיָה, שְׁתַּיִם. וּבְמֹרָא גָּדֹל, שְׁתַּיִם. וּבְאֹתוֹת, שְׁתַּיִם. וּבְמֹפְתִים, שְׁתַּיִם.

אֵלּוּ עֶשֶׂר מַכּוֹת שֶׁהֵבִיא הַקָּדוֹשׁ בָּרוּךְ הוּא עַל הַמִּצְרִים בְּמִצְרַיִם, וְאֵלּוּ הֵן:

With a mighty hand – refers to the pestilence, as it is stated: Behold, the hand of Hashem shall strike your livestock which are in the field, the horses, the donkeys, the camels, the herds, and the flocks – a very severe pestilence.[1]

With an outstretched arm – refers to the sword, as it says: His drawn sword in His hand, outstretched over Jerusalem.[2]

And with great fear – alludes to the revelation of the *Shechinah*, as it says: Has God ever attempted to take unto Himself a nation from the midst of another nation by trials, miraculous signs and wonders, by war and with a mighty hand and outstretched arm and by awesome revelations, as all that Hashem your God did for you in Egypt, before your eyes?[3]

With signs – refers to the miracles performed with the staff as it says: Take this staff in your hand, that you may perform the miraculous signs with it.[4]

With wonders – alludes to the blood, as it says: I will show wonders in the heavens and on the earth:

As each of the words דָּם, *blood*, אֵשׁ, *fire*, and עָשָׁן, *smoke*, is said, a bit of wine is removed from the cup, with the finger or by pouring.
[Rav Shlomo Zalman would pour some wine from his cup.]

Blood, fire, and columns of smoke.[5]

Another explanation of the preceding verse: [Each phrase represents two plagues,] hence: mighty hand – two; outstretched arm – two; great fear – two; signs – two; wonders – two.

These are the ten plagues which the Holy One, Blessed is He, brought upon the Egyptians in Egypt, namely:

---
(1) *Shemos* 9:3. (2) *I Divrei Hayamim* 21:16. (3) *Devarim* 4:34. (4) *Shemos* 4:17. (5) *Yoel* 3:3.

As each of the plagues is mentioned, a bit of wine is removed from the cup. The same is done by each word of Rabbi Yehudah's mnemonic.

דָּם. צְפַרְדֵּעַ. כִּנִּים. עָרוֹב. דֶּבֶר. שְׁחִין. בָּרָד. אַרְבֶּה. חֹשֶׁךְ. מַכַּת בְּכוֹרוֹת.

רַבִּי יְהוּדָה הָיָה נוֹתֵן בָּהֶם סִמָּנִים:

דְּצַ"ךְ עֲדַ"שׁ בְּאַחַ"ב.

The cups are refilled. The wine that was removed is not used.

רַבִּי יוֹסֵי הַגְּלִילִי אוֹמֵר: מִנַּיִן אַתָּה אוֹמֵר שֶׁלָּקוּ הַמִּצְרִים בְּמִצְרַיִם עֶשֶׂר מַכּוֹת וְעַל הַיָּם לָקוּ חֲמִשִּׁים מַכּוֹת? בְּמִצְרַיִם מָה הוּא אוֹמֵר, וַיֹּאמְרוּ הַחַרְטֻמִּם אֶל פַּרְעֹה, אֶצְבַּע אֱלֹהִים הִוא.¹ וְעַל הַיָּם מָה הוּא אוֹמֵר, וַיַּרְא יִשְׂרָאֵל אֶת הַיָּד הַגְּדֹלָה אֲשֶׁר עָשָׂה יהוה בְּמִצְרַיִם, וַיִּירְאוּ הָעָם אֶת יהוה, וַיַּאֲמִינוּ בַּיהוה וּבְמֹשֶׁה עַבְדּוֹ.² כַּמָּה לָקוּ בָאֶצְבַּע? עֶשֶׂר מַכּוֹת. אֱמוֹר מֵעַתָּה, בְּמִצְרַיִם לָקוּ עֶשֶׂר מַכּוֹת, וְעַל הַיָּם לָקוּ חֲמִשִּׁים מַכּוֹת.

רַבִּי אֱלִיעֶזֶר אוֹמֵר. מִנַּיִן שֶׁכָּל מַכָּה וּמַכָּה שֶׁהֵבִיא הַקָּדוֹשׁ בָּרוּךְ הוּא עַל הַמִּצְרִים בְּמִצְרַיִם הָיְתָה שֶׁל אַרְבַּע מַכּוֹת? שֶׁנֶּאֱמַר, יְשַׁלַּח בָּם חֲרוֹן אַפּוֹ — עֶבְרָה, וָזַעַם, וְצָרָה, מִשְׁלַחַת מַלְאֲכֵי רָעִים.³ עֶבְרָה, אַחַת.

וַיַּרְא יִשְׂרָאֵל
Israel saw

When they crossed the Sea of Reeds, the Heavenly cloud was both in front of them and behind them. In other words, even the lowliest of the people (those who traveled behind everyone else) became

As each of the plagues is mentioned, a bit of wine is removed from the cup.
The same is done by each word of Rabbi Yehudah's mnemonic.

**1. Blood 2. Frogs 3. Lice 4. Wild Beasts
5. Pestilence 6. Boils 7. Hail 8. Locusts
9. Darkness 10. Plague of the Firstborn.**

Rabbi Yehudah abbreviated them
by their Hebrew initials:
D'TZACH, ADASH, B'ACHAV.

The cups are refilled. The wine that was removed is not used.

Rabbi Yose the Galilean said: How does one derive that the Egyptians were struck with ten plagues in Egypt, but with fifty plagues at the Sea? – Concerning the plagues in Egypt the Torah states: The magicians said to Pharaoh, "It is the finger of God."[1] However, of those at the Sea, the Torah relates: Israel saw the great "hand" which HASHEM laid upon the Egyptians, the people feared HASHEM and they believed in HASHEM and in His servant Moshe.[2] How many plagues did they receive with the finger? Ten! Then conclude that if they suffered ten plagues in Egypt [where they were struck with a finger], they where stricken with fifty plagues at the Sea [where they were struck with a whole hand].

Rabbi Eliezer said: How does one derive that every plague that the Holy One, Blessed is He, inflicted upon the Egyptians in Egypt was equal to four plagues? – as it says: He sent upon them His fierce anger: wrath, fury, and trouble, a band of emissaries of evil.[3] [Since each plague in Egypt consisted of] 1) wrath,

---

(1) *Shemos* 8:15. (2) *Shemos* 14:31. (3) *Tehillim* 78:49.

---

exalted, for the cloud enveloped them all. Accordingly, a simple maid saw at the sea what even the prophet Yechezkel did not see (Rav Aharon Goldberg, from an unpublished manuscript of Rav Shlomo Zalman Auerbach).

וָזַעַם, שְׁתַּיִם. וְצָרָה, שָׁלֹשׁ. מִשְׁלַחַת מַלְאֲכֵי רָעִים, אַרְבַּע. אֱמוֹר מֵעַתָּה, בְּמִצְרַיִם לָקוּ אַרְבָּעִים מַכּוֹת, וְעַל הַיָּם לָקוּ מָאתַיִם מַכּוֹת.

רַבִּי עֲקִיבָא אוֹמֵר. מִנַּיִן שֶׁכָּל מַכָּה וּמַכָּה שֶׁהֵבִיא הַקָּדוֹשׁ בָּרוּךְ הוּא עַל הַמִּצְרִים בְּמִצְרַיִם הָיְתָה שֶׁל חָמֵשׁ מַכּוֹת? שֶׁנֶּאֱמַר, יְשַׁלַּח בָּם חֲרוֹן אַפּוֹ, עֶבְרָה, וָזַעַם, וְצָרָה, מִשְׁלַחַת מַלְאֲכֵי רָעִים. חֲרוֹן אַפּוֹ, אַחַת. עֶבְרָה, שְׁתַּיִם. וָזַעַם, שָׁלֹשׁ. וְצָרָה, אַרְבַּע. מִשְׁלַחַת מַלְאֲכֵי רָעִים, חָמֵשׁ. אֱמוֹר מֵעַתָּה, בְּמִצְרַיִם לָקוּ חֲמִשִּׁים מַכּוֹת, וְעַל הַיָּם לָקוּ חֲמִשִּׁים וּמָאתַיִם מַכּוֹת.

כַּמָּה מַעֲלוֹת טוֹבוֹת לַמָּקוֹם עָלֵינוּ.

אִלּוּ הוֹצִיאָנוּ מִמִּצְרַיִם,
וְלֹא עָשָׂה בָהֶם שְׁפָטִים, דַּיֵּנוּ.
אִלּוּ עָשָׂה בָהֶם שְׁפָטִים,
וְלֹא עָשָׂה בֵאלֹהֵיהֶם, דַּיֵּנוּ.
אִלּוּ עָשָׂה בֵאלֹהֵיהֶם,
וְלֹא הָרַג אֶת בְּכוֹרֵיהֶם, דַּיֵּנוּ.
אִלּוּ הָרַג אֶת בְּכוֹרֵיהֶם,
וְלֹא נָתַן לָנוּ אֶת מָמוֹנָם, דַּיֵּנוּ.
אִלּוּ נָתַן לָנוּ אֶת מָמוֹנָם,
וְלֹא קָרַע לָנוּ אֶת הַיָּם, דַּיֵּנוּ.
אִלּוּ קָרַע לָנוּ אֶת הַיָּם,
וְלֹא הֶעֱבִירָנוּ בְתוֹכוֹ בֶּחָרָבָה, דַּיֵּנוּ.

2) fury, 3) trouble, and 4) a band of emissaries of evil, therefore conclude that in Egypt they were struck by forty plagues and at the Sea by two hundred!

Rabbi Akiva said: How does one derive that each plague that the Holy One, Blessed is He, inflicted upon the Egyptians in Egypt was equal to five plagues? – as it says: He sent upon them His fierce anger, wrath, fury, trouble, and a band of emissaries of evil. [Since each plague in Egypt consisted of] 1) fierce anger, 2) wrath, 3) fury, 4) trouble, and 5) a band of emissaries of evil, therefore conclude that in Egypt they were struck by fifty plagues and at the Sea by two hundred and fifty!

The Omnipresent has bestowed so many favors upon us!

Had He brought us out of Egypt,
   but not executed judgments against the
  Egyptians,   it would have sufficed us.
Had He executed judgments against them,
   but not acted against their gods,
                              it would have sufficed us.
Had He acted against their gods,
   but not slain their firstborn,
                              it would have sufficed us.
Had He slain their firstborn,
   but not given us their wealth,
                              it would have sufficed us.
Had He given us their wealth,
   but not split the Sea for us,
                              it would have sufficed us.
Had He split the Sea for us,
   but not led us through it on dry land,
                              it would have sufficed us.

אִלּוּ הֶעֱבִירָנוּ בְתוֹכוֹ בֶּחָרָבָה,
וְלֹא שִׁקַּע צָרֵינוּ בְּתוֹכוֹ, דַּיֵּנוּ.
אִלּוּ שִׁקַּע צָרֵינוּ בְּתוֹכוֹ,
וְלֹא סִפֵּק צָרְכֵּנוּ בַּמִּדְבָּר אַרְבָּעִים שָׁנָה, דַּיֵּנוּ.
אִלּוּ סִפֵּק צָרְכֵּנוּ בַּמִּדְבָּר אַרְבָּעִים שָׁנָה,
וְלֹא הֶאֱכִילָנוּ אֶת הַמָּן, דַּיֵּנוּ.
אִלּוּ הֶאֱכִילָנוּ אֶת הַמָּן,
וְלֹא נָתַן לָנוּ אֶת הַשַּׁבָּת, דַּיֵּנוּ.
אִלּוּ נָתַן לָנוּ אֶת הַשַּׁבָּת,
וְלֹא קֵרְבָנוּ לִפְנֵי הַר סִינַי, דַּיֵּנוּ.
אִלּוּ קֵרְבָנוּ לִפְנֵי הַר סִינַי,
וְלֹא נָתַן לָנוּ אֶת הַתּוֹרָה, דַּיֵּנוּ.
אִלּוּ נָתַן לָנוּ אֶת הַתּוֹרָה,

אִלּוּ נָתַן לָנוּ אֶת הַתּוֹרָה
Had He given us the Torah

Many wonder why the Torah has no explicit command to celebrate and rejoice on the day the Torah was given, much as we were commanded to celebrate and rejoice on Pesach, in commemoration of the Exodus, and Sukkos, in commemoration of the Clouds of Glory that were in the desert. Furthermore, the Torah in fact hides the exact day on which the Torah was given.

Indeed, Shavuos (which the Torah itself does not explicitly connect to receiving the Torah) need not always fall out on the sixth day of Sivan (the day tradition ascribes to the giving of the Torah). When we will once again merit having our own Sanhedrin and we will sanctify the months not through our calculated *luach,* but based on testimony that the moon was seen, Shavuos will sometimes also fall on the fifth or seventh of Sivan depending on whether Nisan and Iyar have 29 or 30 days.

The answer is that when Hashem took us out from enslavement to

Had He led us through it on dry land,
 but not drowned our oppressors in it,
  it would have sufficed us.
Had He drowned our oppressors in it,
 but not provided for our needs in the desert
 for forty years, it would have sufficed us.
Had He provided for our needs in the desert
 for forty years,
 but not fed us the manna,
  it would have sufficed us.
Had He fed us the manna,
 but not given us the Shabbos,
  it would have sufficed us.
Had He given us the Shabbos,
 but not brought us before Mount Sinai,
  it would have sufficed us.
Had He brought us before Mount Sinai,
 but not given us the Torah,
  it would have sufficed us.
Had He given us the Torah,

---

freedom we became forever free. Even when we are subservient and apparently enslaved to others, we always remain free men. "Going out" from Egypt was a one-time event in the past, never to recur. Although we mention the Exodus each and every day and night of the year, it is only on the night of the Seder that one must see himself as if he personally went out of Egypt, not on any other night. Thus, we celebrate Pesach seven (or eight) days to recall our Exodus from Egypt, and we celebrate Sukkos "so that your generations will know that I caused the Children of Israel to sit in booths ..." (*Vayikra* 23:43).

The joy at receiving the Torah is different, however, as it was not a one-time occurrence. Of course, we must always remember standing at Mount Sinai with awe and trepidation. The trepidation at that time was so great that the Jewish People refused to accept the Torah out of fear of the great fire until, in His love, Hashem forced them to accept it. Nevertheless, once it was given, there can be no greater joy than

וְלֹא הִכְנִיסָנוּ לְאֶרֶץ יִשְׂרָאֵל, דַּיֵּנוּ.
אִלּוּ הִכְנִיסָנוּ לְאֶרֶץ יִשְׂרָאֵל,
וְלֹא בָנָה לָנוּ אֶת בֵּית הַבְּחִירָה, דַּיֵּנוּ.

עַל אַחַת כַּמָּה, וְכַמָּה טוֹבָה כְפוּלָה וּמְכֻפֶּלֶת לַמָּקוֹם עָלֵינוּ. שֶׁהוֹצִיאָנוּ מִמִּצְרַיִם, וְעָשָׂה בָהֶם שְׁפָטִים, וְעָשָׂה בֵאלֹהֵיהֶם,

the joy of learning Torah, and "those who savor it merit life" (from the Shabbos *Musaf*). In the words of the Gemara (*Berachos* 63b), those who study it "rejoice in it as if it were the day that it was given from Sinai."

Even the quintessence of the mitzvah to study Torah is to rejoice in its study. The Midrash (*Bereishis Rabbah* 97:5) states that "when they hear something new from the Torah they drink it up as thirstily as if they had never heard any Torah."

Furthermore, the total unity of Torah and the Jewish People did not originate on the sixth of Sivan when the Torah was given. That was merely the day on which it became revealed to the public. This total unity already existed before, and indeed predates the Creation of the world. Our father Avraham already kept the entire Torah, although it was not yet given. Even the Midrash recounting how Hashem went from nation to nation asking them if they wanted the Torah does not mean that the Torah could have been given to any other nation. Rather, it means that He asked them if they wanted to upgrade from the seven Noahide mitzvos to 613. The Torah can belong only to the Jewish People, and "If not for the People of Israel there is no Torah" (see *Tanna D'Vei Eliyahu Rabbah* 18).

Accordingly, the Holy One, Blessed is He, did not want to set a limit by explicitly writing in the Holy Torah the day on which He gave us the Torah. We do not celebrate in commemoration of that day — as is the case for Pesach and Sukkos, when we celebrate an event that occurred in the past and is no longer current. Instead, each and every day we praise Hashem and thank Him for choosing us and giving us the Torah, which grants life and joy to those who always study it as if it were just now received from Sinai. Mount Sinai was not a one-time occurrence, rather it is an unceasing day and night continuation, in

but not brought us into the Land of Israel,
                it would have sufficed us.
Had He brought us into the Land of Israel,
but not built the Temple for us,
                it would have sufficed us.

Thus, how much more so should we be grateful to the Omnipresent for all the numerous favors He showered upon us: He brought us out of Egypt; executed judgments against the Egyptians; acted against their

---

the words of *Zohar* (*Parashas Chukas* 179b): "One who toils in Torah study is considered as if he stood the entire day on Mount Sinai and received the Torah."

The Gemara (*Kiddushin* 30a) also states: "Whoever teaches his son and grandson Torah is considered by Scripture to have received it at Sinai, as it says (*Devarim* 4:9): "And make them known to your children and your children's children," which is immediately followed by, "The day that you stood before Hashem, your God, at Horev."

By way of ending, one should always remember the words of our Sages in *Koheles Rabbah* (6:11): "Since a person's days are in vain, numbered and [they pass] like a shadow, what pleasure can there be in life other than being involved in words of Torah which are all life?" The *Midrash* (*Bereishis Rabbah* 13) also says, "A person was created so that he toil. If he has merit, he toils in Torah, if he does not have merit he toils on the land; fortunate is he who toils in Torah" (from *Commentary to Megillas Ruth,* published by *Kol Torah Yeshivah*).

אִלּוּ נָתַן לָנוּ אֶת הַתּוֹרָה וְלֹא הִכְנִיסָנוּ לְאֶרֶץ יִשְׂרָאֵל
Had He given us the Torah but not brought us into the Land of Israel it would have sufficed us

How foolish are those who place the emphasis on the Land of Israel rather than fulfilling the mitzvos of the Torah. On each and every Seder night they say, "Had He given us the Torah but not brought us into the Land of Israel it would have sufficed us." Do their ears not hear what their own mouths say? (*Haggadas Arzei Halevanon,* p. 180).

וְהָרַג אֶת בְּכוֹרֵיהֶם, וְנָתַן לָנוּ אֶת מָמוֹנָם, וְקָרַע לָנוּ אֶת הַיָּם, וְהֶעֱבִירָנוּ בְּתוֹכוֹ בֶּחָרָבָה, וְשִׁקַּע צָרֵינוּ בְּתוֹכוֹ, וְסִפֵּק צָרְכֵּנוּ בַּמִּדְבָּר אַרְבָּעִים שָׁנָה, וְהֶאֱכִילָנוּ אֶת הַמָּן, וְנָתַן לָנוּ אֶת הַשַּׁבָּת, וְקֵרְבָנוּ לִפְנֵי הַר סִינַי, וְנָתַן

וְהָרַג אֶת בְּכוֹרֵיהֶם
Slew their firstborn

Rav Shlomo Zalman was once asked: In the *Ma'ariv* prayers we say, "Who struck with His anger all the firstborn of Egypt and removed His nation from their midst to eternal freedom." This implies that the striking of the firstborn preceded the Exodus itself and in fact the plague against the firstborn actually occurred at midnight, and the Jewish people first left the next morning (as derived by the Gemara, *Berachos* 9a, from the verse [*Bamidbar* 33:3]: "On the day after the Pesach offering the Children of Israel went forth with an upraised hand"). In the *Shacharis* prayer, however, we say, "From Egypt You redeemed us, Hashem, our God, and from the house of slavery You liberated us. All their firstborn You slew, but Your firstborn You redeemed." This seems to indicate that the redemption from Egypt preceded the smiting of the firstborn.

He replied with the following insight: In the introduction to Tractate *Semachos* a contradiction is raised. One verse says, "It was at midnight, and Hashem smote every firstborn in the land of Egypt..." (*Shemos* 12:29). Another verse says, "For every firstborn ... was Mine ... on the day I struck every firstborn in the land of Egypt" (*Bamidbar* 8:17), implying that it was done during the daytime! Rav Yochanan answers that although they were mortally struck at midnight, their souls hovered within them until the morning. Since Hashem wanted the Jewish People to be aware of how the firstborn were punished (much as one who gives food to a child should notify his mother), He kept their souls within them until daylight.

With this idea we can explain the differences between the *Ma'ariv* prayer and the *Shacharis* prayer. In *Ma'ariv*, the reference is to the plague — "Who *struck* with His anger all the firstborn of Egypt." They were indeed struck at midnight, and only afterwards, Hashem "removed His nation from their midst to eternal freedom." In

gods; slew their firstborn; gave us their wealth; split the Sea for us; led us through it on dry land; drowned our oppressors in it; provided for our needs in the desert for forty years; fed us the manna; gave us the Shabbos; brought us close before Mount Sinai; gave

---

Shacharis, however, the reference is to *slaying* the firstborn — the actual death. This indeed occurred after "From Egypt You redeemed us, Hashem, our God, and from the house of slavery You liberated us."

How fitting it is that in the evening prayers we thank Hashem for the miracle that occurred in the nighttime, and in the morning prayers we thank him for the miracle that occurred in the daytime! (*Haggadas Arzei Halevanon*, p. 181).

וְקֵרְבָנוּ לִפְנֵי הַר סִינַי, וְנָתַן לָנוּ אֶת הַתּוֹרָה
Brought us close before Mount Sinai; gave us the Torah.

We Jewish People are unique because Hashem gave us the Torah. The Gemara (*Chagigah* 13a) teaches that one should not study words of Torah with a gentile, as it says (*Tehillim* 147:19-20): "[He relates His Word to Yaakov, His statutes and judgments to Israel;] He did not do so for any other nation; such judgments, they know them not." The reason for this is apparently that studying Torah and mastering it are comparable to writing a Torah scroll, for we find that our Sages compare a Torah sage to a Torah scroll (see e.g., *Kiddushin* 33b). Accordingly, just as a Torah scroll may not be written on just any parchment, but only on parchment with sanctity planted in it by tanning it for the sake of a Torah scroll, so too, the words of Torah can only be "inscribed" on the hearts of people with sanctity — i.e., the Jewish People, who are a holy nation — but not on the hearts of gentiles, who have no sanctity.

A powerful lesson can be learned from this. If only a Torah scholar would appreciate his own worth, he would certainly take great care to refrain from any idle chatter and, even more so, from forbidden speech. Any Jew would be horrified at the desecration of a Torah scroll, specifically when he sees a person actively shaming the Torah and using it for mundane purposes. So how can one who uses his mouth to study Torah — thereby sanctifying himself with a sanctity greater than the sanctity of a Torah scroll — not be afraid to sully that

לָנוּ אֶת הַתּוֹרָה, וְהִכְנִיסָנוּ לְאֶרֶץ יִשְׂרָאֵל, וּבָנָה לָנוּ אֶת בֵּית הַבְּחִירָה, לְכַפֵּר עַל כָּל עֲוֹנוֹתֵינוּ.

רַבָּן גַּמְלִיאֵל הָיָה אוֹמֵר. כָּל שֶׁלֹּא אָמַר שְׁלֹשָׁה דְבָרִים אֵלּוּ בַּפֶּסַח, לֹא יָצָא יְדֵי חוֹבָתוֹ, וְאֵלּוּ הֵן,

פֶּסַח. מַצָּה. וּמָרוֹר.

---

very mouth with idle chatter, or, even worse, prohibited matters?

R' Shimon Bar Yochai, cited in *Yerushalmi* (*Shabbos* 1:2; *Berachos* 1:2, et al.), refers to this idea when he says, "If I would have stood on Mount Sinai when the Torah was given to the Jewish People, I would have demanded and beseeched Hashem to create two mouths for each person, one with which to study Torah and the other with which to do his mundane needs." The reason is as we have explained: Once a mouth has become sanctified through Torah, how can it then be used for mundane matters? (*Sefer Hazikaron Mevakshei Torah, Yom Tov*, p. 585, from an unpublished manuscript of Rav Shlomo Zalman Auerbach).

וְנָתַן לָנוּ אֶת הַתּוֹרָה
And gave us the Torah

The mitzvah of Torah study is the most important mitzvah, as stated in the first *mishnah* in *Pe'ah* : "And Torah study is equivalent to them all." Concerning Torah it is written (*Mishlei* 3:15): "It is more precious than pearls, and all your desires cannot compare to it." *Yerushalmi* comments that not only is everything in the entire world not equal to one word of Torah, but even all the mitzvos are not equal to one word of Torah. Only Torah — which is greater than royalty and priesthood — can provide life for this world and the next.

This is why R' Yochanan was pained regarding those people who are so involved in earning a living that they have no time to study Torah. "With what merit will they be resurrected?" The only solution found for them is based on the verse (*Devarim* 4:4): "But you who cling to Hashem, your God — you are all alive today." The Gemara there asks: "How is it possible to cling to Hashem? After all, it is written, 'For Hashem, your God — He is a consuming fire!' (ibid. v.

us the Torah; brought us to the Land of Israel; and built us the Temple, to atone for all our sins.

Rabban Gamliel used to say: Whoever has not explained the following three things on Pesach has not fulfilled his duty, namely:

Pesach – the *pesach* offering;
Matzah – the unleavened bread;
Maror – the bitter herbs.

---

24). Rather, he who marries his daughter to a Torah scholar, and does business with Torah scholars [benefiting them], is considered by Scripture to cling to Hashem."

In other words, if the parchment of a Torah scroll or a mezuzah is sanctified by the words of Torah written upon it, certainly the Torah inscribed in the heart of a person sanctifies him. As a result, Hashem guards that sanctification and will not allow it to be lost.

Now, just as the accessories of a Torah scroll achieve the sanctity of a Torah scroll, so too, those who support Torah attach themselves to Torah — achieving the sanctity of those who study Torah. They, too, are included in the verse, "But you who cling to Hashem, your God — you are all alive today." Concerning them, the Midrash says (*Midrash Tehillim* 119): "Whoever loves Torah truly only loves life, as is written concerning the Torah (*Mishlei* 3:18): It is a tree of life for those who grasp it, and its supporters are praiseworthy" (from an unpublished manuscript cited in *Pa'amei Kol Torah*).

כָּל שֶׁלֹּא אָמַר שְׁלֹשָׁה דְבָרִים אֵלּוּ בַּפֶּסַח, לֹא יָצָא יְדֵי חוֹבָתוֹ
Whoever has not explained [lit. said] the following three things on Pesach has not fulfilled his duty.

This is not referring to the *kavanah*, intent, one must have when eating the *pesach*, matzah, and *maror*, for then there would be no obligation to *say* anything. Furthermore, it is not so clear that when eating these three there is any specific requirement for intent. Only regarding three mitzvos — *sukkah*, *tefillin*, and *tzitzis* — where there is a specific reason given for the mitzvah, is specific intent required. Rather, the requirement here is to explain the Exodus. One who does not *explain* these three has not fulfilled his duty of explaining the Exodus (Rav Aharon Goldberg, citing his grandfather).

פֶּסַח שֶׁהָיוּ אֲבוֹתֵינוּ אוֹכְלִים בִּזְמַן שֶׁבֵּית הַמִּקְדָּשׁ הָיָה קַיָּם, עַל שׁוּם מָה? עַל שׁוּם שֶׁפָּסַח הַקָּדוֹשׁ בָּרוּךְ הוּא עַל בָּתֵּי אֲבוֹתֵינוּ בְּמִצְרַיִם. שֶׁנֶּאֱמַר, וַאֲמַרְתֶּם, זֶבַח פֶּסַח הוּא לַיהוה, אֲשֶׁר פָּסַח עַל בָּתֵּי בְנֵי יִשְׂרָאֵל בְּמִצְרַיִם בְּנָגְפּוֹ אֶת מִצְרַיִם, וְאֶת בָּתֵּינוּ הִצִּיל, וַיִּקֹּד הָעָם וַיִּשְׁתַּחֲווּ.[1]

The middle matzah is lifted and displayed while the following paragraph is recited.

מַצָּה זוּ שֶׁאָנוּ אוֹכְלִים, עַל שׁוּם מָה? עַל שׁוּם שֶׁלֹּא הִסְפִּיק בְּצֵקָם שֶׁל אֲבוֹתֵינוּ לְהַחֲמִיץ, עַד שֶׁנִּגְלָה עֲלֵיהֶם מֶלֶךְ מַלְכֵי הַמְּלָכִים הַקָּדוֹשׁ בָּרוּךְ הוּא וּגְאָלָם. שֶׁנֶּאֱמַר, וַיֹּאפוּ אֶת הַבָּצֵק אֲשֶׁר הוֹצִיאוּ מִמִּצְרַיִם עֻגֹת מַצּוֹת כִּי לֹא חָמֵץ, כִּי גֹרְשׁוּ מִמִּצְרַיִם, וְלֹא יָכְלוּ לְהִתְמַהְמֵהַּ, וְגַם צֵדָה לֹא עָשׂוּ לָהֶם.[2]

The *maror* is lifted and displayed while the following paragraph is recited.

מָרוֹר זֶה שֶׁאָנוּ אוֹכְלִים, עַל שׁוּם מָה? עַל

מַצָּה זוּ שֶׁאָנוּ אוֹכְלִים
Why do we eat this matzah?

The Torah requires eating two types of matzah. The first is eaten with the *pesach* sacrifice, as it is written (*Bamidbar* 9:11): "With matzos and bitter herbs shall he eat it." This type was eaten even on the first Pesach in Egypt, but it applies only when there is a *pesach* offering. The second type was required *because the dough of our fathers did not have time to become leavened.* This type did not yet apply to the first Pesach in Egypt, but it is required even when there is no *pesach* sacrifice. Rabban Gamliel is thus asking why there is a *continuing* Torah obligation — throughout the generations of the Diaspora — to eat matzah. That question is answered by saying, *Because the dough of our fathers did not have the time to become leavened.* Nevertheless, further research is necessary (from an unpublished manuscript

Pesach – Why did our fathers eat a *pesach* offering during the period when the Temple stood? Because the Holy One, Blessed is He, passed over the houses of our fathers in Egypt, as it says: You shall say: "It is a *pesach* offering for HASHEM, Who passed over the houses of the Children of Israel in Egypt when He struck the Egyptians and spared our houses"; and the people bowed down and prostrated themselves.[1]

<small>The middle matzah is lifted and displayed while the following paragraph is recited.</small>

Matzah – Why do we eat this matzah? Because the dough of our fathers did not have time to become leavened before the King of kings, the Holy One, Blessed is He, revealed Himself to them and redeemed them, as it says: They baked the dough which they had brought out of Egypt into unleavened bread, for it had not fermented, because they were driven out of Egypt and could not delay, nor had they prepared any provisions for the way.[2]

<small>The *maror* is lifted and displayed while the following paragraph is recited.</small>

Maror – Why do we eat this bitter herb? Because the

---

(1) *Shemos* 12:27. (2) *Shemos* 12:39.

---

presented by his grandson, Rav Aharon Goldberg).

The mitzvah of eating matzah also comes to remind us about the creation of the world *ex nihilo*. *Maharam Mintz* writes that ordinarily, bread requires a previous "sourdough" as a starter, creating a never-ending chain of sourdough, dough, sourdough, dough, etc. Eating matzah teaches us that it is possible to start at the beginning and bake a "bread" that satiates even without a pre-existing sourdough. This hints at a world for which there was absolutely nothing before its creation (from an unpublished manuscript presented by his grandson, Rav Aharon Goldberg).

מַצָּה זוּ שֶׁאָנוּ אוֹכְלִים . . . מָרוֹר זֶה שֶׁאָנוּ אוֹכְלִים

Why do we eat this matzah?... Why do we eat this bitter herb?

The mitzvah of this night is to explain the Exodus and tell its tale,

שׁוּם שֶׁמֵּרְרוּ הַמִּצְרִים אֶת חַיֵּי אֲבוֹתֵינוּ בְּמִצְרָיִם. שֶׁנֶּאֱמַר, וַיְמָרְרוּ אֶת חַיֵּיהֶם, בַּעֲבֹדָה קָשָׁה, בְּחֹמֶר וּבִלְבֵנִים, וּבְכָל עֲבֹדָה בַּשָּׂדֶה, אֵת כָּל עֲבֹדָתָם אֲשֶׁר עָבְדוּ בָהֶם בְּפָרֶךְ.[1]

בְּכָל דּוֹר וָדוֹר חַיָּב אָדָם לִרְאוֹת אֶת עַצְמוֹ כְּאִלּוּ הוּא יָצָא מִמִּצְרָיִם. שֶׁנֶּאֱמַר, וְהִגַּדְתָּ לְבִנְךָ בַּיּוֹם הַהוּא לֵאמֹר, בַּעֲבוּר זֶה עָשָׂה יהוה לִי, בְּצֵאתִי מִמִּצְרָיִם.[2] לֹא אֶת אֲבוֹתֵינוּ בִּלְבַד גָּאַל הַקָּדוֹשׁ בָּרוּךְ הוּא, אֶלָּא אַף אוֹתָנוּ גָּאַל עִמָּהֶם. שֶׁנֶּאֱמַר, וְאוֹתָנוּ הוֹצִיא מִשָּׁם, לְמַעַן הָבִיא אֹתָנוּ לָתֶת לָנוּ אֶת הָאָרֶץ אֲשֶׁר נִשְׁבַּע לַאֲבוֹתֵינוּ.[3]

The matzos are covered and the cup is lifted and held until it is to be drunk. According to some customs, however, the cup is put down after the following paragraph, in which case the matzos should once more be uncovered.
[Rav Shlomo Zalman's custom was to hold the cup until it is drunk.]

לְפִיכָךְ אֲנַחְנוּ חַיָּבִים לְהוֹדוֹת, לְהַלֵּל, לְשַׁבֵּחַ, לְפָאֵר, לְרוֹמֵם, לְהַדֵּר, לְבָרֵךְ, לְעַלֵּה, וּלְקַלֵּס, לְמִי שֶׁעָשָׂה לַאֲבוֹתֵינוּ וְלָנוּ אֶת כָּל הַנִּסִּים הָאֵלּוּ, הוֹצִיאָנוּ מֵעַבְדוּת לְחֵרוּת, מִיָּגוֹן לְשִׂמְחָה, וּמֵאֵבֶל לְיוֹם טוֹב, וּמֵאֲפֵלָה לְאוֹר גָּדוֹל, וּמִשִּׁעְבּוּד לִגְאֻלָּה, וְנֹאמַר לְפָנָיו שִׁירָה חֲדָשָׁה, הַלְלוּיָהּ.

---

relating how the dough was not allowed to leaven, how bitter the exile was, etc. Why do we express these thoughts as *explanations* for the mitzvos of the night? Is it not sufficient to mention them only as part of the narrative?

Apparently, this is part of the answer to the Four Questions. In other words, when the Torah tells us (*Shemos* 13:14; *Devarim* 6:20-21):

Egyptians embittered the lives of our fathers in Egypt, as it says: They embittered their lives with hard labor, with mortar and bricks, and with all manner of labor in the field: Whatever service they made them perform was with hard labor.¹

In every generation it is one's duty to regard himself as though he personally had gone out of Egypt, as it says: You shall tell your son on that day: "It was because of this that HASHEM did for 'me' when I went out of Egypt."² It was not only our fathers whom the Holy One, Blessed is He, redeemed from slavery; we, too, were redeemed with them, as it says: He brought "us" out from there so that He might take us to the land which He had promised to our fathers.³

<small>The matzos are covered and the cup is lifted and held until it is to be drunk. According to some customs, however, the cup is put down after the following paragraph, in which case the matzos should once more be uncovered.
[Rav Shlomo Zalman's custom was to hold the cup until it is drunk.]</small>

Therefore it is our duty to thank, praise, pay tribute, glorify, exalt, honor, bless, extol, and acclaim the One Who performed all these miracles for our fathers and for us. He brought us forth from slavery to freedom, from grief to joy, from mourning to festivity, from darkness to great light, and from servitude to redemption. Let us, therefore, recite a new song before Him! Halleluyah!

(1) *Shemos* 1:14. (2) *Shemos* 13:8. (3) *Devarim* 6:23.

"When your son will ask you . . . you shall say to him. . .," the reference is primarily to the mitzvos performed on this night, such as eating the *pesach*, matzah, and *maror*. It is thus not sufficient to say what occurred in Egypt, but rather one must *explain* to his son the reason for eating matzah and *maror* (Rav Aharon Goldberg, citing his grandfather).

וְנֶאֱמַר/וְנֶאֱמַר
Let us, therefore, recite/and there was recited

Mishnah Berurah (473:71) rules in accordance with *Teshuvos*

הַלְלוּיָהּ הַלְלוּ עַבְדֵי יהוה, הַלְלוּ אֶת שֵׁם יהוה. יְהִי שֵׁם יהוה מְבֹרָךְ, מֵעַתָּה וְעַד עוֹלָם. מִמִּזְרַח שֶׁמֶשׁ עַד מְבוֹאוֹ, מְהֻלָּל שֵׁם יהוה. רָם עַל כָּל גּוֹיִם יהוה, עַל הַשָּׁמַיִם כְּבוֹדוֹ. מִי כַּיהוה אֱלֹהֵינוּ, הַמַּגְבִּיהִי לָשָׁבֶת. הַמַּשְׁפִּילִי לִרְאוֹת, בַּשָּׁמַיִם וּבָאָרֶץ. מְקִימִי מֵעָפָר דָּל, מֵאַשְׁפֹּת יָרִים אֶבְיוֹן. לְהוֹשִׁיבִי עִם נְדִיבִים, עִם נְדִיבֵי עַמּוֹ. מוֹשִׁיבִי עֲקֶרֶת הַבַּיִת, אֵם הַבָּנִים שְׂמֵחָה, הַלְלוּיָהּ.¹

בְּצֵאת יִשְׂרָאֵל מִמִּצְרָיִם, בֵּית יַעֲקֹב מֵעַם לֹעֵז. הָיְתָה יְהוּדָה לְקָדְשׁוֹ, יִשְׂרָאֵל מַמְשְׁלוֹתָיו. הַיָּם רָאָה וַיָּנֹס, הַיַּרְדֵּן יִסֹּב לְאָחוֹר. הֶהָרִים רָקְדוּ כְאֵילִים, גְּבָעוֹת כִּבְנֵי צֹאן. מַה לְּךָ הַיָּם כִּי תָנוּס, הַיַּרְדֵּן תִּסֹּב לְאָחוֹר. הֶהָרִים תִּרְקְדוּ כְאֵילִים, גְּבָעוֹת כִּבְנֵי צֹאן. מִלִּפְנֵי אָדוֹן חוּלִי אָרֶץ, מִלִּפְנֵי אֱלוֹהַּ יַעֲקֹב. הַהֹפְכִי הַצּוּר אֲגַם מָיִם, חַלָּמִישׁ לְמַעְיְנוֹ מָיִם.²

<small>According to all customs the cup is lifted
and the matzos covered during the recitation of this blessing.</small>

בָּרוּךְ אַתָּה יהוה אֱלֹהֵינוּ מֶלֶךְ הָעוֹלָם,

Maharshal §88 that the proper vowelization should be *u'ne'emar, and there was recited,* which is past tense, since the meaning is that a new song was recited before Him [in Egypt].

Others defend the standard vowelization of *u'nomar, let us recite,* future tense, since the reference is to a new song to be recited for the redemption in every generation (see *Emek Berachah;* also see *Keser Rosh* §101, who notes that this was the custom of Rav Chaim Volozhin). [Rav Avigdor Nebenzahl, a noted disciple of Rav Shlomo

Halleluyah! Praise, you servants of HASHEM, praise the Name of HASHEM. Blessed is the Name of HASHEM from now and forever. From the rising of the sun to its setting, HASHEM's Name is praised. High above all nations is HASHEM, above the heavens is His glory. Who is like HASHEM, our God, Who is enthroned on high, yet lowers Himself to look upon the heaven and the earth. He raises the destitute from the dust; from the trash heaps He lifts the needy – to seat them with nobles, with nobles of His people. He transforms the barren wife into a glad mother of children. Halleluyah![1]

When Israel went forth from Egypt, Yaakov's household from a people of alien tongue, Yehudah became His sanctuary, Israel His dominion. The Sea saw and fled; the Jordan turned backward. The mountains skipped like rams, and the hills like young lambs. What ails you, O Sea, that you flee? O Jordan, that you turn backward? O mountains, that you skip like rams? O hills, like young lambs? Before HASHEM's presence – tremble, O earth, before the presence of the God of Yaakov, Who turns the rock into a pond of water, the flint into a flowing fountain.[2]

According to all customs the cup is lifted
and the matzos covered during the recitation of this blessing.

Blessed are You, HASHEM, our God, King of the

---

(1) *Tehillim* 113. (2) *Tehillim* 114.

Zalman, understands it as referring to the new song to be inserted at this point when the future redemption occurs. He further notes that *shirah*, song, is a feminine noun, and in the past tense it accords with *v'ne'emrah,* so that a vocalization of *v'ne'emar* is incorrect even for the past tense.]

Rav Shlomo Zalman Auerbach is cited in *V'aleihu Lo Yibol* I, page 177, as ruling that both versions should be recited.

אֲשֶׁר גְּאָלָנוּ וְגָאַל אֶת אֲבוֹתֵינוּ מִמִּצְרַיִם, וְהִגִּיעָנוּ הַלַּיְלָה הַזֶּה לֶאֱכָל בּוֹ מַצָּה וּמָרוֹר. כֵּן יהוה אֱלֹהֵינוּ וֵאלֹהֵי אֲבוֹתֵינוּ, יַגִּיעֵנוּ לְמוֹעֲדִים וְלִרְגָלִים אֲחֵרִים הַבָּאִים לִקְרָאתֵנוּ לְשָׁלוֹם, שְׂמֵחִים בְּבִנְיַן עִירֶךָ וְשָׂשִׂים בַּעֲבוֹדָתֶךָ,

(On *Motzaei Shabbos* the phrase in parentheses substitutes for the preceding phrase.)

וְנֹאכַל שָׁם מִן הַזְּבָחִים וּמִן הַפְּסָחִים [מִן הַפְּסָחִים וּמִן הַזְּבָחִים] אֲשֶׁר יַגִּיעַ דָּמָם עַל קִיר מִזְבַּחֲךָ

אֲשֶׁר גְּאָלָנוּ וְגָאַל אֶת אֲבוֹתֵינוּ
Who redeemed us and redeemed our ancestors

On Pesach we say, *Who redeemed us and redeemed our ancestors*, yet on Purim we say only, *Who has performed miracles for our ancestors*. If a person is required to personally thank Hashem for miracles which occurred to his ancestors — because, ultimately, he is affected as well — then on Purim he should also say ... *miracles for us and for our ancestors*. If, on the other hand, one need not personally thank Hashem for a miracle which occurred to his ancestors, then why do we say *"redeemed us"* **on Pesach?**

The answer seems to be that a miracle that occurs to one's ancestors, i.e., allowing the ancestor to live and bear children, does *not* require the descendant to offer personal thanks. The blessing that is said to express such thanks is, "...Who has performed a miracle for me in this place." How can a person say *for me* when in his present state *no* miracle was performed for him (other than that he would not be in existence had the miracle not occurred to his ancestors)?

This is not the case, however, concerning the slavery in Egypt. Had Hashem not redeemed our ancestors, we would still have been born — but only in the lowly spiritual state of the enslavement, immersed in the fifty gates of defilement. In this case, it *is* appropriate to say "...Who has performed a miracle for me in this place." The miracle He performed *for me* was that my ancestors were redeemed from this spiritual enslavement, thereby changing who *I* am. It is thus appropriate to say, *Who redeemed us and redeemed our ancestors*.

הגדה של פסח [174]

universe, Who redeemed us and redeemed our ancestors from Egypt and enabled us to reach this night that we may eat on it matzah and *maror*. So, HASHEM, our God and God of our fathers, bring us also to future festivals and holidays in peace, gladdened in the building of Your city and joyful at Your service.

(On *Motzaei Shabbos* the phrase in parentheses substitutes for the preceding phrase.)

There we shall eat of the offerings and *pesach* sacrifices (of the *pesach* sacrifices and offerings) whose blood will reach the wall of Your Altar for gracious

---

In a similar vein, it is said that Rav Chaim Volozhin, the famed disciple of the Vilna Gaon, once passed a place in which a miracle had occurred to the Gaon's mother. At that place he recited the blessing ... *Who has performed a miracle for me in this place*. Now, it did not seem that a miracle was performed *for him* in that place; rather, as a result of that miracle, his master the Vilna Gaon came into existence. True, with or without that miracle Rav Chaim would have been born, yet had the Vilna Gaon not been born it would not have been the same Rav Chaim. Would he not have been the benefactor of the Gaon's tutelage he would have never reached those levels of greatness (from an unpublished manuscript presented by Rav Shlomo Zalman's grandson, Rav Aharon Goldberg).

כֵּן ה' ... יַגִּיעֵנוּ לְמוֹעֲדִים וְלִרְגָלִים אֲחֵרִים
So Hashem ... bring us also to future festivals and holidays

What are these future festivals and holidays? They are the festivals alluded to in the verse (*Zechariah* 8:19): "Thus said Hashem, Master of Legions: The fast of the fourth [month; i.e., the seventeenth of Tammuz], the fast of the fifth [month; i.e., the ninth of Av], the fast of the seventh [month; Tzom Gedalyah], and the fast of the tenth [month; the tenth of Teves] will be in the House of Yehudah for joy and for gladness and for happy festivals."

In future days these fasts will be transformed to happy festivals, and we hope and pray that Hashem will speedily bring us to those "future festivals!" (*Haggadas Arzei Halevanon* p. 219).

לְרָצוֹן. וְנוֹדֶה לְךָ שִׁיר חָדָשׁ עַל גְּאֻלָּתֵנוּ וְעַל פְּדוּת נַפְשֵׁנוּ. בָּרוּךְ אַתָּה יהוה, גָּאַל יִשְׂרָאֵל.

Some recite the following before the second cup:

הֲרֵינִי מוּכָן וּמְזֻמָּן לְקַיֵּם מִצְוַת כּוֹס שֵׁנִי מֵאַרְבַּע כּוֹסוֹת. לְשֵׁם יִחוּד קֻדְשָׁא בְּרִיךְ הוּא וּשְׁכִינְתֵּיהּ, עַל יְדֵי הַהוּא טָמִיר וְנֶעְלָם, בְּשֵׁם כָּל יִשְׂרָאֵל. וִיהִי נֹעַם אֲדֹנָי אֱלֹהֵינוּ עָלֵינוּ, וּמַעֲשֵׂה יָדֵינוּ כּוֹנְנָה עָלֵינוּ, וּמַעֲשֵׂה יָדֵינוּ כּוֹנְנֵהוּ:

בָּרוּךְ אַתָּה יהוה אֱלֹהֵינוּ מֶלֶךְ הָעוֹלָם, בּוֹרֵא פְּרִי הַגָּפֶן.

The second cup is drunk while leaning on the left side – preferably the entire cup, but at least most of it.

רָחְצָה

The hands are washed for matzah and the following blessing is recited. It is preferable to bring water and a basin to the head of the household at the Seder table.

בָּרוּךְ אַתָּה יהוה אֱלֹהֵינוּ מֶלֶךְ הָעוֹלָם, אֲשֶׁר קִדְּשָׁנוּ בְּמִצְוֹתָיו, וְצִוָּנוּ עַל נְטִילַת יָדָיִם.

בּוֹרֵא פְּרִי הַגָּפֶן
Who creates the fruit of the vine.

It is our custom to recite a separate *Borei pri hagafen* for each of the four cups of wine. In fact, there is a great dispute concerning this point among the *Rishonim*, and the *Shulchan Aruch* and *Rema* (474:1) dispute the final ruling. The *Shulchan Aruch* rules that one recites the blessing only on the first and third cups, whereas *Rema* rules that each cup requires its own blessing. Ashkenazi custom, as usual, follows *Rema*. The *Shulchan Aruch's* rule is based on the general principle that a blessing remains viable until it is removed from the mind. In this case, the Grace After Meals recited between the second and third cups breaks the concentration and obligates a separate

acceptance. We shall then sing a new song of praise to You for our redemption and for the liberation of our souls. Blessed are You, HASHEM, Who has redeemed Israel.

Some recite the following before the second cup:

Behold, I am prepared and ready to fulfill the mitzvah of the second of the Four Cups. For the sake of the unification of the Holy One, Blessed is He, and His Presence, through Him Who is hidden and inscrutable — [I pray] in the name of all Israel. May the pleasantness of my Lord, our God, be upon us — may He establish our handiwork for us; our handiwork may He establish.

Blessed are You, HASHEM, our God, King of the universe, Who creates the fruit of the vine.

The second cup is drunk while leaning on the left side — preferably the entire cup, but at least most of it.

RACHTZAH

The hands are washed for matzah and the following blessing is recited. It is preferable to bring water and a basin to the head of the household at the Seder table.

Blessed are You, HASHEM, our God, King of the universe, Who has sanctified us with His commandments, and has commanded us concerning the washing of the hands.

---

blessing on the third cup. *Rema,* on the other hand, reasons that each cup involves the fulfillment of a separate mitzvah, thereby requiring a separate blessing for each cup.

Perhaps an example from other laws can illustrate the principle of separate mitzvos requiring separate blessings. The rabbi who performs the marriage ceremony begins the marriage ceremony by reciting *Borei pri hagafen.* The prevalent Ashkenazi custom is that the rabbi does not drink from the wine; only the bride and groom do. The seven blessings (*Sheva Berachos*) of *nissuin* are then recited, which begin with another blessing of *Borei pri hagafen.* It is quite possible that the very same rabbi will be honored with that blessing. Once again he recites the blessing and only the bride and groom drink from the wine. What is the purpose of repeating the *Borei pri hagafen*? Did

מוֹצִיא / מַצָּה

Some recite the following before the blessing *hamotzi*:

הִנְנִי מוּכָן וּמְזֻמָּן לְקַיֵּם מִצְוַת אֲכִילַת מַצָּה. לְשֵׁם יִחוּד קֻדְשָׁא בְּרִיךְ הוּא וּשְׁכִינְתֵּיהּ, עַל יְדֵי הַהוּא טָמִיר וְנֶעְלָם, בְּשֵׁם כָּל יִשְׂרָאֵל. וִיהִי נֹעַם אֲדֹנָי אֱלֹהֵינוּ עָלֵינוּ, וּמַעֲשֵׂה יָדֵינוּ כּוֹנְנָה עָלֵינוּ, וּמַעֲשֵׂה יָדֵינוּ כּוֹנְנֵהוּ:

The following two blessings are recited over matzah; the first is recited over matzah as food, and the second for the special mitzvah of eating matzah on the night of Pesach. [The latter blessing is to be made with the intention that it also apply to the "sandwich" and the *afikoman*.]

---

the bride and groom not remain in the very same spot beneath the *chuppah*?

The answer, of course, is that *kiddushin* and *nissuin* are separate mitzvos. The first *Borei pri hagafen* was recited as part of the *kiddushin* process. After the groom places a ring on the bride's finger, the process of *nissuin* begins and the seven blessings are recited. These blessings of praise must also be recited over a cup of wine, and since *nissuin* involves a new mitzvah, a new blessing is recited over the wine.

The same is true for the four cups of wine at the Seder. Each of them is considered a separate mitzvah, and so a separate blessing is recited over each cup (from a lecture on the laws of Pesach given by Rav Shlomo Zalman in 1970).

מַצָּה / Matzah

◈§ How much matzah must one eat?

Each person should eat a *kezayis* (literally, the measure of an olive; or the volume of half a large egg) from each of the top two matzos. The customary value for this measure is 27 milliliters (.913 fluid ounces) which, for matzah, weighs between 13.5 and 15 grams (.476-.529 ounces) (Rav Shlomo Zalman Auerbach cited in *Yom Tov Sheni K'hilchasah* 1:198).[1]

In Rav Shlomo Zalman's house, each participant was given three hand matzos before the Seder, so that each person would be able to

---

1. Also Rav Y.S. Elyashiv, ibid., *Kovetz Teshuvos* II.

MOTZI / MATZAH

Some recite the following before the blessing *hamotzi*:

Behold, I am prepared and ready to fulfill the mitzvah of eating matzah. For the sake of the unification of the Holy One, Blessed is He, and His Presence, through Him who is hidden and inscrutable – [I pray] in the name of all Israel. May the pleasantness of my Lord, our God, be upon us – may He establish our handiwork for us; our handiwork may He establish.

The following two blessings are recited over matzah; the first is recited over matzah as food, and the second for the special mitzvah of eating matzah on the night of Pesach. [The latter blessing is to be made with the intention that it also apply to the *"sandwich"* and the *afikoman*.]

---

take his own two *kezayis*-measures without having to spend too much time between washing *netilas yadayim* and eating the matzos (as cited by his grandson, Rav Pinchas Bondy, in *Kol HaTorah*, Nisan 5756.)[1]

Rav Shlomo Zalman himself ate the two *kezayis*-measures quickly and without pausing, but a piece at a time (as reported by his grandson, Rav Aharon Goldberg).

In his final years he would dip the matzah in water to make it easier to chew and swallow in the requisite time frame (*Kol HaTorah*, Nisan 5756, citing his grandson, Rav Pinchas Bondy).

Children who understand the concepts of Pesach should also eat the requisite measure of matzah within the requisite time period. If they cannot, then they should not recite the blessing *Al achilas matzah*. Nevertheless, in their case, one can be lenient in considering

---

1. *Rema, Orach Chaim* 167:1 states that on [an ordinary] Shabbos, one "has to give each participant a *kezayis* measure from the *lechem mishneh*, the two loaves upon which *Hamotzi* is recited." Rav Shlomo Zalman Auerbach is quoted (in *Shemiras Shabbos K'hilchasah* 55:5 [15]) as stating that perhaps it is sufficient if each of the participants eats less than a *kezayis* from the *lechem mishneh*. Rav Shlomo Zalman went on to explain: The reasoning of the *Rema* is not due to *lechem mishneh* considerations; but is because it is preferable to consume a *kezayis* before speaking. However, many people are lenient regarding this halachah. Therefore, it is possible that it is fully permissible to fulfill one's *lechem mishneh* requirement by eating less than a *kezayis* from the one who recites the blessing. This is especially true for the Shabbos and *Yom Tov* meals of Pesach, where it is virtually impossible to give each participant a *kezayis*-sized piece from two matzos. One who wishes to be stringent can eat a *kezayis* from another matzah. (Also see the citation there from Rav Moshe Feinstein and the reported practice of Rav Y.S. Elyashiv.)

The head of the household raises all the matzos on the Seder plate and recites the following blessing:

בָּרוּךְ אַתָּה יהוה אֱלֹהֵינוּ מֶלֶךְ הָעוֹלָם, הַמּוֹצִיא לֶחֶם מִן הָאָרֶץ.

The bottom matzah is put down and the following blessing is recited while the top (whole) matzah and the middle (broken) piece are still raised.

בָּרוּךְ אַתָּה יהוה אֱלֹהֵינוּ מֶלֶךְ הָעוֹלָם, אֲשֶׁר קִדְּשָׁנוּ בְּמִצְוֹתָיו, וְצִוָּנוּ עַל אֲכִילַת מַצָּה.

Each participant is required to eat an amount of matzah equal in volume to an egg. Since it is usually impossible to provide a sufficient amount of matzah from the two matzos for all members of the household, the other matzos should be available at the head of the table from which to complete the required amounts. However, each participant should receive a piece from each of the top two matzos. The matzos are to be eaten while reclining on the left side and without delay; they need not be dipped in salt.

מָרוֹר

The head of the household takes a half-egg volume of maror, dips it into charoses, and gives each participant a like amount.

Some recite the following before maror:

הִנְנִי מוּכָן וּמְזוּמָּן לְקַיֵּם מִצְוַת אֲכִילַת מָרוֹר. לְשֵׁם יִחוּד קֻדְשָׁא בְּרִיךְ הוּא וּשְׁכִינְתֵּיהּ, עַל יְדֵי הַהוּא טָמִיר וְנֶעְלָם, בְּשֵׁם כָּל יִשְׂרָאֵל. וִיהִי נֹעַם אֲדֹנָי אֱלֹהֵינוּ עָלֵינוּ, וּמַעֲשֵׂה יָדֵינוּ כּוֹנְנָה עָלֵינוּ, וּמַעֲשֵׂה יָדֵינוּ כּוֹנְנֵהוּ:

---

bichdei achilas pras as allowing up to nine minutes (Rav Shlomo Zalman Auerbach cited in *Shemiras Shabbos K'hilchasah* II 54 130).

מָרוֹר / Maror

◆§ The Kezayis of Maror

Referring to the *pesach* sacrifice, the Torah says (*Bamidbar* 9:11): "With matzos and bitter herbs shall he eat it." The primary obligation is to eat *maror* along with the *pesach* sacrifice. Accordingly, in our times, when the *pesach* sacrifice is not offered, there is no Torah obligation to eat *maror*. (Matzah, on the other hand, has an additional verse from *Shemos* 12:18: "In the evening shall you eat matzos,"

The head of the household raises all the matzos on the Seder plate and recites the following blessing:

Blessed are You, HASHEM, our God, King of the universe, Who brings forth bread from the earth.

The bottom matzah is put down and the following blessing is recited while the top (whole) matzah and the middle (broken) piece are still raised.

Blessed are You, HASHEM, our God, King of the universe, Who has sanctified us with His commandments, and has commanded us concerning the eating of the matzah.

Each participant is required to eat an amount of matzah equal in volume to an egg. Since it is usually impossible to provide a sufficient amount of matzah from the two matzos for all members of the household, the other matzos should be available at the head of the table from which to complete the required amounts. However, each participant should receive a piece from each of the top two matzos. The matzos are to be eaten while reclining on the left side and without delay; they need not be dipped in salt.

MAROR

The head of the household takes a half-egg volume of maror, dips it into charoses, and gives each participant a like amount.

Some recite the following before maror:

Behold, I am prepared and ready to fulfill the mitzvah of eating maror. For the sake of unification of the Holy One, Blessed is He, and His Presence, through Him Who is hidden and inscrutable – [I pray] in the name of all Israel. May the pleasantness of my Lord, our God, be upon us – may He establish our handiwork for us; our handiwork may He establish.

---

which obligates eating matzah in every generation.)

The requirement to eat a *kezayis* of matzah is derived from the requirement to "eat" (in the above-mentioned verse in *Shemos* 12:18), since any mandated eating refers to a *kezayis*. Rosh, in his commentary to *Pesachim* (10:28), states that there was never a Torah requirement to eat a *kezayis* measure of *maror*, since the only form of "eat" in the verse, "With matzos and bitter herbs shall he eat it," refers to "it," the *pesach* offering, and not to the *maror*. The requirement to eat a *kezayis* of *maror* is a Rabbinic requirement, because "eating," *achilah*, is mentioned in the blessing on *maror*: *Al achilas maror*, and *eating* requires a *kezayis*. Since the whole requirement for a *kezayis* originates from a Rabbinic enactment,

The following blessing is recited with the intention that it also apply to the maror *of the "sandwich." The* maror *is eaten without reclining, and without delay.*

בָּרוּךְ אַתָּה יהוה אֱלֹהֵינוּ מֶלֶךְ הָעוֹלָם, אֲשֶׁר קִדְּשָׁנוּ בְּמִצְוֺתָיו, וְצִוָּנוּ עַל אֲכִילַת מָרוֹר.

כּוֹרֵךְ

The bottom (thus far unbroken) matzah is now taken. From it, with the addition of other matzos, each participant receives a half-egg volume of matzah with an equal-volume portion of maror *(dipped into* charoses *which is shaken off). The following paragraph is recited and the "sandwich" is eaten while reclining. [Rav Shlomo Zalman recited the paragraph after eating the "sandwich."]*

---

however, there is room for greater leniency in this measure. Nevertheless, others (e.g., *Yerei'im* 94) explain the "shall he eat it" of the above-cited verse as referring to the *maror* as well. They agree that there is no Torah requirement in our times to eat *maror*, but since a *kezayis* was mandated when there was a *pesach* sacrifice, today's Rabbinic obligation is somewhat more stringent (from a lecture on the laws of Pesach given by Rav Shlomo Zalman in 1970).

As mentioned above, Rav Shlomo Zalman maintained that a *kezayis* of matzah was 27 cubic centimeters. This is based on the assumption that a *kezayis* is the volume of half an egg, as ruled by the *Shulchan Aruch* 866:1. However, the *Mishnah Berurah* (ad loc.) states that, according to Rambam, a *kezayis* is only one-*third* of an egg. He concludes that for Torah mitzvos one should conduct himself according to the stringent opinion that it is the volume of half an egg (except for sick people and the like, who can rely on Rambam). There is more room for leniency, however, for *maror* and other Rabbinic mitzvos, and if necessary, one can rely on the opinion that it is only one-third of an egg — i.e., 17.3 cubic centimeters according to Rav Shlomo Zalman.

If there is room for leniency regarding the quantity of *maror*, there is also room for leniency regarding the time frame in which the required measure must be consumed. If necessary, one can take up to nine minutes to eat the required quantity of *maror*. Certainly a child, who cannot recite the blessing unless he eats the minimum measure in the required time (the view attributed to Rav Shlomo Zalman in *Chinuch Habanim L'mitzvos*, p.15, note 72), may take nine minutes to

*The following blessing is recited with the intention
that it also apply to the maror of the "sandwich."
The maror is eaten without reclining, and without delay.*

Blessed are You, HASHEM, our God, King of the universe, Who has sanctified us with His commandments, and has commanded us concerning the eating of *maror*.

KORECH

*The bottom (thus far unbroken) matzah is now taken. From it, with the addition of other matzos, each participant receives a half-egg volume of matzah with an equal volume portion of maror (dipped into charoses which is shaken off). The following paragraph is recited and the "sandwich" is eaten while reclining.
[Rav Shlomo Zalman recited the paragraph after eating the "sandwich."]*

consume the *kezayis* (Rav Shlomo Zalman, as cited in *Shemiras Shabbos K'hilchasah* Chapter 54, note 130).[1]

A sick person who cannot swallow *maror* may not chew *maror* and then spit it out. One fulfills the requirement of eating *maror* only when it is actually swallowed (*Minchas Shlomo* I:91).

◆§ Charoses

There are various Kabbalistic reasons for dipping the *maror* into *charoses*. On a simple level it is either to nullify the poisonous nature of the *maror*, or to symbolize the mortar with which the Children of Israel worked in Egypt, as is mentioned in the Gemara (*Pesachim* 116a) (from a lecture on the laws of Pesach given by Rav Shlomo Zalman in 1970).

כּוֹרֵךְ / Korech

When the *Beis HaMikdash* stood, Hillel would make a sandwich out of matzah, *maror* [and the *pesach* sacrifice — Rashi on the Gemara there] and eat them together to fulfill the literal meaning of the verse (*Bamidbar* 9:11): "With matzos and bitter herbs shall he eat it." The Sages disagree and rule that he fulfills his obligation by eating each element on its own.

Since it is not clear whether we follow Hillel or the Sages, we first eat a piece of matzah by itself and then a piece of *maror* by itself. Then we

---

1. However, he is cited as granting the same leniency to children eating a *kezayis* of matzah.

זֵ**כֶר** לְמִקְדָּשׁ כְּהִלֵּל. כֵּן עָשָׂה הִלֵּל בִּזְמַן שֶׁבֵּית הַמִּקְדָּשׁ הָיָה קַיָּם. הָיָה כּוֹרֵךְ [פֶּסַח] מַצָּה וּמָרוֹר וְאוֹכֵל בְּיַחַד. לְקַיֵּם מַה שֶּׁנֶּאֱמַר, עַל מַצּוֹת וּמְרֹרִים יֹאכְלֻהוּ.[1]

שֻׁלְחָן עוֹרֵךְ

The meal should be eaten in a combination of joy and solemnity, for the meal, too, is a part of the Seder service. While it is desirable that *zemiros* and discussion of the laws and events of Pesach be part of the meal, extraneous conversation should be avoided. It should be remembered that the *afikoman* must be eaten while there is still some appetite for it. In fact, if one is so sated that he must literally force himself to eat it, he is not credited with the performance of the mitzvah of *afikoman*. Therefore, it is unwise to eat more than a moderate amount during the meal.

---

take an additional piece of matzah and an additional piece or *maror* and eat them together, as did Hillel.

However, one might ask: Why not follow Hillel's opinion? If one must eat matzah and *maror,* what harm can there be in combining them? The answer is that, today, *maror* is a Rabbinic obligation, and that changes the situation. Even Hillel would agree today that matzah and *maror* must be eaten separately. Otherwise, the Rabbinic *maror* in one's mouth would overpower the taste of the Torah-mandated matzah being eaten along with it and nullify it. Therefore, we must first eat a piece of matzah which is Torah mandated.

Now another question arises. Why must we eat *maror* on its own? Perhaps, halachically, the best option would be to proceed straight to *Korech*? Do the Sages object if one eats *maror* together with a piece of matzah? Again, we apply the same principle, albeit differently. If the Halachah accords with the Sages, and the person has already fulfilled his matzah requirement, the taste of another piece of nonrequired matzah along with the required *maror* would nullify the *maror*.

The results of these deliberations are: If it were clear that the Halachah accords with the Sages, then we would eat only matzah by itself and then *maror* by itself. Conversely, if it were clear that the Halachah accords with Hillel, then nowadays we would eat matzah by itself followed by a matzah-*maror* sandwich. Since, however, we do not know with whom the Halachah accords, we eat matzah by itself,

In remembrance of the Temple we do as Hillel did in Temple times: He would combine (the *pesach* offering,) matzah and *maror* in a sandwich and eat them together, to fulfill what it says: They shall eat it with matzos and bitter herbs.[1]

SHULCHAN ORECH

The meal should be eaten in a combination of joy and solemnity, for the meal, too, is a part of the Seder service. While it is desirable that *zemiros* and discussion of the laws and events of Pesach be part of the meal, extraneous conversation should be avoided. It should be remembered that the *afikoman* must be eaten while there is still some appetite for it. In fact, if one is so sated that he must literally force himself to eat it, he is not credited with the performance of the mitzvah of *afikoman*. Therefore, it is unwise to eat more than a moderate amount during the meal.

(1) *Bamidbar* 9:11.

---

maror by itself, and then a matzah-*maror* sandwich (from a lecture on the laws of Pesach given by Rav Shlomo Zalman in 1970, published in *Kuntres Seder Pesach*).

שֻׁלְחָן עוֹרֵךְ / Shulchan Orach

◆§ Eggs and Salt Water

Rema (476:2) cites the custom of eating an egg on the Seder night. He explains the custom as a sign of mourning, since Tishah B'Av always comes out on the same day of the week as the first day of Pesach. See *Biur HaGra* (ibid.) for an alternate reason. *Rema* (475:1) in another ruling states that matzah is not dipped into salt, and consequently many people do not place salt at the table. Subsequently, when eating the egg and finding no other salt, people began dipping it into the salt water which *was* on the table. Others followed the custom brought by *Rema* (476:2) that one should not dip more than two times on this night (from a lecture on the laws of Pesach given by Rav Shlomo Zalman in 1970, published in *Kuntres Seder Pesach*).

◆§ Finishing the meal after chatzos

R' Avraham of Sochaczew (*Avnei Nezer, Orach Chaim* 381:5), a great man who could not extend the Seder as long as he wished and still eat the *afikoman* before *chatzos*, resolved the problem ingeniously

צָפוּן

From the *afikoman* matzah (and from additional matzos to make up the required amount) a half-egg's volume portion — according to some, a full egg's volume portion — is given to each participant. It should be eaten before midnight, while reclining, without delay, and uninterruptedly. Nothing may be eaten or drunk after the *afikoman* (with the exception of water and the like) except for the last two Seder cups of wine.

Some recite the following before eating the *afikoman*:

הִנְנִי מוּכָן וּמְזוּמָּן לְקַיֵּם מִצְוַת אֲכִילַת אֲפִיקוֹמָן. לְשֵׁם יִחוּד קֻדְשָׁא בְּרִיךְ הוּא וּשְׁכִינְתֵּיהּ, עַל יְדֵי הַהוּא טָמִיר וְנֶעְלָם, בְּשֵׁם כָּל יִשְׂרָאֵל. וִיהִי נְעַם אֲדֹנָי אֱלֹהֵינוּ עָלֵינוּ, וּמַעֲשֵׂה יָדֵינוּ כּוֹנְנָה עָלֵינוּ, וּמַעֲשֵׂה יָדֵינוּ כּוֹנְנֵהוּ:

---

by eating the *afikoman* twice with the following condition:

The requirement to eat the *afikoman* by a certain time, and the prohibition to eat other foods after the *afikoman*, are both based upon a dispute between R' Elazar ben Azaryah and R' Akiva concerning the permitted time to eat the *pesach* sacrifice. According to R' Elazar ben Azaryah, the *pesach* sacrifice can only be eaten until *chatzos*. The *afikoman*, substituting for the sacrifice, must, therefore, also be eaten before *chatzos*. However, the Sochaczewer asked, when does the prohibition of eating after the *afikoman* end? Surely, one may eat the next morning. He explained that this prohibition exists only during the time period in which the *pesach* sacrifice may be eaten. Thus, according to R' Elazar ben Azaryah who says that the *pesach* sacrifice is eaten only until *chatzos*, eating should be permitted after *chatzos*! As for R' Akiva, who says that the *pesach* offering may be eaten until dawn, the *afikoman* is also eaten until dawn, and after eating the *afikoman* all other eating is prohibited until dawn.

Therefore the Sochaczewer suggested taking a piece of matzah shortly before *chatzos* and saying before eating it, "If the Halachah follows R' Elazar ben Azaryah, then let this matzah be my *afikoman*; but if the Halachah follows R' Akiva, then let this be an ordinary piece of matzah and I will eat my *afikoman* later." In either case, he is allowed to continue eating after *chatzos*. According to R' Elazar ben Azaryah, he may continue to eat because it is no longer the time period in which a person eats the *pesach* offering. According to R' Akiva, he can continue to eat because, even though in this time

TZAFUN

From the *afikoman* matzah (and from additional matzos to make up the required amount) a half-egg's volume portion – according to some, a full egg's volume portion – is given to each participant. It should be eaten before midnight, while reclining, without delay, and uninterruptedly. Nothing may be eaten or drunk after the *afikoman* (with the exception of water and the like) except for the last two Seder cups of wine.

Some recite the following before eating the *afikoman*:

Behold, I am prepared and ready to fulfill the mitzvah of eating the *afikoman*. For the sake of the unification of the Holy One, Blessed is He, and his Presence, through Him Who is hidden and inscrutable – [I pray] in the name of all Israel. May the pleasantness of my Lord, our God, be upon us – may He establish our handiwork for us; our handiwork may He establish.

---

period it is still legitimate to eat both the *pesach* sacrifice and *afikoman*, he has not yet eaten the "real" *afikoman*. Only after eating his "second" *afikoman* before the Grace After Meals is he prohibited eating until dawn[1] (from a lecture on the laws of Pesach given by Rav Shlomo Zalman in 1970, published in *Kuntres Seder Pesach*).

צָפוּן / Tzafun

◈§ Why isn't mayim acharonim listed in the order of the Seder?

The *simanim* order of the Seder include *Kadesh, U'rechatz,* and *Rachtzah*. Why don't we also list *mayim acharonim* (the washing after the meal)? In the special *yotzer* addition recited on *Shabbos Hagadol* (authored by R' Yosef Tov-Elem), *mayim acharonim* is indeed listed in the order!

There is a dispute as to the reason for using *mayim acharonim*. According to one view, there may be "Sodomite" salt (which may have mixed into the standard salt) on the fingers, which could cause blindness if not washed away. The other view is that, in the process of

---

1. The Brisker Rav held that, *if* this works, it should work without explicitly stating this condition as well. Rav Moshe Feinstein, on the other hand, maintained that the condition does not work at all, and the *afikoman* must be eaten before *chatzos*.

Rav Avigdor Nebenzahl notes that this condition applies only to the *afikoman*. It cannot work with regard to *Hallel* and the four cups. Those who hold that *Hallel* must be recited before *chatzos,* and that the four cups of wine must be drunk by that time, cannot rely on this condition.

בָּרֵךְ

The third cup is poured and *Bircas Hamazon* (Grace After Meals) is recited.
According to some customs, the Cup of Eliyahu is poured at this point.

שִׁיר הַמַּעֲלוֹת, בְּשׁוּב יהוה אֶת שִׁיבַת צִיּוֹן, הָיִינוּ כְּחֹלְמִים. אָז יִמָּלֵא שְׂחוֹק פִּינוּ וּלְשׁוֹנֵנוּ רִנָּה, אָז יֹאמְרוּ בַגּוֹיִם, הִגְדִּיל יהוה לַעֲשׂוֹת עִם אֵלֶּה. הִגְדִּיל יהוה לַעֲשׂוֹת עִמָּנוּ, הָיִינוּ שְׂמֵחִים. שׁוּבָה יהוה אֶת שְׁבִיתֵנוּ, כַּאֲפִיקִים בַּנֶּגֶב. הַזֹּרְעִים בְּדִמְעָה בְּרִנָּה יִקְצֹרוּ. הָלוֹךְ יֵלֵךְ וּבָכֹה נֹשֵׂא מֶשֶׁךְ הַזָּרַע, בֹּא יָבֹא בְרִנָּה, נֹשֵׂא אֲלֻמֹּתָיו.[1]

---

eating, the hands get dirty and one may not recite a blessing (i.e., the Grace After Meals) with dirty hands. This view is learned from the verse (*Vayikra* 20:7): "You shall sanctify yourselves and you will be holy"; *You shall sanctify yourselves* by washing before eating bread, and *you will be holy* by washing after the meal (*mayim acharonim*). [See *Eruvin* 17b; *Berachos* 53b; *Mishnah Berurah* 181:1.]

Apparently, the order of the Seder reflects the first reason for *mayim acharonim,* the possibility of Sodomite salt. Since on this night, in accordance with the ruling of the *Rema* (471:1), we do not dip the matzah into salt, and there is no obligation to have salt on any other food (indeed, there is no *obligation* to eat *any* specific food), there is no absolute obligation to wash *mayim acharonim.*

The author of the *yotzer,* on the other hand, understood that the main reason for *mayim acharonim* is to clean the hands. This reason clearly applies to the Seder night, even when no salt is used. Accordingly he included it in his order.

In summation: Washing with *mayim acharonim* is very important on the Seder night, and should not be omitted.[1] The only reason it is not

---

1. See *Leket Yosher* I, *Orach Chaim* 36:3, who writes, "I remember that the author of *Terumas Hadeshen* [a late *Rishon*] did not wash with *mayim acharonim* at all, except for the first two nights of Pesach." His reason was that as a result of the preciousness of the miracle of Pesach one should act more stringently.

BARECH

The third cup is poured and Bircas Hamazon (Grace After Meals) is recited. According to some customs, the Cup of Eliyahu is poured at this point.

A song of Ascents. When HASHEM brings back the exiles to Tziyon, we will have been like dreamers. Then our mouth will be filled with laughter, and our tongue with glad song. Then will it be said among the nations: HASHEM has done great things for these, HASHEM has done great things for us, and we rejoiced. Restore our captives, HASHEM, like streams in the dry land. Those who sow in tears shall reap in joy. Though the farmer bears the measure of seed to the field in tears, he shall come home with joy, bearing his sheaves.[1]

(1) *Tehillim* 126.

---

included in our order of the Seder is that the author of the order held that since there did not have to be any salt used at the Seder, it was not an absolute obligation (from a lecture on the laws of Pesach given by Rav Shlomo Zalman in 1970, published in *Kuntres Seder Pesach*).

בָּרֵךְ / *Barech*

◈§ The "Cup of Eliyahu"

The four cups of wine correspond to the four expressions of redemption used by God in His promise to Moshe in *Shemos* 6:6-7: "1) I shall *take you out* from under the burdens of Egypt; 2) I shall *rescue* you from their servitude; 3) I shall *redeem* you with an outstretched arm and with great judgments; 4) I shall *take* you to Me for a people and I shall be a God to you."

Actually, the end of the last verse, *I shall be a God to you*, can be understood as a fifth expression of redemption. Indeed, there is a dispute among the *Rishonim* regarding whether a fifth cup should be drunk at the Seder or not. Some *Rishonim* did in fact drink a fifth cup of wine. Today, there may be some communities where they drink

---

Rav Shlomo Zalman himself certainly washed with *mayim acharonim* on the Seder night (*Kol HaTorah,* Nisan 5756, citing Rav Shlomo Zalman's grandson, Rav Pinchas Bondy).

Some recite the following before *Bircas Hamazon*:

הִנְנִי מוּכָן וּמְזוּמָן לְקַיֵּם מִצְוַת עֲשֵׂה שֶׁל בִּרְכַּת הַמָּזוֹן, כַּכָּתוּב, וְאָכַלְתָּ וְשָׂבָעְתָּ וּבֵרַכְתָּ אֶת יהוה אֱלֹהֶיךָ עַל הָאָרֶץ הַטֹּבָה אֲשֶׁר נָתַן לָךְ:

If three or more males, aged thirteen or older, participated in the meal, the leader is required to formally invite the others to join him in the recitation of Grace After Meals. Following is the *zimun*, or formal invitation.

The leader begins:

רַבּוֹתַי נְבָרֵךְ.

The group responds:

יְהִי שֵׁם יהוה מְבֹרָךְ מֵעַתָּה וְעַד עוֹלָם.[1]

The leader continues:

יְהִי שֵׁם יהוה מְבֹרָךְ מֵעַתָּה וְעַד עוֹלָם.[1]

If ten men join in the *zimun*, the words (in parentheses) are included.

בִּרְשׁוּת מָרָנָן וְרַבָּנָן וְרַבּוֹתַי, נְבָרֵךְ [אֱלֹהֵינוּ] שֶׁאָכַלְנוּ מִשֶּׁלּוֹ.

The group responds:

בָּרוּךְ [אֱלֹהֵינוּ] שֶׁאָכַלְנוּ מִשֶּׁלּוֹ וּבְטוּבוֹ חָיִינוּ.

The leader continues:

בָּרוּךְ [אֱלֹהֵינוּ] שֶׁאָכַלְנוּ מִשֶּׁלּוֹ וּבְטוּבוֹ חָיִינוּ.

The following line is recited if ten men join in the *zimun*.

בָּרוּךְ הוּא וּבָרוּךְ שְׁמוֹ.

בָּרוּךְ אַתָּה יהוה אֱלֹהֵינוּ מֶלֶךְ הָעוֹלָם, הַזָּן אֶת הָעוֹלָם כֻּלּוֹ, בְּטוּבוֹ, בְּחֵן בְּחֶסֶד וּבְרַחֲמִים, הוּא נוֹתֵן לֶחֶם לְכָל בָּשָׂר, כִּי לְעוֹלָם חַסְדּוֹ[2] וּבְטוּבוֹ הַגָּדוֹל, תָּמִיד לֹא חָסַר לָנוּ, וְאַל יֶחְסַר לָנוּ מָזוֹן לְעוֹלָם וָעֶד. בַּעֲבוּר שְׁמוֹ הַגָּדוֹל,

---

five cups of wine, but the general custom is to drink four cups of wine.

Because there is doubt, however, a fifth cup is poured and placed in the middle of the table. This is as if to say that this cup will stay until Eliyahu the Prophet comes and teaches us whether we should drink

Some recite the following before Bircas Hamazon:

Behold, I am prepared and ready to fulfill the mitzvah of Grace After Meals, as it is written; "And you shall eat and you shall be satisfied and you shall bless HASHEM, your God, for the good land which He gave you."

If three or more males, aged thirteen or older, participated in the meal, the leader is required to formally invite the others to join him in the recitation of Grace After Meals. Following is the zimun, *or formal invitation.*

The leader begins:
Gentlemen, let us bless.
The group responds:
Blessed is the Name of HASHEM from this moment and forever!¹
The leader continues:
Blessed is the Name of HASHEM from this moment and forever!¹

If ten men join in the zimun, *the words (in parentheses) are included.*
With the permission of the distinguished people present, let us bless [our God] for we have eaten from what is His.
The group responds:
Blessed is He [our God] of Whose we have eaten and through Whose goodness we live.
The leader continues:
Blessed is He [our God] of Whose we have eaten and through Whose goodness we live.

The following line is recited if ten men join in the zimun.
Blessed is He and Blessed is His Name.

Blessed are You, HASHEM, our God, King of the universe, Who nourishes the entire world, in His goodness – with grace, with kindness, and with mercy. He gives nourishment to all flesh, for His kindness is eternal.² And through His great goodness, we have never lacked, and may we never lack, nourishment, for all eternity. For the sake of His Great Name,

---

(1) Tehillim 113:2. (2) Tehillim 136:25.

---

this fifth cup or not. That is why a cup is called the "Cup of Eliyahu."
It is not, as people think, that this cup is poured *for* Eliyahu the

כִּי הוּא אֵל זָן וּמְפַרְנֵס לַכֹּל, וּמֵטִיב לַכֹּל, וּמֵכִין מָזוֹן לְכָל בְּרִיּוֹתָיו אֲשֶׁר בָּרָא. בָּרוּךְ אַתָּה יהוה, הַזָּן אֶת הַכֹּל.

נוֹדֶה לְךָ יהוה אֱלֹהֵינוּ, עַל שֶׁהִנְחַלְתָּ לַאֲבוֹתֵינוּ אֶרֶץ חֶמְדָּה טוֹבָה וּרְחָבָה. וְעַל שֶׁהוֹצֵאתָנוּ יהוה אֱלֹהֵינוּ מֵאֶרֶץ מִצְרַיִם, וּפְדִיתָנוּ מִבֵּית עֲבָדִים, וְעַל בְּרִיתְךָ שֶׁחָתַמְתָּ בִּבְשָׂרֵנוּ, וְעַל תּוֹרָתְךָ שֶׁלִּמַּדְתָּנוּ, וְעַל חֻקֶּיךָ שֶׁהוֹדַעְתָּנוּ, וְעַל חַיִּים חֵן וָחֶסֶד שֶׁחוֹנַנְתָּנוּ, וְעַל אֲכִילַת מָזוֹן שָׁאַתָּה זָן וּמְפַרְנֵס אוֹתָנוּ תָּמִיד, בְּכָל יוֹם וּבְכָל עֵת וּבְכָל שָׁעָה.

וְעַל הַכֹּל יהוה אֱלֹהֵינוּ אֲנַחְנוּ מוֹדִים לָךְ, וּמְבָרְכִים אוֹתָךְ, יִתְבָּרַךְ שִׁמְךָ בְּפִי כָּל חַי תָּמִיד לְעוֹלָם וָעֶד. כַּכָּתוּב, וְאָכַלְתָּ וְשָׂבָעְתָּ, וּבֵרַכְתָּ אֶת יהוה אֱלֹהֶיךָ, עַל הָאָרֶץ הַטֹּבָה אֲשֶׁר נָתַן לָךְ.[1] בָּרוּךְ אַתָּה יהוה, עַל הָאָרֶץ וְעַל הַמָּזוֹן.

רַחֶם יהוה אֱלֹהֵינוּ עַל יִשְׂרָאֵל עַמֶּךָ, וְעַל יְרוּשָׁלַיִם עִירֶךָ, וְעַל צִיּוֹן מִשְׁכַּן כְּבוֹדֶךָ, וְעַל מַלְכוּת בֵּית דָּוִד מְשִׁיחֶךָ, וְעַל הַבַּיִת הַגָּדוֹל וְהַקָּדוֹשׁ שֶׁנִּקְרָא שִׁמְךָ עָלָיו.

Prophet. We are not in the habit of pouring cups for Eliyahu or anyone else who is not truly present. Rather, we await his advent to teach us the requirement, if any, for a fifth cup. This concept is the basis of the Talmud's difficult concluding, unresolved questions, with the phrase

because He is God Who nourishes and sustains all, and benefits all, and He prepares food for all of His creatures which He has created. Blessed are You, HASHEM, Who nourishes all.

We thank You, HASHEM, our God, because You have given to our forefathers as a heritage a desirable, good, and spacious land; because You removed us, HASHEM, our God, from the land of Egypt and You redeemed us from the house of bondage; for Your covenant which You sealed in our flesh; for Your Torah which You taught us and for Your statutes which You made known to us; for life, grace, and kindness which You granted us; and for the provision of food with which You nourish and sustain us constantly, in every day, in every season, and in every hour.

For everything, HASHEM, our God, we thank You and bless You. May Your Name be blessed by the mouth of all the living, continuously for all eternity. As it is written: "And you shall eat and you shall be satisfied, and you shall bless HASHEM, your God, for the good land which He gave you."[1] Blessed are You, HASHEM, for the land and for the nourishment.

Have mercy, HASHEM, our God, on Israel Your people; on Yerushalayim, Your city, on Tziyon, the rest-ing place of Your Glory; on the monarchy of the House of David, Your anointed; and on the great and holy House upon which Your Name is called.

---

(1) *Devarim* 8:10.

תיקו, *Teiku*, an acronym for: תִּשְׁבִּי יְתָרֵץ קוּשְׁיוֹת וְאִבָּעְיוֹת — *the Tishbite (Eliyahu) shall resolve questions and problems* (from a lecture on the laws of Pesach given by Rav Shlomo Zalman in 1970, published in *Kuntres Seder Pesach*).

אֱלֹהֵינוּ אָבִינוּ רְעֵנוּ זוּנֵנוּ פַּרְנְסֵנוּ וְכַלְכְּלֵנוּ וְהַרְוִיחֵנוּ, וְהַרְוַח לָנוּ יהוה אֱלֹהֵינוּ מְהֵרָה מִכָּל צָרוֹתֵינוּ. וְנָא אַל תַּצְרִיכֵנוּ יהוה אֱלֹהֵינוּ, לֹא לִידֵי מַתְּנַת בָּשָׂר וָדָם, וְלֹא לִידֵי הַלְוָאָתָם, כִּי אִם לְיָדְךָ הַמְּלֵאָה הַפְּתוּחָה הַקְּדוֹשָׁה וְהָרְחָבָה, שֶׁלֹּא נֵבוֹשׁ וְלֹא נִכָּלֵם לְעוֹלָם וָעֶד.

On Shabbos add the following paragraph.

רְצֵה וְהַחֲלִיצֵנוּ יהוה אֱלֹהֵינוּ בְּמִצְוֹתֶיךָ, וּבְמִצְוַת יוֹם הַשְּׁבִיעִי הַשַּׁבָּת הַגָּדוֹל וְהַקָּדוֹשׁ הַזֶּה, כִּי יוֹם זֶה גָּדוֹל וְקָדוֹשׁ הוּא לְפָנֶיךָ, לִשְׁבָּת בּוֹ וְלָנוּחַ בּוֹ בְּאַהֲבָה כְּמִצְוַת רְצוֹנֶךָ, וּבִרְצוֹנְךָ הָנִיחַ לָנוּ יהוה אֱלֹהֵינוּ, שֶׁלֹּא תְהֵא צָרָה וְיָגוֹן וַאֲנָחָה בְּיוֹם מְנוּחָתֵנוּ, וְהַרְאֵנוּ יהוה אֱלֹהֵינוּ בְּנֶחָמַת צִיּוֹן עִירֶךָ, וּבְבִנְיַן יְרוּשָׁלַיִם עִיר קָדְשֶׁךָ, כִּי אַתָּה הוּא בַּעַל הַיְשׁוּעוֹת וּבַעַל הַנֶּחָמוֹת

אֱלֹהֵינוּ וֵאלֹהֵי אֲבוֹתֵינוּ, יַעֲלֶה, וְיָבֹא, וְיַגִּיעַ, וְיֵרָאֶה, וְיֵרָצֶה, וְיִשָּׁמַע, וְיִפָּקֵד, וְיִזָּכֵר זִכְרוֹנֵנוּ וּפִקְדוֹנֵנוּ, וְזִכְרוֹן אֲבוֹתֵינוּ, וְזִכְרוֹן מָשִׁיחַ בֶּן דָּוִד עַבְדֶּךָ, וְזִכְרוֹן יְרוּשָׁלַיִם עִיר קָדְשֶׁךָ, וְזִכְרוֹן כָּל עַמְּךָ בֵּית יִשְׂרָאֵל לְפָנֶיךָ, לִפְלֵיטָה לְטוֹבָה לְחֵן וּלְחֶסֶד וּלְרַחֲמִים, לְחַיִּים וּלְשָׁלוֹם בְּיוֹם חַג הַמַּצּוֹת הַזֶּה. זָכְרֵנוּ יהוה אֱלֹהֵינוּ בּוֹ לְטוֹבָה, וּפָקְדֵנוּ בוֹ לִבְרָכָה, וְהוֹשִׁיעֵנוּ בוֹ לְחַיִּים. וּבִדְבַר יְשׁוּעָה וְרַחֲמִים, חוּס וְחָנֵּנוּ וְרַחֵם עָלֵינוּ וְהוֹשִׁיעֵנוּ, כִּי אֵלֶיךָ עֵינֵינוּ, כִּי אֵל חַנּוּן וְרַחוּם אָתָּה.[1]

Our God, our Father – tend us, nourish us, sustain us, support us, relieve us; HASHEM, our God, grant us speedy relief from all our troubles. Please, make us not needful – HASHEM, our God – of the gifts of human hands nor of their loans, but only of Your Hand that is full, open, holy, and generous, that we not feel inner shame nor be humiliated for all eternity.

> On Shabbos add the following paragraph.
>
> May it please You to strengthen us, HASHEM, our God, in Your commandments, and in the commandment of the seventh day, this great and holy Shabbos. For this day is great and holy before You to rest on it and be content on it in love, as ordained by Your will. May it be Your will, HASHEM, our God, that there be no distress, grief, or lament on this day of our contentment. And show us, HASHEM, our God, the consolation of Tziyon, Your city, and the rebuilding of Yerushalayim, city of Your holiness, for You are the Master of salvations and Master of consolations.

Our God and God of our forefathers, may there rise, come, reach, be noted, be favored, be heard, be considered, and be remembered – the remembrance and consideration of ourselves; the remembrance of our forefathers; the remembrance of Mashiach, son of David, Your servant; the remembrance of Yerushalayim, the city of Your Holiness; the remembrance of all the House of Israel – before You for deliverance, for goodness, for grace, for kindness, and for compassion, for life, and for peace on this day of the Festival of Matzos. Remember us on it, HASHEM, our God, for goodness; consider us on it for blessing; and help us on it for life. In the matter of salvation and compassion, pity, be gracious and compassionate with us and help us, for our eyes are turned to You, because You are God, the gracious, and compassionate.[1]

---

(1) *Nechemiah* 9:31.

וּבְנֵה יְרוּשָׁלַיִם עִיר הַקֹּדֶשׁ בִּמְהֵרָה בְיָמֵינוּ. בָּרוּךְ אַתָּה יהוה, בּוֹנֵה [בְּרַחֲמָיו] יְרוּשָׁלָיִם. אָמֵן.

בָּרוּךְ אַתָּה יהוה אֱלֹהֵינוּ מֶלֶךְ הָעוֹלָם, הָאֵל אָבִינוּ מַלְכֵּנוּ אַדִּירֵנוּ בּוֹרְאֵנוּ גּוֹאֲלֵנוּ יוֹצְרֵנוּ קְדוֹשֵׁנוּ קְדוֹשׁ יַעֲקֹב, רוֹעֵנוּ רוֹעֵה יִשְׂרָאֵל, הַמֶּלֶךְ הַטּוֹב וְהַמֵּטִיב לַכֹּל, שֶׁבְּכָל יוֹם וָיוֹם הוּא הֵטִיב, הוּא מֵטִיב, הוּא יֵיטִיב לָנוּ. הוּא גְמָלָנוּ הוּא גוֹמְלֵנוּ הוּא יִגְמְלֵנוּ לָעַד, לְחֵן וּלְחֶסֶד וּלְרַחֲמִים וּלְרֶוַח הַצָּלָה וְהַצְלָחָה, בְּרָכָה וִישׁוּעָה נֶחָמָה פַּרְנָסָה וְכַלְכָּלָה וְרַחֲמִים וְחַיִּים וְשָׁלוֹם וְכָל טוֹב, וּמִכָּל טוּב לְעוֹלָם אַל יְחַסְּרֵנוּ.

הָרַחֲמָן הוּא יִמְלוֹךְ עָלֵינוּ לְעוֹלָם וָעֶד. הָרַחֲמָן הוּא יִתְבָּרַךְ בַּשָּׁמַיִם וּבָאָרֶץ. הָרַחֲמָן הוּא יִשְׁתַּבַּח לְדוֹר דּוֹרִים, וְיִתְפָּאַר בָּנוּ לָעַד וּלְנֵצַח נְצָחִים, וְיִתְהַדַּר בָּנוּ לָעַד וּלְעוֹלְמֵי עוֹלָמִים. הָרַחֲמָן הוּא יְפַרְנְסֵנוּ בְּכָבוֹד. הָרַחֲמָן הוּא יִשְׁבּוֹר עֻלֵּנוּ מֵעַל צַוָּארֵנוּ, וְהוּא יוֹלִיכֵנוּ קוֹמְמִיּוּת לְאַרְצֵנוּ. הָרַחֲמָן הוּא יִשְׁלַח לָנוּ בְּרָכָה מְרֻבָּה בַּבַּיִת הַזֶּה, וְעַל שֻׁלְחָן זֶה שֶׁאָכַלְנוּ עָלָיו. הָרַחֲמָן הוּא יִשְׁלַח לָנוּ אֶת אֵלִיָּהוּ הַנָּבִיא זָכוּר לַטּוֹב, וִיבַשֵּׂר לָנוּ בְּשׂוֹרוֹת טוֹבוֹת יְשׁוּעוֹת וְנֶחָמוֹת.

Rebuild Yerushalayim, the Holy City, soon in our days. Blessed are You, HASHEM, Who rebuilds Yerushalyim (in His mercy). Amen.

Blessed are You, HASHEM, our God, King of the universe, the Almighty, our Father, our King, our Sovereign, our Creator, our Redeemer, our Maker, our Holy One, Holy One of Yaakov, our Shepherd, the Shepherd of Israel, the King Who is good, and Who does good for all. For every single day He did good, He does good, and He will do good to us. He was bountiful with us, He is bountiful with us, and He will forever be bountiful with us – with grace and with kindness and with mercy, with relief, salvation, success, blessing, help, consolation, sustenance, support, mercy, life, peace, and all good; and of all good things may He never deprive us.

The compassionate One! May He reign over us forever. The compassionate One! May He be blessed in heaven and on earth. The compassionate One! May He be praised throughout all generations, may He be glorified through us forever to the ultimate ends, and be honored through us forever and for all eternity. The compassionate One! May He sustain us in honor. The compassionate One! May He break the yoke of oppression from our necks and guide us erect to our Land. The compassionate One! May He send us abundant blessing to this house and upon this table at which we have eaten. The compassionate One! May He send us Eliyahu Hanavi – he is remembered for good – to proclaim to us good tidings, salvations, and consolations.

The Talmud (*Berachos* 46a) gives a rather lengthy text of the blessing that a guest inserts here for the host. It is quoted with minor variations in *Shulchan Aruch* (*Orach Chaim* 201) and many authorities are at a loss to explain why the prescribed text has fallen into disuse in favor of the briefer version commonly used. The text found in *Shulchan Aruch* is:

יְהִי רָצוֹן שֶׁלֹּא יֵבוֹשׁ וְלֹא יִכָּלֵם בַּעַל הַבַּיִת הַזֶּה, לֹא בָעוֹלָם הַזֶּה וְלֹא בָעוֹלָם הַבָּא, וְיַצְלִיחַ בְּכָל נְכָסָיו, וְיִהְיוּ נְכָסָיו מוּצְלָחִים וּקְרוֹבִים לָעִיר, וְאַל יִשְׁלוֹט שָׂטָן בְּמַעֲשֵׂה יָדָיו, וְאַל יִזְדַּקֵּק לְפָנָיו שׁוּם דְּבַר חֵטְא וְהִרְהוּר עָוֹן, מֵעַתָּה וְעַד עוֹלָם.

הָרַחֲמָן הוּא יְבָרֵךְ

Guests recite the following.
Children at their parents' table add words in parentheses.

אֶת [אָבִי מוֹרִי] בַּעַל הַבַּיִת הַזֶּה, וְאֶת [אִמִּי מוֹרָתִי] בַּעֲלַת הַבַּיִת הַזֶּה,

Those eating at their own table recite the following, adding the appropriate parenthesized phrases:

אוֹתִי [וְאֶת אִשְׁתִּי/בַּעְלִי. וְאֶת זַרְעִי] וְאֶת כָּל אֲשֶׁר לִי.

All guests recite the following:

אוֹתָם וְאֶת בֵּיתָם וְאֶת זַרְעָם וְאֶת כָּל אֲשֶׁר לָהֶם.

All continue here:

אוֹתָנוּ וְאֶת כָּל אֲשֶׁר לָנוּ, כְּמוֹ שֶׁנִּתְבָּרְכוּ אֲבוֹתֵינוּ אַבְרָהָם יִצְחָק וְיַעֲקֹב בַּכֹּל מִכֹּל כֹּל, כֵּן יְבָרֵךְ אוֹתָנוּ כֻּלָּנוּ יַחַד בִּבְרָכָה שְׁלֵמָה, וְנֹאמַר, אָמֵן.

בַּמָּרוֹם יְלַמְּדוּ עֲלֵיהֶם וְעָלֵינוּ זְכוּת, שֶׁתְּהֵא לְמִשְׁמֶרֶת שָׁלוֹם. וְנִשָּׂא בְרָכָה מֵאֵת יהוה, וּצְדָקָה מֵאֱלֹהֵי יִשְׁעֵנוּ, וְנִמְצָא חֵן וְשֵׂכֶל טוֹב בְּעֵינֵי אֱלֹהִים וְאָדָם.[1]

The Talmud (*Berachos* 46a) gives a rather lengthy text of the blessing that a guest inserts here for the host. It is quoted with minor variations in *Shulchan Aruch* (*Orach Chaim* 201) and many authorities are at a loss to explain why the prescribed text has fallen into disuse in favor of the briefer version commonly used. The text found in *Shulchan Aruch* is:

May it be God's will that this host not be shamed nor humiliated in this world or in the World to Come. May he be successful in all his dealings. May his dealings be successful and conveniently close at hand. May no evil impediment reign over his handiwork, and may no semblance of sin or iniquitous thought attach itself to him from this time and forever.

The compassionate One! May He bless

Guests recite the following.
Children at their parents' table add words in parentheses.

(my father, my teacher) the master of this house, and (my mother, my teacher) lady of this house,

Those eating at their own table recite the following, adding the appropriate parenthesized phrases:

me (my wife/husband and family) and all that is mine,

All guests recite the following:

them, their house, their family and all that is theirs,

All continue here:

ours and all that is ours – just as our forefathers Avraham, Yitzchak, and Yaakov were blessed with everything, from everything, with everything. So may He bless all of us together, with a perfect blessing. And let us say: Amen!

On high, may merit be pleaded upon them and upon us, for a safeguard of peace. May we receive a blessing from HASHEM and just kindness from the God of our salvation, and find favor and good understanding in the eyes of God and man.[1]

---

(1) Cf. *Mishlei* 3:4.

On Shabbos add the following sentence:

הָרַחֲמָן הוּא יַנְחִילֵנוּ יוֹם שֶׁכֻּלוֹ שַׁבָּת וּמְנוּחָה לְחַיֵּי הָעוֹלָמִים.

The words in parentheses are added
on the two Seder nights in some communities.

הָרַחֲמָן הוּא יַנְחִילֵנוּ יוֹם שֶׁכֻּלוֹ טוֹב. [יוֹם שֶׁכֻּלוֹ אָרוּךְ. יוֹם שֶׁצַּדִּיקִים יוֹשְׁבִים וְעַטְרוֹתֵיהֶם בְּרָאשֵׁיהֶם וְנֶהֱנִים מִזִּיו הַשְּׁכִינָה וִיהִי חֶלְקֵנוּ עִמָּהֶם.]

הָרַחֲמָן הוּא יְזַכֵּנוּ לִימוֹת הַמָּשִׁיחַ וּלְחַיֵּי הָעוֹלָם הַבָּא. מִגְדּוֹל יְשׁוּעוֹת מַלְכּוֹ וְעֹשֶׂה חֶסֶד לִמְשִׁיחוֹ לְדָוִד וּלְזַרְעוֹ עַד עוֹלָם.[1] עֹשֶׂה שָׁלוֹם בִּמְרוֹמָיו, הוּא יַעֲשֶׂה שָׁלוֹם עָלֵינוּ וְעַל כָּל יִשְׂרָאֵל. וְאִמְרוּ, אָמֵן.

יְראוּ אֶת יהוה קְדֹשָׁיו, כִּי אֵין מַחְסוֹר לִירֵאָיו. כְּפִירִים רָשׁוּ וְרָעֵבוּ, וְדֹרְשֵׁי יהוה לֹא יַחְסְרוּ כָל טוֹב.[2] הוֹדוּ לַיהוה כִּי טוֹב, כִּי לְעוֹלָם חַסְדּוֹ.[3] פּוֹתֵחַ אֶת יָדֶךָ, וּמַשְׂבִּיעַ לְכָל חַי רָצוֹן.[4] בָּרוּךְ הַגֶּבֶר אֲשֶׁר יִבְטַח בַּיהוה, וְהָיָה יהוה מִבְטַחוֹ.[5] נַעַר הָיִיתִי גַּם זָקַנְתִּי, וְלֹא רָאִיתִי צַדִּיק נֶעֱזָב, וְזַרְעוֹ מְבַקֶּשׁ לָחֶם.[6] יהוה עֹז לְעַמּוֹ יִתֵּן, יהוה יְבָרֵךְ אֶת עַמּוֹ בַשָּׁלוֹם.[7]

Upon completion of *Bircas Hamazon* the blessing over wine is recited and the third cup is drunk while reclining on the left side. It is preferable to drink the entire cup, but at the very least, most of the cup should be drained.

> On Shabbos add the following sentence:
> **The compassionate One! May He cause us to inherit the day which will be completely a Shabbos and rest day for eternal life.**

The words in parentheses are added on the two Seder nights in some communities.

The compassionate One! May He cause us to inherit that day which is altogether good (that everlasting day, the day when the just will sit with crowns on their heads, enjoying the reflection of God's majesty – and may our portion be with them!).

The compassionate One! May He make us worthy of the days of Mashiach and the life of the World to Come. He Who is a tower of salvations to His king and does kindness for His anointed, to David and to his descendants forever.[1] He Who makes peace in His heights, may He make peace upon us and upon all Israel. Now respond: Amen!

Fear HASHEM, you, His holy ones, for there is no deprivation for His reverent ones. Those who deny God may become poor and starve, but those who seek HASHEM will not lack any goodness.[2] Give thanks to God for He is good; His kindness endures forever.[3] You open up Your hand and satisfy every living thing with contentment.[4] Blessed is the man who trusts in HASHEM, then HASHEM will be his security.[5] I was a youth and also have aged, and I have not seen a righteous man forsaken, with his children begging for bread.[6] HASHEM will give might to His people; HASHEM will bless His people with peace.[7]

Upon completion of Bircas Hamazon the blessing over wine is recited and the third cup is drunk while reclining on the left side. It is preferable to drink the entire cup, but at the very least, most of the cup should be drained.

---

(1) *II Shmuel* 22:51. (2) *Tehillim* 34:10-11. (3) *Tehillim* 136:1.
(4) *Tehillim* 145:16. (5) *Yirmiyahu* 17:7.
(6) *Tehillim* 37:25. (7) *Tehillim* 29:11.

Some recite the following before the third cup:

הִנְנִי מוּכָן וּמְזוּמָּן לְקַיֵּם מִצְוַת כּוֹס שְׁלִישִׁי שֶׁל אַרְבַּע כּוֹסוֹת. לְשֵׁם יִחוּד קֻדְשָׁא בְּרִיךְ הוּא וּשְׁכִינְתֵּיהּ, עַל יְדֵי הַהוּא טָמִיר וְנֶעְלָם, בְּשֵׁם כָּל יִשְׂרָאֵל. וִיהִי נֹעַם אֲדֹנָי אֱלֹהֵינוּ עָלֵינוּ, וּמַעֲשֵׂה יָדֵינוּ כּוֹנְנָה עָלֵינוּ, וּמַעֲשֵׂה יָדֵינוּ כּוֹנְנֵהוּ:

בָּרוּךְ אַתָּה יהוה אֱלֹהֵינוּ מֶלֶךְ הָעוֹלָם, בּוֹרֵא פְּרִי הַגָּפֶן.

The fourth cup is poured. According to most customs, the Cup of Eliyahu is poured at this point, after which the door is opened in accordance with the verse, "It is a guarded night." Then the following paragraph is recited.

שְׁפֹךְ חֲמָתְךָ אֶל הַגּוֹיִם אֲשֶׁר לֹא יְדָעוּךָ וְעַל מַמְלָכוֹת אֲשֶׁר בְּשִׁמְךָ לֹא קָרָאוּ. כִּי אָכַל אֶת יַעֲקֹב וְאֶת נָוֵהוּ הֵשַׁמּוּ.[1] שְׁפָךְ עֲלֵיהֶם זַעְמֶךָ וַחֲרוֹן אַפְּךָ יַשִּׂיגֵם.[2] תִּרְדֹּף בְּאַף וְתַשְׁמִידֵם מִתַּחַת שְׁמֵי יהוה.[3]

הַלֵּל

The door is closed and the recitation of the Haggadah is continued.

לֹא לָנוּ יהוה לֹא לָנוּ, כִּי לְשִׁמְךָ תֵּן כָּבוֹד, עַל חַסְדְּךָ עַל אֲמִתֶּךָ. לָמָּה יֹאמְרוּ הַגּוֹיִם,

◆§ Leil Shimurim

On this night, the Jewish People became sanctified and betrothed (the same Hebrew word is used for both: *Niskadshu*) to Hashem, much as a bride is to her groom. *Maharal* (as well as earlier sources) notes that seven blessings are recited before the matzah is eaten, comparable to the seven blessings recited at a wedding.

This is the reason why our Sages compare one who eats matzah on *Erev Pesach* to one who is intimate with his betrothed in her father's house. Eating matzah before the seven blessings are recited is the equivalent of one who is intimate with his betrothed before the seven blessings of *nissuin* are recited (also see *Levush* 471:72).

This provides an alternate translation for *Leil Shimurim*. The standard translation is "a guarded night," but *Rashi*, in his commentary to

Some recite the following before the third cup:

Behold, I am prepared and ready to fulfill the mitzvah of the third of the Four Cups. For the sake of the unification of the Holy One, Blessed is He, and His presence, through Him Who is hidden and inscrutable – [I pray] in the name of all Israel. May the pleasantness of my Lord, our God, be upon us – may He establish our handiwork for us; our handiwork may He establish.

Blessed are You, HASHEM, our God, King of the universe, Who creates the fruit of the vine.

The fourth cup is poured. According to most customs, the Cup of Eliyahu is poured at this point, after which the door is opened in accordance with the verse, "It is a guarded night." Then the following paragraph is recited.

Pour Your wrath upon the nations that do not recognize You and upon the kingdoms that do not invoke Your Name. For they have devoured Yaakov and destroyed His habitation.[1] Pour Your fury upon them and let Your fierce anger overtake them.[2] Pursue them with wrath and annihilate them from beneath the heavens of HASHEM.[3]

HALLEL

The door is closed and the recitation of the Haggadah is continued.

Not for us, HASHEM, not for us, but for Your Name give glory, for the sake of Your kindness and Your truth! Why should the nations say,

---

(1) *Tehillim* 79:6-7. (2) *Tehillim* 69:25. (3) *Eichah* 3:66.

(*Shemos* 12:42), explains that the Holy One, Blessed is He, was *keeping this night in mind and looking forward to it*. We propose that *Leil Shimurim* is the night to which He looked forward to sanctify (*Kiddushin*) His betrothed — the Jewish People. With what did He sanctify them? Through the mitzvos associated with this night (from an unpublished manuscript provided by his grandson, Rav Aharon Goldberg).

הַלֵּל / *Hallel*

◈§ *Why do we say Hallel on Pesach?*

The Gemara (*Megillah* 10a; *Arachin* 10b) differentiates between

Purim, when *Hallel* is not recited, and Pesach, when it is, by citing the verse form *Hallel* (*Tehillim* 113:1): "Praise, you servants of Hashem..." The Gemara explains that only completely free people, who serve no one else, are considered "servants of Hashem" and can praise Him through *Hallel*. The Purim miracle did not achieve that goal; post-Purim *Bnei Yisrael* were still "servants of Achashverosh." In this passage "servants of Achashverosh" is not taken literally; rather it represents all subsequent rulers to whom the Jewish People were subservient. All those rulers are, figuratively, an extension and continuation of Achashverosh and his servitude.

Rav Shlomo Zalman asked: If we are still subservient to other rulers, why are we not still considered "servants of Pharaoh" as well? Why don't we see the subsequent rulers as figurative successors to Pharaoh? The fact remains that even in our times, and in our land, we are still not free to do as we please. We are still subservient to the ruling nations and we cannot go against their wishes. If so, how can we recite *Hallel* on Pesach?

The answer is very basic, and everyone should know this principle. There is no comparison between the terrible slavery we underwent in Egypt and other subsequent enslavements in the course of history. Indeed, it is concerning the slavery of Egypt that we recite each night in our *Ma'ariv* prayers, "Who ... removed His nation from their [Egypt's] midst to *eternal freedom*" [italics added]. In fact, the Jewish People in Egypt had descended to such a nadir that their very essence was one of slaves, almost as if they were genetically predisposed to slavery. Even after leaving Egypt and seeing all the great miracles, they *still* wanted to return to Egypt! The only explanation for such puzzling behavior is the slave mentality that had totally taken over their essence. They were actually happy to be slaves!

Being happy as a slave is the lowest level to which a human being can sink. As long as some part of a person still regrets being a slave, he has some interest in freedom. If he is actually happy to be a slave, he has disassociated himself from any type of freedom. It is out of the depths of this level of slavery that Hashem took us out to eternal freedom. Now, and for all eternity, that type of slavery will never be repeated. The reciting of *Hallel* celebrates that eternal freedom.

There is a related distinction between the slavery in Egypt and all subsequent enslavements. The Jewish People were redeemed from slavery in Egypt so that they would "serve God on this mountain"

(*Shemos* 3:12). In other words, they were redeemed so that they could receive the Torah on Mount Sinai. True, while in Egypt they had reached the deepest depths of slavery, as explained above; but when they received the Torah, they were redeemed from their status as slaves and, by the power of the Torah, they became free with *eternal freedom*.

[Actually, since the essence of the redemption was receiving the Torah, they should have received the Torah as soon as they left Egypt. Nevertheless, they were so far from being prepared, it was necessary to count fifty days before being given the Torah. Our Sages compare the relationship between Klal Yisrael and Hashem to that of a husband and wife. A woman must count seven clean days before reuniting with her husband; similarly, the Jewish People had to count seven weeks before they were ready to receive the Torah.]

We now understand why we recite *Hallel* on Pesach, but not on Purim. On Purim there was never a total freedom, since "we are still slaves of Achashverosh." As for Pesach, however, we were redeemed from being the slaves of Pharaoh, and began the process of becoming eternal servants of Hashem. Accordingly, *Praise, you servants of Hashem*.

With this principle we can answer another question. The mishnah in *Megillah* (20b) states that *Hallel* is one of those mitzvos which applies only in the daytime — one may not even recite it between dawn and sunrise. (If he went against the law and recited it by night he fulfilled his requirement, but it certainly should not be done that way.) How, then, do we recite *Hallel* on the Seder night? The answer is, as was explained previously, that this redemption does not resemble other redemptions, and it is eternal. Consequently, the *Hallel* celebrating this eternal redemption does not resemble other recitations of *Hallel*. On this very night that we were redeemed from dreadful slavery to eternal freedom, a special *Hallel*, not bound by the constraints of ordinary *Hallel*, is said with great joy.

This distinction is also indicated by the special name of this *Hallel*. Although in the order of the Seder it is called *Hallel*, the Mishnah in *Pesachim* (117b) refers to it as *Birkas HaShir* — the blessing in song, a song of praise to Hashem. If it were truly "*Hallel*," then it would be forbidden to divide it up, saying the first two chapters, then breaking off to eat a meal, and then resuming the *Hallel*. Rather, it is a song of praise to Hashem, and to emphasize this point we divide it into two parts, unlike the standard *Hallel*.

We can further add to this idea by noting that the first two chapters,

אַיֵּה נָא אֱלֹהֵיהֶם. וֵאלֹהֵינוּ בַשָּׁמָיִם, כֹּל אֲשֶׁר חָפֵץ עָשָׂה. עֲצַבֵּיהֶם כֶּסֶף וְזָהָב, מַעֲשֵׂה יְדֵי אָדָם. פֶּה לָהֶם וְלֹא יְדַבֵּרוּ, עֵינַיִם לָהֶם וְלֹא יִרְאוּ. אָזְנַיִם לָהֶם וְלֹא יִשְׁמָעוּ, אַף לָהֶם וְלֹא יְרִיחוּן. יְדֵיהֶם וְלֹא יְמִישׁוּן, רַגְלֵיהֶם וְלֹא יְהַלֵּכוּ, לֹא יֶהְגּוּ בִּגְרוֹנָם. כְּמוֹהֶם יִהְיוּ עֹשֵׂיהֶם, כֹּל אֲשֶׁר בֹּטֵחַ בָּהֶם. יִשְׂרָאֵל בְּטַח בַּיהוה, עֶזְרָם וּמָגִנָּם הוּא. בֵּית אַהֲרֹן בִּטְחוּ בַיהוה, עֶזְרָם וּמָגִנָּם הוּא. יִרְאֵי יהוה בִּטְחוּ בַיהוה, עֶזְרָם וּמָגִנָּם הוּא.

יהוה זְכָרָנוּ יְבָרֵךְ, יְבָרֵךְ אֶת בֵּית יִשְׂרָאֵל, יְבָרֵךְ אֶת בֵּית אַהֲרֹן. יְבָרֵךְ יִרְאֵי יהוה, הַקְּטַנִּים עִם הַגְּדֹלִים. יֹסֵף יהוה עֲלֵיכֶם, עֲלֵיכֶם וְעַל בְּנֵיכֶם. בְּרוּכִים אַתֶּם לַיהוה, עֹשֵׂה שָׁמַיִם וָאָרֶץ. הַשָּׁמַיִם שָׁמַיִם לַיהוה, וְהָאָרֶץ נָתַן לִבְנֵי אָדָם. לֹא הַמֵּתִים יְהַלְלוּ יָהּ, וְלֹא כָּל יֹרְדֵי דוּמָה. וַאֲנַחְנוּ נְבָרֵךְ יָהּ, מֵעַתָּה וְעַד עוֹלָם, הַלְלוּיָהּ.[1]

---

which discuss the Exodus from Egypt, are known as *Hallel Mitzrayim* (the *Hallel* of Egypt), whereas the remainder deals with the exile of the *Shechinah*, with the Jewish People, and their connection with the Holy One, Blessed is He (cf. Maharil, *Minhagim Seder Hahaggadah*). Accordingly, it was divided so that we recite the first two chapters and sing a song of thanks to Hashem for redeeming us from Egypt, before we proceed to fulfill the mitzvos of eating matzah and *maror* (from a lecture on the laws of Pesach given by Rav Shlomo Zalman in 1970, published in *Kuntres Seder HaPesach*. See also page above, s.v. *V'hayu mesaprim*).

הגדה של פסח [206]

"Where is their God now?" Our God is in the heavens; whatever He pleases, He does! Their idols are silver and gold, the handiwork of man. They have a mouth, but cannot speak; they have eyes, but cannot see; they have ears, but cannot hear; they have a nose, but cannot smell; their hands – they cannot feel; their feet – they cannot walk; nor can they utter a sound with their throat. Those who make them should become like them, whoever trusts in them! O Israel! Trust in HASHEM; He is their help and their shield! House of Aharon! Trust in HASHEM! He is their help and their shield! You who fear HASHEM – trust in HASHEM, He is their help and their shield!

HASHEM Who has remembered us will bless – He will bless the House of Israel; He will bless the House of Aharon; He will bless those who fear HASHEM, the small as well as the great. May HASHEM increase upon you, upon you and upon your children! You are blessed of HASHEM, Maker of heaven and earth. As for the heavens – the heavens are HASHEM's, but the earth He has given to mankind. Neither can the dead praise God, nor any who descend into silence; but we will bless God from this time and forever. Halleluyah![1]

---

(1) *Tehillim* 115.

לֹא הַמֵּתִים יְהַלְלוּ יָהּ, וְלֹא כָּל יֹרְדֵי דוּמָה
Neither can the dead praise God,
nor any [lit. *all*] *who descend into silence;*

Why the lack of symmetry in the verse? Why does it not say, "Neither can *all* who are dead ...," much as it says, "all who descend"?

The answer is that there actually are some dead who *do* praise God. The Gemara (*Yevamos* 97a) states that when one repeats Torah in the name of a deceased person, "His [the deceased] lips speak in the grave." Thus, it is entirely possible that the lips of a dead person will indeed speak in praise of Hashem. The latter part of the verse, "All

[207] THE RAV SHLOMO ZALMAN HAGGADAH

אָהַבְתִּי, כִּי יִשְׁמַע יהוה אֶת קוֹלִי, תַּחֲנוּנָי. כִּי הִטָּה אָזְנוֹ לִי, וּבְיָמַי אֶקְרָא. אֲפָפוּנִי חֶבְלֵי מָוֶת, וּמְצָרֵי שְׁאוֹל מְצָאוּנִי, צָרָה וְיָגוֹן אֶמְצָא. וּבְשֵׁם יהוה אֶקְרָא, אָנָּה יהוה מַלְּטָה נַפְשִׁי. חַנּוּן יהוה וְצַדִּיק, וֵאלֹהֵינוּ מְרַחֵם. שֹׁמֵר פְּתָאיִם יהוה, דַּלּוֹתִי וְלִי יְהוֹשִׁיעַ. שׁוּבִי נַפְשִׁי לִמְנוּחָיְכִי, כִּי יהוה גָּמַל עָלָיְכִי. כִּי חִלַּצְתָּ נַפְשִׁי מִמָּוֶת, אֶת עֵינִי מִן דִּמְעָה, אֶת רַגְלִי מִדֶּחִי. אֶתְהַלֵּךְ לִפְנֵי יהוה, בְּאַרְצוֹת הַחַיִּים. הֶאֱמַנְתִּי כִּי אֲדַבֵּר, אֲנִי עָנִיתִי מְאֹד. אֲנִי אָמַרְתִּי בְחָפְזִי, כָּל הָאָדָם כֹּזֵב.

מָה אָשִׁיב לַיהוה, כָּל תַּגְמוּלוֹהִי עָלָי. כּוֹס יְשׁוּעוֹת אֶשָּׂא, וּבְשֵׁם יהוה אֶקְרָא. נְדָרַי לַיהוה אֲשַׁלֵּם, נֶגְדָה נָּא לְכָל עַמּוֹ. יָקָר בְּעֵינֵי יהוה, הַמָּוְתָה לַחֲסִידָיו. אָנָּה יהוה כִּי אֲנִי עַבְדֶּךָ, אֲנִי עַבְדְּךָ, בֶּן אֲמָתֶךָ, פִּתַּחְתָּ לְמוֹסֵרָי. לְךָ אֶזְבַּח זֶבַח תּוֹדָה, וּבְשֵׁם יהוה אֶקְרָא.

---

who descend into silence," refers to those who descend to *Gehinnom*. Absolutely none who descend there can praise Hashem; thus the word "all" is appropriate *(Haggadas Arzei Halevanon, p. 287)*.

לְךָ אֶזְבַּח זֶבַח תּוֹדָה, וּבְשֵׁם יהוה אֶקְרָא
*To You I will sacrifice thanksgiving offerings,
and the Name of Hashem will I invoke.*

The entire purpose of sacrificing thanksgiving offerings is to be able to call out in the Name of Hashem.

The Gemara (*Berachos* 54b) states: "Four are required to offer *todah* (thanksgiving) sacrifices: Those who go down to the sea, those

I love Him, for HASHEM hears my voice, my supplications. For He has inclined His ear to me, so in my days shall I call. The ropes of death encircled me; the confines of the grave have found me; trouble and sorrow have I found. Then I called upon the Name of HASHEM: "Please, HASHEM, save my soul." Gracious is HASHEM and righteous, our God is merciful. HASHEM protects the simple; I was brought low, but He saved me. Return, my soul, to your rest; for HASHEM has been kind to you. You delivered my soul from death, my eyes from tears, my feet from stumbling. I shall walk before HASHEM in the lands of the living. I kept faith although I say: "I suffer exceedingly." I said in my haste: "All mankind is deceitful."

How can I repay (or respond to) HASHEM? All His benevolence is upon me! I will raise the cup of salvations and I will invoke the Name of HASHEM. My vows to HASHEM I will pay, in the presence, now, of His entire people. Precious in the eyes of HASHEM is the death of His devout ones. Please, HASHEM – for I am Your servant, I am Your servant, son of Your handmaid — You have released my bonds. To You I will sacrifice thanksgiving offerings, and the Name of HASHEM I will

---

who travel through the desert, one who was ill and recovered, and one who was incarcerated in a prison and was freed." The Gemara connects these four to the four times it says in *Tehillim* 107 (8,15,21,31): "Let them give thanks to Hashem for His kindness, and His wonders to the children of man." In other words, the purpose of giving thanks is to emphasize that He is the Source, rather than to believe that the salvation came through the laws of nature. Actually, this is explicitly stated in the Torah (*Devarim* 32:39): "See, now, that I, I am He ... I struck down and I will heal, and there is no rescuer from My hand."

Even the various torments that a person undergoes are implemented by the agents of God faithfully serving their Master (see

נְדָרַי לַיהוה אֲשַׁלֵּם, נֶגְדָה נָּא לְכָל עַמּוֹ. בְּחַצְרוֹת בֵּית יהוה, בְּתוֹכֵכִי יְרוּשָׁלָֽיִם הַלְלוּיָהּ.¹

הַלְלוּ אֶת יהוה, כָּל גּוֹיִם, שַׁבְּחֽוּהוּ כָּל הָאֻמִּים. כִּי גָבַר עָלֵֽינוּ חַסְדּוֹ, וֶאֱמֶת יהוה לְעוֹלָם, הַלְלוּיָהּ.²

[According to Rav Shlomo Zalman, the leader recites each of the following four lines out loud, and the others respond, הוֹדוּ לַהּ כִּי טוֹב כִּי לְעוֹלָם חַסְדּוֹ.]

הוֹדוּ לַיהוה כִּי טוֹב,   כִּי לְעוֹלָם חַסְדּוֹ.
יֹאמַר נָא יִשְׂרָאֵל,   כִּי לְעוֹלָם חַסְדּוֹ.
יֹאמְרוּ נָא בֵית אַהֲרֹן,   כִּי לְעוֹלָם חַסְדּוֹ.
יֹאמְרוּ נָא יִרְאֵי יהוה,   כִּי לְעוֹלָם חַסְדּוֹ.

מִן הַמֵּצַר קָרָֽאתִי יָּהּ, עָנָֽנִי בַמֶּרְחָב יָהּ. יהוה לִי לֹא אִירָא, מַה יַּעֲשֶׂה לִי אָדָם. יהוה לִי בְּעֹזְרָי, וַאֲנִי אֶרְאֶה בְשֹׂנְאָי. טוֹב לַחֲסוֹת בַּיהוה, מִבְּטֹֽחַ בָּאָדָם. טוֹב לַחֲסוֹת בַּיהוה, מִבְּטֹֽחַ בִּנְדִיבִים. כָּל גּוֹיִם סְבָבֽוּנִי, בְּשֵׁם יהוה כִּי אֲמִילַם. סַבּֽוּנִי גַם סְבָבֽוּנִי, בְּשֵׁם יהוה כִּי אֲמִילַם. סַבּֽוּנִי כִדְבֹרִים דֹּעֲכוּ כְּאֵשׁ קוֹצִים, בְּשֵׁם יהוה כִּי אֲמִילַם. דָּחֹה דְחִיתַֽנִי לִנְפֹּל,

---

Avodah Zarah 55a). Thus, in reciting the blessing *Refa'einu* (Heal us) in the *Shemoneh Esrei* prayers, we say, "For You are our praise." In other words, we realize that the Source of healing can only be Hashem, and only He deserves praise.

    The Gemara at the beginning of Tractate *Avodah Zarah* states that three days before pagan festivals one should not cause an idolater to praise his idols. We can certainly learn from here not to praise the gods of nature and medicine. This is the underlying principle of the thanksgiving offering, to proclaim to all and to *oneself* that only He

invoke. My vows to HASHEM I will pay in the presence, now, of His entire people. In the courtyards of the House of HASHEM, in your midst, O Yerushalayim, Halleluyah!¹

Praise HASHEM, all nations; extol Him, all the states! For His kindness has overwhelmed us, and the truth of HASHEM is eternal, Halleluyah!²

[According to Rav Shlomo Zalman, the leader recites each of the following four lines out loud, and the others respond, *Give thanks to Hashem for He is good; His kindness endures forever.*]

Give thanks to HASHEM for He is good;
>His kindness endures forever!

Let Israel say: His kindness endures forever!

Let the House of Aharon say:
>His kindness endures forever!

Let those who fear HASHEM say:
>His kindness endures forever!

From the straits did I call to God; God answered me with expansiveness. HASHEM is for me; I have no fear; what can man possibly do to me? HASHEM is for me through my helpers; therefore I can face my foes. It is better to take refuge in HASHEM than to rely on man. It is better to take refuge in HASHEM than to rely on princes. All the nations surround me; but in the Name of HASHEM I cut them down! They encircle me; they surround me; but in the Name of HASHEM I cut them down! They encircle me like bees, but they are extinguished as a fire does thorns; in the Name of HASHEM I cut them down! You pushed me hard that I might fall,

---

(1) *Tehillim* 116. (2) *Tehillim* 117.

---

can heal; salvation can only come from Him. Accordingly, the Midrash (*Vayikra Rabbah* 9:7) states that in the future all sacrifices will be canceled, other than the thanksgiving offering — for that publicizes that we serve only Hashem, and not nature or medicine *(Haggadas Arzei Halevanon,* p. 288).

וַיהוה עֲזָרָנִי. עָזִּי וְזִמְרָת יָהּ, וַיְהִי לִי לִישׁוּעָה. קוֹל רִנָּה וִישׁוּעָה, בְּאָהֳלֵי צַדִּיקִים, יְמִין יהוה עֹשָׂה חָיִל. יְמִין יהוה רוֹמֵמָה, יְמִין יהוה עֹשָׂה חָיִל. לֹא אָמוּת כִּי אֶחְיֶה, וַאֲסַפֵּר מַעֲשֵׂי יָהּ. יַסֹּר יִסְּרַנִּי יָּהּ, וְלַמָּוֶת לֹא נְתָנָנִי. פִּתְחוּ לִי שַׁעֲרֵי צֶדֶק, אָבֹא בָם אוֹדֶה יָהּ. זֶה הַשַּׁעַר לַיהוה, צַדִּיקִים יָבֹאוּ בוֹ. אוֹדְךָ כִּי עֲנִיתָנִי, וַתְּהִי לִי לִישׁוּעָה. אוֹדְךָ כִּי עֲנִיתָנִי, וַתְּהִי לִי לִישׁוּעָה. אֶבֶן מָאֲסוּ הַבּוֹנִים, הָיְתָה לְרֹאשׁ פִּנָּה. אֶבֶן מָאֲסוּ הַבּוֹנִים, הָיְתָה לְרֹאשׁ פִּנָּה. מֵאֵת יהוה הָיְתָה זֹּאת, הִיא נִפְלָאת בְּעֵינֵינוּ. מֵאֵת יהוה הָיְתָה זֹּאת, הִיא נִפְלָאת בְּעֵינֵינוּ. זֶה הַיּוֹם עָשָׂה יהוה, נָגִילָה וְנִשְׂמְחָה בוֹ. זֶה הַיּוֹם עָשָׂה יהוה, נָגִילָה וְנִשְׂמְחָה בוֹ.

[According to Rav Shlomo Zalman, the next four verses are recited responsively, first by the leader then by the others.]

אָנָּא יהוה הוֹשִׁיעָה נָּא.
אָנָּא יהוה הוֹשִׁיעָה נָּא.
אָנָּא יהוה הַצְלִיחָה נָּא.
אָנָּא יהוה הַצְלִיחָה נָּא.

בָּרוּךְ הַבָּא בְּשֵׁם יהוה, בֵּרַכְנוּכֶם מִבֵּית יהוה. בָּרוּךְ הַבָּא בְּשֵׁם יהוה, בֵּרַכְנוּכֶם מִבֵּית יהוה. אֵל יהוה וַיָּאֶר לָנוּ, אִסְרוּ חַג בַּעֲבֹתִים, עַד קַרְנוֹת הַמִּזְבֵּחַ. אֵל יהוה וַיָּאֶר לָנוּ, אִסְרוּ חַג בַּעֲבֹתִים, עַד קַרְנוֹת הַמִּזְבֵּחַ. אֵלִי אַתָּה וְאוֹדֶךָּ, אֱלֹהַי אֲרוֹמְמֶךָּ. אֵלִי אַתָּה וְאוֹדֶךָּ, אֱלֹהַי

but HASHEM assisted me. My strength and song is God. He became my salvation. The sound of rejoicing and salvation is in the tents of the righteous: "The right hand of HASHEM does valiantly! The right hand of HASHEM is raised triumphantly! The right hand of HASHEM does valiantly!" I shall not die, but I shall live and relate the deeds of God. God afflicted me exceedingly but He did not let me die. Open for me the gates of righteousness, I will enter them and thank God. This is the gate of HASHEM; the righteous shall enter through it. I thank You for You answered me and became my salvation! I thank You for You answered me and became my salvation! The stone which the builders despised has become the cornerstone! The stone which the builders despised has become the cornerstone! This emanated from HASHEM; it is wondrous in our eyes! This emanated from HASHEM; it is wondrous in our eyes! This is the day HASHEM has made; we will rejoice and be glad in Him! This is the day HASHEM has made; we will rejoice and be glad in Him!

[According to Rav Shlomo Zalman, the next four verses are recited responsively, first by the leader then by the others.]

O, HASHEM, please save us!
O, HASHEM, please save us!
O, HASHEM, please make us prosper!
O, HASHEM, please make us prosper!

Blessed is he who comes in the Name of HASHEM; we bless you from the House of HASHEM. Blessed is he who comes in the Name of HASHEM; we bless you from the House of HASHEM. HASHEM is God and He illuminated for us; bind the festival offering with cords to the corners of the Altar. HASHEM is God and He illuminated for us; bind the festival offering with cords to the corners of the Altar. You are my God, and I shall thank You; my God, and I shall exalt You. You are my God, and I shall thank You; my God,

אֲרוֹמְמֶךָ. הוֹדוּ לַיהוה כִּי טוֹב, כִּי לְעוֹלָם
חַסְדּוֹ. הוֹדוּ לַיהוה כִּי טוֹב, כִּי לְעוֹלָם חַסְדּוֹ.[1]

יְהַלְלוּךָ יהוה אֱלֹהֵינוּ כָּל מַעֲשֶׂיךָ, וַחֲסִידֶיךָ צַדִּיקִים עוֹשֵׂי רְצוֹנֶךָ, וְכָל עַמְּךָ בֵּית יִשְׂרָאֵל בְּרִנָּה יוֹדוּ וִיבָרְכוּ וִישַׁבְּחוּ וִיפָאֲרוּ וִירוֹמְמוּ וְיַעֲרִיצוּ וְיַקְדִּישׁוּ וְיַמְלִיכוּ אֶת שִׁמְךָ מַלְכֵּנוּ, כִּי לְךָ טוֹב לְהוֹדוֹת וּלְשִׁמְךָ נָאֶה לְזַמֵּר, כִּי מֵעוֹלָם וְעַד עוֹלָם אַתָּה אֵל.

הוֹדוּ לַיהוה כִּי טוֹב   כִּי לְעוֹלָם חַסְדּוֹ.
הוֹדוּ לֵאלֹהֵי הָאֱלֹהִים
    כִּי לְעוֹלָם חַסְדּוֹ.
הוֹדוּ לַאֲדֹנֵי הָאֲדֹנִים   כִּי לְעוֹלָם חַסְדּוֹ.
לְעוֹשֵׂה נִפְלָאוֹת גְּדֹלוֹת לְבַדּוֹ
    כִּי לְעוֹלָם חַסְדּוֹ.
לְעוֹשֵׂה הַשָּׁמַיִם בִּתְבוּנָה   כִּי לְעוֹלָם חַסְדּוֹ.
לְרוֹקַע הָאָרֶץ עַל הַמָּיִם   כִּי לְעוֹלָם חַסְדּוֹ.
לְעוֹשֵׂה אוֹרִים גְּדֹלִים   כִּי לְעוֹלָם חַסְדּוֹ.
אֶת הַשֶּׁמֶשׁ לְמֶמְשֶׁלֶת בַּיּוֹם
    כִּי לְעוֹלָם חַסְדּוֹ.
אֶת הַיָּרֵחַ וְכוֹכָבִים לְמֶמְשְׁלוֹת בַּלָּיְלָה
    כִּי לְעוֹלָם חַסְדּוֹ.
לְמַכֵּה מִצְרַיִם בִּבְכוֹרֵיהֶם   כִּי לְעוֹלָם חַסְדּוֹ.
וַיּוֹצֵא יִשְׂרָאֵל מִתּוֹכָם   כִּי לְעוֹלָם חַסְדּוֹ.
בְּיָד חֲזָקָה וּבִזְרוֹעַ נְטוּיָה   כִּי לְעוֹלָם חַסְדּוֹ.

and I shall exalt You. Give thanks to Hashem, for He is good; His kindness endures forever. Give thanks to Hashem, for He is good; His kindness endures forever![1]

They shall praise You, Hashem our God, for all Your works, along with Your pious followers, the righteous, who do Your will, and Your entire people, the House of Israel, with joy will thank, bless, praise, glorify, exalt, revere, sanctify, and coronate Your Name, our King! For to You it is fitting to give thanks, and unto Your Name it is proper to sing praises, for from eternity to eternity You are God.

Give thanks to Hashem, for He is good;
          His kindness endures forever!
Give thanks to the God of gods;
          His kindness endures forever!
Give thanks to the Master of masters;
          His kindness endures forever!
To Him Who alone does great wonders;
          His kindness endures forever!
To Him Who makes the heaven with understanding;
          His kindness endures forever!
To Him Who stretched out the earth over the waters;
          His kindness endures forever!
To Him Who makes great luminaries;
          His kindness endures forever!
The sun for the reign of the day;
          His kindness endures forever!
The moon and the stars for the reign of the night;
          His kindness endures forever!
To Him Who smote Egypt through their firstborn;
          His kindness endures forever!
And took Israel out from their midst;
          His kindness endures forever!
With strong hand and outstretched arm;
          His kindness endures forever!

---

(1) *Tehillim* 118.

לְגֹזֵר יַם סוּף לִגְזָרִים	כִּי לְעוֹלָם חַסְדּוֹ.
וְהֶעֱבִיר יִשְׂרָאֵל בְּתוֹכוֹ	כִּי לְעוֹלָם חַסְדּוֹ.
וְנִעֵר פַּרְעֹה וְחֵילוֹ בְיַם סוּף	כִּי לְעוֹלָם חַסְדּוֹ.
לְמוֹלִיךְ עַמּוֹ בַּמִּדְבָּר	כִּי לְעוֹלָם חַסְדּוֹ.
לְמַכֵּה מְלָכִים גְּדֹלִים	כִּי לְעוֹלָם חַסְדּוֹ.
וַיַּהֲרֹג מְלָכִים אַדִּירִים	כִּי לְעוֹלָם חַסְדּוֹ.
לְסִיחוֹן מֶלֶךְ הָאֱמֹרִי	כִּי לְעוֹלָם חַסְדּוֹ.
וּלְעוֹג מֶלֶךְ הַבָּשָׁן	כִּי לְעוֹלָם חַסְדּוֹ.
וְנָתַן אַרְצָם לְנַחֲלָה	כִּי לְעוֹלָם חַסְדּוֹ.
נַחֲלָה לְיִשְׂרָאֵל עַבְדּוֹ	כִּי לְעוֹלָם חַסְדּוֹ.
שֶׁבְּשִׁפְלֵנוּ זָכַר לָנוּ	כִּי לְעוֹלָם חַסְדּוֹ.
וַיִּפְרְקֵנוּ מִצָּרֵינוּ	כִּי לְעוֹלָם חַסְדּוֹ.
נֹתֵן לֶחֶם לְכָל בָּשָׂר	כִּי לְעוֹלָם חַסְדּוֹ.
הוֹדוּ לְאֵל הַשָּׁמָיִם	כִּי לְעוֹלָם חַסְדּוֹ.[1]

נֹתֵן לֶחֶם לְכָל בָּשָׂר כִּי לְעוֹלָם חַסְדּוֹ
He gives food to all living creatures;
His kindness endures forever!

The Gemara (*Pesachim* 111a) states that [providing] a person's food is as difficult as splitting the Sea of Reeds. This is derived from the placement of the statement, "He gives food to all living creatures," which appears several *pesukim* after, "To Him Who divided the Sea of Reeds into parts." The connection between these two statements is rather obscure and requires explanation.

The Gemara (*Sanhedrin* 22a) states that finding a match for a person is as difficult as splitting the Sea of Reeds. This is based on the verse in *Tehillim* (68:7): "God settles the solitary into a family, He releases those bound in *kosharos,* fetters." *Bakosharos*, generally translated as *in fetters*, is understood by the Gemara to refer to being redeemed in a season that is *kosher*, neither too hot nor too cold. Regardless, this too is difficult to understand, for *releasing those bound in fetters* refers to the Exodus from Egypt, not to the splitting of

To Him Who divided the Sea of Reeds into parts;
> His kindness endures forever!

And caused Israel to pass through it;
> His kindness endures forever!

And threw Pharaoh and his army into the Sea of Reeds;
> His kindness endures forever!

To Him Who led His people through the Wilderness;
> His kindness endures forever!

To Him Who smote great kings;
> His kindness endures forever!

And slew mighty kings;
> His kindness endures forever!

Sichon, king of the Emorites;
> His kindness endures forever!

And Og, king of Bashan;
> His kindness endures forever!

And gave their land as an inheritance;
> His kindness endures forever!

An inheritance to Israel His servant;
> His kindness endures forever!

Who remembered us in our lowliness;
> His kindness endures forever!

And released us from our foes;
> His kindness endures forever!

He gives food to all living creatures;
> His kindness endures forever!

Give thanks to God of heaven;
> His kindness endures forever![1]

---

(1) *Tehillim* 136.

---

the Sea. Accordingly, it should have compared finding a match for a person to the Exodus, not the splitting of the Sea. Furthermore, what connection is there between the pleasant season in which the Jewish People were taken out of Egypt and *settling the solitary into a family*, which refers to finding a match for a person?

The answer seems to be that the Torah (*Shemos* 14:27) writes

נִשְׁמַת כָּל חַי תְּבָרֵךְ אֶת שִׁמְךָ יהוה אֱלֹהֵינוּ וְרוּחַ כָּל בָּשָׂר תְּפָאֵר וּתְרוֹמֵם זִכְרְךָ מַלְכֵּנוּ תָּמִיד. מִן הָעוֹלָם וְעַד הָעוֹלָם אַתָּה אֵל וּמִבַּלְעָדֶיךָ אֵין לָנוּ מֶלֶךְ גּוֹאֵל וּמוֹשִׁיעַ פּוֹדֶה וּמַצִּיל וּמְפַרְנֵס וּמְרַחֵם בְּכָל עֵת צָרָה וְצוּקָה. אֵין לָנוּ מֶלֶךְ אֶלָּא אָתָּה. אֱלֹהֵי הָרִאשׁוֹנִים וְהָאַחֲרוֹנִים אֱלוֹהַּ כָּל בְּרִיּוֹת אֲדוֹן כָּל תּוֹלָדוֹת הַמְהֻלָּל בְּרֹב הַתִּשְׁבָּחוֹת הַמְנַהֵג עוֹלָמוֹ בְּחֶסֶד וּבְרִיּוֹתָיו בְּרַחֲמִים וַיהוה לֹא יָנוּם וְלֹא יִישָׁן הַמְעוֹרֵר יְשֵׁנִים וְהַמֵּקִיץ נִרְדָּמִים וְהַמֵּשִׂיחַ אִלְּמִים וְהַמַּתִּיר אֲסוּרִים וְהַסּוֹמֵךְ נוֹפְלִים וְהַזּוֹקֵף כְּפוּפִים לְךָ לְבַדְּךָ אֲנַחְנוּ מוֹדִים. אִלּוּ פִינוּ מָלֵא שִׁירָה כַּיָּם וּלְשׁוֹנֵנוּ רִנָּה כַּהֲמוֹן גַּלָּיו וְשִׂפְתוֹתֵינוּ שֶׁבַח כְּמֶרְחֲבֵי רָקִיעַ וְעֵינֵינוּ מְאִירוֹת כַּשֶּׁמֶשׁ וְכַיָּרֵחַ וְיָדֵינוּ פְרוּשׂוֹת כְּנִשְׁרֵי שָׁמָיִם וְרַגְלֵינוּ קַלּוֹת כָּאַיָּלוֹת

---

concerning the splitting of the Sea of Reeds: "The water reverted to its original power [*l'eisano*]." The Midrash (*Shemos Rabbah* 21:6) expounds this reference as if it said, "*lisna'o*" — to its original stipulation, meaning it was ordained from the six days of Creation that the sea would split before the Jewish People. According to this Midrash, no miracle occurred at all; rather, the sea merely expressed a natural tendency placed within it during the sixth day of Creation! The miraculous occurrence was clothed in natural occurrences, as Hashem blew a powerful easterly wind all night long. The Egyptians believed this to be the cause of the Sea's splitting and, as a result, they saw no reason not to go into the sea (see Ramban ad loc. 15:8). Even the Jewish People understood it to be a natural event, and thought that the Egyptians would be coming out elsewhere (see Rashi ad loc. 14:30). This hot wind went against the behavior of *bakosharos*, which

The soul of every living being shall bless Your Name, HASHEM our God; the spirit of all flesh shall always glorify and exalt Your remembrance, our King. From eternity to eternity You are God, and other than You we have no king, redeemer or savior. Liberator, Rescuer, Sustainer, and Merciful One in every time of trouble and anguish, we have no king but You – God of the first and of the last, God of all human beings, Master of all generations, Who is extolled through a multitude of praises, Who guides His world with kindness and His creatures with mercy. HASHEM neither slumbers nor sleeps; He rouses the sleepers and awakens the slumberers; He makes the mute speak and releases the bound; He supports the fallen and straightens the bent. To You alone we give thanks. Were our mouth as full of song as the sea, and our tongue as full of jubilation as its multitude of waves, and our lips as full of praise as the breadth of the heavens, and our eyes as brilliant as the sun and the moon, and our hands as outspread as eagles of the sky and our feet as swift as hinds –

---

is a temperate, fair climate as explained above, but was necessary to make the miracle appear to be natural.

The same applies to finding a person's match. The above-cited Gemara in *Sotah* mentions that forty days before the forming of a child a Heavenly Echo decrees, "This one's daughter to that one." This decree is also hidden "by an easterly wind" which makes it appear to be a natural occurrence when they are brought together. Thus, this matching is compared to the splitting of the Sea; both are miracles camouflaged as nature.

Finally, the same applies to the statement that [providing] a person's food is as difficult as splitting the Sea of Reeds. The key to a person's sustenance is in the Hands of Hashem, and "a person's sustenance is set for him from Rosh Hashanah" (*Beitzah* 15a). So what is so difficult? Here, too, there is an "easterly wind," seemingly natural circumstances which clothe the bounty which is only through Heavenly decree *(Haggadas Arzei Halevanon,* p. 306).

אֵין אֲנַחְנוּ מַסְפִּיקִים לְהוֹדוֹת לְךָ יהוה אֱלֹהֵינוּ וֵאלֹהֵי אֲבוֹתֵינוּ וּלְבָרֵךְ אֶת שְׁמֶךָ עַל אַחַת מֵאֶלֶף אֶלֶף אַלְפֵי אֲלָפִים וְרִבֵּי רְבָבוֹת פְּעָמִים הַטּוֹבוֹת [נִסִּים וְנִפְלָאוֹת] שֶׁעָשִׂיתָ עִם אֲבוֹתֵינוּ וְעִמָּנוּ. מִמִּצְרַיִם גְּאַלְתָּנוּ יהוה אֱלֹהֵינוּ וּמִבֵּית עֲבָדִים פְּדִיתָנוּ בְּרָעָב זַנְתָּנוּ וּבְשָׂבָע כִּלְכַּלְתָּנוּ מֵחֶרֶב הִצַּלְתָּנוּ וּמִדֶּבֶר מִלַּטְתָּנוּ וּמֵחֳלָיִם רָעִים וְנֶאֱמָנִים דִּלִּיתָנוּ. עַד הֵנָּה עֲזָרוּנוּ רַחֲמֶיךָ וְלֹא עֲזָבוּנוּ חֲסָדֶיךָ וְאַל תִּטְּשֵׁנוּ יהוה אֱלֹהֵינוּ לָנֶצַח. עַל כֵּן אֵבָרִים שֶׁפִּלַּגְתָּ בָּנוּ וְרוּחַ וּנְשָׁמָה שֶׁנָּפַחְתָּ בְּאַפֵּינוּ וְלָשׁוֹן אֲשֶׁר שַׂמְתָּ בְּפִינוּ הֵן הֵם יוֹדוּ וִיבָרְכוּ וִישַׁבְּחוּ וִיפָאֲרוּ וִירוֹמְמוּ וְיַעֲרִיצוּ וְיַקְדִּישׁוּ וְיַמְלִיכוּ אֶת שִׁמְךָ מַלְכֵּנוּ. כִּי כָל פֶּה לְךָ יוֹדֶה וְכָל לָשׁוֹן לְךָ תִשָּׁבַע וְכָל בֶּרֶךְ לְךָ תִכְרַע וְכָל קוֹמָה לְפָנֶיךָ תִשְׁתַּחֲוֶה וְכָל לְבָבוֹת יִירָאוּךָ וְכָל קֶרֶב וּכְלָיוֹת יְזַמְּרוּ לִשְׁמֶךָ. כַּדָּבָר שֶׁכָּתוּב כָּל עַצְמוֹתַי תֹּאמַרְנָה יהוה מִי כָמוֹךָ מַצִּיל עָנִי מֵחָזָק מִמֶּנּוּ וְעָנִי וְאֶבְיוֹן מִגֹּזְלוֹ. מִי יִדְמֶה לָּךְ וּמִי יִשְׁוֶה לָּךְ וּמִי יַעֲרָךְ לָךְ הָאֵל הַגָּדוֹל הַגִּבּוֹר וְהַנּוֹרָא אֵל עֶלְיוֹן קֹנֵה שָׁמַיִם וָאָרֶץ. נְהַלֶּלְךָ וּנְשַׁבֵּחֲךָ וּנְפָאֶרְךָ וּנְבָרֵךְ אֶת שֵׁם קָדְשֶׁךָ כָּאָמוּר לְדָוִד בָּרְכִי נַפְשִׁי אֶת יהוה וְכָל קְרָבַי אֶת שֵׁם קָדְשׁוֹ:

הָאֵל בְּתַעֲצֻמוֹת עֻזֶּךָ הַגָּדוֹל בִּכְבוֹד שְׁמֶךָ הַגִּבּוֹר לָנֶצַח וְהַנּוֹרָא בְּנוֹרְאוֹתֶיךָ הַמֶּלֶךְ הַיּוֹשֵׁב עַל כִּסֵּא רָם וְנִשָּׂא:

we still could not sufficiently thank You, HASHEM our God and God of our forefathers, and to bless Your Name for even one of the thousands upon thousands, and myriads upon myriads of the favors (miracles and wonders) that You performed for our ancestors and for us. You redeemed us from Egypt, HASHEM our God, and liberated us from the house of bondage. In famine You nourished us and in plenty You sustained us. From sword You saved us; from plague You let us escape; and You spared us from severe and enduring diseases. Until now Your mercy has helped us and Your kindness has not forsaken us; do not abandon us, HASHEM our God, forever. Therefore, the limbs which You have set within us, and the spirit and soul which You have breathed into our nostrils, and the tongue which You have placed in our mouth – they shall thank, bless, praise, glorify, exalt, revere, sanctify, and do homage to Your Name, our King. For every mouth shall offer thanks to You; every tongue shall vow allegiance to You; every knee shall bend to You; all who stand erect shall bow before You; all hearts shall fear You, and all men's innermost feelings and thoughts shall sing praises to Your Name, as it is written: "All my bones declare: 'HASHEM, who is like You?' You save the poor man from one stronger than he, the poor and destitute from one who would rob him." Who is like unto You? Who is equal to You? Who can be compared to You? O great, mighty, and awesome God, supreme God, Maker of heaven and earth. We shall praise, acclaim, and glorify You and bless Your holy Name, as it is said: "Of David: Bless HASHEM, O my soul, and let all my innermost being bless His holy Name!"

O God, in the omnipotence of Your strength, great in the honor of Your Name, powerful forever and awesome through Your awesome deeds, O King enthroned upon a high and lofty throne!

שׁוֹכֵן עַד מָרוֹם וְקָדוֹשׁ שְׁמוֹ. וְכָתוּב רַנְּנוּ צַדִּיקִים בַּיהוה לַיְשָׁרִים נָאוָה תְהִלָּה: בְּפִי יְשָׁרִים תִּתְהַלָּל וּבְדִבְרֵי צַדִּיקִים תִּתְבָּרַךְ וּבִלְשׁוֹן חֲסִידִים תִּתְרוֹמָם וּבְקֶרֶב קְדוֹשִׁים תִּתְקַדָּשׁ:

וּבְמַקְהֲלוֹת רִבְבוֹת עַמְּךָ בֵּית יִשְׂרָאֵל בְּרִנָּה יִתְפָּאֵר שִׁמְךָ מַלְכֵּנוּ בְּכָל דּוֹר וָדוֹר שֶׁכֵּן חוֹבַת כָּל הַיְצוּרִים לְפָנֶיךָ יהוה אֱלֹהֵינוּ וֵאלֹהֵי אֲבוֹתֵינוּ לְהוֹדוֹת לְהַלֵּל לְשַׁבֵּחַ לְפָאֵר לְרוֹמֵם לְהַדֵּר לְבָרֵךְ לְעַלֵּה וּלְקַלֵּס עַל כָּל דִּבְרֵי שִׁירוֹת וְתִשְׁבְּחוֹת דָּוִד בֶּן יִשַׁי עַבְדְּךָ מְשִׁיחֶךָ.

יִשְׁתַּבַּח שִׁמְךָ לָעַד מַלְכֵּנוּ הָאֵל הַמֶּלֶךְ הַגָּדוֹל וְהַקָּדוֹשׁ בַּשָּׁמַיִם וּבָאָרֶץ כִּי לְךָ נָאֶה יהוה אֱלֹהֵינוּ וֵאלֹהֵי אֲבוֹתֵינוּ שִׁיר וּשְׁבָחָה הַלֵּל וְזִמְרָה עֹז וּמֶמְשָׁלָה נֶצַח גְּדֻלָּה וּגְבוּרָה תְּהִלָּה וְתִפְאֶרֶת קְדֻשָּׁה וּמַלְכוּת בְּרָכוֹת וְהוֹדָאוֹת מֵעַתָּה וְעַד עוֹלָם: בָּרוּךְ אַתָּה יהוה אֵל מֶלֶךְ גָּדוֹל בַּתִּשְׁבָּחוֹת אֵל הַהוֹדָאוֹת אֲדוֹן הַנִּפְלָאוֹת הַבּוֹחֵר בְּשִׁירֵי זִמְרָה מֶלֶךְ אֵל חֵי הָעוֹלָמִים.

The blessing over wine is recited and the fourth cup is drunk while reclining to the left side. It is preferable that the entire cup be drunk.

Some recite the following before the fourth cup:

הִנְנִי מוּכָן וּמְזֻמָּן לְקַיֵּם מִצְוַת כּוֹס רְבִיעִי שֶׁל אַרְבַּע כּוֹסוֹת. לְשֵׁם יִחוּד קֻדְשָׁא בְּרִיךְ הוּא וּשְׁכִינְתֵּיהּ, עַל יְדֵי הַהוּא טָמִיר וְנֶעְלָם, בְּשֵׁם כָּל יִשְׂרָאֵל. וִיהִי נֹעַם אֲדֹנָי אֱלֹהֵינוּ עָלֵינוּ, וּמַעֲשֵׂה יָדֵינוּ כּוֹנְנָה עָלֵינוּ, וּמַעֲשֵׂה יָדֵינוּ כּוֹנְנֵהוּ:

He Who abides forever, exalted and holy is His Name. And it is written: "Rejoice in HASHEM, you righteous; for the upright, praise is fitting." By the mouth of the upright You shall be lauded; by the words of the righteous You shall be praised; by the tongue of the pious You shall be exalted; and amid the holy You shall be sanctified.

And in the assemblies of the myriads of Your people, the House of Israel, with jubilation shall Your Name, our King, be glorified, in every generation. For such is the duty of all creatures – before You, HASHEM, our God, and God of our forefathers, to thank, praise, laud, glorify, exalt, adore, bless, raise high, and sing praises – even beyond all expressions of the songs and praises of David the son of Yishai, Your servant, Your anointed.

May Your Name be praised forever, our King, the God, and King Who is great and holy in heaven and on earth; for to You, HASHEM, our God, and the God of our forefathers, it is fitting to render song and praise, lauding and hymns, power and dominion, triumph, greatness and strength, praise and splendor, holiness and sovereignty, blessings and thanksgivings from now and forever. Blessed are You, HASHEM, God, King, great in praises, God of thanksgivings, Master of wonders, Who favors songs of praise – King, God, Life-giver of the world.

The blessing over wine is recited and the fourth cup is drunk while reclining to the left side. It is preferable that the entire cup be drunk.

Some recite the following before the fourth cup:

Behold, I am prepared and ready to fulfill the mitzvah of the fourth of the Four Cups. For the sake of the unification of the Holy One, Blessed is He, and His Presence, through Him Who is hidden and inscrutable – [I pray] in the name of all Israel. May the pleasantness of my Lord, our God, be upon us – may He establish our handiwork for us; our handiwork may He establish.

בָּרוּךְ אַתָּה יהוה אֱלֹהֵינוּ מֶלֶךְ הָעוֹלָם בּוֹרֵא פְּרִי הַגָּפֶן:

After drinking the fourth cup, the concluding blessing is recited.
On Shabbos include the passage in parentheses.

בָּרוּךְ אַתָּה יהוה אֱלֹהֵינוּ מֶלֶךְ הָעוֹלָם עַל הַגֶּפֶן וְעַל פְּרִי הַגֶּפֶן וְעַל תְּנוּבַת הַשָּׂדֶה וְעַל אֶרֶץ חֶמְדָּה טוֹבָה וּרְחָבָה שֶׁרָצִיתָ וְהִנְחַלְתָּ לַאֲבוֹתֵינוּ לֶאֱכוֹל מִפִּרְיָהּ וְלִשְׂבּוֹעַ מִטּוּבָהּ. רַחֶם נָא יהוה אֱלֹהֵינוּ עַל יִשְׂרָאֵל עַמֶּךָ וְעַל יְרוּשָׁלַיִם עִירֶךָ וְעַל צִיּוֹן מִשְׁכַּן כְּבוֹדֶךָ וְעַל מִזְבְּחֶךָ וְעַל הֵיכָלֶךָ. וּבְנֵה יְרוּשָׁלַיִם עִיר הַקֹּדֶשׁ בִּמְהֵרָה בְיָמֵינוּ וְהַעֲלֵנוּ לְתוֹכָהּ וְשַׂמְּחֵנוּ בְּבִנְיָנָהּ, וְנֹאכַל מִפִּרְיָהּ וְנִשְׂבַּע מִטּוּבָהּ וּנְבָרֶכְךָ עָלֶיהָ בִּקְדֻשָּׁה וּבְטָהֳרָה. [וּרְצֵה וְהַחֲלִיצֵנוּ בְּיוֹם הַשַּׁבָּת הַזֶּה] וְשַׂמְּחֵנוּ בְּיוֹם חַג הַמַּצּוֹת הַזֶּה. כִּי אַתָּה יהוה טוֹב וּמֵטִיב לַכֹּל וְנוֹדֶה לְּךָ עַל הָאָרֶץ וְעַל פְּרִי הַגָּפֶן: בָּרוּךְ אַתָּה יהוה עַל הָאָרֶץ וְעַל פְּרִי הַגָּפֶן:

◆§ The Shabbos and Festival additions in the after-berachah

In *Bircas HaMazon* on the festivals we add *Ya'aleh V'yavo*, and on Shabbos *Retzei*. Whenever there is an absolute requirement to eat bread (such as for the first two meals on Shabbos) one must repeat *Bircas Hamazon* if he forgot to recite *Ya'aleh V'yavo*. At the Pesach Seder, since there is an absolute requirement to drink the fourth cup of wine, the same should apply to the special additions to the *Al HaGefen* (the *Berachah Mei'ein Shalosh*) after-blessing; if they are forgotten, one should have to repeat the entire after-blessing.

The premise of this analogy is not correct, however. First, whereas there is an addition recited in *Bircas Hamazon* for Chanukah and

Blessed are You, HASHEM, our God, King of the universe, Who creates the fruit of the vine.

<small>After drinking the fourth cup, the concluding blessing is recited. On Shabbos include the passage in parentheses.</small>

Blessed are You, HASHEM, our God, King of the universe, for the vine and the fruit of the vine, and for the produce of the field. For the desirable, good, and spacious land that You were pleased to give our forefathers as a heritage, to eat of its fruit and to be satisfied with its goodness. Have mercy, we beg You, HASHEM, our God, on Israel Your people; on Yerushalayim, Your city; on Tziyon, resting place of Your glory; Your Altar, and Your Temple. Rebuild Yerushalayim the city of holiness, speedily in our days. Bring us up into it and gladden us in its rebuilding, and let us eat from its fruit and be satisfied with its goodness and bless You upon it in holiness and purity. (Favor us and strengthen us on this Shabbos day) and grant us happiness on this Festival of Matzos; for You, HASHEM, are good and do good to all, and we thank You for the land and for the fruit of the vine. Blessed are You, HASHEM, for the land and for the fruit of the vine.

Purim, there is no addition for these holidays in the *Berachah Mei'ein Shalosh*. Furthermore, several authorities (see *Tosafos, Berachos* 44a s.v. *Al ha'etz*) are of the opinion that there never is a requirement to recite additions in this after-*berachah* (see *Sha'ar Hatziyun*, 208:9).

Furthermore, there is no absolute requirement to recite the after-blessing at all, for two reasons. First, one who does not have wine can use certain other beverages for which this after-blessing is not recited at all (rather, *Borei Nefashos* is said). Second, if one drinks less than the requisite amount of wine (a *revi'is;* see *Shulchan Aruch* and *Mishnah Berurah* 192) he has no requirement to say an after-blessing at all. Accordingly, there is no *absolute* requirement to recite the additions, and one who forgets to say them need not repeat the after-blessing (*Hamodia*, 13th of Nisan 5761, citing Rav Shlomo Zalman).

נִרְצָה

חֲסַל סִדּוּר פֶּסַח כְּהִלְכָתוֹ. כְּכָל מִשְׁפָּטוֹ וְחֻקָּתוֹ. כַּאֲשֶׁר זָכִינוּ לְסַדֵּר אוֹתוֹ. כֵּן נִזְכֶּה לַעֲשׂוֹתוֹ: זָךְ שׁוֹכֵן מְעוֹנָה. קוֹמֵם קְהַל עֲדַת מִי מָנָה. בְּקָרוֹב נַהֵל נִטְעֵי כַנָּה. פְּדוּיִם לְצִיּוֹן בְּרִנָּה:

לְשָׁנָה הַבָּאָה בִּירוּשָׁלָיִם:

On the first night recite the following.
On the second night continue on page 228.

וּבְכֵן וַיְהִי בַּחֲצִי הַלַּיְלָה:

בַּלַּיְלָה.	אָז רוֹב נִסִּים הִפְלֵאתָ
הַלַּיְלָה.	בְּרֹאשׁ אַשְׁמוֹרֶת זֶה
לַיְלָה.	גֵּר צֶדֶק נִצַּחְתּוֹ כְּנֶחֱלַק לוֹ
	וַיְהִי בַּחֲצִי הַלַּיְלָה.
הַלַּיְלָה.	דַּנְתָּ מֶלֶךְ גְּרָר בַּחֲלוֹם
לַיְלָה.	הִפְחַדְתָּ אֲרַמִּי בְּאֶמֶשׁ
לַיְלָה.	וַיָּשַׂר יִשְׂרָאֵל לְמַלְאָךְ וַיּוּכַל לוֹ
	וַיְהִי בַּחֲצִי הַלַּיְלָה.
הַלַּיְלָה.	זֶרַע בְּכוֹרֵי פַתְרוֹס מָחַצְתָּ בַּחֲצִי
בַּלַּיְלָה.	חֵילָם לֹא מָצְאוּ בְּקוּמָם
לַיְלָה.	טִיסַת נְגִיד חֲרֹשֶׁת סִלִּיתָ בְּכוֹכְבֵי
	וַיְהִי בַּחֲצִי הַלַּיְלָה.
בַּלַּיְלָה.	יָעַץ מְחָרֵף לְנוֹפֵף אִוּוּי הוֹבַשְׁתָּ פְגָרָיו
לַיְלָה.	כָּרַע בֵּל וּמַצָּבוֹ בְּאִישׁוֹן

NIRTZAH

The Seder is now concluded in accordance with its laws, with all its ordinances and statutes. Just as we were privileged to arrange it, so may we merit to perform it. O Pure One, Who dwells on high, raise up the countless congregation, soon guide the offshoots of Your plants, redeemed to Tziyon with glad song.

NEXT YEAR IN YERUSHALAYIM

On the first night recite the following.
On the second night continue on page 228.

It came to pass at midnight.

You have, of old, performed many wonders
                by night.
At the head of the watches of   this night.
To the righteous convert (Avraham),
   You gave triumph by dividing for him   the night.
      It came to pass at midnight.

You judged the king of Gerar (Avimelech),
   in a dream   by night.
You frightened the Aramean (Lavan),
   in the dark   of night.
Israel (Yaakov) fought with an angel
   and overcame him   by night.
      It came to pass at midnight.

Egypt's firstborn You crushed   at midnight.
Their host they found not upon arising   at night.
The army of the prince of Charoshes (Sisera)
   You swept away with stars of   the night.
      It came to pass at midnight.

The blasphemer (Sancheriv) planned to raise his hand against Yerushalayim —
   but You withered his corpses   by night.
Bel was overturned with its pedestal,
   in the darkness   of night.

לַיְלָה.	לְאִישׁ חֲמוּדוֹת נִגְלָה רָז חֲזוֹת
	וַיְהִי בַּחֲצִי הַלַּיְלָה.
בַּלַּיְלָה.	**מִ**שְׁתַּכֵּר בִּכְלֵי קֹדֶשׁ נֶהֱרַג בּוֹ
לַיְלָה.	**נ**וֹשַׁע מִבּוֹר אֲרָיוֹת פּוֹתֵר בְּעִתּוּתֵי
בַּלַּיְלָה.	**שִׂ**נְאָה נָטַר אֲגָגִי וְכָתַב סְפָרִים
	וַיְהִי בַּחֲצִי הַלַּיְלָה.
לַיְלָה.	**ע**וֹרַרְתָּ נִצְחֲךָ עָלָיו בְּנֶדֶד שְׁנַת
מִלַּיְלָה.	**פּ**וּרָה תִדְרוֹךְ לְשׁוֹמֵר מַה
לַיְלָה.	**צ**ָרַח כַּשּׁוֹמֵר וְשָׂח אָתָא בֹקֶר וְגַם
	וַיְהִי בַּחֲצִי הַלַּיְלָה.
לַיְלָה.	**ק**ָרֵב יוֹם אֲשֶׁר הוּא לֹא יוֹם וְלֹא
הַלַּיְלָה.	**ר**ָם הוֹדַע כִּי לְךָ הַיּוֹם אַף לְךָ
	שׁוֹמְרִים הַפְקֵד לְעִירְךָ
הַלַּיְלָה.	כָּל הַיּוֹם וְכָל
לַיְלָה.	**תָּ**אִיר כְּאוֹר יוֹם חֶשְׁכַּת
	וַיְהִי בַּחֲצִי הַלַּיְלָה.

On the second night recite the following.
On the first night continue on page 232.

וּבְכֵן וַאֲמַרְתֶּם זֶבַח פֶּסַח:

בַּפֶּסַח.	**אֹ**מֶץ גְּבוּרוֹתֶיךָ הִפְלֵאתָ
פֶּסַח.	**בְּ**רֹאשׁ כָּל מוֹעֲדוֹת נִשֵּׂאתָ
פֶּסַח.	**גִּ**לִּיתָ לְאֶזְרָחִי חֲצוֹת לֵיל
	וַאֲמַרְתֶּם זֶבַח פֶּסַח.
בַּפֶּסַח.	**דְּ**לָתָיו דָּפַקְתָּ כְּחֹם הַיּוֹם

To the man of Your delights (Daniel)
was revealed the mystery of the visions of night.
    It came to pass at midnight.
He (Belshazzar) who caroused from the holy vessels
was killed that very night.
From the lions' den was rescued he (Daniel)
who interpreted the "terrors" of the night.
The Agagite (Haman) nursed hatred
and wrote decrees at night.
    It came to pass at midnight.
You began Your triumph over him when You
disturbed (Achashverosh's) sleep at night.
Trample the winepress to help those who ask the
watchman, "What of the long night?"
He will shout, like a watchman, and say:
"Morning shall come after night."
    It came to pass at midnight.
Hasten the day (of Mashiach),
that is neither day nor night.
Most High — make known that Yours
are day and night.
Appoint guards for Your city,
all the day and all the night.
Brighten like the light of day
the darkness of night.
    It came to pass at midnight.

<small>On the second night recite the following.
On the first night continue on page 232.</small>

And you shall say: This is the feast of Pesach.

You displayed wondrously Your
mighty powers on Pesach.
Above all festivals You elevated Pesach.
To the Oriental (Avraham) You revealed
the future midnight of Pesach.
    And you shall say: This is the feast of Pesach.
At his door You knocked in the
heat of the day on Pesach;

הִסְעִיד נוֹצְצִים עֻגּוֹת מַצּוֹת	בַּפֶּסַח.
וְאֶל הַבָּקָר רָץ זֵכֶר לְשׁוֹר עֵרֶךְ	פֶּסַח.
וַאֲמַרְתֶּם זֶבַח פֶּסַח.	
זוֹעֲמוּ סְדוֹמִים וְלוֹהֲטוּ בָּאֵשׁ	בַּפֶּסַח.
חֻלַּץ לוֹט מֵהֶם וּמַצּוֹת אָפָה בְּקֵץ	פֶּסַח.
טִאטֵאתָ אַדְמַת מוֹף וְנוֹף בְּעָבְרְךָ	בַּפֶּסַח.
וַאֲמַרְתֶּם זֶבַח פֶּסַח.	
יָהּ רֹאשׁ כָּל אוֹן מָחַצְתָּ בְּלֵיל שִׁמּוּר	פֶּסַח.
כַּבִּיר עַל בֵּן בְּכוֹר פָּסַחְתָּ בְּדַם	פֶּסַח.
לְבִלְתִּי תֵּת מַשְׁחִית לָבֹא בִּפְתָחַי	בַּפֶּסַח.
וַאֲמַרְתֶּם זֶבַח פֶּסַח.	
מְסֻגֶּרֶת סֻגְּרָה בְּעִתּוֹתֵי	פֶּסַח.
נִשְׁמְדָה מִדְיָן בִּצְלִיל שְׂעוֹרֵי עֹמֶר	פֶּסַח.
שׂוֹרְפוּ מִשְׁמַנֵּי פּוּל וְלוּד בִּיקַד יְקוֹד	פֶּסַח.
וַאֲמַרְתֶּם זֶבַח פֶּסַח.	
עוֹד הַיּוֹם בְּנֹב לַעֲמוֹד	
עַד גָּעָה עוֹנַת	פֶּסַח.
פַּס יָד כָּתְבָה לְקַעֲקֵעַ צוּל	בַּפֶּסַח.
צָפֹה הַצָּפִית עָרוֹךְ הַשֻּׁלְחָן	בַּפֶּסַח.
וַאֲמַרְתֶּם זֶבַח פֶּסַח.	
קָהָל כִּנְּסָה הֲדַסָּה צוֹם לְשַׁלֵּשׁ	בַּפֶּסַח.
רֹאשׁ מִבֵּית רָשָׁע מָחַצְתָּ	
בְּעֵץ חֲמִשִּׁים	בַּפֶּסַח.
שְׁתֵּי אֵלֶּה רֶגַע תָּבִיא לְעוּצִית	בַּפֶּסַח.

He satiated the angels with matzah-cakes on Pesach.
And he ran to the herd — symbolic of
the sacrificial beast   of Pesach.
 And you shall say: This is the feast of Pesach.

The Sodomites provoked (God) and were devoured
by fire   on Pesach;
Lot was withdrawn from them — he had baked
matzos at the time   of Pesach.
You swept clean the soil of Mof and Nof (in Egypt)
when You passed through   on Pesach.
 And you shall say: This is the feast of Pesach.

God, You crushed every firstborn of On (in Egypt)
on the watchful night   of Pesach.
But Master – Your own firstborn, You skipped
by merit of the blood   of Pesach,
Not to allow the Destroyer to enter my doors
                                                   on Pesach.
 And you shall say: This is the feast of Pesach.

The beleaguered (Yericho) was besieged on Pesach.
Midyan was destroyed with a barley cake,
from the Omer   of Pesach.
The mighty nobles of Pul and Lud (Assyria) were
consumed in a great conflagration   on Pesach.
 And you shall say: This is the feast of Pesach.

He (Sancheriv) would have stood that day at Nob,
but for the advent   of Pesach.
A hand inscribed the destruction of
Tzul (Babylon)   on Pesach.
As the watch was set, and the royal
table decked   on Pesach.
 And you shall say: This is the feast of Pesach.

Hadassah (Esther) gathered a congregation
for a three-day fast   on Pesach.
You caused the head of the evil clan (Haman) to be
hanged on a fifty-cubit gallows   on Pesach.
Doubly, will You bring in an instant
upon Utzis (Edom)   on Pesach.

תָּעֹז יָדְךָ וְתָרוּם יְמִינֶךָ
כְּלֵיל הִתְקַדֶּשׁ חַג פֶּסַח.
וַאֲמַרְתֶּם זֶבַח פֶּסַח.

On both nights continue here:

כִּי לוֹ נָאֶה, כִּי לוֹ יָאֶה:

אַדִּיר בִּמְלוּכָה, בָּחוּר כַּהֲלָכָה, גְּדוּדָיו יֹאמְרוּ לוֹ, לְךָ וּלְךָ, לְךָ כִּי לְךָ, לְךָ אַף לְךָ, לְךָ יהוה הַמַּמְלָכָה, כִּי לוֹ נָאֶה, כִּי לוֹ יָאֶה.

דָּגוּל בִּמְלוּכָה, הָדוּר כַּהֲלָכָה, וָתִיקָיו יֹאמְרוּ לוֹ, לְךָ וּלְךָ, לְךָ כִּי לְךָ, לְךָ אַף לְךָ, לְךָ יהוה הַמַּמְלָכָה, כִּי לוֹ נָאֶה, כִּי לוֹ יָאֶה.

זַכַּאי בִּמְלוּכָה, חָסִין כַּהֲלָכָה, טַפְסְרָיו יֹאמְרוּ לוֹ, לְךָ וּלְךָ, לְךָ כִּי לְךָ, לְךָ אַף לְךָ, לְךָ יהוה הַמַּמְלָכָה, כִּי לוֹ נָאֶה, כִּי לוֹ יָאֶה.

יָחִיד בִּמְלוּכָה, כַּבִּיר כַּהֲלָכָה, לִמּוּדָיו יֹאמְרוּ לוֹ, לְךָ וּלְךָ, לְךָ כִּי לְךָ, לְךָ אַף לְךָ, לְךָ יהוה הַמַּמְלָכָה, כִּי לוֹ נָאֶה, כִּי לוֹ יָאֶה.

מוֹשֵׁל בִּמְלוּכָה, נוֹרָא כַּהֲלָכָה, סְבִיבָיו יֹאמְרוּ לוֹ, לְךָ וּלְךָ, לְךָ כִּי לְךָ, לְךָ אַף לְךָ, לְךָ יהוה הַמַּמְלָכָה, כִּי לוֹ נָאֶה, כִּי לוֹ יָאֶה.

עָנָיו בִּמְלוּכָה, פּוֹדֶה כַּהֲלָכָה, צַדִּיקָיו יֹאמְרוּ לוֹ, לְךָ וּלְךָ, לְךָ כִּי לְךָ, לְךָ אַף לְךָ, לְךָ יהוה הַמַּמְלָכָה, כִּי לוֹ נָאֶה, כִּי לוֹ יָאֶה.

קָדוֹשׁ בִּמְלוּכָה, רַחוּם כַּהֲלָכָה, שִׁנְאַנָּיו יֹאמְרוּ לוֹ, לְךָ וּלְךָ, לְךָ כִּי לְךָ, לְךָ אַף לְךָ, לְךָ יהוה הַמַּמְלָכָה, כִּי לוֹ נָאֶה, כִּי לוֹ יָאֶה.

Let Your hand be strong, and Your right arm exalted, as on that night when You hallowed the festival of Pesach.
And you shall say: This is the feast of Pesach.

On both nights continue here:

To Him praise is due! To Him praise is fitting!

Mighty in majesty, perfectly distinguished, His companies of angels say to Him: Yours and only Yours; Yours, yes Yours; Yours, surely Yours; Yours, HASHEM, is the sovereignty. To Him praise is due! To Him praise is fitting!

Supreme in kingship, perfectly glorious, His faithful say to Him: Yours and only Yours; Yours, yes Yours; Yours, surely Yours; Yours, HASHEM, is the sovereignty. To Him praise is due! To Him praise is fitting!

Pure in kingship, perfectly mighty, His angels say to Him: Yours and only Yours; Yours, yes Yours; Yours, surely Yours; Yours, HASHEM, is the sovereignty. To Him praise is due! To Him praise is fitting!

Alone in kingship, perfectly omnipotent, His scholars say to Him: Yours and only Yours; Yours, yes Yours; Yours, surely Yours; Yours, HASHEM, is the sovereignty. To Him praise is due! To Him praise is fitting!

Commanding in kingship, perfectly wondrous, His surrounding (angels) say to Him: Yours and only Yours; Yours, yes Yours; Yours, surely Yours; Yours, HASHEM, is the sovereignty. To Him praise is due! To Him praise is fitting!

Modest in dominion, perfectly the Redeemer, His righteous say to Him: Yours and only Yours; Yours, yes Yours; Yours, surely Yours; Yours, HASHEM, is the sovereignty. To Him praise is due! To Him praise is fitting!

Holy in kingship, perfectly merciful, His troops of angels say to Him: Yours and only Yours; Yours, yes Yours; Yours, surely Yours; Yours, HASHEM, is the sovereignty. To Him praise is due! To Him praise is fitting.

תַּקִּיף בִּמְלוּכָה, תּוֹמֵךְ כַּהֲלָכָה, תְּמִימָיו יֹאמְרוּ לוֹ, לְךָ וּלְךָ, לְךָ כִּי לְךָ, לְךָ אַף לְךָ, לְךָ יהוה הַמַּמְלָכָה, כִּי לוֹ נָאֶה, כִּי לוֹ יָאֶה.

אַדִּיר הוּא יִבְנֶה בֵיתוֹ בְּקָרוֹב, בִּמְהֵרָה, בִּמְהֵרָה, בְּיָמֵינוּ בְּקָרוֹב. אֵל בְּנֵה, אֵל בְּנֵה, בְּנֵה בֵיתְךָ בְּקָרוֹב.

בָּחוּר הוּא. גָּדוֹל הוּא. דָּגוּל הוּא. יִבְנֶה בֵיתוֹ בְּקָרוֹב, בִּמְהֵרָה, בִּמְהֵרָה, בְּיָמֵינוּ בְּקָרוֹב. אֵל בְּנֵה, אֵל בְּנֵה, בְּנֵה בֵיתְךָ בְּקָרוֹב.

הָדוּר הוּא. וָתִיק הוּא. זַכַּאי הוּא. חָסִיד הוּא. יִבְנֶה בֵיתוֹ בְּקָרוֹב, בִּמְהֵרָה, בִּמְהֵרָה, בְּיָמֵינוּ בְּקָרוֹב. אֵל בְּנֵה, אֵל בְּנֵה, בְּנֵה בֵיתְךָ בְּקָרוֹב.

טָהוֹר הוּא. יָחִיד הוּא. כַּבִּיר הוּא. לָמוּד הוּא. מֶלֶךְ הוּא. נוֹרָא הוּא. סַגִּיב הוּא. עִזּוּז הוּא. פּוֹדֶה הוּא. צַדִּיק הוּא. יִבְנֶה בֵיתוֹ בְּקָרוֹב, בִּמְהֵרָה, בִּמְהֵרָה, בְּיָמֵינוּ בְּקָרוֹב. אֵל בְּנֵה, אֵל בְּנֵה, בְּנֵה בֵיתְךָ בְּקָרוֹב.

קָדוֹשׁ הוּא. רַחוּם הוּא. שַׁדַּי הוּא. תַּקִּיף הוּא. יִבְנֶה בֵיתוֹ בְּקָרוֹב, בִּמְהֵרָה, בִּמְהֵרָה, בְּיָמֵינוּ בְּקָרוֹב. אֵל בְּנֵה, אֵל בְּנֵה, בְּנֵה בֵיתְךָ בְּקָרוֹב.

The *Omer* is counted from the second night of Pesach until the night before Shavuos. While most communities begin to count the *Omer* at *Maariv*, some have the custom to begin counting at the Seder. The Counting of the *Omer* can be found on pg. 255.

אֶחָד מִי יוֹדֵעַ? אֶחָד אֲנִי יוֹדֵעַ. אֶחָד אֱלֹהֵינוּ שֶׁבַּשָּׁמַיִם וּבָאָרֶץ.

שְׁנַיִם מִי יוֹדֵעַ? שְׁנַיִם אֲנִי יוֹדֵעַ. שְׁנֵי לֻחוֹת

Almighty in kingship, perfectly sustaining, His perfect ones say to Him: Yours and only Yours; Yours, yes Yours; Yours, surely Yours; Yours, Hᴀsʜᴇᴍ, is the sovereignty. To Him praise is due! To Him praise is fitting!

He is most mighty. May He soon rebuild His House, speedily, yes speedily, in our days, soon. God, rebuild, God, rebuild, rebuild Your House soon!

He is distinguished, He is great, He is exalted. May He soon rebuild His House, speedily, yes speedily, in our days, soon. God, rebuild, God, rebuild, rebuild Your House soon!

He is all glorious, He is faithful, He is faultless, He is kind. May He soon rebuild His House, speedily, yes speedily, in our days, soon. God, rebuild, God, rebuild, rebuild Your House soon!

He is pure, He is unique, He is powerful, He is all-wise, He is King, He is awesome, He is sublime, He is all-powerful, He is the Redeemer, He is the all-righteous. May He soon rebuild His House, speedily, yes speedily, in our days, soon. God, rebuild, God, rebuild, rebuild Your House soon!

He is holy, He is compassionate, He is Almighty, He is omnipotent. May He soon rebuild His House, speedily, yes speedily, in our days, soon. God, rebuild, God, rebuild, rebuild Your House soon!

The *Omer* is counted from the second night of Pesach until the night before Shavuos. While most communities begin to count the *Omer* at *Maariv,* some have the custom to begin counting at the Seder. The Counting of the *Omer* can be found on pg. 255.

Who knows one? I know one: One is our God, in heaven and on earth.

Who knows two? I know two: two are the Tablets of

הַבְּרִית, אֶחָד אֱלֹהֵינוּ שֶׁבַּשָּׁמַיִם וּבָאָרֶץ.

שְׁלֹשָׁה מִי יוֹדֵעַ? שְׁלֹשָׁה אֲנִי יוֹדֵעַ. שְׁלֹשָׁה אָבוֹת, שְׁנֵי לֻחוֹת הַבְּרִית, אֶחָד אֱלֹהֵינוּ שֶׁבַּשָּׁמַיִם וּבָאָרֶץ.

אַרְבַּע מִי יוֹדֵעַ? אַרְבַּע אֲנִי יוֹדֵעַ. אַרְבַּע אִמָּהוֹת, שְׁלֹשָׁה אָבוֹת, שְׁנֵי לֻחוֹת הַבְּרִית, אֶחָד אֱלֹהֵינוּ שֶׁבַּשָּׁמַיִם וּבָאָרֶץ.

חֲמִשָּׁה מִי יוֹדֵעַ? חֲמִשָּׁה אֲנִי יוֹדֵעַ. חֲמִשָּׁה חֻמְשֵׁי תוֹרָה, אַרְבַּע אִמָּהוֹת, שְׁלֹשָׁה אָבוֹת, שְׁנֵי לֻחוֹת הַבְּרִית, אֶחָד אֱלֹהֵינוּ שֶׁבַּשָּׁמַיִם וּבָאָרֶץ.

שִׁשָּׁה מִי יוֹדֵעַ? שִׁשָּׁה אֲנִי יוֹדֵעַ. שִׁשָּׁה סִדְרֵי מִשְׁנָה, חֲמִשָּׁה חֻמְשֵׁי תוֹרָה, אַרְבַּע אִמָּהוֹת, שְׁלֹשָׁה אָבוֹת, שְׁנֵי לֻחוֹת הַבְּרִית, אֶחָד אֱלֹהֵינוּ שֶׁבַּשָּׁמַיִם וּבָאָרֶץ.

שִׁבְעָה מִי יוֹדֵעַ? שִׁבְעָה אֲנִי יוֹדֵעַ. שִׁבְעָה יְמֵי שַׁבַּתָּא, שִׁשָּׁה סִדְרֵי מִשְׁנָה, חֲמִשָּׁה חֻמְשֵׁי תוֹרָה, אַרְבַּע אִמָּהוֹת, שְׁלֹשָׁה אָבוֹת, שְׁנֵי לֻחוֹת הַבְּרִית, אֶחָד אֱלֹהֵינוּ שֶׁבַּשָּׁמַיִם וּבָאָרֶץ.

שְׁמוֹנָה מִי יוֹדֵעַ? שְׁמוֹנָה אֲנִי יוֹדֵעַ. שְׁמוֹנָה יְמֵי מִילָה, שִׁבְעָה יְמֵי שַׁבַּתָּא, שִׁשָּׁה סִדְרֵי מִשְׁנָה, חֲמִשָּׁה חֻמְשֵׁי תוֹרָה, אַרְבַּע אִמָּהוֹת, שְׁלֹשָׁה אָבוֹת, שְׁנֵי לֻחוֹת הַבְּרִית, אֶחָד אֱלֹהֵינוּ שֶׁבַּשָּׁמַיִם וּבָאָרֶץ.

תִּשְׁעָה מִי יוֹדֵעַ? תִּשְׁעָה אֲנִי יוֹדֵעַ. תִּשְׁעָה יַרְחֵי לֵדָה, שְׁמוֹנָה יְמֵי מִילָה, שִׁבְעָה יְמֵי שַׁבַּתָּא, שִׁשָּׁה סִדְרֵי מִשְׁנָה, חֲמִשָּׁה חֻמְשֵׁי

the Covenant; One is our God, in heaven and on earth.

Who knows three? I know three: three are the Patriarchs; two are the Tablets of the Covenant; One is our God, in heaven and on earth.

Who knows four? I know four: four are the Matriarchs; three are the Patriarchs; two are the Tablets of the Covenant; One is our God, in heaven and on earth.

Who knows five? I know five: five are the Books of Torah; four are the Matriarchs; three are the Patriarchs; two are the Tablets of the Covenant; One is our God, in heaven and on earth.

Who knows six? I know six: six are the Orders of the Mishnah; five are the Books of the Torah; four are the Matriarchs; three are the Patriarchs; two are the Tablets of the Covenant; One is our God, in heaven and on earth.

Who knows seven? I know seven: seven are the days of the week; six are the Orders of the Mishnah; five are the Books of the Torah; four are the Matriarchs; three are the Patriarchs; two are the Tablets of the Covenant; One is our God, in heaven and on earth.

Who knows eight? I know eight: eight are the days of circumcision; seven are the days of the week; six are the Orders of the Mishnah; five are the Books of the Torah; four are the Matriarchs; three are the Patriarchs; two are the Tablets of the Covenant; One is our God, in heaven and on earth.

Who knows nine? I know nine: nine are the months of pregnancy; eight are the days of circumcision; seven are the days of the week; six are the Orders of the Mishnah; five are the Books of the

תּוֹרָה, אַרְבַּע אִמָּהוֹת, שְׁלֹשָׁה אָבוֹת, שְׁנֵי לֻחוֹת הַבְּרִית, אֶחָד אֱלֹהֵינוּ שֶׁבַּשָּׁמַיִם וּבָאָרֶץ.

עֲשָׂרָה מִי יוֹדֵעַ? עֲשָׂרָה אֲנִי יוֹדֵעַ. עֲשָׂרָה דִבְּרַיָּא, תִּשְׁעָה יַרְחֵי לֵדָה, שְׁמוֹנָה יְמֵי מִילָה, שִׁבְעָה יְמֵי שַׁבַּתָּא, שִׁשָּׁה סִדְרֵי מִשְׁנָה, חֲמִשָּׁה חֻמְשֵׁי תוֹרָה, אַרְבַּע אִמָּהוֹת, שְׁלֹשָׁה אָבוֹת, שְׁנֵי לֻחוֹת הַבְּרִית, אֶחָד אֱלֹהֵינוּ שֶׁבַּשָּׁמַיִם וּבָאָרֶץ.

אַחַד עָשָׂר מִי יוֹדֵעַ? אַחַד עָשָׂר אֲנִי יוֹדֵעַ. אַחַד עָשָׂר כּוֹכְבַיָּא, עֲשָׂרָה דִבְּרַיָּא, תִּשְׁעָה יַרְחֵי לֵדָה, שְׁמוֹנָה יְמֵי מִילָה, שִׁבְעָה יְמֵי שַׁבַּתָּא, שִׁשָּׁה סִדְרֵי מִשְׁנָה, חֲמִשָּׁה חֻמְשֵׁי תוֹרָה, אַרְבַּע אִמָּהוֹת, שְׁלֹשָׁה אָבוֹת, שְׁנֵי לֻחוֹת הַבְּרִית, אֶחָד אֱלֹהֵינוּ שֶׁבַּשָּׁמַיִם וּבָאָרֶץ.

שְׁנֵים עָשָׂר מִי יוֹדֵעַ? שְׁנֵים עָשָׂר אֲנִי יוֹדֵעַ. שְׁנֵים עָשָׂר שִׁבְטַיָּא, אַחַד עָשָׂר כּוֹכְבַיָּא, עֲשָׂרָה דִבְּרַיָּא, תִּשְׁעָה יַרְחֵי לֵדָה, שְׁמוֹנָה יְמֵי מִילָה, שִׁבְעָה יְמֵי שַׁבַּתָּא, שִׁשָּׁה סִדְרֵי מִשְׁנָה, חֲמִשָּׁה חֻמְשֵׁי תוֹרָה, אַרְבַּע אִמָּהוֹת, שְׁלֹשָׁה אָבוֹת, שְׁנֵי לֻחוֹת הַבְּרִית, אֶחָד אֱלֹהֵינוּ שֶׁבַּשָּׁמַיִם וּבָאָרֶץ.

שְׁלֹשָׁה עָשָׂר מִי יוֹדֵעַ? שְׁלֹשָׁה עָשָׂר אֲנִי יוֹדֵעַ. שְׁלֹשָׁה עָשָׂר מִדַּיָּא, שְׁנֵים עָשָׂר שִׁבְטַיָּא, אַחַד עָשָׂר כּוֹכְבַיָּא, עֲשָׂרָה דִבְּרַיָּא, תִּשְׁעָה יַרְחֵי לֵדָה, שְׁמוֹנָה יְמֵי מִילָה, שִׁבְעָה יְמֵי שַׁבַּתָּא, שִׁשָּׁה סִדְרֵי מִשְׁנָה, חֲמִשָּׁה חֻמְשֵׁי תוֹרָה, אַרְבַּע

Torah; four are the Matriarchs; three are the Patriarchs; two are the Tablets of the Covenant; One is our God, in heaven and on earth.

Who knows ten? I know ten: ten are the Ten Commandments; nine are the months of pregnancy; eight are the days of circumcision; seven are the days of the week; six are the Orders of the Mishnah; five are the Books of the Torah; four are the Matriarchs; three are the Patriarchs; two are the Tablets of the Covenant; One is our God, in heaven and on earth.

Who knows eleven? I know eleven: eleven are the stars (in Yosef's dream); ten are the Ten Commandments; nine are the months of pregnancy; eight are the days of circumcision; seven are the days of the week; six are the Orders of the Mishnah; five are the Books of the Torah; four are the Matriarchs; three are the Patriarchs; two are the Tablets of the Covenant; One is our God, in heaven and on earth.

Who knows twelve? I know twelve: twelve are the tribes; eleven are the stars (in Yosef's dream); ten are the Ten Commandments; nine are the months of pregnancy; eight are the days of circumcision; seven are the days of the week; six are the Orders of the Mishnah; five are the Books of the Torah; four are the Matriarchs; three are the Patriarchs; two are the Tablets of the Covenant; One is our God, in heaven and on earth.

Who knows thirteen? I know thirteen: thirteen are the attributes of God; twelve are the tribes; eleven are the stars (in Yosef's dream); ten are the Ten Commandments; nine are the months of pregnancy; eight are the days of circumcision; seven are the days of the week; six are the Orders of the Mishnah; five are the Books of the Torah; four are

אִמָּהוֹת, שְׁלֹשָׁה אָבוֹת, שְׁנֵי לֻחוֹת הַבְּרִית, אֶחָד אֱלֹהֵינוּ שֶׁבַּשָּׁמַיִם וּבָאָרֶץ.

חַד גַּדְיָא, חַד גַּדְיָא, דְּזַבִּין אַבָּא בִּתְרֵי זוּזֵי, חַד גַּדְיָא חַד גַּדְיָא.

וְאָתָא שׁוּנְרָא וְאָכְלָה לְגַדְיָא, דְּזַבִּין אַבָּא בִּתְרֵי זוּזֵי, חַד גַּדְיָא חַד גַּדְיָא.

וְאָתָא כַלְבָּא וְנָשַׁךְ לְשׁוּנְרָא, דְּאָכְלָא לְגַדְיָא, דְּזַבִּין אַבָּא בִּתְרֵי זוּזֵי, חַד גַּדְיָא חַד גַּדְיָא.

וְאָתָא חוּטְרָא וְהִכָּה לְכַלְבָּא, דְּנָשַׁךְ לְשׁוּנְרָא, דְּאָכְלָה לְגַדְיָא, דְּזַבִּין אַבָּא בִּתְרֵי זוּזֵי, חַד גַּדְיָא חַד גַּדְיָא.

וְאָתָא נוּרָא וְשָׂרַף לְחוּטְרָא, דְּהִכָּה לְכַלְבָּא, דְּנָשַׁךְ לְשׁוּנְרָא, דְּאָכְלָה לְגַדְיָא, דְּזַבִּין אַבָּא בִּתְרֵי זוּזֵי, חַד גַּדְיָא חַד גַּדְיָא.

וְאָתָא מַיָּא וְכָבָה לְנוּרָא, דְּשָׂרַף לְחוּטְרָא, דְּהִכָּה לְכַלְבָּא, דְּנָשַׁךְ לְשׁוּנְרָא, דְּאָכְלָה לְגַדְיָא, דְּזַבִּין אַבָּא בִּתְרֵי זוּזֵי, חַד גַּדְיָא חַד גַּדְיָא.

וְאָתָא תוֹרָא וְשָׁתָה לְמַיָּא, דְּכָבָה לְנוּרָא, דְּשָׂרַף לְחוּטְרָא, דְּהִכָּה לְכַלְבָּא, דְּנָשַׁךְ לְשׁוּנְרָא, דְּאָכְלָה לְגַדְיָא, דְּזַבִּין אַבָּא בִּתְרֵי זוּזֵי, חַד גַּדְיָא חַד גַּדְיָא.

וְאָתָא הַשּׁוֹחֵט וְשָׁחַט לְתוֹרָא, דְּשָׁתָא לְמַיָּא, דְּכָבָה לְנוּרָא, דְּשָׂרַף לְחוּטְרָא, דְּהִכָּה לְכַלְבָּא, דְּנָשַׁךְ לְשׁוּנְרָא, דְּאָכְלָה לְגַדְיָא, דְּזַבִּין אַבָּא בִּתְרֵי זוּזֵי, חַד גַּדְיָא חַד גַּדְיָא.

וְאָתָא מַלְאַךְ הַמָּוֶת וְשָׁחַט לְשׁוֹחֵט, דְּשָׁחַט לְתוֹרָא, דְּשָׁתָה לְמַיָּא, דְּכָבָה לְנוּרָא, דְּשָׂרַף לְחוּטְרָא, דְּהִכָּה לְכַלְבָּא, דְּנָשַׁךְ לְשׁוּנְרָא, דְּאָכְלָה

the Matriarchs; three are the Patriarchs; two are the Tablets of the Covenant; One is our God, in heaven and on earth.

A kid, a kid, that father bought for two zuzim, a kid, a kid.

A cat then came and devoured the kid that father bought for two zuzim, a kid, a kid.

A dog then came and bit the cat, that devoured the kid that father bought for two zuzim, a kid, a kid.

A stick then came and beat the dog, that bit the cat, that devoured the kid that father bought for two zuzim, a kid, a kid.

A fire then came and burnt the stick, that beat the dog, that bit the cat, that devoured the kid that father bought for two zuzim, a kid, a kid.

Water then came and quenched the fire, that burnt the stick, that beat the dog, that bit the cat, that devoured the kid that father bought for two zuzim, a kid, a kid.

An ox then came and drank the water, that quenched the fire, that burnt the stick, that beat the dog, that bit the cat, that devoured the kid that father bought for two zuzim, a kid, a kid.

A slaughterer then came and slaughtered the ox, that drank the water, that quenched the fire, that burnt the stick, that beat the dog, that bit the cat, that devoured the kid that father bought for two zuzim, a kid, a kid.

The angel of death then came and killed the slaughterer, who slaughtered the ox, that drank the water, that quenched the fire, that burnt the stick, that beat the dog, that bit the cat, that devoured

לְגַדְיָא, דְזַבִּין אַבָּא בִּתְרֵי זוּזֵי, חַד גַּדְיָא חַד גַּדְיָא.
וְאָתָא הַקָּדוֹשׁ בָּרוּךְ הוּא וְשָׁחַט לְמַלְאַךְ הַמָּוֶת, דְשָׁחַט לְשׁוֹחֵט, דְשָׁחַט לְתוֹרָא, דְשָׁתָה לְמַיָּא, דְכָבָה לְנוּרָא, דְשָׂרַף לְחוּטְרָא, דְהִכָּה לְכַלְבָּא, דְנָשַׁךְ לְשׁוּנְרָא, דְאָכְלָה לְגַדְיָא, דְזַבִּין אַבָּא בִּתְרֵי זוּזֵי, חַד גַּדְיָא חַד גַּדְיָא.

Although the Haggadah formally ends at this point,
one should continue to occupy himself with the story of the Exodus,
and the laws of Pesach, until sleep overtakes him.

the kid that father bought for two zuzim, a kid, a kid.

The Holy One, Blessed is He, then came and slew the angel of death, who killed the slaughterer, who slaughtered the ox, that drank the water, that quenched the fire, that burnt the stick, that beat the dog, that bit the cat, that devoured the kid that father bought for two zuzim, a kid, a kid.

> Although the Haggadah formally ends at this point,
> one should continue to occupy himself with the story of the Exodus,
> and the laws of Pesach, until sleep overtakes him.

שיר השירים

Many recite שִׁיר הַשִּׁירִים, *Song of Songs*, after the Haggadah.

פרק א

א שִׁיר הַשִּׁירִים אֲשֶׁר לִשְׁלֹמֹה. ב יִשָּׁקֵנִי מִנְּשִׁיקוֹת פִּיהוּ, כִּי טוֹבִים דֹּדֶיךָ מִיָּיִן. ג לְרֵיחַ שְׁמָנֶיךָ טוֹבִים, שֶׁמֶן תּוּרַק שְׁמֶךָ, עַל כֵּן עֲלָמוֹת אֲהֵבוּךָ. ד מָשְׁכֵנִי אַחֲרֶיךָ נָּרוּצָה, הֱבִיאַנִי הַמֶּלֶךְ חֲדָרָיו, נָגִילָה וְנִשְׂמְחָה בָּךְ. נַזְכִּירָה דֹדֶיךָ מִיַּיִן, מֵישָׁרִים אֲהֵבוּךָ. ה שְׁחוֹרָה אֲנִי וְנָאוָה, בְּנוֹת יְרוּשָׁלָיִם, כְּאָהֳלֵי קֵדָר, כִּירִיעוֹת שְׁלֹמֹה. ו אַל תִּרְאוּנִי שֶׁאֲנִי שְׁחַרְחֹרֶת, שֶׁשֱּׁזָפַתְנִי הַשָּׁמֶשׁ, בְּנֵי אִמִּי נִחֲרוּ בִי, שָׂמֻנִי נֹטֵרָה אֶת הַכְּרָמִים, כַּרְמִי שֶׁלִּי לֹא נָטָרְתִּי. ז הַגִּידָה לִּי, שֶׁאָהֲבָה נַפְשִׁי, אֵיכָה תִרְעֶה, אֵיכָה תַּרְבִּיץ בַּצָּהֳרָיִם, שַׁלָּמָה אֶהְיֶה כְּעֹטְיָה עַל עֶדְרֵי חֲבֵרֶיךָ. ח אִם לֹא תֵדְעִי לָךְ, הַיָּפָה בַּנָּשִׁים, צְאִי לָךְ בְּעִקְבֵי הַצֹּאן, וּרְעִי אֶת גְּדִיֹּתַיִךְ עַל מִשְׁכְּנוֹת הָרֹעִים. ט לְסֻסָתִי בְּרִכְבֵי פַרְעֹה דִּמִּיתִיךְ, רַעְיָתִי. י נָאווּ לְחָיַיִךְ בַּתֹּרִים, צַוָּארֵךְ בַּחֲרוּזִים. יא תּוֹרֵי זָהָב נַעֲשֶׂה לָּךְ, עִם נְקֻדּוֹת הַכָּסֶף. יב עַד שֶׁהַמֶּלֶךְ בִּמְסִבּוֹ, נִרְדִּי נָתַן רֵיחוֹ. יג צְרוֹר הַמֹּר דּוֹדִי לִי, בֵּין שָׁדַי יָלִין. יד אֶשְׁכֹּל הַכֹּפֶר דּוֹדִי לִי, בְּכַרְמֵי עֵין גֶּדִי. טו הִנָּךְ יָפָה, רַעְיָתִי, הִנָּךְ יָפָה, עֵינַיִךְ יוֹנִים. טז הִנְּךָ יָפֶה, דוֹדִי, אַף נָעִים, אַף עַרְשֵׂנוּ רַעֲנָנָה. יז קֹרוֹת בָּתֵּינוּ אֲרָזִים, רָהִיטֵנוּ בְּרוֹתִים.

פרק ב

א אֲנִי חֲבַצֶּלֶת הַשָּׁרוֹן, שׁוֹשַׁנַּת הָעֲמָקִים. ב כְּשׁוֹשַׁנָּה בֵּין הַחוֹחִים, כֵּן רַעְיָתִי בֵּין הַבָּנוֹת. ג כְּתַפּוּחַ בַּעֲצֵי הַיַּעַר, כֵּן דּוֹדִי בֵּין הַבָּנִים, בְּצִלּוֹ חִמַּדְתִּי וְיָשַׁבְתִּי, וּפִרְיוֹ מָתוֹק לְחִכִּי. ד הֱבִיאַנִי אֶל בֵּית הַיָּיִן, וְדִגְלוֹ עָלַי אַהֲבָה. ה סַמְּכוּנִי בָּאֲשִׁישׁוֹת, רַפְּדוּנִי בַּתַּפּוּחִים, כִּי חוֹלַת אַהֲבָה אָנִי. ו שְׂמֹאלוֹ תַּחַת לְרֹאשִׁי, וִימִינוֹ תְּחַבְּקֵנִי. ז הִשְׁבַּעְתִּי אֶתְכֶם, בְּנוֹת יְרוּשָׁלַיִם, בִּצְבָאוֹת אוֹ בְּאַיְלוֹת הַשָּׂדֶה, אִם תָּעִירוּ וְאִם תְּעוֹרְרוּ אֶת הָאַהֲבָה עַד שֶׁתֶּחְפָּץ. ח קוֹל דּוֹדִי הִנֵּה זֶה בָּא, מְדַלֵּג עַל הֶהָרִים, מְקַפֵּץ עַל הַגְּבָעוֹת. ט דּוֹמֶה דוֹדִי לִצְבִי, אוֹ לְעֹפֶר הָאַיָּלִים, הִנֵּה זֶה עוֹמֵד אַחַר כָּתְלֵנוּ, מַשְׁגִּיחַ מִן הַחֲלֹּנוֹת, מֵצִיץ מִן הַחֲרַכִּים. י עָנָה דוֹדִי וְאָמַר לִי, קוּמִי לָךְ, רַעְיָתִי, יָפָתִי, וּלְכִי לָךְ. יא כִּי הִנֵּה הַסְּתָו עָבָר, הַגֶּשֶׁם חָלַף הָלַךְ לוֹ. יב הַנִּצָּנִים נִרְאוּ בָאָרֶץ, עֵת הַזָּמִיר הִגִּיעַ, וְקוֹל הַתּוֹר נִשְׁמַע בְּאַרְצֵנוּ. יג הַתְּאֵנָה חָנְטָה פַגֶּיהָ, וְהַגְּפָנִים סְמָדַר נָתְנוּ רֵיחַ, קוּמִי לָךְ, רַעְיָתִי, יָפָתִי, וּלְכִי לָךְ. יד יוֹנָתִי, בְּחַגְוֵי הַסֶּלַע, בְּסֵתֶר הַמַּדְרֵגָה, הַרְאִינִי אֶת מַרְאַיִךְ, הַשְׁמִיעִינִי אֶת קוֹלֵךְ, כִּי קוֹלֵךְ עָרֵב, וּמַרְאֵיךְ נָאוֶה. טו אֶחֱזוּ לָנוּ שֻׁעָלִים, שֻׁעָלִים קְטַנִּים, מְחַבְּלִים כְּרָמִים, וּכְרָמֵינוּ סְמָדַר. טז דּוֹדִי לִי, וַאֲנִי לוֹ, הָרֹעֶה בַּשּׁוֹשַׁנִּים. יז עַד שֶׁיָּפוּחַ הַיּוֹם,

וְנָסוּ הַצְּלָלִים, סֹב דְּמֵה לְךָ, דוֹדִי, לִצְבִי אוֹ לְעֹפֶר הָאַיָּלִים, עַל הָרֵי בָתֶר.

פרק ג

א עַל מִשְׁכָּבִי בַּלֵּילוֹת בִּקַּשְׁתִּי אֵת שֶׁאָהֲבָה נַפְשִׁי, בִּקַּשְׁתִּיו וְלֹא מְצָאתִיו. ב אָקוּמָה נָּא וַאֲסוֹבְבָה בָעִיר, בַּשְּׁוָקִים וּבָרְחֹבוֹת, אֲבַקְשָׁה אֵת שֶׁאָהֲבָה נַפְשִׁי, בִּקַּשְׁתִּיו וְלֹא מְצָאתִיו. ג מְצָאוּנִי הַשֹּׁמְרִים הַסֹּבְבִים בָּעִיר, אֵת שֶׁאָהֲבָה נַפְשִׁי רְאִיתֶם. ד כִּמְעַט שֶׁעָבַרְתִּי מֵהֶם, עַד שֶׁמָּצָאתִי אֵת שֶׁאָהֲבָה נַפְשִׁי, אֲחַזְתִּיו וְלֹא אַרְפֶּנּוּ, עַד שֶׁהֲבֵיאתִיו אֶל בֵּית אִמִּי, וְאֶל חֶדֶר הוֹרָתִי. ה הִשְׁבַּעְתִּי אֶתְכֶם, בְּנוֹת יְרוּשָׁלִַם, בִּצְבָאוֹת אוֹ בְּאַיְלוֹת הַשָּׂדֶה, אִם תָּעִירוּ וְאִם תְּעוֹרְרוּ אֶת הָאַהֲבָה עַד שֶׁתֶּחְפָּץ. ו מִי זֹאת עֹלָה מִן הַמִּדְבָּר, כְּתִימְרוֹת עָשָׁן, מְקֻטֶּרֶת מֹר וּלְבוֹנָה, מִכֹּל אַבְקַת רוֹכֵל. ז הִנֵּה מִטָּתוֹ שֶׁלִּשְׁלֹמֹה, שִׁשִּׁים גִּבֹּרִים סָבִיב לָהּ, מִגִּבֹּרֵי יִשְׂרָאֵל. ח כֻּלָּם אֲחֻזֵי חֶרֶב, מְלֻמְּדֵי מִלְחָמָה, אִישׁ חַרְבּוֹ עַל יְרֵכוֹ, מִפַּחַד בַּלֵּילוֹת. ט אַפִּרְיוֹן עָשָׂה לוֹ הַמֶּלֶךְ שְׁלֹמֹה מֵעֲצֵי הַלְּבָנוֹן. י עַמּוּדָיו עָשָׂה כֶסֶף, רְפִידָתוֹ זָהָב, מֶרְכָּבוֹ אַרְגָּמָן, תּוֹכוֹ רָצוּף אַהֲבָה מִבְּנוֹת יְרוּשָׁלִָם. יא צְאֶינָה וּרְאֶינָה, בְּנוֹת צִיּוֹן, בַּמֶּלֶךְ שְׁלֹמֹה, בָּעֲטָרָה שֶׁעִטְּרָה לּוֹ אִמּוֹ, בְּיוֹם חֲתֻנָּתוֹ, וּבְיוֹם שִׂמְחַת לִבּוֹ.

פרק ד

א הִנָּךְ יָפָה, רַעְיָתִי, הִנָּךְ יָפָה, עֵינַיִךְ יוֹנִים, מִבַּעַד לְצַמָּתֵךְ, שַׂעְרֵךְ כְּעֵדֶר הָעִזִּים, שֶׁגָּלְשׁוּ מֵהַר גִּלְעָד. ב שִׁנַּיִךְ כְּעֵדֶר הַקְּצוּבוֹת שֶׁעָלוּ מִן הָרַחְצָה, שֶׁכֻּלָּם מַתְאִימוֹת, וְשַׁכֻּלָה אֵין בָּהֶם. ג כְּחוּט הַשָּׁנִי שִׂפְתוֹתַיִךְ, וּמִדְבָּרֵךְ נָאוֶה, כְּפֶלַח הָרִמּוֹן רַקָּתֵךְ, מִבַּעַד לְצַמָּתֵךְ. ד כְּמִגְדַּל דָּוִיד צַוָּארֵךְ, בָּנוּי לְתַלְפִּיּוֹת, אֶלֶף הַמָּגֵן תָּלוּי עָלָיו, כֹּל שִׁלְטֵי הַגִּבּוֹרִים. ה שְׁנֵי שָׁדַיִךְ כִּשְׁנֵי עֳפָרִים, תְּאוֹמֵי צְבִיָּה, הָרוֹעִים בַּשּׁוֹשַׁנִּים. ו עַד שֶׁיָּפוּחַ הַיּוֹם, וְנָסוּ הַצְּלָלִים, אֵלֶךְ לִי אֶל הַר הַמּוֹר, וְאֶל גִּבְעַת הַלְּבוֹנָה. ז כֻּלָּךְ יָפָה, רַעְיָתִי, וּמוּם אֵין בָּךְ. ח אִתִּי מִלְּבָנוֹן, כַּלָּה, אִתִּי מִלְּבָנוֹן תָּבוֹאִי, תָּשׁוּרִי מֵרֹאשׁ אֲמָנָה, מֵרֹאשׁ שְׂנִיר וְחֶרְמוֹן, מִמְּעֹנוֹת אֲרָיוֹת, מֵהַרְרֵי נְמֵרִים. ט לִבַּבְתִּנִי, אֲחוֹתִי כַלָּה, לִבַּבְתִּנִי בְּאַחַת מֵעֵינַיִךְ, בְּאַחַד עֲנָק מִצַּוְּרֹנָיִךְ. י מַה יָּפוּ דֹדַיִךְ, אֲחוֹתִי כַלָּה, מַה טֹּבוּ דֹדַיִךְ מִיַּיִן, וְרֵיחַ שְׁמָנַיִךְ מִכָּל בְּשָׂמִים. יא נֹפֶת תִּטֹּפְנָה שִׂפְתוֹתַיִךְ, כַּלָּה, דְּבַשׁ וְחָלָב תַּחַת לְשׁוֹנֵךְ, וְרֵיחַ שַׂלְמֹתַיִךְ כְּרֵיחַ לְבָנוֹן. יב גַּן נָעוּל אֲחֹתִי כַלָּה, גַּל נָעוּל, מַעְיָן חָתוּם. יג שְׁלָחַיִךְ פַּרְדֵּס רִמּוֹנִים, עִם פְּרִי מְגָדִים, כְּפָרִים עִם נְרָדִים. יד נֵרְדְּ וְכַרְכֹּם, קָנֶה וְקִנָּמוֹן, עִם כָּל עֲצֵי לְבוֹנָה, מֹר וַאֲהָלוֹת, עִם כָּל רָאשֵׁי בְשָׂמִים. טו מַעְיַן גַּנִּים, בְּאֵר מַיִם חַיִּים, וְנֹזְלִים מִן לְבָנוֹן. טז עוּרִי צָפוֹן, וּבוֹאִי

תֵּימָן, הָפִיחִי גַנִּי, יִזְּלוּ בְשָׂמָיו, יָבֹא דוֹדִי לְגַנּוֹ, וְיֹאכַל פְּרִי מְגָדָיו.

פרק ה

א בָּאתִי לְגַנִּי, אֲחֹתִי כַלָּה, אָרִיתִי מוֹרִי עִם בְּשָׂמִי, אָכַלְתִּי יַעְרִי עִם דִּבְשִׁי, שָׁתִיתִי יֵינִי עִם חֲלָבִי, אִכְלוּ רֵעִים, שְׁתוּ וְשִׁכְרוּ דּוֹדִים. ב אֲנִי יְשֵׁנָה וְלִבִּי עֵר, קוֹל דּוֹדִי דוֹפֵק, פִּתְחִי לִי, אֲחֹתִי, רַעְיָתִי, יוֹנָתִי, תַמָּתִי, שֶׁרֹּאשִׁי נִמְלָא טָל, קְוֻצּוֹתַי רְסִיסֵי לָיְלָה. ג פָּשַׁטְתִּי אֶת כֻּתָּנְתִּי, אֵיכָכָה אֶלְבָּשֶׁנָּה, רָחַצְתִּי אֶת רַגְלַי, אֵיכָכָה אֲטַנְּפֵם. ד דּוֹדִי שָׁלַח יָדוֹ מִן הַחֹר, וּמֵעַי הָמוּ עָלָיו. ה קַמְתִּי אֲנִי לִפְתֹּחַ לְדוֹדִי, וְיָדַי נָטְפוּ מוֹר, וְאֶצְבְּעֹתַי מוֹר עֹבֵר, עַל כַּפּוֹת הַמַּנְעוּל. ו פָּתַחְתִּי אֲנִי לְדוֹדִי, וְדוֹדִי חָמַק עָבָר, נַפְשִׁי יָצְאָה בְדַבְּרוֹ, בִּקַּשְׁתִּיהוּ וְלֹא מְצָאתִיהוּ, קְרָאתִיו וְלֹא עָנָנִי. ז מְצָאֻנִי הַשֹּׁמְרִים הַסֹּבְבִים בָּעִיר, הִכּוּנִי פְצָעוּנִי, נָשְׂאוּ אֶת רְדִידִי מֵעָלַי שֹׁמְרֵי הַחֹמוֹת. ח הִשְׁבַּעְתִּי אֶתְכֶם, בְּנוֹת יְרוּשָׁלָיִם, אִם תִּמְצְאוּ אֶת דּוֹדִי, מַה תַּגִּידוּ לוֹ שֶׁחוֹלַת אַהֲבָה אָנִי. ט מַה דּוֹדֵךְ מִדּוֹד, הַיָּפָה בַּנָּשִׁים, מַה דּוֹדֵךְ מִדּוֹד, שֶׁכָּכָה הִשְׁבַּעְתָּנוּ. י דּוֹדִי צַח וְאָדוֹם, דָּגוּל מֵרְבָבָה. יא רֹאשׁוֹ כֶּתֶם פָּז, קְוֻצּוֹתָיו תַּלְתַּלִּים, שְׁחֹרוֹת כָּעוֹרֵב. יב עֵינָיו כְּיוֹנִים עַל אֲפִיקֵי מָיִם, רֹחֲצוֹת בֶּחָלָב, יֹשְׁבוֹת עַל מִלֵּאת. יג לְחָיָו כַּעֲרוּגַת הַבֹּשֶׂם, מִגְדְּלוֹת

מֶרְקָחִים, שִׂפְתוֹתָיו שׁוֹשַׁנִּים, נֹטְפוֹת מוֹר עֹבֵר. יד יָדָיו גְּלִילֵי זָהָב, מְמֻלָּאִים בַּתַּרְשִׁישׁ, מֵעָיו עֶשֶׁת שֵׁן, מְעֻלֶּפֶת סַפִּירִים. טו שׁוֹקָיו עַמּוּדֵי שֵׁשׁ, מְיֻסָּדִים עַל אַדְנֵי פָז, מַרְאֵהוּ כַּלְּבָנוֹן, בָּחוּר כָּאֲרָזִים. טז חִכּוֹ מַמְתַקִּים, וְכֻלּוֹ מַחֲמַדִּים, זֶה דוֹדִי וְזֶה רֵעִי, בְּנוֹת יְרוּשָׁלָיִם.

פרק ו

א אָנָה הָלַךְ דּוֹדֵךְ, הַיָּפָה בַּנָּשִׁים, אָנָה פָּנָה דוֹדֵךְ, וּנְבַקְשֶׁנּוּ עִמָּךְ. ב דּוֹדִי יָרַד לְגַנּוֹ, לַעֲרֻגוֹת הַבֹּשֶׂם, לִרְעוֹת בַּגַּנִּים וְלִלְקֹט שׁוֹשַׁנִּים. ג אֲנִי לְדוֹדִי, וְדוֹדִי לִי, הָרוֹעֶה בַּשּׁוֹשַׁנִּים. ד יָפָה אַתְּ רַעְיָתִי כְּתִרְצָה, נָאוָה כִּירוּשָׁלָיִם, אֲיֻמָּה כַּנִּדְגָּלוֹת. ה הָסֵבִּי עֵינַיִךְ מִנֶּגְדִּי, שֶׁהֵם הִרְהִיבֻנִי, שַׂעְרֵךְ כְּעֵדֶר הָעִזִּים, שֶׁגָּלְשׁוּ מִן הַגִּלְעָד. ו שִׁנַּיִךְ כְּעֵדֶר הָרְחֵלִים, שֶׁעָלוּ מִן הָרַחְצָה, שֶׁכֻּלָּם מַתְאִימוֹת, וְשַׁכֻּלָה אֵין בָּהֶם. ז כְּפֶלַח הָרִמּוֹן רַקָּתֵךְ, מִבַּעַד לְצַמָּתֵךְ. ח שִׁשִּׁים הֵמָּה מְלָכוֹת, וּשְׁמֹנִים פִּילַגְשִׁים, וַעֲלָמוֹת אֵין מִסְפָּר. ט אַחַת הִיא יוֹנָתִי תַמָּתִי, אַחַת הִיא לְאִמָּהּ, בָּרָה הִיא לְיוֹלַדְתָּהּ, רָאוּהָ בָנוֹת וַיְאַשְּׁרוּהָ, מְלָכוֹת וּפִילַגְשִׁים, וַיְהַלְלוּהָ. י מִי זֹאת הַנִּשְׁקָפָה כְּמוֹ שָׁחַר, יָפָה כַלְּבָנָה, בָּרָה כַּחַמָּה, אֲיֻמָּה כַּנִּדְגָּלוֹת. יא אֶל גִּנַּת אֱגוֹז יָרַדְתִּי לִרְאוֹת בְּאִבֵּי הַנָּחַל, לִרְאוֹת הֲפָרְחָה הַגֶּפֶן, הֵנֵצוּ

הָרִמּוֹנִים. יב לֹא יָדַעְתִּי, נַפְשִׁי שָׂמַתְנִי, מַרְכְּבוֹת עַמִּי נָדִיב.

פרק ז

א שׁוּבִי שׁוּבִי, הַשּׁוּלַמִּית, שׁוּבִי שׁוּבִי וְנֶחֱזֶה בָּךְ, מַה תֶּחֱזוּ בַּשּׁוּלַמִּית, כִּמְחֹלַת הַמַּחֲנָיִם. ב מַה יָּפוּ פְעָמַיִךְ בַּנְּעָלִים, בַּת נָדִיב, חַמּוּקֵי יְרֵכַיִךְ כְּמוֹ חֲלָאִים, מַעֲשֵׂה יְדֵי אָמָּן. ג שָׁרְרֵךְ אַגַּן הַסַּהַר, אַל יֶחְסַר הַמָּזֶג, בִּטְנֵךְ עֲרֵמַת חִטִּים, סוּגָה בַּשּׁוֹשַׁנִּים. ד שְׁנֵי שָׁדַיִךְ כִּשְׁנֵי עֳפָרִים, תָּאֳמֵי צְבִיָּה. ה צַוָּארֵךְ כְּמִגְדַּל הַשֵּׁן, עֵינַיִךְ בְּרֵכוֹת בְּחֶשְׁבּוֹן, עַל שַׁעַר בַּת רַבִּים, אַפֵּךְ כְּמִגְדַּל הַלְּבָנוֹן, צוֹפֶה פְּנֵי דַמָּשֶׂק. ו רֹאשֵׁךְ עָלַיִךְ כַּכַּרְמֶל, וְדַלַּת רֹאשֵׁךְ כָּאַרְגָּמָן, מֶלֶךְ אָסוּר בָּרְהָטִים. ז מַה יָּפִית וּמַה נָּעַמְתְּ, אַהֲבָה בַּתַּעֲנוּגִים. ח זֹאת קוֹמָתֵךְ דָּמְתָה לְתָמָר, וְשָׁדַיִךְ לְאַשְׁכֹּלוֹת. ט אָמַרְתִּי, אֶעֱלֶה בְתָמָר, אֹחֲזָה בְּסַנְסִנָּיו, וְיִהְיוּ נָא שָׁדַיִךְ כְּאֶשְׁכְּלוֹת הַגֶּפֶן, וְרֵיחַ אַפֵּךְ כַּתַּפּוּחִים. י וְחִכֵּךְ כְּיֵין הַטּוֹב, הוֹלֵךְ לְדוֹדִי לְמֵישָׁרִים, דּוֹבֵב שִׂפְתֵי יְשֵׁנִים. יא אֲנִי לְדוֹדִי, וְעָלַי תְּשׁוּקָתוֹ. יב לְכָה דוֹדִי, נֵצֵא הַשָּׂדֶה, נָלִינָה בַּכְּפָרִים. יג נַשְׁכִּימָה לַכְּרָמִים, נִרְאֶה אִם פָּרְחָה הַגֶּפֶן, פִּתַּח הַסְּמָדַר, הֵנֵצוּ הָרִמּוֹנִים, שָׁם אֶתֵּן אֶת דֹּדַי לָךְ. יד הַדּוּדָאִים נָתְנוּ רֵיחַ, וְעַל פְּתָחֵינוּ כָּל מְגָדִים, חֲדָשִׁים גַּם יְשָׁנִים, דּוֹדִי, צָפַנְתִּי לָךְ.

פרק ח

א מִי יִתֶּנְךָ כְּאָח לִי, יוֹנֵק שְׁדֵי אִמִּי, אֶמְצָאֲךָ בַחוּץ אֶשָּׁקְךָ, גַּם לֹא יָבוּזוּ לִי. ב אֶנְהָגְךָ, אֲבִיאֲךָ אֶל בֵּית אִמִּי, תְּלַמְּדֵנִי, אַשְׁקְךָ מִיַּיִן הָרֶקַח, מֵעֲסִיס רִמֹּנִי. ג שְׂמֹאלוֹ תַּחַת רֹאשִׁי, וִימִינוֹ תְּחַבְּקֵנִי. ד הִשְׁבַּעְתִּי אֶתְכֶם, בְּנוֹת יְרוּשָׁלָיִם, מַה תָּעִירוּ וּמַה תְּעֹרְרוּ אֶת הָאַהֲבָה עַד שֶׁתֶּחְפָּץ. ה מִי זֹאת עֹלָה מִן הַמִּדְבָּר, מִתְרַפֶּקֶת עַל דּוֹדָהּ, תַּחַת הַתַּפּוּחַ עוֹרַרְתִּיךָ, שָׁמָּה חִבְּלַתְךָ אִמֶּךָ, שָׁמָּה חִבְּלָה יְלָדַתְךָ. ו שִׂימֵנִי כַחוֹתָם עַל לִבֶּךָ, כַּחוֹתָם עַל זְרוֹעֶךָ, כִּי עַזָּה כַמָּוֶת אַהֲבָה, קָשָׁה כִשְׁאוֹל קִנְאָה, רְשָׁפֶיהָ רִשְׁפֵּי אֵשׁ, שַׁלְהֶבֶתְיָה. ז מַיִם רַבִּים לֹא יוּכְלוּ לְכַבּוֹת אֶת הָאַהֲבָה, וּנְהָרוֹת לֹא יִשְׁטְפוּהָ, אִם יִתֵּן אִישׁ אֶת כָּל הוֹן בֵּיתוֹ בָּאַהֲבָה, בּוֹז יָבוּזוּ לוֹ. ח אָחוֹת לָנוּ קְטַנָּה, וְשָׁדַיִם אֵין לָהּ, מַה נַּעֲשֶׂה לַאֲחוֹתֵנוּ בַּיּוֹם שֶׁיְּדֻבַּר בָּהּ. ט אִם חוֹמָה הִיא, נִבְנֶה עָלֶיהָ טִירַת כָּסֶף, וְאִם דֶּלֶת הִיא, נָצוּר עָלֶיהָ לוּחַ אָרֶז. י אֲנִי חוֹמָה, וְשָׁדַי כַּמִּגְדָּלוֹת, אָז הָיִיתִי בְעֵינָיו כְּמוֹצְאֵת שָׁלוֹם. יא כֶּרֶם הָיָה לִשְׁלֹמֹה בְּבַעַל הָמוֹן, נָתַן אֶת הַכֶּרֶם לַנֹּטְרִים, אִישׁ יָבִא בְּפִרְיוֹ אֶלֶף כָּסֶף. יב כַּרְמִי שֶׁלִּי לְפָנָי, הָאֶלֶף לְךָ שְׁלֹמֹה, וּמָאתַיִם לְנֹטְרִים אֶת פִּרְיוֹ. יג הַיּוֹשֶׁבֶת בַּגַּנִּים, חֲבֵרִים מַקְשִׁיבִים לְקוֹלֵךְ, הַשְׁמִיעִנִי. יד בְּרַח דּוֹדִי, וּדְמֵה לְךָ לִצְבִי, אוֹ לְעֹפֶר הָאַיָּלִים, עַל הָרֵי בְשָׂמִים.

ספירת העומר

ספירת העומר

The *Omer* is counted from the second night of Pesach
until the night before Shavuos.
While most communities begin to count the *Omer* at *Maariv*,
some have the custom to begin counting at the Seder.

∽§ Sefiras Ha'Omer: The connection between the Exodus and receiving the Torah

The Midrash (*Bamidbar Rabbah*, beginning of *Nasso*) comments, "The verse (*Bamidbar* 4:22), 'Take a census of the sons of Gershon as well,' is what is meant by the verse (*Mishlei* 3:15), 'It is more precious than pearls, and all your desires cannot compare to it.' For we have learned [in the Gemara *Horiyos* 13a] that a wise man precedes a king and a king precedes a *Kohen Gadol*.... A *Kohen Gadol* precedes a prophet .... When? When they are otherwise equal. But if the *mamzer* [who is last] is a Torah scholar, he precedes a *Kohen Gadol*, albeit unlearned, who enters the Holiest of Holies."

The reasoning of the Midrash is that Torah is more precious than all desires — even Heavenly desires such as entering the Holiest of Holies. What is it about Torah that makes it so precious?

We know that God's main wish is that the world exist. It is the Torah that maintains all worlds, those above and those below, as so thoroughly explained in *Nefesh Hachaim* (1:3). Many statements of the Sages attest to this fact, such as, "Whoever involves himself in Torah for its sake brings peace and completion to the Heavenly Host above and to the Host below on earth" (*Sanhedrin* 99b). Similarly, "One who says, 'Of what use to us are the Rabbis? They study Scripture only for themselves and they study Oral Law only for themselves,' is considered an *apikores*, as well as one who acts insolently toward the Torah, for it is written (*Yirmiyahu* 33:25): 'If not for my Covenant [i.e. the Torah] day and night, I would not have established the statutes of heaven and earth.'" Additionally, it says (*Bereishis* 18:26): "I would spare the entire place on their [the righteous'] account"; this teaches that the world exists because of the merit of those who study Torah. *Nefesh Hachaim* (ibid.) cites *Zohar* as interpreting the verse (*Tehillim* 68:35): "Attribute invincible might to God" as saying that Israel has the power, so to speak, to attribute invincible might to God to maintain all the worlds! Of course it was in

COUNTING THE OMER

The *Omer* is counted from the second night of Pesach
until the night before Shavuos.
While most communities begin to count the *Omer* at *Maariv*,
some have the custom to begin counting at the Seder.

God's power to create the world in other ways so that He would not "need" His own creations, yet that was His will, so that He could give proper reward to the righteous.

On the verse (*Shir HaShirim* 3:11), "Adorned with the crown His mother made for Him," the Midrash (*Shir HaShirim Rabbah* 3:21) comments, "Rabbi Shimon bar Yochai asked Rabbi Elazar son of Rabbi Yossi, 'Did you perhaps hear from your father an explanation of the [above] verse?' He replied ... 'It is comparable to a king who had an only daughter whom he loved excessively. Initially, he called her "my daughter." As his love for her grew, he called her "my sister." When his love for her grew even stronger, he called her "my mother." So, too, the Holy One, Blessed is He, loves His People exceedingly, and He called them "My daughter," as it is written (*Tehillim* 45:11): "Hear, O daughter, and see." Later, out of His increasing love, He called them "My sister," as it is written (*Shir HaShirim* 5:2): "Open to Me, My sister, My love." His love continued to increase, until He called them "My mother," as it says (*Yeshayahu* 51:4): "Pay attention to Me, My people; give ear to Me, My nation. *My nation — le'umi —* [can be interpreted as] *l'imi —* My mother'" Rav Shimon bar Yochai stood up, kissed him on his head, and said, 'If I would come only to hear just this from your mouth, it would be sufficient.' "

What does this Midrash mean? Isn't a father's love for his daughter greater than for his sister and even his mother? It seems that the Midrash is referring to the level of influence in the special relationship between Hashem and His people. First He called them "My daughter," because it is the father who begets his daughter and influences her in a one-sided way; He created us, took care of our needs, and influenced us. Then, He personally watched over us, with no intermediaries, and allowed us to all but become His partners. This is the level of "sister," since a brother and sister are relatively equal and each has influence on the other. Finally, He called us "Mother." Just as a mother influences her child, so too, the Jewish People influence Hashem. The

Many recite the following Kabbalistic prayer before the counting of the Omer.

לְשֵׁם יִחוּד קוּדְשָׁא בְּרִיךְ הוּא וּשְׁכִינְתֵּיהּ, בִּדְחִילוּ וּרְחִימוּ לְיַחֵד שֵׁם יוּ"ד הֵ"א בְּוָא"ו הֵ"א בְּיִחוּדָא שְׁלִים, בְּשֵׁם כָּל יִשְׂרָאֵל. הִנְנִי מוּכָן וּמְזוּמָּן לְקַיֵּם מִצְוַת עֲשֵׂה שֶׁל סְפִירַת הָעוֹמֶר כְּמוֹ שֶׁכָּתוּב בַּתּוֹרָה: וּסְפַרְתֶּם לָכֶם מִמָּחֳרַת הַשַּׁבָּת מִיּוֹם הֲבִיאֲכֶם אֶת עֹמֶר הַתְּנוּפָה שֶׁבַע שַׁבָּתוֹת תְּמִימֹת תִּהְיֶינָה. עַד מִמָּחֳרַת הַשַּׁבָּת הַשְּׁבִיעִת תִּסְפְּרוּ חֲמִשִּׁים יוֹם וְהִקְרַבְתֶּם מִנְחָה חֲדָשָׁה לַיהוה.[1]

---

profound influence that a person can have can be seen from the verses in *Iyov* (22:23-28), in which Elifaz the Temanite tells Iyov: "If you would return to the Almighty, you will be built up; if you would drive iniquity from your tent...You would utter a decree and it would be done." Furthermore, the Gemara (*Mo'ed Katan* 16b), in discussing the verse (II *Shmuel* 23:3): "...A righteous one rules fear of God," quotes God: "I rule over man, and who rules over Me? The righteous one. For I issue a decree and he cancels it."

This power can only come from the Torah, the medium through which Creation came about, as stated by the *Zohar*, "The Holy One, Blessed is He, looked in the Torah and created the world." Thus, although service in the *Beis HaMikdash* is of great importance, the power that maintains the universe is the power of Torah. Accordingly, "Torah study equals them all," as explained in the Mishnah at the beginning of Tractate *Pe'ah*, and a Torah scholar is considered on a higher level than a *Kohen Gadol*. Thus, in the dark world in which we live, it is especially important to strengthen our fulfillment of the mitzvah of Torah study.

We should also emphasize that the status of the Jewish People as a nation is not dependent on a homeland; it is dependent on Torah. There can be no continued existence for the Jewish People without the Torah. Thus, the essence of remembering the Exodus is recalling the enslavement and the freedom which led to the imminent

Many recite the following Kabbalistic prayer before the counting of the Omer.

For the sake of the unification of the Holy One, Blessed is He, and His Presence, in fear and love to unify the Name Yud-Kei with Vav-Kei in perfect unity, in the name of all Israel. Behold I am prepared and ready to perform the commandment of counting the Omer, as it is written in the Torah: "You are to count for yourselves from the morrow of the rest day, from the day you brought the Omer-offering that is waved — they are to be seven complete weeks — until the morrow of the seventh week you are to count fifty days, and then offer a new meal-offering to HASHEM."[1]

(1) *Leviticus* 23:15-16.

---

receiving of the Torah. Accordingly, we say at the beginning of the Seder, "This is the bread of affliction that our fathers ate in the land of Egypt," referring to the enslavement and subsequent freedom. If the ultimate purpose of the Exodus was to become a nation and enter the Land of Israel, we would instead celebrate the day of entry into the Land.

Furthermore, the sixteenth day of Nisan, the day after we celebrate the day of the Exodus, the Torah permits us to harvest and eat the new wheat crop. Simultaneously, we are commanded to remember the poor and the stranger and to share the produce of the land with them (see *Vayikra* 23:22). This teaches that though we may have toiled on land that is supposedly ours, we do not own the land exclusively. This all serves the ultimate purpose of realizing that our becoming a nation was not to have a land of our own from which we can harvest wheat, but to receive the Torah. In this way, these days of harvesting the new crop are intimately connected with the other role of these days — the anticipation of receiving the Torah. This connection is fortified with the counting of the *Omer* from the day of the harvest until the day the Torah was given. Through this, we teach ourselves that "This day you have become a people" (*Devarim* 27:9) — but only through the Torah. Indeed, it is in the merit of the Torah that the future redemption will come (from an unpublished manuscript presented by his grandson, Rav Aharon Goldberg).

וִיהִי נֹעַם יְהוָה אֱלֹהֵינוּ עָלֵינוּ וּמַעֲשֵׂה יָדֵינוּ כּוֹנְנָה עָלֵינוּ וּמַעֲשֵׂה יָדֵינוּ כּוֹנְנֵהוּ.

בָּרוּךְ אַתָּה יְיָ אֱלֹהֵינוּ מֶלֶךְ הָעוֹלָם, אֲשֶׁר קִדְּשָׁנוּ בְּמִצְוֹתָיו וְצִוָּנוּ עַל סְפִירַת הָעוֹמֶר.

הַיּוֹם יוֹם אֶחָד לָעוֹמֶר.

הָרַחֲמָן הוּא יַחֲזִיר לָנוּ עֲבוֹדַת בֵּית הַמִּקְדָּשׁ לִמְקוֹמָהּ, בִּמְהֵרָה בְיָמֵינוּ אָמֵן סֶלָה.

לַמְנַצֵּחַ בִּנְגִינֹת מִזְמוֹר שִׁיר. אֱלֹהִים יְחָנֵּנוּ וִיבָרְכֵנוּ, יָאֵר פָּנָיו אִתָּנוּ, סֶלָה. לָדַעַת בָּאָרֶץ דַּרְכֶּךָ, בְּכָל גּוֹיִם יְשׁוּעָתֶךָ. יוֹדוּךָ עַמִּים אֱלֹהִים, יוֹדוּךָ עַמִּים כֻּלָּם. יִשְׂמְחוּ וִירַנְּנוּ לְאֻמִּים, כִּי תִשְׁפֹּט עַמִּים מִישֹׁר, וּלְאֻמִּים בָּאָרֶץ תַּנְחֵם סֶלָה. יוֹדוּךָ עַמִּים אֱלֹהִים, יוֹדוּךָ עַמִּים כֻּלָּם. אֶרֶץ נָתְנָה יְבוּלָהּ, יְבָרְכֵנוּ אֱלֹהִים אֱלֹהֵינוּ. יְבָרְכֵנוּ אֱלֹהִים, וְיִירְאוּ אוֹתוֹ כָּל אַפְסֵי אָרֶץ.[2]

אָנָּא בְּכֹחַ גְּדֻלַּת יְמִינְךָ תַּתִּיר צְרוּרָה.
קַבֵּל רִנַּת עַמְּךָ שַׂגְּבֵנוּ טַהֲרֵנוּ נוֹרָא.
נָא גִבּוֹר דּוֹרְשֵׁי יִחוּדְךָ כְּבָבַת שָׁמְרֵם.
בָּרְכֵם טַהֲרֵם רַחֲמֵם צִדְקָתְךָ תָּמִיד גָּמְלֵם.

May the pleasantness of my Lord, our God, be upon us — may He establish our handiwork for us; our handiwork, may He establish.¹

Blessed are You, Hashem, our God, King of the universe, Who has sanctified us with His commandments and has commanded us regarding the counting of the Omer.

Today is one day of the Omer.

The Compassionate One! May He return for us the service of the Temple to its place, speedily, in our days. Amen, selah!

For the Conductor, upon Neginos, a psalm, a song. May God favor us and bless us, may He illuminate His countenance with us, Selah. To make known Your way on earth, among all the nations Your salvation. The peoples will acknowledge You, O God, the peoples will acknowledge You, all of them. Nations will be glad and sing for joy, because You will judge the people fairly and guide the nations on earth, Selah. The peoples will acknowledge You, O God, the peoples will acknowledge You, all of them. The earth has yielded its produce, may God, our own God, bless us. May God bless us and may all the ends of the earth fear him.¹

We beg You! With the strength of Your right hand's greatness, untie the bundled sins. Accept the prayer of Your nation; strengthen us, purify us, O Awesome One. Please, O Strong One — those who foster Your Oneness, guard them like the apple of an eye. Bless them, purify them, show them pity, may Your righteousness always recompense them.

---

(1) *Psalms* 90:17. (2) *Psalms* 67.

חֲסִין קָדוֹשׁ בְּרֹב טוּבְךָ נַהֵל עֲדָתֶךָ.
יָחִיד גֵּאֶה לְעַמְּךָ פְּנֵה זוֹכְרֵי קְדֻשָּׁתֶךָ.
שַׁוְעָתֵנוּ קַבֵּל וּשְׁמַע צַעֲקָתֵנוּ יוֹדֵעַ תַּעֲלֻמוֹת.
בָּרוּךְ שֵׁם כְּבוֹד מַלְכוּתוֹ לְעוֹלָם וָעֶד.

רִבּוֹנוֹ שֶׁל עוֹלָם, אַתָּה צִוִּיתָנוּ עַל יְדֵי מֹשֶׁה עַבְדֶּךָ לִסְפֹּר סְפִירַת הָעוֹמֶר, כְּדֵי לְטַהֲרֵנוּ מִקְּלִפּוֹתֵינוּ וּמִטֻּמְאוֹתֵינוּ, כְּמוֹ שֶׁכָּתַבְתָּ בְּתוֹרָתֶךָ. וּסְפַרְתֶּם לָכֶם מִמָּחֳרַת הַשַּׁבָּת מִיּוֹם הֲבִיאֲכֶם אֶת־עֹמֶר הַתְּנוּפָה, שֶׁבַע שַׁבָּתוֹת תְּמִימֹת תִּהְיֶינָה. עַד מִמָּחֳרַת הַשַּׁבָּת הַשְּׁבִיעִת תִּסְפְּרוּ חֲמִשִּׁים יוֹם. כְּדֵי שֶׁיִּטָּהֲרוּ נַפְשׁוֹת עַמְּךָ יִשְׂרָאֵל מִזֻּהֲמָתָם. וּבְכֵן יְהִי רָצוֹן מִלְּפָנֶיךָ יְיָ אֱלֹהֵינוּ וֵאלֹהֵי אֲבוֹתֵינוּ, שֶׁבִּזְכוּת סְפִירַת הָעוֹמֶר שֶׁסָּפַרְתִּי הַיּוֹם, יְתֻקַּן מַה שֶּׁפָּגַמְתִּי בִּסְפִירָה חֶסֶד שֶׁבְּחֶסֶד. וְאֶטָּהֵר וְאֶתְקַדֵּשׁ בִּקְדֻשָּׁה שֶׁל מַעְלָה, וְעַל יְדֵי זֶה יֻשְׁפַּע שֶׁפַע רַב בְּכָל הָעוֹלָמוֹת. וּלְתַקֵּן אֶת נַפְשׁוֹתֵינוּ, וְרוּחוֹתֵינוּ, וְנִשְׁמוֹתֵינוּ, מִכָּל סִיג וּפְגַם, וּלְטַהֲרֵנוּ וּלְקַדְּשֵׁנוּ בִּקְדֻשָּׁתְךָ הָעֶלְיוֹנָה, אָמֵן סֶלָה.

Powerful Holy One, with Your abundant goodness guide Your congregation. One and only Exalted One, turn to Your nation, which proclaims Your holiness. Accept our entreaty and hear our cry, O Knower of mysteries. Blessed is the Name of His glorious Kingdom for all eternity.

Master of the universe, You commanded us through Moses, Your servant, to count the Omer Count in order to cleanse us from our encrustations of evil and from our contaminations, as You have written in Your Torah: You are to count for yourselves from the morrow of the rest day, from the day you brought the Omer-offering that is waved — they are to be seven complete weeks — until the morrow of the seventh week you are to count fifty days,[1] so that the souls of Your people Israel be cleansed from their contamination. Therefore, may it be Your will, HASHEM, our God and the God of our forefathers, that in the merit of the Omer Count that I have counted today, may there be corrected whatever blemish I have caused in the *sefirah chesed shebechesed*. May I be cleansed and sanctified with the holiness of Above, and through this may abundant bounty flow in all the worlds. And may it correct our lives, spirits, and souls from all sediment and blemish; may it cleanse us and sanctify us with Your exalted holiness. Amen, Selah!

---

(1) *Leviticus* 23:15-16.

This volume is part of
THE ARTSCROLL SERIES®
an ongoing project of
translations, commentaries and expositions
on Scripture, Mishnah, Talmud, Halachah,
liturgy, history, the classic Rabbinic writings,
biographies and thought.

For a brochure of current publications
visit your local Hebrew bookseller
or contact the publisher:

Mesorah Publications, ltd
4401 Second Avenue
Brooklyn, New York 11232
(718) 921-9000
www.artscroll.com